Biletzki has written the definitive account of the human rights thinking that emerges from centuries of philosophical conversations. She covers, succinctly and clearly, the most fundamental classical writers, for example Hobbes, Locke, Mill, Rawls, as well as scores of contemporary ones like Arendt, Nussbaum, Balibar and Levinas. She deftly lays out complicated material about the most fundamental issues and conflicts within the field: the relationship between equality and freedom, the ability to have rights and its relationship to state formation, the way our very language shapes our thinking, whether human rights need to be religiously grounded, whether human rights doctrine is inherently Eurocentric, ferociously individualistic, and selectively enforced... If you are looking for one book on the swathe of human rights ideas, their history and practical implications, then this is the book for you.

–*Eve Spangler, Author of* Understanding Israel/Palestine:
Race, Nation, and Human Rights in the Conflict,
Boston College, USA

Anat Biletzki gives us a sophisticated and accessible discourse on pivotal issues of philosophy—how rights are conceived and practiced, contested and reshaped, beaten back and reasserted. *The Philosophy of Human Rights* is both a substantial rendering of the attendant philosophical understandings of rights and illustrations of how rights emerge in lived experience.

–*John Tirman, Executive Director & Principal Research Scientist,*
MIT Center for International Studies, USA

A deeply ethical, beautifully written philosophical exploration of our very notion of "human rights". Anat Biletzki's masterful survey of theory, of practice, and current realities is timely, wise, and desperately needed.

–*Juliet Floyd, Professor of Philosophy,*
Boston University, USA

D0145507

Philosophy of Human Rights

An introductory text to the philosophy of human rights, this book provides an innovative, systematic study of the concepts, ideas, and theories of human rights. It examines the principal philosophical issues that arise in specific areas of rights, such as women's rights, minority rights, or disability rights, and addresses the human rights aspects of world problems such as global poverty and humanitarian intervention. Along with the presentation of these established subjects, the book provides a vibrant critique of both the liberal fundamentals of human rights and the legal and political aspects of the concrete practice by individuals and organizations.

Key Features:

- Presents a thorough philosophical introduction to human rights for anyone from any subject (e.g., international law, politics, public policy, philosophy).
- While grounded in philosophy, demonstrates a clear, organized understanding of real-world aspects of the field, with a deep analysis of vital, current issues.
- Is attentive to critical stances on human rights and to stultifying privations in the field.
- Offers a well-organized overall structure, moving from historical treatment, to conceptual analysis, to a set of current issues, and finally to criticism.

Anat Biletzki is the Albert Schweitzer Professor of Philosophy at Quinnipiac University in Hamden, Connecticut, having previously been at the Philosophy Department at Tel Aviv University for many years. Her publications include: *Talking Wolves: Thomas Hobbes on the Language of Politics and the Politics of Language* (1997), and *(Over)Interpreting Wittgenstein* (2003). She served as chairperson of B'Tselem—the Israeli Information Center for Human Rights in the Occupied Territories (2001–2006) and was nominated among the "1000 Women for the Nobel Peace Prize—2005."

Philosophy of Human Rights

A Systematic Introduction

Anat Biletzki

 Routledge
Taylor & Francis Group

NEW YORK AND LONDON

First published 2020
by Routledge
52 Vanderbilt Avenue, New York, NY 10017

and by Routledge
2 Park Square, Milton Park, Abingdon, Oxon OX14 4RN

Routledge is an imprint of the Taylor & Francis Group, an informa business

Library of Congress Cataloging-in-Publication Data
Names: Biletzki, Anat, author.
Title: Philosophy of human rights : a systematic introduction / Anat Biletzki.
Description: New York : Routledge, 2020. | Includes bibliographical references and index.
Identifiers: LCCN 2019017919 | ISBN 9781138787346 (hardback)
Subjects: LCSH: Human rights--Philosophy.
Classification: LCC JC571 .B54185 2020 | DDC 323.01--dc23
LC record available at https://lccn.loc.gov/2019017919

ISBN: 978-1-138-78734-6 (hbk)
ISBN: 978-1-138-78735-3 (pbk)
ISBN: 978-1-315-76663-8 (ebk)

Typeset in Sabon
by Taylor & Francis Books

To the workers in human rights at *B'Tselem* – The Israeli Information Center for Human Rights in the Occupied Territories.

Contents

Preface and Acknowledgments   xi

Introduction   xvi

PART I
Overview

  1 Fundamentals   3

  2 The Legal Framework   18

  3 Some Questions (about Human Rights)   32

PART II
Philosophical Groundings

  4 Liberal Underpinnings   47

  5 Theories of Rights   59

  6 Theories of Human Rights   73

PART III
Issues in Human Rights

  7 The Universalism of Human Rights   91

  8 Groups and Other Collections   107

  9 Rights on Our Mind   125

  10 Global Economic Rights   151

  11 Security, Sovereignty, and Humanitarian Intervention   170

PART IV
Critique

12   Philosophical Critique of Human Rights   191

13   Back to the Rough Ground   210

A Somewhat Epilogue: On the Ground   232

Formal Documents of Human Rights   236
Bibliography   239
Index   251

Preface and Acknowledgments

A book on the philosophy of human rights must straddle the two very different, sometimes even oppositional contexts of academia and activism. This book has been decades in the making, actually in the thinking; two decades, to be exact. That is when my internally divided life, always weaving between direct action and scholarship, finally came together at the Institute for Advanced Study in Princeton, New Jersey. The theme for that year – the Institute has an annual theme – was "Universalism of Human Rights," and, although I candidly admitted that human rights, for me, was an object of practice, not theory, the scholars there accepted me as an equal interlocutor in the purportedly theoretical exchange on the universalism of human rights. That question – the universalism of human rights – as anyone who has engaged with human rights in legal or philosophical surroundings knows, has moved from being (almost) axiomatic to (usually) adversarial in a relatively short time. It provides the springboard for the move made from praxis to theory and then back again that I perceive as the *philosophy* of human rights.

Another somewhat related and no less problematic dichotomy that seems to pursue any practically oriented philosopher writing about human rights resides in the local-global conundrum. Its manifestation is never far removed from the political and conflictual settings in which the writer finds herself, viz., in this case, Israel-Palestine. International human rights, articulated by non-governmental organizations, the UN, diplomatic international relations, religious and secular social movements, and, of course, the institutions of international law, cannot but play a – *the* – leading role on the stage of the human rights drama of global justice and peace unfolding in our times. But the fulcrum of human rights that is the inescapable focus of another drama – in Israel-Palestine – is never far from the mind of this writer. Paradigm cases of the violations of (Palestinian) human rights inevitably serve as illustrations for the more abstract and theoretical issues that are sometimes thrust to the backdrop of the ostensibly philosophical interchange. And – on the practical level of doing human rights, and in contradistinction to the conventional mandate – this means that for the sake of human rights we think locally, but are called upon to act globally.

My particular "local" (Israeli-Palestinian) human rights setting consisted, during these past decades, of the human rights organization *B'Tselem* – The Israeli Information Center for Human Rights in the Occupied Territories. The name of the organization, its provenance and development, is a story in its own right and uncannily reflects some of the very questions that must be dealt with in a philosophy of human rights. "B'Tselem" literally means "in the image of ..." It is a partial quote from the book of Genesis: "So God created man in his own image, *in the image of* God created he him" (Genesis 1:27, KJV, my emphasis). In Hebrew, the four English words "in the image of" are voiced by only one word: b'tselem ("in the image of God" becoming "b'tselem Elohim"). The interpretation of that verse, and of the idea that man was created "in the image of" God, has, since antiquity, supplied religious and secular thinkers with a panoply of conceptual challenges regarding the human being's likeness to God (in free will, in power, in behavior, in exceptionalism, in incorporeality, etc.). But the modern, explicit reading of the term "b'tselem" calls it to serve as a synonym for dignity: The human essence touted by the claim that we are created in God's image is precisely our inherent dignity. And it is the claim of such essential dignity that initiates, for both believers and non-believers, the concept of human rights. Unsurprisingly, then, the NGO *B'Tselem*, by name and in practice, has also served to expose, in my mind, problems that accompany the investigation of human rights: their religious grounding, their moral bases, their politicization, and their universality, to name just an obvious few.

So terms of vigorous involvement with human rights – universalism, globalism, practice, theory, politicization, religiosity, dignity, and many others – provide a conceptual framework for the philosophical discussion on human rights; just as insistently, they become, themselves, objects of analysis for any philosopher of human rights. The immediate upshot of the strain that attends a philosophy of human rights is that all ideas and all practices harbored in our discourse are immediately subject to deep, abiding, philosophical (and political) criticism. *B'Tselem* was scarcely founded, in 1989, when a philosopher friend, Adi Ophir, wrote an article in the weekend magazine of a popular newspaper (*Davar*), "Documentation as an Act of Resistance," that stopped many human rights do-gooders in their tracks. In the setting of the Israeli occupation of Palestinian lands, despite accepting the presupposition that human rights organizations in that setting were intent on exposing and fighting against the violations of human rights that the Occupation entailed, Ophir showed how working within the system – i.e., as a law-abiding, normative organization – led us into collaboration with the powers that be. Using both conceptual and political argument, Ophir swept the rug out from under our feet, so to speak; he put the seed of doubt into our heretofore complacent enterprise of liberal human rights. And now, almost forty years later, I hold fast to the quaking that that early criticism evoked in us – both activists and philosophers. It is the criticism of the (liberal) idea of human rights but also of the on-the-ground doings of its practitioners that therefore occupies the final chapters of this book.

* * *

Doing the philosophy of human rights has been a decades-long engagement – with students, colleagues, and practitioners. The impossibility of listing them all is a given; as is the need to attempt a thanksgiving, nevertheless. Early on, Aaron Back from the Ford Foundation supported a different project, that subsequently morphed into this one. His vision provided a first validation of my writing. A down-to-earth visionary is Andrew Beck, who discussed with me both the rationale and the execution of the hybrid venture that I was pursuing several years ago. His sensitivity then to the issues that should be addressed in a philosophical introduction (to human rights) has been matched by his patience and encouragement throughout the ensuing years. Similarly significant were the readers of my early sketch of the book; their comprehensive comments – as to structure, content, agenda, and even ideology – followed me to its completion. Jason Culmone aided me with preliminary comprehensive – and questioning – editing. His contribution as well as that of my production and copy editors was vital.

Let me return, though, to the experience that began my formal and unambiguous *academic* immersion into human rights at the Institute for Advanced Study. The group of anthropologists, historians, sociologists, philosophers, and literary persons at the School of Social Studies there were a source of exhilaration. The very different perspectives of Clifford Geertz and Michael Walzer first presented me with the (startling) possibility of not agreeing with them; Thomas Pogge laid the philosophical basis of liberalism in human rights for me without ever asking for acquiescence; and Joan W. Scott opened my eyes – and tongue and pen – to a new way of looking at human rights, and at the scholar-activist life.

At the other, chronological, end of my human rights "research" journey has been the recent year spent at the National Humanities Center in North Carolina. Librarians and administrative staff provided an environment that catered to the need for mental and emotional quiet – especially as I was deeply immersed in the ongoing tragedies of human rights. Invigorating in tight discussion, which created a space for the philosophical questioning that must apply to human rights, were my cohorts there – whose sophisticated commitment to human rights (under many other names) helped me to problematize the (usually liberal) assumptions of human rights study. I gesture gratefully to those with whom that human rights discussion reverberated mightily: Robin Einhorn, Jonathon Glassman, Geoff Harpham, Noah Heringman, Nan Woodruff; along with Judith Ferster, Jimmy Kern, and Irene Silverblatt. Without the NHC, this book would not have finally materialized.

Other educational, and I dare say political, hosts have given me sustenance in the form of welcoming fellowships and affiliations, and my debt to them cannot be overstated. Ioanna Kuçuradi, first at Hacettepe University in Ankara and later at Maltepe University in Istanbul, has been my constant guide in the grinding mission of doing, teaching, and researching human rights all at once. At Boston University, Massachusetts, where I was Findlay Visiting Professor, human rights shone through never-ending interactions with David Lyons, Fred Tauber, Juliet

Floyd, Simon Keller, Charles Griswold, and – now sadly deceased – Jaakko Hintikka. At MIT's Center for International Studies, Massachusetts, where I was a fellow at the Program for Human Rights and Justice, Raj Balakrishnan, John Tirman, and Dick Samuels enriched my understanding of the organization of institutional human rights; my work with them on human rights education continues until today. Alex De Waal, Lisa Avery, and Bridget Conley of the World Peace Foundation at Tufts University, Massachusetts, whom I first met through work on human rights advocacy, always amaze me with their unconventional approach to humanitarianism (through dire constructs such as "mass atrocities" and "mass starvation," among others); their continuous support of my work on human rights has been invaluable.

The University of Bergen, Norway, has enabled me to try out exploratory expositions of human rights in several workshops, symposia, and classes. There I have been able to concentrate on specific but variegated problematics – Hannah Arendt on human rights, human rights in Israel-Palestine, refugee ethics, and the educational structure of an introduction to the Philosophy of Human Rights. Particular thanks for giving me "access" to their thoughts (on human rights) and their students (in human rights) are due to Reidar Lie, Anne Granberg, Alois Pichler, Jesse Tomalty, Gunnar Skirbekk, and Harald Johannessen.

Quinnipiac University, Connecticut, where I am associated with the Albert Schweitzer Institute, has become my academic home. It is there that I was able during the past few years, while away from my political home – Israel-Palestine, to teach human rights (alongside "good old analytic philosophy") while writing this book. The intense dialogue and activity pertaining in some way to human rights on campus is due, in no small measure, to the previous and present directors of the Albert Schweitzer Institute, David Ives and Sean Duffy. On pain of clichés, I maintain that words cannot express my thanks to them for their care, their dedication, and their own unsurpassed zeal for human rights. Similar intensity on the part of Sujata Gadkar-Wilcox, also at Quinnipiac University, has brought me into vital mutual immersion in human rights talk with her and with members of the Oxford Consortium for Human Rights, Cheyney Ryan, Nabeel Hamdi, and Deen Chaterjee.

Indeed, these wandering positions have all catered to the necessity of undertaking scholarship on human rights; they were all accompanied with the gratification of *teaching* human rights. At the philosophy departments in Tel Aviv University, Boston University, The University of Bergen, Quinnipiac University, and at the Center for International Studies at MIT, where I have taught classes on human rights, I have encountered the most diverse (in the real sense of the word) group of people that one can dream of meeting. Young (and sometimes not so young) persons from different countries, roots, upbringings, and dreams, have come together in my classes to study human rights with me; but it is I who have learnt from them. The very dissimilar cultural, religious, and political environments which nurtured these students afforded me the opportunity to really probe not only the presuppositions that underlie the liberal conceptualization of human rights, but also the very idea of the possibility of creating a robust philosophy of human rights. Their various challenges of everything I had to say about human rights as coming from a philosophical Weltanschauung could – and still can – only be countered by a sharing of the pains that we attempt to relieve by *doing* human rights. Again, the activism and the academy needed to come together.

* * *

Those anxieties bring me to a final coda of thankyous. I spoke above of awakening to the moral and political critique of human rights; not for naught does the book treat this (mostly negative) evaluation with such trepidation. The philosophical disparagement of (the mostly liberal perception of) human rights is sadly matched, in many quarters, by the concrete reproach of human rights in practice. Beyond such censure, sometimes in its wake but oft-times merely as a result of thoughtful realism, one is often privy to a certain mood of despair that enlists the dealers in human rights. Such despair is not an emotional phenomenon; it is rather a rational extrapolation from the accurate valuation of things as they are.

While writing this book, I have wavered between rational despair and (irrational?) hope. It is only fellow travelers who have sometimes swayed me to the latter; to them I owe the greatest debt. These include the members of the Boston reading group in moral psychology: Larry Blum, Steve Nathanson, Sally Haslanger, Margaret Rhodes, Chris Zurn, Lisa Rivera, Adam Hosein, and Naomi Scheman. Years of philosophical conversation with these deep thinkers on subjects that almost always touch upon human rights can be sensed in every page of this book. Additional immense gratitude is owed the sisters and brothers in arms (what an inept metaphor!) in Israel-Palestine and Boston, who link scholarship and political morality, and from whom I never cease to learn: Susan Akram, Diana Buttu, Leila Farsakh, Irene Gendzier, Susannah Heschel, Hannan Hever, Orly Lubin, Adi Ophir, Hilary Rantisi, Alice Rothchild, Sara Roy, Eve Spangler, and Salim Tamari. Ronny Talmor, one of the founders of *B'Tselem*, Ovadia Ezra, a leading Israeli philosopher of human rights, and Ruth Anna and Hilary Putnam, friends and mentors, died before the book came to fruition; I mourn them while thanking them.

Finally, there are the real workers in human rights – the staff, field workers, and members of the board of *B'Tselem*. Hope for human rights resides with them and it is to them I dedicate this book.

Introduction

> The urge to explain one's own ideas, not simply, not in a story, but by means of a "systematic account," is powerful indeed.
>
> Paul Feyerabend, *Against Method* (1975, 179–80)

"Human Rights" has become a catchphrase in current international and local political praxis, in countless legal arenas, and in popular discourse, from media to academia to personal interactions. It came into such standing, we usually claim, after the atrocities carried out by humans against humans in World War II. The working hypothesis of this book is that it is worthy of philosophical elucidation and analysis not just by dint of its prominence in these contemporary areas of human conduct, but also due to its inherently philosophical nature. The multitudinous variety of articles, books, and journalistic pieces on human rights now on offer – not to mention the uses of the term in both layperson and professional conversation – is less often found in philosophical frameworks than in legal or political ones. Still, although there is no institutionalized or disciplinary "philosophy of human rights," we are now witnessing a welcome surge in philosophical interest – that is to say, a diverse body of philosophical work that has been executed regarding both theoretical and applied aspects of human rights thought. On the other side, as it were, in the working fields of human rights (mostly in the legal arena, but also in politics and policy making, and even in professional human rights activism), there have been noteworthy excursions into investigations of human rights that could not ignore erupting philosophical issues. The philosophy of human rights undertaken in this book purports to straddle this divide between the academy and the field precisely by providing a common philosophical foundation for both sides.

The past two decades of burgeoning human rights research have seen "theory and practice" tomes on human rights, functioning at the same time as primers on the subject. Such are the erstwhile prerequisites of human rights study such as Orend's *Human Rights: Concept and Context* (2002), Nickel's *Making Sense of Human Rights* (2007), Boersema's *Philosophy of Human Rights: Theory and Practice* (2011), or Donnelly's *Universal Human Rights in Theory and Practice* (2013). Another brand of sophisticated philosophical contributions to the scholarship on human rights is in no way introductory, instead presenting theoretical positions in and on the philosophy of human rights, some of which even grapple with the traditional, conventional (almost always liberal), standard story. I like to call them "Advanced Philosophy of Human Rights." Noticeable signposts of such philosophies of human rights are Perry's *The Idea of Human Rights: Four Inquiries* (1998), where religion is posited as the only true ideational basis of human rights, and the more recent wave of offerings such as Griffin's novel treatment, in *On Human Rights* (2008), of human rights making possible normative agency under limits of practical considerations; Beitz, who in *The Idea of Human Rights* (2009) concentrates on the place of global political practice in the clarification of human rights; Tasioulas's "Towards a Philosophy of Human Rights" (2012) that gives us ways of connecting human rights culture with the natural rights tradition, while taking into consideration more contemporary human rights justifications; or Buchanan's *The Heart of Human Rights* (2013), where the methodology that philosophers are advised to adopt in treating human rights is centered on the practice of human rights law. Notably, these erudite additions to philosophical thought on human rights have come out of the familiar, liberalism-focused, story that we have traditionally been telling about human rights; they are "advanced" in virtue of coming out of it and taking it to new places – to individual, professional, philosophical theses on how we are to read human rights today.

Given a standard (liberal) narrative of human rights and the more innovative (but still liberal) developments of the philosophy of that narrative, more so – given the intense interest exhibited in human rights in the corridors of academe, it is no wonder that we now come upon contemplative engagement with the complexities, and even convolutions, that accompany such philosophical musings. Unsurprisingly, some more recent books have taken the shape of edited volumes that exhibit the array of perspectives in the philosophical conversation on the subject of human rights. The explicitly probing ones are Ernst and Heilinger's *The Philosophy of Human Rights: Contemporary Controversies* (2012), Corradetti's *Philosophical Dimensions of Human Rights* (2012), Cushman's *Handbook of Human Rights* (2012), Holder and Reidy's *Human Rights: The Hard Questions* (2013), and Cruft, Liao, and Renzo's *Philosophical Foundations of Human Rights* (2015). These currently pertinent volumes allow one to be immersed in the detailed and intricate discussions in the human rights conversation – on the history, foundations, justifications, categorizations, positioning, problematics, inter-relationships, and criticisms of human rights – in their most cutting-edge displays; that is to say, their most particularized, independent, and updated elaborations.

Consequently, the study of the philosophy of human rights takes one of three roads. It can take place on the introductory, perhaps less philosophical, level, adhering to the conventional "theory and practice" model which usually nods at philosophical questions and is engrossed in a typically non-structural presentation of human rights issues.[1] It may, in more developed fashion, engage in an original thesis concerning human rights and proceed to cultivate it as arising from an articulated philosophical position. Finally, having fully employed these two standard modes in the philosophical treatment of human rights, the philosophy of human rights seems poised, at this point in time, to be involved in deep debates that stem both from conceptual and legal dealings in human rights and from the complicated workings of human rights "on the ground."[2]

This introductory text is not a "theory and practice" book. Neither is it a self-standing proposal to view human rights through a particular philosophical or practical (legal or political) lens, and still less does it mount an innovative philosophical debate on human rights. It is an *introduction* to the philosophy of human rights aiming to supply a fundamental analysis and exposition of the idea of human rights. But it aims at more: it wants to provide a *systematic* study of the conceptual and historical dealings with the term and of the roots of the practice, leading to an understanding of current discourse and its context. As such, it is, in a sense, a "survey" text with expository goals. It intends to clarify the concept of "human rights" by examining its derivation from classical theories of *rights*, on through commonly accepted theories of *human rights*, all the way to existing reflective uses. This obviously entails access to the terminology and modern-day documents that are constitutive of the human rights arena. It also demands a study of how foundational questions apply to the human rights issues now so much with us, and how philosophical critique of human rights (also now so much with us) plays such a meaningful part in the deep-thinking of the field.

A Systematic Structure

The structure of the book reflects these intended systematic meanderings. It consists of four parts – Part I "Overview" (Chapters 1–3), Part II "Philosophical Groundings" (Chapters 4–6), Part III "Issues in Human Rights" (Chapters 7–11), and Part IV "Critique" (Chapters 12–13).

The somewhat long Part I ("Overview") holds "background" chapters presenting the history and terminology of human rights language, the modern-day legal documents that are constitutive of the human rights turf in action, and an articulation of some basic questions – later to be returned to all along the text – that turn the engine of the *philosophy* of human rights. Chapter 1 ("Fundamentals") provides a short historical outline and the terminological basis for the entire discussion of human rights, introducing the (orthodox) structure of individual-state-international authorities that underlies the subject. It also lays out the conventional categorizations of civil-political rights and economic-social-cultural rights, and discusses the difference between human rights and civil rights. The necessary legal background which grounds the contemporary practice of human rights is provided in Chapter 2 ("The Legal Framework"), elaborating on the fundamental documents of international human rights law, common legal human rights instruments, and the (related, but different) elements of humanitarian law (the laws of war). Central philosophical questions of human rights are first introduced in Chapter 3 ("Some Questions (about Human Rights)"): Who holds human rights? How are they justified? Do they exist? Are they absolute? And the most basic concept of all – What is dignity?

Moving from general surveyal to philosophical brick-laying, Part II ("Philosophical Groundings") begins with the historical philosophical grounding of human rights in liberalism and then expounds on theories of rights in general and theories of human rights in particular. This is philosophy in its systematic, even inferential, essence: political liberalism provides the grounds for the idea of rights, and that, in turn, cannot but establish and then initiate human rights. Chapter 4 ("Liberal Underpinnings") presents philosophical liberalism as the historical genesis of human rights theories, using four protagonists: Thomas Hobbes, John Locke, John Stuart Mill, and John Rawls. In Chapter 5 ("Theories of Rights"), after a detour into Hohfield's legalistic theory of rights, three contemporary philosophers' perceptions of rights are expounded: H. L. A. Hart, Ronald Dworkin, and Joseph Raz. And in Chapter 6 ("Theories of Human Rights") we finally arrive at the theoretical core of our exposition – theories of human rights. First, the general category of religious justifications of human rights is established, and then three eminent non-religious positions are spelt out – Alan Gewirth's two basic human rights to freedom and well-being, Martha Nussbaum's capability approach to human rights, and Thomas Pogge's articulation of institutional duties (to respect human rights).

Part III ("Issues in Human Rights") is the place where theory and practice meet, but not in the naïve sense of applied theory. Instead, a group of fundamental human rights issues are sequentially entertained; they are, in some sense, connected, each conversing with more general philosophical matters (raised in Part II) and thereby impacting one another. Drawing on the philosophical universalism/relativism debate, in Chapter 7 ("The Universalism of Human Rights") the painful human rights issue of cultural relativity is seen as an essential test in any examination of human rights. Philosophers such as Charles Taylor and Jeremy Waldron are called upon for their nuanced analysis of the universalism of human rights, and the accusation of imperialistic (i.e., Western) universalism is thence considered. In Chapter 8 ("Groups and Other Collections"), the liberal rights tradition is brought to bear, and is then questioned, on the matter of group rights that, although prioritized nowadays in the human rights conversation, may go against individual rights. Not unrelated to this are minority rights and indigenous rights that also play a crucial part in this discussion. Chapter 9 ("Rights on Our Mind") investigates women's rights, disability rights, and refugee rights – now so much on our human rights mind – and presents their challenges both in the context of the liberal rights tradition and through some more critical, non-liberal perspectives. This leads, unsurprisingly, to other types of rights that are in some ways outliers in the liberal tradition. Thus, in Chapter 10 ("Global Economic Rights"), economic rights, their explicit violation in the case of poverty, and questions of equality between individuals and between states (in the context of liberalism) become the focus of our conversation. Finally, Chapter 11 ("Security, Sovereignty, and Humanitarian Intervention") brings up the double role of the construct of security in human rights as a basic personal human right but also as a trump in the violation of (other) human rights. This tension is exposed as a conceptual challenge, leading to related questions about torture, sovereignty, and humanitarian intervention.

These intra- and inter-issue strains cannot but bring to an interrogation of sorts that rises, willy-nilly, to the level of criticism. This comes about both directly and explicitly in Part IV ("Critique"), where our questions become troublesome, perhaps even distressing. On the one hand, the philosophy of human rights must re-investigate the supposed axioms of the idea of human rights, believed to inhere in liberalism, and is called upon to unearth some questionable basics. On the other hand, the concrete contexts in which human rights practice is carried out are discovered – were actually discovered far earlier – to also contain intolerable frictions. It is when these are seen as self-defeating that the philosophy of human rights might be perceived as turning upon itself. Accordingly, in Chapter 12 ("Philosophical Critique of Human Rights"), several philosophers are called upon to illuminate the profound drawbacks of the liberal conception of human rights. From Marx to Rorty, different conceptions are entertained and alternative systems (such as those of Foucault, Levinas, Balibar, and Arendt) are seen to invigorate a philosophical view of human rights, which sees them as "political" in a different, deeper sense of that word. But Chapter 13 ("Back to the Rough Ground") returns us to the politics we know and seem to have always known. Human rights is now investigated by philosophers who insist on the practice's essentialistic legal and political moorings. That, however, brings us to more concrete criticism carrying moral weight and ethical dilemmas and lodged against the widespread discourse, the institutional practice, and the human rights community at large. These are addressed in this last chapter, and the crucial question of foreseeable good and bad expectations of the human rights agenda is – unavoidably – entertained.

Method

What do we mean by systematic philosophy? How committed is a philosophy of human rights to philosophical methodology? And how do we face up to the recognition that there are distinct and different philosophical methods? Even without spelling out an obligatory definition of "philosophy" and a corresponding characterization of "systematicity," we must explain what our requirements are for a *philosophy* of human rights.[3] Our philosophical ideology, in a manner of speaking, first views philosophy as an activity of questioning. Yes, our philosophical questions merit answers; but the focus on questioning emphasizes the pluralistic, non-dogmatic, never-ending nature of philosophy. Our next characterization of philosophy, that is, of philosophical questioning, consists of insisting on three keynotes that attach to our questions: conceptual, analytical, and critical. In short shrift – philosophy is, first and foremost, an activity of questioning. Our questions interrogate concepts, such interrogation analyzes the concepts at hand, and no answer is accepted at face value without critical response. So the philosophy of human rights will ask about the concepts "human," "rights," "liberty," "equality," "dignity," "politics," "security," "torture," and oh-so-many others; and this activity of conceptual questioning will be accomplished through analytical method and critical attitude.

Where and how do replies to our questions fit into this methodology? That is the part of our project that is in the nature of a "survey," and the survey is systematic. Conventional wisdom accords human rights a history and a creed predicated on liberalism. Still, within that orthodoxy, one encounters a diversity of stories on and analyses of human rights. Surveying that multiplicity of (admittedly liberal) theories of human rights is a large part of a philosophy of human rights. But it is not the exclusive part – for two reasons. First, the conventional, even if only liberal, story is too detailed, too variegated, too densely populated by thinkers and actors for us to be able to really "survey" it all in an introductory text. Second, the critique of the canon is no less meaningful for our understanding of human rights; indeed, it might be more so.

Subsequently, our systematic introduction surveys the historical thinkers – Thomas Hobbes, John Locke, and John Stuart Mill – who laid the groundwork for liberalism, and adds on the great liberal philosopher of the twentieth century – John Rawls. Just as systematically it surveys liberal theories of rights and theories of human rights coming out of that same wellspring of liberalism. And it goes on to address several issues now prevalent in the matter of human rights – universalism, group rights, women's rights, refugee rights, economic rights, security, humanitarian intervention, and several others. These are all impacted by liberal theories of human rights – but are dealt with differently by various philosophers and philosophies. Some conduct an internal-to-liberalism dispute; others provide the more radical views that criticize, and even negate, the standard (liberal) story. Systematically, then, it behooves us to address the critique with as much gravity as we do the "regular" narrative and analysis. But then, given this multi-branched and variously-layered, albeit still systematic, presentation of the philosophy of human rights, it is foreseeable that certain questions, topics, theories, and especially philosophers make several appearances in the book. (Such are, for example, Hannah Arendt, John Rawls, or Wendy Brown.) If we were to map the subjects and issues that play their part in the story of human rights, looking for a graphic or visual representation of our "system," we would find roads going back and forth, intersecting and crisscrossing, all still leading to a philosophical understanding of human rights.

The weight we have put on the surveyability of (liberal and non-liberal) theories of human rights and the attendant systematicity of an introduction to the philosophy of human rights corresponds with questions of comprehensiveness and emphasis. The illusory goal of covering the entire field of study – even if it be only the field of the philosophy of that study – is obviously flawed. But the other extreme, of adopting a particular, articulated philosophical thesis regarding human rights, is also not our agenda. Neither do we develop an independent theory of human rights and attempt to respond according to that theory to the questions raised in our review of theories, of issues, of questions, and answers.

Still, and significantly, an author – even if she is only a systematic surveyor or a philosophical introducer – has the prerogative to select the topics of (her) interest and to emphasize the subjects of (her) notice. So the choice of thinkers and theories that populate Part II of our systematic introduction is based on both their historical importance and representative prowess, but also upon the particular contribution they make to *our* philosophical views on human rights. The emphasis put upon universalism and its questionable role in Western imperialism, the overriding interest in the human-rights-related plight of marginalized people and peoples, or the abhorrence of security-centered torture are, among other attention grabbers, a reflection of *our* ethical leanings in human rights. And even the weight put upon the non-liberal critique of certain conceptions of human rights echoes *our* philosophical proclivity to always question.

Perhaps similarly significant are decisions made regarding subjects that are omitted from this book. For example, animal rights, environmental rights, and questions of technology as it pertains to human rights have not received their (due?) respect in our discussions. The problem of the status of animal rights in the context of human rights is, indeed, both a conceptual and ethical challenge. In a sense, it is a meta-problem that should engage intimately with some of the conceptual questions raised in our story, such as the meaning of "human" and the status of having rights. Both environmental rights and technology-oriented human rights are, as we write, headline concerns. Precisely because of their novelty they were deemed less "classical" than other subjects taken up in our survey. But that is not to say that these three topics are not deserving of equal attention in the philosophy of human rights.

Finally, it is verily unattainable for an author to adopt a supposedly neutral, objective, unbiased position on a subject with such weighty ethical import as human rights. Hiding behind the label of "systematic introduction," with its insistence on aspects of surveyability, is the recognition that since the beginning (whenever that may be) there have been different ways of looking at human rights. We will be charting the historical, political, and legal facets of the terrain of human rights, but using the philosophical perspective on it to do more: to address these human rights "stories" in comparing them, assessing them, and trying to adjudicate between them. Indeed, presenting the traditional, liberal outlook on human rights in all its garb as a springboard for a view to less standard philosophical standpoints transports this book from a "systematic account" of human rights to a more comprehensive, yet perhaps more tentative, story, not just of issues and critique but, inevitably, of self-critique.

Notes

1 Orend's *Concept and Context* is differently balanced, affording most of its attention to the conceptual rather than contextual issues.
2 Coincidentally with these developments in the philosophy of human rights, the literature invigorating their discussion is immeasurable. The bibliography at the end of the book is made up of the exemplary representatives of these fundamental directions in the *philosophy* of human rights that is associated with these developments.
3 This is the place to also note that, along the text, "human rights" is sometimes used in plural, other times in singular form. The distinction is suspiciously nebulous, but nevertheless necessary. In the concrete use of "human rights" that refers to the rights themselves, that is, to particular rights that are characterized as human rights (such as the right to vote, the right to movement, the right to freely assemble), we will use the natural plural form, saying, for example, that "human rights are inalienable," or that "the rights that are violated by governments should be enforced." In the general use that points to the institution of human rights, to the field of human rights, to the idea of human rights, and the like, we will talk about the institution, the field, the idea and so on in the singular. Thus, we will say, for instance, that "human rights is all the rage." The pedant may insist that we ought to elaborate (by saying "the discussion on human rights is all the rage," or even by using reference quotes, as in "'human rights' is all the rage"). We find such meticulousness unnecessary, misleading, and sometimes even wrong.

Part I

Overview

1 Fundamentals

Human rights are the rights human beings have by virtue of being human. Although this claim seems simple enough, even superficial, perhaps even tautological, it is – as we shall see in this book – a statement that holds many philosophical questions. Just to begin with typical philosophical, conceptual questions, we might ask: What does it mean to be human? What is a right? What does it mean to have a right? And, finally – what is hiding behind that phrase "by virtue of"? In other words: what is it about being human that entitles us, as human beings, to something that is due precisely, exclusively, and universally, to human beings?

The conversation about human rights has various beginnings, but it is usually seen as starting in the middle of the twentieth century. Indeed, the story of human rights is typically told in the context of twentieth-century history and, more exactly, against the background of that most egregious of human tragedies, the Holocaust. It is after such atrocities as were perpetrated in the Holocaust, we are told, that the community of humankind awoke to the realization that a fundamental obligation had been breached, allowing humanity to perform actions which are absolutely prohibited. The search for the basis of that fundamental obligation led naturally to the concept of human rights. And that conceptual basis just as naturally resulted in what some have called the bible of human rights: the Universal Declaration of Human Rights of 1948.

This is not to say that our discussion here will start there – in 1948. In fact, since we are intent on asking conceptual, philosophical questions about human rights, there are several different ways of marking the beginning of the discussion. First, one can reject any chronological or historical perspective on human rights and aspire to be purely "analytical." This would mean that we propose to analyze the concepts "human" and "right," and pretend that we can provide a satisfactory understanding of human rights by analysis alone. Such is not necessarily a moot exercise in the semantics of only those two words. This analysis would certainly be asked to elaborate on questions such as "what are the objects of human rights?", "what are the criteria of being human?", "why are human rights more significant than other rights?", etc. But such analyses could not be responsible for the historical, contextual *use* of the term "human rights" or the practical *doings* of the community that is today labeled as the "human rights community." It would be a truly conceptual analysis.

A very different project would tell the historical story of human rights, deciding in some well-explained fashion, or perhaps in a more arbitrary one, where that history begins. We have mentioned that common wisdom puts its beginning after World War II. But since human rights are a sub-category of rights in general, it might behoove the teller of the story to begin where the concept of "rights" began. Without going into minute textual investigation, it is generally safe to say that the idea of rights belongs in seventeenth-century philosophy with the advent of philosophical-political liberal thought. So our story would begin in the seventeenth century with the usual suspects – famous protagonists like Thomas Hobbes, John Locke, and Jean Jacques Rousseau. It would, however, need to identify the intellectual point in time where rights in general gave way to human rights. And it would have to address other challenges to that conventional 1948 birth of human rights, propounded by historians and scholars of a more political or historical bent who look to the current *praxis* of human rights and identify its beginnings in various concrete rather than merely legalistic or formalistic contexts.[1]

Our aim in this book is to provide a working philosophical synthesis of both of these perspectives. In other words, we aspire to treat the conceptual framework of human rights simultaneously in both an analytic and contextual manner: the terms "human" and "rights" – along with their amalgamation and derivatives – will be examined not in a purely meaning-ridden enquiry but rather as items of a discourse and practice that carry both historical baggage and contemporary weight. In this chapter we begin with some terminological clarifications for such a synthesis.

The Basic Building Blocks

Human rights are the rights to which humans are entitled; or, to put it more accurately, human rights concepts articulate what it is that humans are entitled to. It should be immediately stressed that entitlement is not – as it might sound to some – a matter of privilege. The entitlement of which we speak here is an entitlement of necessity, not of indulgence. Saying that human beings are entitled to something does not thereby make that something an object to be fashionably coveted or popularly desired. It rather implies that these are things without which a human life is not complete or properly human. The entitlement associated with human rights is a requirement of certain things due to any human being.

A common axiom of human rights (which will, in the sequel, be questioned and discussed, despite being sometimes considered axiomatic) is that it is the *individual* human being who is owed these rights. Such individualism is a staple of modern liberal thought, coming on the heels of the Enlightenment recognition of the human individual – rather than the family, the tribe, the religious group, the community, the society, or the nation – as a source of rational and sometimes even moral authority. We will soon examine the issue of authority but, for the meantime, it is a relatively straightforward insight that places the single, distinct human being at the center of human rights. Although groups of human beings, like the family, the tribe, the religious group, the community, the society, and the nation, may seem to carry an identifiable existence of their own, and although we may entertain the notion of the rights of such groups,[2] it is the individual who is the emblematic subject of human rights. Saying that individual humans rather than groups, for instance, are entitled to human rights does not preclude asking further questions about which individuals these might be: Each and every human being? Does that include children? And what about prisoners, or disabled persons? These are weighty questions that need answering; but they do not belie the exclusive focus on the singular human being who functions as the main protagonist in the human rights story.

An immediate additional query, after we posit that individuals are owed human rights, is "who (or what) owes these rights?" Here again, in almost axiomatic form, the conventional modern answer is a consequence of a modern political construct – the *state*. True, we might find ourselves saying things like "I have a right to that house that I bought," and surmising that the seller of the house that I bought must deliver on my right. Or we might discuss the issue of students' rights in school and accost a teacher or a principal as responsible for protecting those rights. We might even speak of prisoners' rights in a penitentiary and hold the guards or warden accountable for upholding those prisoners' rights. But in the case of the human rights of individuals, in general, it is the political authority of the state that is looked to for support, protection, defense, and safeguarding; and it is, contrarily, the state which houses the greatest potential for violation of human rights. By saying "the state" we mean the persons, institutions, and roles that together make up and perform the functions of political authority. Political theories, within the context of political science and political philosophy, may be called upon to explicate the essence of these bodies and to elaborate on their functioning. (Some of them will, indeed, come up in subsequent chapters.) Suffice for now to acknowledge the modern state, more often than not a nation-state, as the main player[3] in the international arena and therefore the body that is considered responsible for the individual's human rights.

Individuals, and the states that house them, are subsequently the actors on the human rights stage. But aren't we missing the main actor on the stage? Or perhaps what is needed is a better description of the stage itself. Who, or what, is it that prescribes human rights? Who, or what, is it that formulates the rules for recognizing human rights and their violations? Who, or what, is it that is called upon to enforce the guardianship of human rights by states and then to castigate or punish their violators? Here, it is time to continue climbing the staircase that leads from individuals to states to ... the global order. It is the somewhat abstract level of international authority that is accepted as the power which, from on-high, from "above" the authority of the state itself, must undergird the arena of human rights. Such an international or global body might be seen as a purely theoretical construct – the higher-than-the-state authority which can be discerned in our quest for a general association of humanity. It has, however, acquired more concrete and down-to-earth expression in the workings of international politics and international law. For it is in international agreements, treaties, conventions or covenants, and in global institutions, courts, tribunals, and commissions, that human rights have been "grounded." The legal and political bodies to which we allude will be duly elaborated in the coming chapters, but it is important to note, immediately, that the theoretical structure we are describing – from individuals who hold human rights, to states that are responsible for them, to a world society which ensures their protection – is deceptively simple, tracing, as it seems to do, a progression from the human ground up to a global sky.

Deceptive and simplistic, since it appears to facetiously suggest that states are only conglomerates of individuals and the global order is only an amalgamation of states. Even supposing that we could easily define and identify the individual human who is the "hero" of the human rights story – that is to say, its main protagonist – these two higher levels of state and global authority need the attention given by the disciplines of political science, international relations, and legal studies to analyze their status in the realm of human rights. Think of it this way: Since human rights are to be accorded to all human beings, it is under the purview of a global power to prescribe and ensure their accordance universally. The state seems to be positioned somewhere between that universal authority that is reaching out to individuals and the individuals themselves, and it is the state that is considered the vehicle of providing for human rights (and being called to task if it doesn't). But how are individuals to reach out, beyond or around or above the state, to the world power that governs human rights? And how can that world power access, under or around or below the state, the human beings that need its human rights support and protection? Clearly it is that entity called the state, positioned between the individual and the world, which plays both the political role and the legal functions that either provide for human rights or violate them. And states, rather than individuals or international institutions, might prove to be the indispensable characters in our story of human rights.

Categories of Rights

In the following chapters we will encounter numerous examples of human rights. An immediate, rather intuitive list that is made up of elements we are all familiar with probably looks like this: the right to life, the right to liberty, the right to be recognized before the law, freedom of movement, the right to honorable subsistence, the right not to be subjected to torture, the right to never be a slave, freedom of thought and religion, the right to work, the right to marry whomever one wishes to marry – or the right not to be married at all, the right of free association, the right to healthcare, the right to education. Some readers of this list may think there are basic human rights missing from it; others may feel it includes "rights" that are not, by their light, really human rights. The exact enumeration of those rights that are, or should be, recognized as human rights is one of the issues that a philosopher (of human rights) must elaborate upon; the criteria for including or excluding a right from the category of human rights are something a philosopher (of human rights) must investigate and then clarify. These questions are, in fact, an important part of our agenda in this book. For the moment, however, let us expound more generally on two main categories of human rights that have become part and parcel of the human rights suitcase: a family of human rights called civil and political rights and another family called economic, social, and cultural rights.

When looking at the usual suspects adumbrated in the lists of human rights that we – we who are mostly in the Western World – are accustomed to, like the right to vote, our rights before the law, the freedom to leave and re-enter a country, the right to a nationality, and other obvious candidates for the label of "human rights," it seems clear that these are civil or political rights. That is to say, these are rights that one – an individual – can demand as a citizen of a political entity, usually of a state. There is something inherently political in this type of right, something that is manifested in the civil role that an individual plays *vis à vis* the state of which she is a citizen. Another type of right, seemingly less political, can be discerned in, for instance, the right to health care, the right to a reasonable subsistence, or the right to education. These rights appear to be a matter of one's economic, social, or cultural well-being, not one's political existence. True, these latter rights, if recognized as human rights, are also claimed by the individual facing her state authorities, but they are of a different kind than the evidently political or civil rights of the first group of rights.

Understandably, then, the human rights discussion has evolved (since 1948) to accept two relatively well-defined groups of rights: the civil-political class of human rights and the economic-social-cultural set of human rights.[4] Relatively well-defined, since several problems arise from this handy distinction. First, how are we to situate some prominent human rights, like freedom of movement or the right to free speech? Are these political rights or social rights? And what about the right to education? Is that a civil right or an economic right? Or the rights having to do with marriage – are they political, civil, social, or perhaps even economic? Second, and not unconnected, what is it that justifies our placement of a right – supposing we have agreed that it is a human right – in one of these categories? In the annals of liberal thought, the twosome of freedom and equality have played a central role as the basic concepts that ground liberalism.[5] And in the analysis of human rights it is often claimed that the construct of freedom grounds civil and political rights, while equality is the idea driving economic, social, and cultural rights. But this, of course, needs deep exploration, especially since these two stalwarts of liberalism – and of human rights – have led to some sore complexities in our political life. Not unrelated to this tension are, thirdly, the attitudes towards freedom and equality, and subsequently towards human rights, held by different societies in different parts of the world. Our historical story of the formal advent of human rights (in 1948) will illustrate the debates between various countries on issues of human rights that can be understood precisely through the bifurcation of liberty and equality. Recalling the French Revolution's "liberty, equality, frater-nity,"[6] Martin Buber once famously quipped that liberty went West, equality went East, and fraternity was lost sight of by all (Friedman, 1983, 450). Be that as it may, we will see in the sequel how this essential and deep division between civil-political and economic-social-cultural human rights led to the evolvement of two separate formal-legal bodies of human rights. And we will ask, more philosophically, if this division is warranted and whether it carries essential or practical consequences.

Human Rights or Civil Rights?

> When we call anything a person's right, we mean that he has a valid claim on society to protect him in the possession of it, either by the force of law, or by that of education and opinion ... To have a right, then, is, I conceive, to have something which society ought to defend me in the possession of.
>
> (Mill, *Utilitarianism* 1985 [1861], 25)

Is John Stuart Mill talking here about human rights? About civil rights? About all rights? Consider those earlier founding documents of rights, the American Declaration of Independence (1776), the French Declaration of the Rights of Man and Citizen (1789), and the American Bill of Rights (1791), documents which formulated, introduced, and established the point of our rights as claims on society. Which of them were talking of human rights, and which of civil rights? Or, fast forward and look at the Stanford Ency-clopedia of Philosophy under the entry "Rights": there is some mention of "human rights," but none at all of "civil rights"![7]

In the 1960s, civil rights were at the heart of our political, social, and cultural discourse and action; in the 1980s, and on into the twenty-first century, most of the discussions and organizational practices have moved to center on human rights. These are both conversations that have to do with the concept of "right" itself; a philosophical (and also legal) analysis of that concept will be forthcoming shortly. At this point, it will suffice to pose the preliminary question about the difference and relationship between *human* rights and *civil* rights as they appear in common discourse. For that pur-pose, we can continue on the track established above by the postulate that human rights are the rights human beings have by virtue of being human. In parallel, we can posit that civil rights are the rights that accrue to a person by virtue of being a citizen (of a state) or perhaps a member of a civil society. If asked – and we *will* ask later on – what makes us think that we do all have rights simply because we are human, we can reply religiously by saying that these are God-given rights or metaphysically by saying that these are natural rights.[8] The corresponding query regarding civil rights receives more straightforward answers: civil rights are thought to derive from a *social contract* – the common consent of society at large to the rules under which its members live.[9] In other words, under this conception civil rights originate in the society or community of which we are a part; they are not God-given or naturally determined.

One of the first insights that comes to mind from this initial, supposedly definitional characterization of human rights and civil rights is that the latter might seem more provisional or less absolute than human rights. Indeed, in contrast to human rights, which are perceived as universal rights owing to all human beings, civil rights can have an air of contingency about them – they are dependent on the society or the state in which they are formulated and implemented. Certain liberties might be rescinded: for example, drug or alcohol use, or driving at one's chosen speed. Others might be introduced into the society at a certain time, where they were previously absent, such as the right (of women) to vote, or the right (of Americans) to healthcare. The reason to regard all of these as civil rather than human rights is their dependence on variant forms of social organization, various conditions of societal resources, or even variable *civil* value-systems.

In fact, the questions and debates about the foundation of human rights – are they God-given or natural, and if natural, then which metaphysical faith grounds them – naturally transform into questions and debates about civil law itself. Take, for example, questions about education. When asking about the right to education we should decree, first, whether a human being's nature involves developmental potential. If our answer is "no," then the "right" to free education cannot be posited as a natural human right, depending rather, as it invariably must, on contingent factors such as the wealth of a given society. Some might even go further along the contingency path and claim that even if our answer is "yes" – yes, human nature involves the potential for perfection – the right to free education is still conditional on the circumstances of the civil body in which it is to be realized. Similarly vexing is the right to freedom of movement: is it a basic human right or a derived (from situational conditions) civil right? So too is the even more fundamental right of fair treatment in court: isn't that essential right a function of a society's ideas of justice and fairness? We seem to be heading towards an admission that the identification of certain rights as human rights changes from society to society; obviously, then, so does recognition of diverse civil rights. Reflect, for a moment, on the American Declaration of Independence, which bases the rights of life, liberty, and the pursuit of happiness on "the laws of nature and of nature's God." We view this, traditionally, as building upon John Locke's "natural rights" of life, liberty, and property (Locke 1689). But for that exact reason, Locke believed that these rights should be converted into civil rights, that is to say, they should be protected by the state, which is, in turn, the outcome of the social contract. We seem to have come full circle.

A facile way to answer the question about the connections, or the disconnection, between civil rights and human rights is to turn to our earlier demarcation of civil-political human rights and economic-social-cultural human rights. This type of schematic solution has human rights encompassing civil rights as a semantic category applying to the universal rights to which all human beings are entitled; civil rights then become merely a sub-class, a certain type of human rights (as do social or economic rights). Another, less simplistic, but still fairly structural resolution of this puzzle holds that civil rights are more primary than human rights since rights cannot and do not exist independently of a political-civil society. Human rights, on this reading, are an abstract, theoretical construct having nothing to do with real human beings; civil rights are and should be the object of our strivings. Finally, putting this last evasion of human rights into more concrete relief, we can point to the important difference between the two as residing with the authorities evaluating and enforcing the protection of both types of rights. Civil rights are administered by the state, within which laws concerning rights are formulated, kept and broken. Human rights are considered to be universal, and so we aspire to international bodies that are placed in charge of their appraisal and judgment.

Malcolm X and Hannah Arendt

To be sure, this last was the distinction between human rights and civil rights that Malcolm X was adopting in his assault against the more conventional struggle promulgated by Martin Luther King Junior and the civil rights movement of the 1950s and 1960s. Alternately considered a defamer of anti-violence, a preacher of racism, and a human rights activist, Malcom X is relevant to our deliberations concerning human rights vs. civil rights precisely due to his explicit statement that the fight for civil rights is and ought to be, for all intents and purposes, a fight for human rights. "When you take your case to Washington D.C.," he said, "you're taking it to the criminal who's responsible." His point, presented to civil rights organizations, was that by making the civil rights movement a more expansive human rights movement they would be internationalizing it.

> Once the civil rights movement is expanded to a human rights movement our African brothers and our Asian brothers and Latin American brothers can place it on the agenda at the General Assembly that is coming up this year and Uncle Sam has no more say-so in it then.
>
> (Spellman, 1964)

Working at the level of human rights rather than civil rights meant, for Malcolm X, turning to world jurisdiction. But it also seems clear that Malcolm X was not only harping on the pragmatic agenda of who or what authority can be called on to help the cause.

> Civil rights means you're asking Uncle Sam to treat you right. Human rights are something you were born with. Human rights are your God-given rights. Human rights are the rights that are recognized by all nations of this earth. And any time anyone violates your human rights, you can take them to the world court.[10]

The authority that Malcolm X adduces is an international tribunal, not the American government, which is the culprit itself. But that authority is born of the deep question of where our rights come from; his answer makes them human rights rather than civil rights.

Where Malcolm X wants to associate civil rights and human rights by subordinating the first to the second, Hannah Arendt, one of the twentieth century's most mesmerizing political thinkers, connects the two going in the opposite direction, to civil rights from human rights, and thereby deeply challenging the latter. But Arendt must be considered in context if we are to understand her "attack" on human rights with her intricate turn to civil rights. Writing after World War II, while writing more generally about totalitarianism, she sets the stage:

> [T]he incredible plight of an ever-growing group of innocent people was like a practical demonstration of the totalitarian movements' cynical claims that no such thing as inalienable human rights existed and that the affirmations of the democracies to the contrary were mere prejudice, hypocrisy, and cowardice in the face of the cruel majesty of a new world. The very phrase "human rights" became for all concerned – victims, persecutors, onlookers alike – the evidence of hopeless idealism or fumbling feeble-minded hypocrisy.
>
> (Arendt, 1966 [1951], 269)

Arendt's was a double-pronged attack: One was against totalitarian systems, in which human rights have no existence, in which there is no respect for a person as a human being, and in which the cruelty of the regime is explained precisely by the demise of any ideas of rights for human beings. The other was against the liberal, democratic discourse on human rights which she identified as a farce when used by leaders and politicians. These two critiques must be distinguished, but more importantly they must not be taken to mean that Arendt was "against human rights." She was, rather, despondent about the decline of human rights and despairing of the possibility of their universal achievement or enforcement.

[The] new situation in which "humanity" has in effect assumed the role formerly ascribed to nature or history would mean in this context that the right to have rights or the right of every individual to belong to humanity should be guaranteed by humanity itself. It is by no means certain whether it is possible.

(ibid., 298)

Arendt's stunning designation of "the right to have rights" has been recognized, by many, as an apposite characterization, perhaps even a definition, of human rights. Interestingly, however, it is not only in totalitarian regimes that we might lose the right to have rights; we can and must identify the naïve idealists who talk about human rights without realizing that human rights are used and abused by cynical hypocrites for their own instrumental interests. Consequently, Arendt spells out what must be done to ensure our right to have rights. On the basic, most practical level, the fight against totalitarianism must be joined to liberal democracy and carried out not only in the legal arena (as "human rightists" believe) but in the political and sometimes even the military one as well. Related to this is the business of public intellectuals: they must go beyond the idealistic struggle for human rights and engage in the political pursuit of civil rights. This is because there is a philosophical, substantive level of understanding here. The idea of essential human dignity,[11] lying at the base of human rights, involves a moral demand for *political* equality. "We are not born equal; we become equal as members of a group, on the strength of our decision to guarantee ourselves mutually equal rights" (ibid., 301). In other words, equality arises in and from the political sphere, not from the natural assumption of being human. Born as human means we have moral and civic capabilities; and being a champion of human rights means making them political, that is to say, civil. The upshot of such an analysis seems to be that there is no existential option for human rights unless they are conceived and implemented as civil and political rights.

Admittedly, Hannah Arendt wrote these profoundly philosophical ruminations before the current proliferation of human rights discourse, human rights organizations, human rights communities, human rights commissions and tribunals – the whole "industry" of human rights. In a sense, we can see her call for the politicization of human rights – by insisting they be administered as civil rights – as having been answered. Paradoxically, perhaps, this has not happened exclusively at the level of state-laws, which Arendt considered crucial for the realization of civil rights. Instead, we seem to have entered an era of both international politics and international law, with human rights being addressed, on that level, overtly as human – rather than civil – rights. For Arendt, talk of human rights was bound by the individual and the political state in which he or she functioned as a citizen. In the three-level structure we have adopted, of individual-state-world, the place of human rights might, in the end, be upgraded to fit in the top tier.

Two Provisional Disclaimers

Politics

One term that has made its appearance often up to now is "politics," and its close cousin – "the political." Indeed, we have used it naturally, as it appears in common discourse, in ordinary language, and in the media, without tasking ourselves with questions of its accurate meaning or definition. But its use has not been inconsequential – note, for example, the move from human rights to civil rights that Hannah Arendt makes precisely by insisting on the political aspects of being human. We must, therefore, ask ourselves at this introductory stage about the connection between human rights and politics; very explicitly, we ask "Are human rights political?"

On the one hand, it seems almost trivial to answer positively. Of course human rights are political. They are usually studied in the halls of academia in departments of political science (and sometimes philosophy) under the rubric of "political thought" and "political theory." Then there is the "on-the-ground" sense of the political, involving persons in the corridors of real politics, power, and diplomacy. Here, saying that human rights are political means merely pinpointing the availability and use of the language of human rights and the dealings in issues of human rights for and by professional and semi-professional politicians. These actors are not unaware of human rights, although they surely are often disturbingly unmindful of them. In saying that human rights are political in this sense, one is only alluding to the reality of the political context in which they dwell.

On the other hand, it is surprising that in the field of human rights itself, in both organizational practice and even in (some) concordant theoretical discussions, one is constantly admonished to "never mix up human rights with politics." In fact, it seems that the one seemingly unchanging presupposition that guides human rights activity and has accompanied its phenomenal growth in the past few decades, the one almost consensual mantra in the arena of human rights, is – "human rights are not political." What could be the explanation for such a denial of politics, for such self-distancing of the human rights community from the political doings that seem to be almost automatically linked with human rights? One straightforward, though perhaps naïve, way of apprehending this disconnect between politics and human rights is to say that the whole point of the turn to human rights in the twentieth century was to escape the dependence rights have had, traditionally, on political contexts. Dealing in *human* rights would ensure the rights that human beings have prior to any political circumstance (and would vouch for the priority of human rights over other considerations). Another more down-to-earth look at this disengagement from politics emphasizes the practical status of the maxim and focuses on the need to defend the rights human beings have when facing political authorities; a counterweight to these authorities can be provided, then, by apolitical auspices that challenge the political from a "neutral" standpoint. More pragmatic still is the claim that human rights organizations can be more efficacious, indeed might even make more substantial progress, by not being beholden to or associated with any political entity – by being, as it were, universal[12] in their moral foundations, and thereby apolitical in their actions.

A blatant, distinctive way of being apolitical that the human rights community has espoused is the legal approach, i.e., the theoretical and practical predication of human rights on the law, whether it be domestic law or, more often than not in the human rights context, international human rights law. In fact, the predominant mode of action for human rightists is legal methodology – a law-centered approach to violations, problems, solutions, and recommendations that are under human rights' purview. There is, according to some who assume this legal perspective exclusively, no avenue for addressing human rights that is free of legal vocabulary, and it is this focus that keeps us on the road of "pure" human rights, thus preventing a political side-stepping. We will not, in this book, deny the significant legal anchor of human rights; on the contrary, we will be surveying the legal instruments that are available to us for the formulation of violations, for the determination of problems, and then for the suggestion of solutions and the articulation of recommendations regarding human rights. But our treatment of human rights, while certainly admitting the indispensability of the legal toolbox, will be wider and more inclusive, based on two vital insights. First, without engaging in the philosophy of law explicitly, we make note that the law itself is not an unadulterated, apolitical construct. We cannot here address the several philosophical positions regarding the law – e.g., natural law theory, legal positivism, legal realism, legal formalism, and others – that might guide us in our engagement with politics, but we especially note our affinity with those descriptions and analyses of the law that admit to the impossibility of its divorce from politics. Second, and importantly, we also believe that human rights *are* and *should be* political. That is to say, given the theoretical political context of the concept of human rights and the unavoidable politics of our contemporary life, which pushes human rights into the field of political activism, we will view human rights as political and claim that they cannot be anything but political. So we set the explicit debate on human rights and politics aside, while accepting the legal framework itself as a part of our essentially political perception of human rights.[13]

Religion

A no less thorny subject than politics is religion. The relationship between religion and human rights and, even more so, the attempt to investigate that relationship hold pitfalls for any systematic introduction of the subject. The philosophical challenge regarding religion – and human rights – usually arises in the context of the question regarding the foundation and justification of human rights. Answers to this question may be religious or secular and it is incumbent on us to provide criteria for the legitimacy – not the correctness – of different answers. On the one hand, says the open-minded thinker, any satisfactory examination of the foundations of human rights, including the one that asks about religious fundamentals, should be studied for whatever it is worth. On the other hand, says the secular philosopher, the point of human rights is their humanistic basis. Bringing religion into the conversation takes us off the legitimate course of investigation which decries any articles of faith. On still another level, says the tolerant mediator, if we allow metaphysical arguments into the discussion, why are the irreligious metaphysics of secular philosophy more acceptable than religious essentials of thinkers of faith?

A very different challenge to the discussion of religion and human rights resides concretely in the arena of human rights activism, its motivation, and the localities of its support. Again, we are faced with supposedly contradictory intuitions and experiences. On the institutional level, there are religious houses of worship with their world-wide establishments and adherents – be they of Muslim, Christian, Buddhist, Jewish, Confucian, Hindu and oh-so-many other denominations – that proclaim a profound care and love of humanity and that, more practically, engage in the kind of humanitarian work that is typically allied with the activities of human rights organizations. Contrariwise, however, we are also far too often exposed to the religious agendas of such institutions – again, be they Jewish, Christian, Muslim, Hindu, and others – that deeply and ideologically oppose some of the most central tenets, and therefore activities, of numerous human rights organizations. Issues such as women's rights, or capital punishment, or hierarchical social structures, or even slavery, are exactly the sort of concerns that have become centerpieces of the human rights program all over the world; these are also exactly the places of contention with religious authorities all over the world.

Putting the two levels of questioning together, the theoretical dilemma of what can justify human rights and the practical quandary of how to collaborate with religious institutions, we can ask about the motivation for human rights activism: when a religious person joins a secular one in a march for workers' rights, or at a demonstration against racism, or in a petition for prisoners' privileges – are they partaking of the same activity? Does it matter that the faithless person does it out of a deep conviction in human dignity, with no turn to the divine, while the believer sees his actions as deriving from godly instruction? Even if they both use the expression "human rights," do they really mean the same thing? Does, indeed, the person of faith often use the term "human rights," or will she more likely be speaking about God's commands? Does the different impetus for the same activity make the activity itself of dissimilar worth and meaning? And finally, are there any concrete implications for the results of that activity that come out of their divergent belief systems? When assessing the success or failure of the human rights program, writ large, should we take into consideration the religious-secular divide in human culture?

Differently from the case of politics, we will not make the issue of religion a self-standing topic in our treatment of human rights.[14] But as in the case of politics, we cannot deny the crucial place of religion in human endeavor, in general, and in both the personal and communal engagement in human rights, in particular. In contrast to politics, though, where we are prepared to say unequivocally that human rights are political, the question of religion will remain more opaque. That question – which is, in truth, a dual question: Is the foundation for human rights religious or secular, and does it matter which? – will make itself apparent at several junctures in our discussion, but we will not always be able to offer a final pronouncement. In fact, more often than not, we will have to be satisfied with understanding the consequences of different perspectives, or sometimes only with understanding the question itself. That is how things are in philosophy; that is how they should be in the philosophical inquiry into human rights.

Notes

1 An outstanding example of such revision is Samuel Moyn, *The Last Utopia: Human Rights in History* (2010), who determines a beginning of very different sorts in the 1970s.

2 There is, of course, a difference between the rights of a group *as a group* and the rights of the aggregate of individuals in the group. See Chapter 8 for further discussion.

3 The critique and demise of the nation-state with suggestions for its replacement (an international government, the global community, cosmopolitan authorities, et al) have become a mainstay of current theoretical political thought. Some important contributors to the debate(s) are Zygmunt Bauman, *Culture in a Liquid Modern World* (2011); Seyla Benhabib, *Transformations of Citizenship: Dilemmas of the Nation State in the Era of Globalization* (2001); Gayatri Chakravorty Spivak and Judith Butler, *Who Sings the Nation-State? Language, Politics, Belonging* (2007); Norman Davies, *Vanished Kingdoms: The Rise and Fall of States and Nations* (2011); Linda Basch, Linda Glick Schiller, and Cristina Szanton Blanc, *Nations Unbound: Transnational Projects, Postcolonial Predicaments and Deterritorialized Nation-States* (1993).

4 Sometimes these two types have been referred to as first-generation and second-generation rights, but the moniker hints at a problematic (substantial or chronological) order or even priority that does not really serve us well.

5 Liberalism, as both a political philosophy, a political practice, and a political structure, is consensually perceived as enshrining both freedom and equality. Just as fascinating are the tensions and conflicts between these two concepts that make up the ongoing conversation about and within liberalism.

6 As is well-known, the slogan arising from the French Revolution and popularly inscribed on some Parisian houses was "Liberty, equality, fraternity, or death."

7 https://plato.stanford.edu/entries/rights/

8 This question will engage us in Chapter 6.

9 Usually associated with Jean-Jacques Rousseau's *The Social Contract* (1968 [1762]), the social contract tradition can be traced back to Thomas Hobbes and John Locke, and receives a sustained treatment in John Rawls's political philosophy.

10 From "The Ballot or the Bullet," a public speech delivered on April 3, 1964, at Cory Methodist Church in Cleveland Ohio.

11 We will explore the concept of dignity further in Chapter 3.
12 We will return to the essential issue of universalism several times in the sequel.
13 See Chapters 12 and 13 for a deeper examination of the political in human rights.
14 We will, nevertheless, address certain positions on the religious foundations of human rights in Chapter 6.

2 The Legal Framework

It is commonly accepted that International Human Rights Law developed after World War II. Yet, when we ask about the legal background of current human rights, it is appropriate to refer to earlier legal perceptions and the documents that reflected or established the way we think about them today. We shall not regress here to ancient times and their legal templates – one sometimes hears of the Laws of Noah or the Ten Commandments or the Hebrew prophets or Hammurabi's Code; neither shall we dig up medieval papers, like the Constitution of Medina (622) or the Magna Carta (1215). Ours is not a historical quest for the roots of ethical and legal thinking that might have invigorated, and probably did, ideas of legal *rights*, human or otherwise. It is, rather, fitting to recognize that the significant background of rights as we view them today is a product of modern history,[1] buttressed by the conceptual scaffolding of modern philosophy. In Part II ("Philosophical Groundings"), we will, indeed, follow the steps of that philosophy as it led to the conceptual framework of human rights. But now, since we are focusing on the *legal* background of human rights, we must make mention of the three revolutionary documents that mark the advent of a rights-oriented political mind-set. Those are, as we have seen before, the American Declaration of Independence (1776), the French Declaration of the Rights of Man and Citizen (1789), and the American Bill of Rights (1791). All three documents exhibit the understanding, so basic to human rights, that rights are universal and owing to all humans.[2] Famously, of course, the Declaration of Independence announces that the truths about such rights are "self-evident" – "that all men are created equal, that they are endowed by their Creator with certain inalienable Rights, that among these are Life, Liberty and the pursuit of Happiness." The French document, based on the doctrine of natural rights, just as universally speaks of these rights as being "natural, unalienable and sacred," and lists the basic ones as the rights of "liberty, property, security and resistance to oppression." The Bill of Rights, constituting the first ten amendments to the American Constitution, with less fanfare and fewer explicit universal proclamations, is a list of limits on governmental power, all born of (human) rights such as freedom of religion, freedom of speech, and the right to keep and bear arms.[3]

Importantly, these famous documents, even when talking of "all men" and justifying the rights of all men through universal (also called natural) assumptions, are addressed to a particular government. Universality functions as a justification, not as a concrete framework in which the rights that are based on it can be implemented or enforced. In fact, the demand made of the French and the American governments is to each respect and protect the rights of their own citizens. That these rights originate in a certain universal nature of man is used as an argument for their realization but cannot function beyond the relationship between citizen and state. In this sense, these early articulations of rights that might be viewed as human rights evade the structure of the whole edifice of human rights which was posited in Chapter 1. There it was proposed that human rights are the rights that individuals can demand of the states that govern them, but that there is a higher level, the global or international level, from which human rights emerge and at which they are realized.

International Human Rights Law

There are numerous legal or sometimes semi-legal instruments relating to human rights. There are declarations of principles, guidelines of action, rules, and recommendations; and there are covenants and treaties, statutes and protocols, conventions and contracts. The legal status of all of these "pieces of paper" is a perplexing question. In general, we can proffer that declarations, guidelines, and statements do not have any binding legal force; they do, however, carry moral weight and can provide practical guidance for states and other governing bodies. Treaties, covenants, and conventions are more legalistically grounded. Depending on their terms and conditions, they carry legal effect for the parties that sign them, accede to them, or ratify them. Even these, however, must be investigated for their provenance, their implementation, and their enforcement.

International human rights law developed, as we know it today, after World War II. The addressees of the law are almost always states and the rights involved are almost always the rights of individuals, claimed of their state authorities. Like in domestic law, there is a distinction between customary law (expected of all states) and treaty-based law (required of those states who have signed onto a treaty). These conventions, treaties, and even declarations are the basic building blocks of international human rights law, but just as significant are the various legal organizational frameworks for the protection of human rights and the enforcement mechanisms that exist, some on the global level, others in more circumscribed geographical areas, for their employment. Thus, for example, the United Nations houses the Human Rights Council, tasked with the "promotion and protection of all human rights around the globe." On more localized levels we have the just-as-ambitious European Council's Commissioner for Human Rights, the African Commission on Human and People's Rights, the Inter-American Commission on Human Rights, and others.

No less important than such protection is judicial enforcement of human rights. Again, on the global level we look to the United Nations. There, since 1945, we have had the International Court of Justice (ICJ), based in The Hague. Despite its promising name, the ICJ is not the court of choice in matters of human rights violations, since it is charged with adjudication of disputes between states. Although a state may submit a case in the name of one of its citizens against another state which has violated the rights of that citizen, the ICJ has no jurisdiction over complaints submitted directly by individuals or other human rights bodies.[4] Again, localized and more pointedly defined courts, such as the European Court of Human Rights, the African Court of Human and People's Rights, and the Inter-American Court of Human Rights, are the venues where human rights violations can have their day in court. Most significant in the context of human rights law and its enforcement is a recent development – the International Criminal Court (ICC), based in The Hague beginning in 2002, as established by the Rome Statute of 1998. Although the conference in Rome, out of which the Rome Statute emerged, was convened by the UN, the ICC is an international tribunal whose existence and jurisdiction are independent of the UN, its functioning due to the multilateral treaty which obliges the states who sign and ratify it.[5] The ICC's unique responsibility is to attend to *individuals* who have perpetrated crimes of genocide, crimes against humanity, war crimes, and the crime of aggression;[6] just as significant is its openness to accept not only accusations and submissions from states and the UN Security Council, but information from "individuals, intergovernmental or nongovernmental organizations, or any other reliable sources" that can initiate an investigation (and consequent rulings).

The International Bill of Human Rights

In 1948 the United Nations General Assembly adopted the Universal Declaration of Human Rights (UDHR) "as a common standard of achievement for all peoples and all nations" concerning human rights. That short document – no longer than 2000 words – was the harbinger of more elaborate articulations of the set of rights accepted, to various degrees, by all member states of the UN. The two additional treaties, the International Covenant on Civil and Political Rights (ICCPR) and the International Covenant on Economic, Social and Cultural Rights (ICESCR), that were submitted to the UN in 1966 (along with the Optional Protocols attached to them), became, after sufficient ratifications by member countries by 1976, the binding legal documents for international human rights. Together these three documents have been titled the International Bill of Human Rights. Although the UDHR is "only" a declaration, while the ICCPR and ICESCR are formal treaties, we will survey and examine the former for its concise and principled formulation of purportedly global standards of human rights; afterwards, we will inquire into the added value – if there is any – of the two more detailed, more formal, official documents.

The Universal Declaration of Human Rights

If one were a historian or an archivist, one might seriously be interested in the story of the coming to be of the Universal Declaration of Human Rights (UDHR). How the idea – of drafting an obligating document on human rights in a world organization dedicated to peace – came to be; where it germinated; who was involved in its formulation; what circumstances and tensions characterized its progress; how much it included, how much was left out – and why. These wonderings are all germane to the narrative accompanying the UDHR.[7] Our concern here is not to tell stories, however; our purview is to understand the document under philosophical aegis (complemented, perhaps, by legal and political facets).

The UDHR consists of a Preamble and 30 Articles. Like many legal documents, especially contracts, the preamble begins with a set of "whereas" statements, that is to say, the set of justifications, motivations, and presuppositions that might serve to explicate the need for such a document being formulated. And indeed, the first few paragraphs of the declaration voice a motley group of "whereas" statements, two of which are of particular interest to us. One of them (actually the second in the text) spells out, in no uncertain terms, the historical reason for the document: "*Whereas* disregard and contempt for human rights have resulted in barbarous acts which have outraged the conscience of mankind ..." The nations of the world were reeling, in the post-war years, from what states and human beings could do to other human beings. The UDHR was a result of, and a testament to, that trauma. Another key paragraph (actually the first in the text) is no less unequivocal about its ideational object: "*Whereas* recognition of the inherent dignity and of the equal and inalienable rights of all members of the human family is the foundation of freedom, justice and peace in the world..." It is both the particular historical circumstances of the twentieth century as they relate to human rights and the essential dignity and absolute status of rights of all human beings that together served as stimuli for the UDHR.

Simplistically, it is tempting to say that the 30 articles of the UDHR enumerate 30 human rights; but things are a little more complicated (though not much more intricate) than that. A first, general categorization goes like this: The first two articles provide the fundamental thoughts of the drafters (and then one could ask how these are different from the Preamble), the next 19 articles lay out civil and political human rights, one further article advocates the basis of economic, social and cultural rights, which are then itemized in five more articles. The three final articles are odd – they seem to be afterthoughts to the list of human rights, adding elements which are either crucial or formalistic and rounding out the declarative discussion about human rights going on throughout the UDHR.

Article 1 begins with the statement that has been acknowledged by all and sundry as the quintessential proclamation of human rights: "All human beings are born free and equal in dignity and rights." Notice that this is not an elaboration of rights; it does not say that human beings have the right to freedom, equality, or dignity. Rather it assumes this characterization of all human beings, almost to the tune of an origin story – that they are free and that they are equal in dignity and rights. We will presently probe this crucial assumption for its philosophical implications concerning human beings. But for now, let us add to it another assumption, or rather injunction, that relates to these fundamentals. Article 2 gives the additional requirement that evolves out of the first three words of Article 1 – "all human beings." The universality that is assumed for universal human rights has to be explicitly laid down as correlative to the absence of any type of discrimination. "Everyone is entitled to all the rights and freedoms set forth in this Declaration, without distinction of any kind, such as race, color, sex, language, religion, political or other opinion, national or social origin, property, birth or other status."[8] More so, this universality is a universality of persons, human beings, individuals – unrelated to the political status of the place they live in, be it one of independence, mandate, occupied territory, or any other invention of international relations.

The next nineteen articles are the familiar list of human rights that are usually addressed in both the colloquial and academic conversation on the subject. We can, if we so desire, categorize them in various ways.[9] We opt, instead, to make some general remarks about them all and to note the oft-recognized problematic aspects that some of them exhibit. Famously, Article 3, the most basic of articles about human rights, tells us that "[e]veryone has the right to life, liberty and security of person."[10] Articles 4 and 5 provide the prohibitions on what are usually considered the most heinous crimes of governments against persons – slavery and torture. Articles 6–11 elaborate on the relationship between an individual and the law – i.e., the rights that individuals hold in the legal arena as a defense against government actions – and include recognition as a person before the law, equal protection of the law, effective remedy, no arbitrary arrest, impartial tribunal, and the like. The next few articles each deal independently with a different facet of our civil existence: privacy, movement, asylum, nationality, marriage, property, conscience and religion, opinion and speech, association and assembly, and, finally, active service and government.

This list raises classic queries: Do these rights rely on one another? Is this in any way a homogeneous list? Are some rights more important than others? Are some absolute while others can be laid aside in certain circumstances? Can they be portrayed systematically according to any theoretical template? Such queries obviously crop up in the legal frameworks of rights discourse; they are also noticeably impacted by conceptual thinking about them. Our substantive remark, at this point, is to note that all of these rights belong to what we have called above civil-political rights. That is what distinguishes them from those that now appear in the last few articles of the UDHR.

Article 22 seems anomalous to begin with:

> Everyone, as a member of society, has the right to social security and is entitled to realization, through national effort and international co-operation and in accordance with the organization and resources of each State, of the economic, social and cultural rights indispensable for his dignity and the free development of his personality.

Whereas the first group of rights (those in the first 21 articles) deals with "all human beings," devoid of any characteristic trait (indeed, we are instructed to ignore any such trait), there is in Article 22 an essential feature of the human being that makes him or her a holder of certain rights: being a member of society. Although human rights are rights of individuals, the individuals reflected here are not just isolated atoms; they are a part of society and, *as such*, they are deserving of rights that have to do, essentially, with society. Article 22, like Articles 1 and 2, does not detail any particular right but rather lays the ground for the next few articles, which do give such an elaboration.

That elaboration, in Articles 23–27, is what have come to be called economic, social and cultural rights. They range from rights that have to do with work and labor (equal pay, right to unionize, just remuneration, work conditions, etc.) to the right to leisure and rest; from rights of well-being (health, food, clothing, housing, etc.) to several rights having to do with education; and from that to the "right to participate in the cultural life of the community" (which includes both the arts and the sciences, with the added tack of copyright). As an interesting list indeed, this family of rights has merited less consensual acceptance than the civil-political rights of the first 21 articles. As we mentioned above,[11] these rights appear to be concerned with equality more than with freedom and were championed more emphatically, as could be expected, by the countries of Eastern Europe and China than by those of the liberal West.[12]

Let us conclude with a few words about the last three articles of the UDHR. These closing articles may be depicted as concluding remarks, as formal legalities often seen in contracts, or, perhaps, as even contributing something of more substance to the listing of rights that they follow. Indeed, Article 28 is, on the one hand, a final right but is, on the other hand, a meta-right, so to speak, which necessitates, for all people, a "social and international order" in which all the previous rights enumerated in the Declaration are realized. Article 29, oddly enough, introduces concepts which are not mere rights – such as those of "duties," of "morality," and of "democratic society" – and goes on to insist that the binding context of the declaration is "the purposes and principles of the United Nations." And Article 30, in true legalistic formulation, protects the Declaration, as a whole, from any internal contradiction that might undermine its original intent. Thus ends the monumental document that has come to be called the Bible of Human Rights.

Two International Human Rights Covenants

The decision to draft a foundation document of human rights was adopted by the United Nations in 1947, but when work on its formulation began, several different functions and goals became independently evident. A first bifurcation involved the distinction between a declaration of principles and a legal covenant of specific rights, their limitations and their implementation. It is not surprising, therefore, that that first pronouncement, which continued indeed to be called a Declaration, was more easily and quickly articulated and then accepted by the UN (on December 10, 1948).[13] It is just as plausible that not only did the purported legal treaty, later called a covenant, involve more detailed and problematic work, but that it itself also split, in 1951, into two covenants, one on civil and political rights and the other on economic, social, and cultural rights. Although the General Assembly suggested that the two covenants include as many identical rights as possible, it became clear that the human rights agendas of these two avenues of thought were, in some crucial respects, dissimilar. Further desiderata, like an article-by-article discussion, and the aim of including as many states as possible in the conversation and taking into consideration the public opinion of as large a public as possible, brought the preparation of these two covenants to the year 1966. We shall not present the minutiae of these two documents – they are, as we have stated, legal treaties concluded between the member-states of the UN. Let us, instead, take notice of two especially outstanding features of the covenants that are ostentatiously absent from the UDHR.

We have seen, and emphasized, that the idea of human rights, from its inception in the modern era and as voiced in the UDHR, is centered on *individual* human rights. But when one contemplates the political, historical times in which the covenants were being drafted, one cannot but acknowledge that these were the heated moments of anti-colonialism, anti-imperialism, and the independence struggles of countless ethnic and national groups. It is no wonder, then, that the idea of a group's rights, as a *group* (rather than merely as a conglomerate of individuals), made its way into the mindset of the persons formulating these covenants. Indeed, in both covenants we find an identical *first* article:

Article 1
1   All peoples have the right of self-determination. By virtue of that right they freely determine their political status and freely pursue their economic, social and cultural development.
2   All peoples may, for their own ends, freely dispose of their natural wealth and resources without prejudice to any obligations arising out of international economic co-operation, based upon the principle of mutual benefit, and international law. In no case may a people be deprived of its own means of subsistence.

3   The States Parties to the present Covenant, including those having responsibility for the administration of Non-Self-Governing and Trust Territories, shall promote the realization of the right of self-determination, and shall respect that right, in conformity with the provisions of the Charter of the United Nations.

We shall investigate the issue of group rights presently.[14] Suffice to notice now a few vital, conceptual elements of this article, which dwells in both the ICCPR and the ICESCR. First, the rights of the article are not rights of individuals but rather rights of "peoples."[15] Second, the primary, crucial right is that of "self-determination." Not only does self-determination appear, at first sight, to be a political right which is just as explicitly presented in the ICESCR as in the ICCPR, but there is, additionally, no explication as to what self-determination consists in. Third, the following section in this right of peoples – still in the same article – is concerned with their "natural wealth and resources," rather than with any other political rights; is this thereby an economic right? It too is identically presented in both covenants. Finally, the third section of the article expands to the duties of other states, duties which derive from respect for the rights of peoples. This article, then, is an instance of a human right that, even in its succinct and relatively abrupt formulation, manages to explicitly straddle the issues of individuals vs. groups, political vs. economic rights, and rights vs. duties.

We asked above, yet with no resolution, about the relative standing of different rights. A closely related question is that of the absoluteness of (all or some) human rights. Are human rights unconditional on circumstances or on situations in which they might be criticized or challenged? Can they be temporalized, relativized, or in other ways abstained from for a variety of reasons? The very famous metaphor of human rights being considerations that *trump* all others (Dworkin, 1984) seems to place human rights *above* all other arguments. But does this make them absolute? In the UDHR, Article 29 (and actually the three final articles in general) spoke, in familiar legalistic style, about limitations on rights and freedoms – on all rights and freedoms, be they civil-political or economic-social-cultural ones – being only allowed if and when they "are determined by law solely for the purpose of securing due recognition and respect for the rights and freedoms of others and of meeting the just requirements of morality, public order and the general welfare in a democratic society." In other words, the rights spelled out in the Declaration itself are almost absolute; they can be limited only under an ideological umbrella that assumes a democratic system of government. Interestingly, however, the covenants part ways on this seemingly convoluted question. The ICESCR, like the UDHR, limits all of the rights under its purview to human-rights focused law; in other words, none of its rights may be disposed of for any non-human-rights related reason. It is the ICCPR which makes a remarkable distinction between two groups of rights; let us call them absolute and non-absolute rights. In Article 4, which has no correlative in the ICESPR, we find:

Article 4

1 In time of public emergency which threatens the life of the nation and the existence of which is officially proclaimed, the States Parties to the present Covenant may take measures derogating from their obligations under the present Covenant to the extent strictly required by the exigencies of the situation, provided that such measures are not inconsistent with their other obligations under international law and do not involve discrimination solely on the ground of race, colour, sex, language, religion or social origin.

2 No derogation from articles 6, 7, 8 (paragraphs 1 and 2), 11, 15, 16 and 18 may be made under this provision.

Human rights, then, are not absolute at all; neither do they trump other considerations at all times and in all circumstances. At certain times *which threaten the life of the nation*, a state may "derogate" from upholding human rights, if that is what is assessed to be necessary to save the nation. We shall not engage here with the political queries of how we evaluate such threats, of who evaluates these threats, or of what is meant exactly by "the life of the nation." Those are deep, troubling questions in political theory and, more so, in political practice. But we make note of section 2 in Article 4, where the covenant does seem to recognize that certain human rights are, nonetheless, absolute. In other words, they cannot be derogated under any circumstances. These are, fascinatingly enough, the rights which come to mind most naturally in any list of human rights: the right to life, the right not to be tortured, the right not to be enslaved, the protection from imprisonment due to debt, freedom from retroactive laws, the right to recognition before the law, and freedom of thought, conscience, and religion. These are absolute human rights, and it is in the covenant on civil and political rights that their absoluteness is made explicit. Such explicitness highlights even more the bewildering yet enticing balance that is attempted here, in this seminal political document, between the idealistic concept of (absolute) human rights and the realistic awareness of threats to "the life of a nation."

Additional International Human Rights Instruments

The International Bill of Human Rights, consisting of a declaration and two covenants, is the basic and fundamental text which legally grounds human rights law all over the world. We have seen that in its first iteration, as the Universal Declaration of Human Rights, it does not carry formal legality but this is not to say that it does not function, in a more abstract and public framework, as the holy grail of human rights. Still, it had to be fleshed out and then enriched and established as a contractual text, in the form of the International Covenant on Civil and Political Rights and the International Covenant on Economic, Social and Cultural Rights, before the United Nations and its member states could embrace it as a legally binding document. And like these two covenants, there are other official conventions of international human rights law that have legal authority.

Very concretely, such documents of international law can only obligate states if they are adopted according to rules and regulations of international law. This involves a systematic procedure of signature and ratification of (or accession to) a treaty that is spelled out in exact detail by the United Nations. Of great interest to us is the difference between a state's signature to a treaty or convention and its ratification of that treaty. (There is also the option of acceding to a convention, which is a shortcut that joins together the signature and ratification.) By signing an international convention, a state does not thereby incur any legal obligations; it rather expresses its intention to sometime in the future take the appropriate steps which will indeed so obligate it. Those steps, however, are contingent on a state's domestic law, which prescribes the procedure mandated for ratifying the international treaty, such as legislation by parliament in the state's own legal system. Only then does a state ratify the treaty at the international level; and only then is it legally bound to implement it. Treaties also have to wait, as you might say, for a sufficient number of ratifications by states before they enter into force (and obligate the states that have ratified them). Finally, even upon ratifying an international treaty, states may formally express reservations about the treaty and by so doing exclude certain parts of the treaty or change some of its effects. This, of course, may raise the question: Isn't a reservation on a convention self-defeating? Precisely for that reason, the regulations concerning treaties are cleverly formulated, enjoining states to refrain from reservations that absolutely contradict the object of the treaty. Just as effective is the process that allows other states to object to a state's reservations, opening up an exchange between states by which they attempt to clarify problems until they are solved.[16]

Beyond these two central international covenants, we are at the time of writing aware of seven other human rights treaties considered by the U.N. to be the core international human rights instruments. Each of them is not only an international treaty, signed and ratified by enough countries so as to come into force, i.e., to obligate those countries, but is also supervised and monitored by formal UN committees, entrusted with ensuring their implementation. (Some also have optional protocols that accompany them, independently signed and ratified as well.) These treaties deal with foundational human rights topics such as racial discrimination, discrimination against women, torture, the rights of children, the rights of migrant workers, protection against forced disappearance, and the rights of people with disabilities.[17] And then there are the tens of other declarations, conventions, statements of rules and principles, and other legal instruments that, together, provide the human rightist with the legal wherewithal to address various concerns of human rights.[18] Some of the more preeminent ones are well-known in the public sphere. These include the United Nations Millennium Declaration (2000) and the 2030 Agenda for Sustainable Development (2015), in which leaders of the world articulated their goals concerning human rights, humanitarian law (more on that in the next section), and sustainable development; the General Assembly has gone on to speak about and monitor implementation of these declarations. A more uneven issue in the ongoing international discussion of human rights is the question of indigenous rights. There, again, we see a conglomeration of declarations and conventions but witness the UN finding it hard to achieve a document which can legally oblige all countries of the world.[19] Similarly multifaceted are several conventions dealing with discrimination – discrimination in employment and occupation, discrimination in education, or discrimination based on religious belief. And indeed, the general conventions having to do with discrimination against women or the rights of children, both of which have garnered official documents, also receive more particularistic – and no less important – attention in specific declarations such as the Declaration on the Elimination of Violence against Women or the Minimum Age Convention.

A comprehensive list, then, of the matters which populate the many documents of international human rights – some very formal and legal sounding, others more declarative but no less influential for that – is understandably rich and variegated. Notably, one of the earliest conventions is the Convention on the Prevention and Punishment of the Crime of Genocide (1948). The date of the establishment of the United Nations and its obvious circumstances made this concern a natural object of a convention of international law. But in addition to this striking statement, the various documents at hand consist of a roster of rights, from well-known and oft-mentioned issues to some slightly less ubiquitous topics to those that might seem particularistic to a fault. Accordingly, these range from women's rights, indigenous rights, or rights of disabled persons; to rights of older persons, rights of prisoners, rights and limitations of marriage, rights of migrants or rights of refugees; to the specific topic of smuggling of migrants, trafficking in persons, or the right to organize and collective bargaining, to name a few. The status of signature and ratification of these instruments (i.e., contracts, conventions, treaties, declarations, statements) that put all of these human rights into play on the international arena is, itself, a complicated piece of data and legal acumen. Such is the field of international human rights law.

Humanitarian Law

We will encounter, in this book, two distinct uses of the word "humanitarian." The more obvious one, which is the one more in use in ordinary parlance, is that meaning of "humanitarian" which points to the aspiration to improve the human condition or to support and promote human welfare. Thus, we speak of humanitarian organizations, humanitarian aid, humanitarian affairs, and, of course, humanitarianism itself. Though we shall engage with all these contexts and their natural relationship with human rights, in the present framework of legal affairs we are dealing with a very specific – and different – use of "humanitarian": We are referring here to *humanitarian law*, which is the name given to laws and rules that have to do with the conduct of war.

The semantics involved here is fascinating. War, as we know, is the least humanitarian of human activities. The end and means of war are a matter of victory (or defeat), domination (or servitude), and methods of warfare that inflict great suffering. Still, from the beginnings of human history involving combative conflicts, there has been an awareness of the illegitimacy of particular ways and means that come into play in war-situations. In other words, there have been attempts to formulate the rules that can guide the parties to battle concerning what may or may not be done – even in that most reprehensible of human deeds, even in killing, even in war. Since wars were usually fought between nations, it is reasonable to expect that within the framework of international law we can find the regulations that apply to what belligerent states may do in wartime. But it also makes sense to examine what other actors such as collaborative states, neutral states, and individuals – whether representatives of states or individual in essence, and whether combatants or non-combatants – can and cannot be permitted to carry out in a war situation.

So when we say "humanitarian law" we are taken to mean the laws of war, that is to say, the laws which limit and control the effects of armed conflict for humanitarian reasons; differently put, these are laws that attempt to balance humanitarian and military interests. Importantly for us in the context of human rights, there is a nuanced distinction that is made between laws of war that relate to what armies (usually of states) may do to one another – who are considered their soldiers, what are legitimate battle goals, and, most notably, what means are accepted as legitimate means to carry out those goals – and those laws of war that relate to what armies may or may not do to those who are not, or who are no longer, an active part of an enemy army. These are the *civilians* who are non-combatants; they can also be those who are wounded, those who are taken prisoner, those who are shipwrecked, or those who are sick. The first group of laws attending the former circumstances were put together in The Hague Conventions of 1899 and 1907; they were sometimes called the laws of war proper. The second group, pertaining to the latter distinction, were those articulated in Geneva, first in the nineteenth century, and then, after several revisions in the twentieth century, put together in their current form in 1949 and termed humanitarian law. It is now widely perceived, however, especially after additional protocols were added to the Geneva Conventions in 1977 and after some more conventions restricting certain weapons were added on as international legal instruments, that international humanitarian law encompasses all the laws of war.

The central and vital documents of international humanitarian law are the four Geneva Conventions. The First Geneva Convention is entrusted with "the Amelioration of the Condition of the Wounded and Sick in Armed

Forces in the Field"; the Second attends to "the Amelioration of the Condition of Wounded, Sick and Shipwrecked Members of Armed Forces at Sea"; the Third is "relative to the Treatment of Prisoners of War." But it is the Fourth Geneva Convention that garners the most interest on human rights agendas, for it is "relative to the Protection of Civilian Persons in Time of War." All the countries that are members of the United Nations have signed and ratified the four Geneva Conventions; this cannot be said, however, about the additional protocols to the conventions, which relate to protection of victims of both international and internal conflicts and which are therefore very relevant to human rights law. Still, one can safely say that international humanitarian law is widely accepted and respected, having achieved a level of compliance, authority, implementation, and enforcement that is a universal standard. Interestingly, it is the International Committee of the Red Cross that is explicitly named in the Geneva Conventions as the authority to regulate, evaluate, and adjudicate the application of humanitarian law; and it is the international courts – both the International Court of Justice and the International Criminal Court, and also the ad hoc tribunals (the International Criminal Tribunal for the Former Yugoslavia and the International Criminal Tribunal for Rwanda) – that are authorized, by these same conventions and the Rome Statute, to administer humanitarian justice.

Notes

1 When we say "modern" in this context, we are speaking of the modern era and modern philosophy, i.e., the new way of looking at the world that began – approximately – in the sixteenth century.
2 It is, of course, a well-known point that the universality of humans proclaimed in these documents was restricted and far from what we would consider "universal" today. Women, slaves, persons of meager property, among others, were not eligible for these "universal" rights.
3 Note that religion does, and does not, play an important role in these documents. The Declaration of Independence mentions the Creator and the Declaration of the Rights of Man and Citizen describes these rights as sacred. Interestingly, the Bill of Rights (along with the American Constitution) does not allude to God at all.
4 The ICJ is also authorized to give advisory opinions on legal questions coming from UN bodies. For instance, in December 2003, the ICJ's advisory opinion on "Legal Consequences of the Construction of a Wall in the Occupied Palestinian Territory" was requested by the General Assembly (www.icj-cij.org/files/case-rela ted/131/1497.pdf).
5 As of May 2019, one hundred and twenty-two states were party to the statute. Thirty-one states were signatories, but had not ratified the statute, and four of those (Sudan, Israel, Russia, and the United States) have alerted the UN that they do not intend to become parties to the statute, despite their earlier signature.
6 We will shortly address the distinction between human rights law and the laws of wartime, termed humanitarian law.
7 For such tales, see especially Johannes Morsink, *The Universal Declaration of Human Rights: Origins, Drafting, and Intent* (1999) and Mary Ann Glendon, *A World Made New: Eleanor Roosevelt and the Universal Declaration of Human Rights* (2002).

8 We shall, shortly, inquire about other limitations on universality, such as those pertaining to children or prisoners or differently disabled persons, and the philosophical groundings of these limitations. See especially Chapter 9.

9 Beyond the most obvious categorization into civil and political rights, on the one hand, and economic, social, and cultural rights, on the other hand, there are other possible groupings – such as negative/positive rights (or duties) and individual/collective rights – that have also received legal and philosophical attention.

10 One item that is worth comparative discussion lies in the choice of these basic rights: Locke speaks of the right to life, liberty and property; the French Declaration posits liberty, property, security, and resistance to oppression; the American Declaration talks of life, liberty and the pursuit of happiness; and the UDHR insists on life, liberty, and security of person.

11 See Chapter 1, p. 8.

12 Here we can reiterate that there are many "stories" illustrating the different political and cultural proclivities of the countries that were involved in the drafting of the UDHR, resulting in its nuances and peculiarities. See Note 7.

13 But see Morsink (1999) and Glendon (2002) for intimations of a cantankerous process that was not at all easy or quick.

14 See Chapter 8.

15 The semantics here is important. The covenants use "peoples," not "nations," assumedly because the issues of nations and nationalism are inherently problematic. The official French translation, as well, uses "peuples," the German "Völker," the Italian "popoli," but other languages, such as Hebrew, use the vernacular "nations."

16 Note the (in)famous case of the U.S.'s reservation to Article 6 of the ICCPR, which prohibits capital punishment (U.S. Reservation to Article 6 of the ICCPR, UN Doc. ST/LEG/SER.E/13, p. 175).

17 The official list of conventions is available at: www.ohchr.org/EN/ProfessionalIn terest/Pages/CoreInstruments.aspx

18 The official list of instruments is available at: www.ohchr.org/EN/ProfessionalIn terest/Pages/UniversalHumanRightsInstruments.aspx

19 The details of this challenge will be discussed in Chapter 8.

3 Some Questions (about Human Rights)

If we look for the academic disciplines or the general professional fields where exchanges about human rights are conducted, the first two obvious candidates are political science (which includes both empirical studies of politics and the more theoretical aspects of political thought) and the law. In pointing to political science here, we are speaking of the theoretical, academic engagement in human rights, not the activist conversation or policy-making talk. Those areas must, and will, occupy us later – after we have asked the preliminary questions that might be thought of as basic to questions of law or of political thought, i.e., the philosophical questions. These are conceptual investigations, interrogating the terms, the notions, the very words we use when we talk about human rights. This is not to say that human rights in practice are not a part of our investigation; it is merely to insist that first we must travel further along the philosophical road of human rights.

Who Holds Human Rights?

In asking philosophical questions about human rights we delve, first, into that most basic of concepts: the "human." (Though it might seem odd, we will postpone the parallel question about the concept of "rights" that is included in "human rights" to an independent, subsequent Chapter 5.) Two related issues crop up as obvious questions: "Who holds human rights?" and "What does it mean to be human?" These queries may sound suspiciously identical or, at the very least, as so intimately linked that we can treat them together in the same ideational examination. The reason for this is that the obvious reply to "who holds human rights?" is ... the human being. And that answer sounds suspiciously tautological, thrusting us immediately into the terminological, semantic, and conceptual exploration of the meaning of being human. The biological-zoological definitions will not do here: We cannot adopt a formulation such as "a bipedal primate belonging to the genus Homo, especially Homo sapiens" and stop there, satisfied with thinking that it is bipedal primates that belong to the genus Homo who hold human rights. Evidently, we are insinuating much more than this when we claim that human rights are due all human beings solely by virtue of being human.

Other definitions of "human" are rife in philosophy. We have two so-called definitions attributed to Aristotle, namely that humans are rational beings (*bios logicos*) and that humans are political animals (*zoon politicon*). We have learned, from Kant and Sartre, that humans are essentially – that is, by definition – free and autonomous entities. We know from Rousseau that human beings, as opposed to other animals, are capable of improvement and perfectibility. Some philosophers, like Marx, tell us that our social and moral proclivities, that is to say, our inborn relationships with and responsibility for others, are what make us human. Such various accounts of being human are rampant. So the decision to adopt one essential trait rather than another, or more than one, or none or all of the above characterizations, is a philosophically grounded conclusion that impacts what we understand by "human" rights and how we answer the question regarding who holds them. Even if we accept that *only* humans are entitled to human rights because *only* they have these essential properties – in other words, that animals or machines do not enter this conversation[1] – we have not yet deciphered what it is that we mean, exactly, by saying that *all* humans are entitled to human rights. Do *all* humans have the (favored) traits that make us human and in deference to which we have human rights?

Think, for example, of children. We are all somewhat sanguine about not according to children all of the same human rights that are assumed to be owing to adults. And asked to answer why we so naturally limit children's rights, we could look to the attributes above, attributes which are so basic that we think they are definitive of being human, and point out that they are missing – necessarily missing – in children. Thus, although children might be, and probably are, capable of improvement and future perfectibility, we would not attribute to them full-grown rationality, responsibility or autonomy. And we would probably continue to deliberate – philosophically and psychologically – about their freedom and sociality. Children, in fact, can make us reconsider the difference between essential characteristics and necessary or sufficient characteristics. They might be potentially responsible – it is a part of their essence as human beings, though not as children – but not yet responsible enough to merit human rights.

Similarly problematic is the assessment of the essential human characteristics of the mentally disabled – either cognitively or emotionally. Are they entitled to the same human rights as all and any human beings? And the question also arises, but now in very different form, when we ask about the human rights of the incarcerated criminal. Here the perplexity originates not from our attempt to identify that which in the human being is humanly worthy of human rights; rather, there is a moral question now about the possibility of abdicating those rights (intentionally or not) by one's actions. Are people who are mentally disabled and therefore without certain attributes – not even potential attributes – that speak to the holding of human rights thereby not entitled to them? Are people who have violated someone else's rights thereby to be seen as having relinquished their own human rights? We must admit that the philosophical identification of the "human," far from being an abstract deliberation insulated conceptually and analytically, serves as an inescapable anchor for our most urgent human rights concerns and questions.

How are Human Rights Justified?

In Chapter 6, we will inquire about specific philosophical justifications of human rights. Here we want to distinguish, on an ostensible meta-level, between three general methods of accounting for the legitimacy and necessity of human rights: the legal justification, the political justification, and the philosophical justification.

We cannot engage in the comprehensive philosophy of law here – the highbrow context in which one asks about the status of the law in general and of specific laws in particular. But clearly that is the overall framework in which we find ourselves when we ask about the justification for human rights law. And the answers here are not much different from those of any other laws. The two main paths that philosophers of law travel are either ethics-oriented or positivistic conceptions of law. The former recognizes the presence of morality and ethical considerations prior to any legal propositions and considers the laws – humanly formulated laws of our actual legal systems – as based on that morality. The latter sees human law-making as constitutive of itself, or sometimes as having social, conventional, or political explanation, and recognizes no need to justify the laws of our legal systems in any external or moral respect. Laws are justified simply by being a part of the legal system. Both these ways of validation of the law may be called upon in the case of human rights *law*. We are here doubtful of the second option – the one which says that human rights law is merely positivistic law, in need of no external (to itself) explication. Taking the other path, however, and going in a moralistic direction means asking about the moral norms and arguments that ground human rights law.[2] And that means basing human rights themselves – not only the laws we recognize as human rights laws – on some system of ethics. Such an ethics-centered project catapults us from legal into philosophical grounds; first, though, let us reflect for a moment about the political justification of human rights.

What do we mean by requiring a political justification or political reasoning for human rights? In very deliberate terms, we recognize that there is a political practice, i.e., actions that are perpetrated by political actors (usually states, sometimes other political institutions), which involves the rights of human beings under those actors' control. This practice is very closely related to the legal practice that accompanies it; but concentrating on the political aspect of human rights practice means emphasizing the questions about political interests that are served – or not – by that practice. International political interests having to do with human rights are those of stability, or peace, or even global justice; domestic political interests that engage with human rights might be more attuned to certain groups, or to demands of equality, or to individual freedoms. But linking the account of human rights to either domestic or international interests means showing that the pursuit of stability or peace or justice (or equality and freedom) can serve, and is better served by, the observance of human rights regulations in the political sphere. More so, justifying human rights politically provides policy makers with a motivation that recognizes interests other than those of well-known Hobbesian "psychological egotism." In fact, the concept of interests itself may be widened when we associate it with the human rights lexicon.

Have we not here, however, narrowed the scope of political justification to the very concrete essence of politics as practiced in the corridors of power? Should we not move on to political thought, i.e., to considerations of political theory rather than only political practice? If we do so, we are well on the way to ethics, and ethics is admittedly a part of philosophy. So talking about the ethical foundations of human rights requires that we transfer our focus from practical, concrete political justification for human rights to ivory-tower philosophical reasoning about them. Grounding human rights philosophically means rooting them in a philosophical, ethical theory that can explain their why and wherefore. That will be our objective in the upcoming chapters, where we will go deeply into the ethical, conceptual analysis that undergirds theories of rights in general and theories of human rights in particular. Whether we examine moral deontology, instrumentalism, contractualism, or other moral theories, our view will be to provide a foundation of human rights that is philosophically – and ethically – robust.

Nevertheless, one basic point must not be overlooked. Conceptual borders and boundaries are neither exact nor precise and, indeed, need not be. Our concepts meld into one another, they mutually bear upon each other, and they travel in and out of fields of discourse. Talking of political justification for human rights is not that different from talking about their moral justification: There is no unequivocal borderline between politics and morality (and some would say there should not be). So it should not be surprising to encounter, for example, John Rawls's *A Theory of Justice* or, even more so, his *Law of Peoples*, treated at times as a tract in political theory and at other times as a manifesto in ethics. Especially in the matter of human rights, it is perfectly warranted to make use of Rawls's theory in terms of either political or moral justification of human rights, as has often been done.[3] This does not pertain only to the supposed divide between political and moral deliberation: The legal sphere is just as facilely linked to moral discussion and political interests. So, although we will, in the following chapters, try to keep our semantics clear and distinct and our positioning as well-defined as possible, we cannot – and do not want to – avoid the interplay between law, politics, and ethics. Undeniably, the point of engaging in the *philosophy* of human rights is asking conceptual questions about their legal, political, and ethical foundations and justifications.

Do Human Rights Exist?

Now, after we have conceptualized ourselves to the hilt, we must still ask whether human rights exist. What can possibly be meant by that? Without facetiously asking "what is the meaning of 'exist'?" (and that, as is well-known, is a classic, foundational question in philosophy), we must expound on the facets of existence that may be attributed to human rights. Obviously, when I say that I have a right to something, I am not referring to a material possession that can be recognized by my senses. Neither are rights ideational or abstract objects that we "own" (and what does it mean to say that I "have" an idea?). Having a right is our colloquial way of talking about demands that we can make on the (typically political) authorities that control our life; more than that, having rights is our idiomatic way of giving reasons for those demands. But how, then, do rights exist? Where or in whose abode can we locate them? And what happens when they are violated? Do they then cease to exist?

Legal rights are the abstract derivatives of contractual documents, constitutional statements, or even oral agreements to which people commit. If, for example, two people sign a contract entailing that one sells his house to the other, the seller has a right to the money agreed upon in the contract and the buyer has a right to the house. If one person promises another person that he will give her something – rather than sell her that same something – then the latter has a right to receive the object promised. This second example is hardly in the legal field (though, in many legal systems, an oral promise counts as a contract); it would be more appropriate to term it a moral right. Still, by dealing with contracts or promises we can locate the rights that are created by these contracts and promises in our legal and moral systems. Importantly, the fact that the contract is not satisfied or the promise is not kept does in no way cancel the right, annul it, or make it disappear. The right arising from a contract or promise continues to exist, even if it is not respected or implemented.

The case of human rights is similar, but also distinctly dissimilar. Legally speaking, we could point to the various human rights treaties we have mentioned – all of which are legal documents – and claim that they have created the set of human rights that are articulated in them. Even if we accept the justification of human rights by their constitution in legal documents – and we have said above that we find that type of justification inadequate – we tread upon unstable foundations here that give rise to legal and conceptual difficulties. The signatories to human rights "contracts," be they "treaties," "covenants," or "conventions," are states and political bodies that, by becoming parties to these treaties, are expected to protect the human rights of individuals. The holders of the rights so constituted are not parties to the treaties; they are, rather, the persons mentioned in the treaties. Their rights exist as posited by these legal documents whether or not they are protected, implemented, or violated.

We could, then, move away from the legalistic stance and ask, instead, about human rights that are held by human beings, dependent on a certain moral theory (that might even be seen as justifying the legalism) – but we may still be stumped by the question of the existence of these rights. Where and how do these human rights exist? Ironically, though, we would be correct in replying just as we did in the legalistic context. Talking about the *existence* of human rights, no matter how we justify them, means claiming something for an individual from some powers that be and giving good reasons for that claim. The rights we are speaking of exist, however one parses "exist," because we have explained their moral provenance and necessity. If they are not respected or supported or manifested by whoever or whatever it is that is responsible for respecting or supporting or manifesting them, they do not thereby become nonexistent. On the contrary, human rights *are there*, even if they have been disrespected, violated, or trampled upon. They do not, in any way, cease to exist – though they might not be realized.

Are Human Rights Absolute? Are they Universal?

These two questions come from the same philosophical impetus that relates to the nature of human rights. In Chapter 7 we will investigate the heated debate that is – and has been for a while now – enveloping the human rights activist community and its theorists concerning cultural relativity. Here, for a moment, we harken back to the general philosophical dispute regarding the construct of "relativism" itself, and attempt to describe the conceptual basis that underlies its more concrete bout in the setting of human rights.

In philosophy, when we talk about relativism, it is usually located as opposed to absolutism or universalism. In fact, it helps to think of two families of "isms" that are in tension, each comprised of related ideas. The first includes absolutism, universalism, objectivism, globalism, internationalism, externalism, and sometimes realism. The second begins with relativism and goes on to list subjectivism, contextualism, pluralism, historicism, and sometimes pragmatism. Notice, when looking at these two sets of philosophical stances, that in one sense or another the elements of the first family have something comprehensive and all-encompassing about them while those of the second group exhibit an aspect of contingency. In philosophical discussion these views can be treated as metaphysical theories, as epistemological notions, or as ethical Weltanschauungen. Take objectivism, for instance: We can believe that there are objective metaphysical truths about the world or we can claim that any "truth" is subjectively held. We can go on and assert that such truths can be objectively known or we can consider our knowledge of all "truths" as a subjective product. Finally, we can posit moral truths that "really" exist unrelated to any particular perspective or avow that morality is always a subjective assessment.[4]

In the second half of the twentieth century we can ascertain, to be sure, a move to a more relativistic mood in philosophy and in other academic and intellectual pursuits. Whether this is born of the postmodern critique of enlightenment rationalism (which saw the rational human being in an essentialistic, universalistic, generic mode) or of the growing awareness of social and cultural diversity in human endeavor, relativism has been on the ascent in various scholarly and real-world contexts. The philosophical debate itself is invigorating, for it lays to waste our confidence in the type of absolute truths that seem to have been a traditional staple of philosophical theories.[5] In the matter of human rights, though, two players in the first family of our general dualism have inestimable significance: absolutism and universalism. Countering both is the broadly relativistic viewpoint, even if we finesse it by calling it historicist or cultural, pluralistic or contextual.

Let us inquire first, then, about the first contrast – absolutism vs. relativism in human rights. The question of absolutism is easily seen as patently asking whether human rights are absolute rights – i.e., do they always trump and, if so, what do they trump? We have already encountered this problem in the context of the international law of human rights. And, in fact, it was the legal scholar Ronald Dworkin who gave us that tool – of "trumping" – with which to analyze and then claim the status of human rights as the peak consideration in any moral-political deliberation we might encounter (Dworkin, 1984). But saying that human rights trump all other factors opens us up to both an external and internal tension. Externally, the question that arises is what other factors there might be that might disarm the absolute trump that human rights seem to have; internally, our query is whether there is any scale of priority among human rights themselves: Are some rights more obligating than others and can we decide, in the cases where rights conflict, which ones to disown in favor of others that are (more) absolute? Philosophically speaking, then, all these formulations boil down to the question of absolutism: Are human rights absolute (in the sense that nothing may be accepted as a justified violation of them)? Are some more absolute than others?

We saw, in Chapter 2, that although the Universal Declaration of Human Rights did not explicitly trouble itself with either the external or the internal absoluteness of human rights, the International Covenant on Civil and Political Rights did so in no uncertain terms, regarding any external factors competing with human rights. However, it is interesting to note that the only external circumstance which was thought, in that covenant, to disable the trump of human rights was a "threat to the life of the nation." That is to say, when on the one hand we are faced with the option of reneging on a human right and, on the other, we are in a situation which puts the life of a nation at mortal risk, we are permitted to derogate from the human right in question in order to ensure the nation's existence, the nation's "life." However – and here is a very weighty "however" – this kind of imbalance does not carry through for all the human rights expounded in the covenant.

There are human rights that must invariably be protected and respected, no matter what dire circumstances the nation might be encountering. As we have seen, these are the right to life, the prohibition of torture and enslavement, the protection against debt-incurred imprisonment, the proscription against retroactive laws, recognition before the law, and freedom of thought, conscience and religion. In other words, we can certainly identify the very specific human rights enumerated in Article 4.3 of the ICCPR as *absolute* human rights: There is no social situation or political circumstance which allows us to violate them; they trump all other – external – considerations.

The issue of internal absoluteness seems more common but, oddly, less acute, and essentially becomes a question of precedence. When different priorities and preferences are involved, and when human rights subsequently appear to contradict one another or, at the very least, to hinder each other's realization, there is always a question about the criterion by which we select one over another. We can easily imagine cases where such clashes may occur, some abstract and hypothetical, others more ordinary and commonsensical. The right to life and freedom of movement, for example, very naturally obstruct each other in the everyday context of traffic and transportation. Your right to move freely– within your vehicle – wherever and whenever you desire almost automatically threatens my right to life and (physical) well-being. Less simplistic cases abound: We can entertain questions concerning the scale of importance of different rights – freedom of movement and residence within the borders of a state as opposed to the right of free exit from and return to one's country; the right to life in general as competing with the right to a dignified life; the right to integrity of body (of a mother) versus the right to life (of a fetus); and so many others. In all of these examples we are up against scenarios that challenge us: Which human right trumps another human right? How are we to order the scale on which human rights are weighed and decide on their relative importance? Fortuitously, ethical theories and legal systems address precisely these sorts of quandaries. We do not have to invent a new set of considerations just for human-rights clashes; human rights are to be adjudicated by human rights law and by ethics. We can adopt already finely honed ethical philosophies and apply them to our human rights dilemmas or we can, even more simply, turn to legal systems that have taught us how to deal with such predicaments. By doing so, we give up on the internal absoluteness of *each and every* human right but not on the well-based insight that human rights, as a unified system, are still an absolute trump.

Questioning the universalism of human rights is more challenging, nary to be disposed of by turning to this or that ethical theory and even less so by conscripting the law. Raising a question about the universalism of human rights means taxing the most common presupposition we have encountered in our talk of human rights: Do human rights apply to all people, at all times, in all places, and during all circumstances, in the same way? But was not that, unerringly, the axiom from which the idea of human rights was derived? Did we not assume universalism in the very definition of human rights? How can we possibly deny that the rights humans are entitled to by virtue of being human are universally applicable? Is there not a definitional, inherent universalism in the very idea of human rights? Is not our foundational text the *Universal* Declaration of Human Rights?

Fragments of this difficulty were already perceived when we questioned who holds human rights. Suppose, for the moment, that we could discover sufficient and necessary conditions that make a person human – that is to say, a human being entitled to human rights. It seems that even then we could not avoid the immediate follow-up: Are all humans equally entitled to the same human rights in the same manner? If not, what grounds the fleshing out of a negative answer, and have we not now descended – or ascended – into relativism? Beyond the conceptual dissection of universalistic vs. relativistic attitudes, the question of the universalism of human rights has added concrete, practical implications. We tread here into the waters of cultural relativism – the awareness that in different locales, which house different cultures, the values that undergird the very idea of human rights may be a function of those places and those cultures. Strikingly, we realize that the universalism which we have assumed as a linchpin of human rights – that *all* human beings are entitled to *the same* human rights *in the same* manner – is itself a value which is in danger of being relativized. This becomes a far more pressing question than the abstract philosophical problem of (metaphysical, epistemic, ethical) relativism; it instructs us to fathom how to relate to, and include, societies and communities that are very different from our own – different even, and especially, in their conceptions of both humans and rights, and therefore in all matters of human rights. This is one of the most demanding conundrums in the current human rights conversation; it will consequently merit a chapter of its own (Chapter 7).

What is Dignity?

We have already come across the first article of the Universal Declaration of Human Rights (1948): "All human beings are born free and equal in dignity and rights." While it seems abundantly clear that human rights and dignity "go together," it behooves us to inquire, particularly when we investigate the concept of human rights, not only about the concept of dignity *per se* but also about the relationship, if there is one, between human rights and dignity. If they are related, how are they related? Does one analytically precede the other? Does one presuppose the other? Are they symmetrically conjoined – "no human rights without dignity, no dignity without human rights"? Can the discussion of one preclude attendance to the other? Is one just a synonym of, or perhaps a misnomer for, the other? And suppose we have a good idea of what we mean by human rights, already presented legalistically and soon to be further fleshed out; can the same be said about dignity?

A natural way to look at these questions – and answer them – is to structurally posit three options. First, the most common perception at hand holds that human dignity functions as the motive for recognition of human rights. In other words, dignity comes first, then human rights follow – buttressed by, justified by, or based on human dignity. The second formal position turns things around, suggesting that human rights are prior to dignity and that it is precisely the respect for human rights that bestows dignity on the human person. Third is the stance that identifies the analysis of human rights with talk of dignity. This last view of human rights and dignity garners insights that derive from a semantic delving into the meaning of dignity as precisely the capacity to make (human rights) claims – that is to say, a person's dignity is no more and no less than their position as deserving of human rights; and this can even lead to the deprecatory reduction of the very significance of dignity as being no more than its fancy implementation in place of ordinary ethics talk.[6] The second view, that which places human rights "before" dignity, entails that dignity is indeed bestowed upon someone by the respect for their human rights; differently put, one acquires dignity by being respected by others and that means having one's rights respected by others. An even more intricate version of this positioning puts the right to have one's dignity respected as simply one human right, among others. In this case, the question of which comes first, dignity or human rights, becomes either very complex, or moot (Rosen, 2012, 58–60).

Let us return, then, to the first alternative – the conventional understanding of dignity and human rights: Dignity is the inherent, inviolable, essential attribute that human beings possess, and it grounds – in a way to somehow be revealed – the idea of human rights. Why and wherefrom? What is the source of such dignity and on what can we base the notion of an intrinsic dignity that characterizes all human beings? Before turning to one of the most remarkable philosophical answers to this question – Immanuel Kant's ethics – we take a detour for just one moment in a different direction, going the way of the religious concept of dignity. According to the religions which recognize a deity, and in particular the Abrahamic religions (Judaism, Christianity, and Islam), humans were created by God. Indeed, the world and everything in it was created by God. The creation of the human, however, has "preeminence" (Eccles. 3:19) over all other things and animals, and this status is explained by the fact that God created humans "in his own image" (Gen. 1:27). It might be thought that, since all creation is creation by God, consistency requires that we treat all things and animals in the world with the respect due to all God's creations. But the religious tale makes it explicitly clear that God's attitude towards his favored creation – the human being – is a special one and that the likeness between God and the human endows the latter with a singular standing. It is that station, of being created in God's image and thereby being worthy of a distinct respect, that can justify the endowment of innate dignity to the human being. The religious version of human creation thus becomes a straightforward, unproblematic account of dignity. Whether that type of dignity can also lead to a consequent account of human rights is a different query.[7]

If dignity is not God-given, what is its origin? Is it common to all human beings? If so, what is it about human beings that makes us all holders of inherent dignity? And, finally, how does it function as the herald of human rights? There are a few philosophical attempts to answer these questions in a consistent manner; the one that will serve as our chosen illustration is Immanuel Kant's theory of morality in the *Groundwork to the Metaphysics of Morals* (1785). It is in that book that Kant bequeathed us the Categorical Imperative – the moral commandment which is contingent on no other directive and which can be discovered and then formulated using only our reason. Famously, the Categorical Imperative is articulated by Kant first as "act only in accordance with that maxim through which you can at the same time will that it become a universal law" (*GMM*, 421). In other words, the ultimate moral dictate that a person must follow is the one which that person can generalize from, indeed universalize to apply to everyone. Other versions follow – we shall immediately enumerate them and show how, together, they provide a moral reading of dignity, from which human rights can be derived.

Three basic conceptual blocks are needed for this building – rationality, autonomy, and law. The first is axiomatic; indeed, as Kant says explicitly, he is not speaking of human beings here, but rather of rational beings. "... [T]he ground of obligation here is to be sought not in the nature of the human being or the circumstances of the world in which he is placed, but *a priori* solely in concepts of pure reason. ..." (*GMM*, 389). It is reason, held by any rational being, that leads to other versions of the categorical imperative. These arise from the acknowledgment that just as foundational for the moral imperative as the rationality of these beings is their autonomy. And this leads to the "formula of autonomy" version of the imperative – "the idea of the will of every rational being as a will giving universal law." Emphatically, this rational being is perceived as "legislating to itself" and its will "grounds itself on no interest" and is "subject only to his own and yet universal legislation" (*GMM*, 431–432). Clearly, then, our rationality is necessary for the maxim and it is also rational analysis that shows that "the principle of autonomy is the sole principle of morals" (*GMM*, 440).

In the versions of the Categorical Imperative that we have met – usually called the formula of universal law[8] and the formula of autonomy – the concepts of law and legislation have already made their appearance. But this is made unequivocally obvious in the last version of the imperative. Based on the insight that "every rational being must act as if it were through its maxims always a legislative member in a universal realm of ends," the final articulation that Kant offers is "Act in accordance with maxims of a universally legislative member for a merely possible realm of ends" (*GMM*, 438). What can this "realm of ends" possibly refer to? We shall ask about ends in a minute; let us begin with realms, for these are "the systematic combination of various rational beings through communal laws" (*GMM*, 433). While the earlier version of the Categorical Imperative dealt with one's willing the maxim to be a law, only this last account talks explicitly of one's being a legislator in a realm, which is itself defined as existing through laws. Each person in this realm legislates both for herself and for others; this is what makes the law universally compulsory. Indeed, a rational being belongs to the realm of ends as a member precisely because she legislates universal laws and is subject to those laws herself.

It is now the realm of *ends*, not just any realm, in which the rational human is a legislator, that opens up the vista of dignity. Kant provides us with a rich, analytical explanation of dignity – in German, Würde: worth, value. This begins with the penultimate formula (after the formula of universal law and the formula of the law of nature) of the Categorical Imperative: "Act so that you use humanity, as much in your own person as in the person of every other, always at the same time as end and never merely as means" (*GMM*, 429). How is this attained? Reason, which rules itself by itself, is present in all persons (or all rational beings) and provides a sure basis to treat them all as of equal value and therefore worthy of equal honor, i.e., dignity. It is through this third formulation of the Categorical Imperative that the rational, autonomous person becomes a moral subject and object. This means that that person must never be seen as only a means but always also as an end. Our recognition of the humanity – in ourselves and in the other – as not only a means, but as also always an end, is what posits in humanity a value that is not substitutable by, or dependent on, any other value. "What has a price," says Kant,

> is such that something else can also be put in its place as its equivalent; by contrast, that which is elevated above all price, and admits of no equivalent, has a dignity ... that which constitutes the condition under which alone something can be an end in itself does not have merely a relative worth, i.e., a price, but rather an inner worth, i.e., dignity.
>
> (*GMM*, 435)

The categorical moral imperative, which is based on human rationality and autonomy and is reliant on the self-legislative and other-legislative capability and duty of the autonomous human of reason, necessitates a notion of human value that is an absolute, inner worth residing, essentially, in all humans; this is what is termed "dignity." Significantly, this Kantian idea of dignity is adjoined to the human being analytically, even *a priori*. And this makes the move to human rights, or, more pedantically, the connection between dignity and human rights, so fundamentally comprehensive. The characterization of the human being as one of intrinsic dignity is basic, but not axiomatically dogmatic. This is because the human's dignity is inextricably tied to his rationality and autonomy, and rationality and autonomy are precisely what make up a person's humanity – which is always (also) an end. Consequently, human rights are the legal and political constructs that arise from the moral idea of human dignity.[9]

Notes

1 This is not to say that there is no place for a philosophical discussion of animal rights; only that this, being the discussion of *human* rights, is not that place.
2 But see also Chapters 12 and 13, in which we engage with very different conceptions of human rights, some predicated on practice and discourse rather than on (moral) theory.
3 For example, we will presently investigate Thomas Pogge's work on human rights coming directly out of (and arguing with) John Rawls.
4 Note that these three – metaphysics, epistemology, ethics – are not exhaustive of philosophical areas (we can think of linguistic objectivism, scientific objectivism, and the like); still, there are philosophical grounds for the claim that they are not unrelated to one another.
5 This is not to say that relativism itself – as a philosophical theory – has not been noticed since ancient Greece (usually attributed to Protagoras, 490–420 BC).
6 Emblematic of such a reductive stance is Ruth Macklin's "Dignity is a useless concept: It means no more than respect for persons or their autonomy" (2003). For a less strident approach, see Feinberg and Narveson, "The nature and value of rights" (1970).
7 Intuitively, one encounters two irksome questions that hinder the move from such God-given dignity to human rights. One has to do with the inclusiveness of the term "religion" and the question of dignity as arising exclusively from its God-given provenance. Another is the issue of the absolute authority of God, which can, at will, rescind rights, belying the humanistic core of "right." For more on these questions, see Chapter 6.
8 A variant of this version is the Formula of the Law of Nature: "So act as if the maxim of your action were to become through your will a universal law of nature" (*GMM*, 421).
9 But see Jeremy Waldron's *Dignity, Rank, and Rights* (2012) for an analysis of human dignity that confounds both the religious and Kantian assumptions, showing that viewing dignity through legal, rather than moral, spectacles is more conducive to human rights.

Part II
Philosophical Groundings

4   Liberal Underpinnings

"Rights," as a word, term, and concept that undergird human rights, began their relevant philosophical life in the seventeenth century. It might seem astounding that rights as a philosophical (or even a political and legal) construct are so young, so to speak, but when we follow the intellectual development of the word itself ("right"), although we find its first appearance in English in the twelfth century, it is only in the seventeenth century's revolution of ideas, usually termed the Enlightenment, sometimes called less flamboyantly Modern Philosophy, that we encounter rights in their new garb. A right speaks of something that someone is entitled to; and it is important, at this point, to notice that we are not yet speaking of human rights, but of rights in general. The critical questions that arise in modern philosophy's novel conversation about rights are usually "Who holds which rights?" and "What justifies such holding?"

In the conventional story about rights it is usually Liberalism, capital L intended, as a philosophical or political worldview, that is credited with "inventing" rights. What is there in classical liberalism that caters so well to the topic of rights? Typically perceived as based on ethical considerations, classical liberalism derives from, or is at the least tightly associated with, ideas that involved natural law and natural reason. The natural law tradition recognized the standards (or rules or laws) of morality as being entailed by the nature of the world and the nature of human beings. (This could be, but need not necessarily be, congruent with divine standards or rules or laws.) Given the rational nature of human beings (and some thought even of the world itself), natural reason could serve both to discover natural moral law and to regulate human action according to it. The move to natural rights in such a conceptual setting, and to natural duties as well, was … well, natural. Two additional fulcra of liberalism have already been discussed in Chapter 1 and both have invigorated the internal discussion within liberal thought that cannot be easily laid to rest. One is the liberal emphasis on the individual and the ensuing questions on his or her position in and relationship with society. The other is the liberal emphasis on freedom and the ensuing vacillation, within liberal discourse, between liberty and equality. The liberal focus on individual freedoms rather than on the autonomy of a society as a whole and the supposed priority given to liberty over equality in liberal thought have both been reviewed from the very beginnings of liberalism. With the passage from natural law theories (that were not necessarily liberal) to investigations of (natural) rights within liberalism, these musings became explicit deliberations. As we shall see in our forthcoming chapters, debates about community and group rights and the insistence on equality as no less important than freedom intensify even more in the context of *human* rights.

The usual protagonists paraded as heroes of the liberal story are John Locke and John Stuart Mill.[1] Not that other philosophers did not contribute important and profound insights and analyses to the story; but only that in telling a distinct, mostly headline-carrying narrative, those two philosophers are called on to present the basic stepping stones of the tale. We do not shy away from presenting that traditional and somewhat standard story here as a bulwark to our later, more nuanced discussion of human rights, but we will add on to that skeletal scheme two more central figures – Thomas Hobbes, chronologically even earlier than John Locke, and John Rawls, chronologically after John Stuart Mill. Karl Marx, who provides us with one of the most exceptional views of rights – and especially liberal rights – will be noticed, but is left, for obvious structural reasons, to a later chapter which concentrates, quite explicitly, on critique of human rights.

Thomas Hobbes

Although the philosopher most often credited with originating the liberal conception of rights – i.e., liberal rights as we know and speak of them today – is John Locke, it is fair to say that there would have been no Locke if there had not first been a Hobbes. This is not the facetious pointing to any philosopher's words and ideas as being obviously a development of and preceded by some other philosophical pioneer, but an essential assessment: Not only is Locke's work, in several instances, an engagement with and a response to Hobbes's thoughts but, more emphatically, Locke's self-same ideas essentially come on the heels of Hobbes's philosophy. The intellectual context here is that of seventeenth-century British philosophy, grounded in the historical context of the British Civil War (1640–1660), which is our first instance of a true debate, and then a battle and a war, over the two grounds of political authority: monarchy or republic (sometimes termed a Commonwealth). And it is in that historical and political context that Thomas Hobbes devoted himself to providing the philosophical justification – and grounding, and description, and hypotheses – of political power.

A fascinating aspect of Hobbes is his conventional, public reputation – as the hyper-conservative who bequeathed to us the idea of a "state of nature" which is characterized as a "war of all against all," with human life being "solitary, poor, nasty, brutish, and short" (Hobbes, *Leviathan*, 2010 [1651]). In this state of nature, so the Hobbesian interpretive tradition tells us, we are ruled by fear; being, though, at the same time, rational creatures, we proceed to contract with one another and to enact a sovereign who can provide us with protection from the ills of an unregulated state of nature. What has given Hobbes the bad reputation that he has is his depiction of that rationally adopted sovereign as an absolute ruler. And that is, I agree, not something to be shrugged away in a discussion of political power and especially in the context of rights – for it seems to prescribe that the citizens of the commonwealth ruled by that absolute sovereign have no rights at all. It is important, therefore, to return to Hobbes's exact words and see what he really does claim in the matter of rights that will later correspond with our own engagement with human rights.

Famously, Hobbes begins by defining the concept of "natural right":

> The right of nature ... is the liberty each man hath to use his own power as he will himself for the preservation of his own nature; that is to say, of his own life; and consequently, of doing anything which, in his own judgement and reason, he shall conceive to be the aptest means thereunto.
>
> (*Leviathan*, chapter 14)

Since man[2] is trapped, to begin with, in the state of nature, which is a war of all against all, and since his natural right bespeaks the liberty to do anything for self-preservation, it follows (less famously, but very strikingly) that "in such a condition every man has a right to every thing, even to one another's body" (ibid.). No other proclamation of basic, natural rights of the human being is as sweeping and fundamental. We all have a basic, natural right to anything and everything in the name of our own survival.

Hobbes's path from such an extensive axiom of natural rights – in the state of nature – to the final, almost rights-less condition of the subject – in the state of the commonwealth – is logical, even if off-putting. It leads, if man is also axiomatically perceived as a creature of reason, from the constant and ubiquitous state of war to a voluntary contract between men, who give up their rights to everything in favor of one authority – the sovereign – who can provide protection of all from all. In rough hues this can be seen as the concession and transfer of all individual rights to one individual who holds all rights and proceeds, from this powerful position, to decide on all laws. Hobbes is nothing if not meticulous in presenting and enumerating the sovereign's rights; but they are not of interest to us here.[3] It remains to ask what rights, if any, are left for the subject in the odd situation where, seemingly, he has conceded them all to the sovereign. What has endured of the individual's original right to everything? Differently put, how can we countenance the absolute power – and therefore rights and laws – of the sovereign with the "true liberty of a subject" (*Leviathan*, chapter 21)? Recognition of this tension is behind the various interpretive debates in the matter of the individual's right to refuse to sacrifice his life (or implicate himself) in service of the commonwealth. It seems that these rights are still inalienable (in our modern terminology) and one cannot be expected to renege on them, unless, Hobbes seems to be saying, "the defence of the Commonwealth" so requires, i.e., the commonwealth itself is in danger. This convoluted issue has stayed an open question in the interpretation of Hobbes's passage from the universal right of all men to everything to an ostensible absence of all rights in the commonwealth.

Still, even if we accept this tale of a logical, rational move from a state of nature which holds unlimited rights to a commonwealth ruled by an absolute sovereign which precludes (almost) all of the subject's rights, in Hobbes's assumptions about natural man there are some outstanding novelties. First, this account of human political endeavor is, at this point, devoid of any religious over-tones or under-tones. So the sovereign's laws are man-made, i.e., they are civil laws. Second, the acceptance of political structure is contingent upon human rationality and mutual consent. Third – and most significantly for our upcoming questions of human rights – in this view of rights there is a presupposition of human equality. All men are equally entitled to their natural rights (to anything) in the state of nature and they can be seen as functioning subjects of the common-wealth (and its absolute sovereign) with full awareness of that assumption (though with the paradoxical transfer of those rights to the sovereign). Ian Shapiro puts it succinctly: "Despite the awesome power Hobbes gives to the regulative state, he provides the conceptual tools for perpetual attacks on it" (Shapiro, 1986, 78). Subsequently, this will be our guiding light in the matter of human rights.

John Locke

Perhaps it is Hobbes's posit of an absolute ruler that has deprived him of recognition as a necessary protagonist in any discussion of the development of liberal human rights. Or perhaps it is a misunderstanding of the relative weight of individual rights vs. state power in his work that has kept him out of the conventional narrative. In any case, it is John Locke who is usually given the title of "father of political liberalism" in general and, conse-quently, the accepted purveyor of the concept of natural rights (that later became human rights). Secular individualism was posited by Hobbes as leading to a contract version of the state – the Commonwealth – but the subsequent priority of that state over that individual usually deprived Hobbes of any recognized title to liberalism.[4] In Locke's hands that balance was turned around, with the individual (*sans* the secularism) attaining pride of place; thus, Locke is termed the father of liberalism. How does that relate to his concept of rights?

The interesting relationship between natural law and natural right is more traditional, in a sense, in Locke than in Hobbes. Natural law is God's doing, and God's presence and will are a necessary part of Locke's move to rights.

Locke, too, sees man as inhabiting an original state of nature, but this state of nature is ruled by God; and, naturally, we all hold duties to God arising from the laws of nature, the first of which is our duty of self-preservation. However, that basic duty, which is definitional for our existence in the state of nature, in order to lead to basic rights must take an indirect path: First, our self-preservation is dependent on our ability to defend ourselves against dangers that threaten our life and our liberty; otherwise, how could we ensure our subsistence? Famously, Locke also posits a requirement to have more material means of self-preservation, which he calls personal property. So we must have fundamental rights to life, liberty, and property.

> Man being born, as has been proved, with a title to perfect freedom, and an uncontrolled enjoyment of all the rights and privileges of the law of nature, equally with any other man, or number of men in the world, hath by nature a power, not only to preserve his property, that is, his life, liberty and estate, against the injuries and attempts of other men ...
> (Locke, *Two Treatises of Civil Government*, §87)

Note that all of this transpires before any thought of state or sovereignty arises. And indeed, the reason for contracting between men and creating a political authority at all is precisely the protection of such rights. The Lockean state has an explicit goal: to protect and promote those rights to life, liberty, and property of the individuals who have contracted with the sovereign to fulfill that goal. Three extremely vital points must be recognized in this scenario. First, the contract that is enacted between men in the state of nature leading to the existence of the political state is a contract between these men and the sovereign himself. This, importantly, leads to the second point – that the idea of government in this sense necessarily involves the idea of representation. Different from the men of Hobbes's Commonwealth, who gave up all their rights to the (absolute or not) sovereign, the men of Locke's polity are represented by their sovereign. Most emphatically, one might say that it is the persons of the state who are the sovereign, and it is they who are represented by the governing body. This leads to the third, no less significant point. Because the contract involves the government itself, and because that government represents the subjects of the polity, the limits of government are clearly marked. Government cannot do anything that might violate the rights of its subjects, the protection of whom being the very reason it was instituted. A very stark contrast to Hobbes's absolute government!

Not for nothing, then, has Locke been touted as the father of liberalism. If liberalism be conceived as prioritizing the individual and setting limits to government, then we have in Locke the explicit justification for a liberal, political worldview. The added value to this skeletal concept of liberalism is its basis in the additional concept of natural right. Locke's springboard of the unassailable right to life, liberty, and property that is owed to any man – a very basic foundation, from which the rest of our political rights are born – can easily and naturally be seen as an obvious precursor of the (liberal) idea of human rights.

Still, it is interesting to see some additional contrasts between Hobbes and Locke and try to ascertain which of them is the more "liberal" thinker. For Hobbes, the entire hypothetical exercise of man in the state of nature leading to the constitution of the commonwealth is a secular, rational progression, from rights to (civic) laws. For Locke, without God the exercise – even if it is only an exercise – fumbles: First there is the natural law conscribed by God and only then can we derive the rights for life, liberty, and property (which enable us to fulfill the duty we owe to God). In a sense then, Locke's postulate of rights, usually accepted by readers as just that – a basic postulate – is dependent on God as a lawgiver; Hobbes's posit of rights is a basic axiom having nothing to do with religion. Related to this is the progression from natural law to natural rights – established by Locke in that direction. For Hobbes the move seems to be in the opposite direction, from the rights that all men have in the state of nature to laws prescribed by the lawgiver, the political sovereign. There is also the question "which laws?" Hobbes's man in the state of nature, we have seen, has a right to "every thing"; Locke is far more well-defined, speaking, in one place, about the rights to "life, health, liberty, or possessions," a little later of "the life, the liberty, health, limb, or goods," (Locke, *Two Treatises*, Book II, chapter II, §6), and finally of "life, liberty, and estate" (*Two Treatises*, Book II, chapter VII, §87). Given this seeming expansion of rights in Hobbes and reduction in Locke, it becomes fascinating to consider the consequences of their supposed, respective leniency. For the final fruit of their rights-based labor is, paradoxically, at odds: Hobbes has arrived at an absolute government that may impinge on all its subjects' rights (except, perhaps, the right to life, which then permits some type of resistance) while Locke's achievement is what has come to be known as the liberal state – the political authority which gets its *raison d'être* precisely from its protection of those rights and the limitation on its ability to violate them.

John Stuart Mill

We fast-forward now to the nineteenth century, to another name which is consensually associated with liberalism and, accordingly, with questions of rights. In fact, John Stuart Mill wrote what is often considered to be the founding manifesto of a brand of liberalism that prioritizes individual liberty, *On Liberty* (1977 [1859]), but this must be conjoined with his other great contribution to philosophy, *Utilitarianism* (1985 [1861]), a book that offered the moral theory of that same name and which must be made to square with the rights born of liberalism.

Utilitarianism is a moral theory; liberalism is a social-political philosophy. The two are unsurprisingly linked, with various inter-relationships between them. We will assume a definitional acquaintance with utilitarianism and the principle of utility: "It is the greatest happiness of the greatest number that is the measure of right and wrong" (Bentham, 1988 [1776]).[5] Importantly, too, the emphasis in utilitarianism is on the consequences of actions (rather than the intent of the actor, or any a priori criterion) and these determine their moral worth. Liberalism of the Millian type raises the question of the liberty of the human being as against the powers of government or society. Mill begins *On Liberty* with the words: "The subject of this essay is … civil or social liberty: the nature and limits of the power which can be legitimately exercised by society over the individual" (*On Liberty*, chapter 1). But there is no way of talking about the limits on society and government without asking what it is that human beings are entitled to which would so limit society's exercise. The definition of such human demands, also known as rights, is given (as we saw in Chapter 1) in *Utilitarianism*: "When we call anything a person's right, we mean that he has a valid claim on society to protect him in the possession of it, either by the force of law, or by that of education and opinion" (*Utilitarianism*, chapter 5).

This might seem to verge on the tautological. Asked about the limits on government, we point to the individual's demands, and asked about his demands, that is to say his rights, we turn to a "valid claim" on society. But Mill's work on his moral theory – Utilitarianism – and his corresponding investigation of the relations between man and government – Liberalism – is ultimately fascinating, yet complex. It is not that utility and rights contradict each other at all; rather, it is difficult to put these two systems together in a systematic, coherent structure. And even if we attempt to focus on the rights in liberalism alone,[6] we cannot ignore the definitive connection that Mill insists on making between them and utility. He puts its strikingly in another stipulation of what rights are:

> To have a right, then, is, I conceive, to have something which society ought to defend me in the possession of. If the objector goes on to ask why it ought, I can give him no other reason than general utility.
>
> (*Utilitarianism*, chapter 5)

How is the connection made? Very comprehensively:

> While I dispute the pretensions of any theory which sets up an imaginary standard of justice not grounded on utility, I account the justice which is grounded on utility to be the chief part, and incomparably the most sacred and binding part, of all morality. Justice is a name for certain classes of moral rules which concern the essentials of human well-being more nearly, and are therefore of more absolute obligation, than any other rules for the guidance of life; and the notion which we have found to be of the essence of the idea of justice—that of a right residing in an individual—implies and testifies to this more binding obligation.
>
> (ibid.)

So morality – a utilitarian morality – is at the basis of rights, but what are these rights? What is it that a person is naturally entitled to, by moral fiat, in facing her society? The hint is already there in *On Liberty*, when Mill refuses talk of rights as abstract, or as perhaps metaphysical entities.

> It is proper to state that I forego any advantage which could be derived to my argument from the idea of abstract right as a thing independent of utility. I regard utility as the ultimate appeal on all ethical questions; but it must be utility in the largest sense, grounded on the permanent interests of man as a progressive being.
>
> (*On Liberty*, chapter 1)

We are finally at the explicit rendering of real rights, rights as connected to interests, with those interests being attributed to a certain conception of man. But Mill's first, fundamental idea is that man's interests, or goods, or desires, are not something which is under any public auspice. The sole end which men can treat as allowing them to interfere in other men's liberty is self-protection. So the only reason society might have to brandish power over men is to prevent any harm to other men. Very significantly, then, men are autonomous regarding actions which pertain to themselves; they are only obligated to society in actions that are inter-subjective. And their liberty can be curtailed only in cases where there might be harm to others. But now, recall utility and its original rendition as aspiring to happiness. Mill's "progressive" being is one who engages in deliberative discussion, one who reaches a happiness that is deep and reflective. The rights of such a person are spelled out in *Utilitarianism* as those that are necessary for manifesting that progressive nature. Not unexpectedly, Mill posits freedom of expression, going on to elaborate on more basic rights – he calls them liberties – of three categories: liberties of conscience and expression; liberties of tastes, pursuits, and life-plans; and liberties of association. He goes on to tell us that there are priorities to consider when liberties conflict and that these liberties can be curtailed if their fulfillment clearly harms someone else.

Before leaving Mill and going on to the twentieth century, it is useful to note, in passing, three results of his liberal analysis of rights, or of liberties, that are closely tied in to our contemporary discussion about human rights. First, in *On Liberty* we are confronted with the on-going tension between individual rights and the "tyranny of the majority." That is to say, Mill is cognizant of the threat that democracy might hold for rights of minorities. Second, Mill provides us with an articulated criterion for the holders of liberties – they must be normatively competent. And third, Mill connects the idea of such basic rights with the ideas of equality and impartiality; for example, great recognition is given in his work to women's rights (especially in *The Subjection of Women*, 1984 [1869]). Suffice here to end with Mill's own words, yet again:

The entire history of social improvement has been a series of transitions, by which one custom or institution after another, from being supposed a primary necessity of social existence, has passed into the rank of universally stigmatized injustice and tyranny. So it has been with the distinctions of slaves and freemen, nobles and serfs, patricians and plebeians; and so it will be, and in part already is, with the aristocracies of colour, race, and sex.

(*Utilitarianism*, chapter 5)

John Rawls

We have arrived, finally, at contemporary times, with the philosopher who is considered to be, by a wide array of distinct philosophical communities, the greatest political philosopher of the twentieth century. Rawls's *A Theory of Justice* (1971) has been likened to Kant's *Groundwork for the Metaphysics of Morals* (1785) as the basis for a philosophical foundation in moral theory relating to political thought. (Rawls is, indeed, self-described as a Kantian.) In his lifetime, Rawls published – after *A Theory of Justice* – three additional crucial texts (and several definitive articles): *Political Liberalism* (1993) and "Justice as Fairness" (1985) were both political, ethical, analytical, and practical elaborations of *A Theory of Justice; The Law of Peoples* (1999) was an expansion of the "domestic" vision, having to do with relationships between individuals and between society and individual, to the realm of international relations. Here we will treat only of the domestic texts, leaving the discussion on international issues to a later chapter.[7] In fact, Rawls's moral-political theory is of great breadth, but is used here – as were Hobbes, Locke, and Mill – as a philosophical pivot for our dealings with human rights. And that philosophy is, avowedly, a player in the liberal tradition.

Rawlsian terms and constructs have become a virtual *lingua franca* of contemporary political philosophy. Let us familiarize ourselves with some of its anchors. Reminiscent of Hobbes's and Locke's (and also Rousseau's) concepts of "state of nature" and "social contract" are some of Rawls's ideas, which answer to a different vocabulary and have their own unique aspects. But whereas Hobbes and Locke begin with a hypothetical or historical (the debate wavers) state of nature and advance from that to a social contract, Rawls's methodology is an explicit thought experiment. Given that we are talking about an ideal just society, we need to imagine a situation in which all individuals are represented and where their representatives agree on principles of justice that decide the ways of political institutions. It is this imaginary situation which Rawls calls the *original position*, an abstract meeting place of representatives who are equal in their (original) powers and who exist behind a *veil of ignorance*: None of them know the gender, class, race, income, talents, or any other traits of the groups who are being represented (others and their own); or about the social, economic, political, or cultural makeup of the society in which they live. It is from this putatively neutral position that all of them are said to come to an agreement (a contract) concerning the principles of their political system. Ostensibly, this system will be a just, fair system.

What makes a just system? Rawls is celebrated for the mantra *justice as fairness*, which provides us with not only a slogan but also a moral compass with which to assess our ideas of justice. Where liberalism had struggled with its two basic ideas of freedom and equality, Rawls postulates two principles of justice which purport to make peace, as it were, between freedom and equality and furthermore to lead us to the fairness we expect as constituting justice. The first principle says that each person must have an equal right to a total system of basic liberties which is compatible with the same system of liberties for all. The second principle deals with inequality, requiring that social and economic inequalities (a) are attached to offices and positions that are open to all under conditions of fair equality of opportunity (*equal opportunity*), and (b) are to the greatest benefit of the least-advantaged members of society (*the difference principle*). We will not here dive into the sea of moral and political complexities that accompany this orderly articulation of the principles of justice. It will do to notice that not only do they address the interesting tension between the two towers of liberalism – freedom and equality – but that Rawls also provides us with a criterion for prioritizing our demands for justice. The first principle takes pride of place, meaning that a right protected by it can never be surrendered for economic well-being; between the two parts of the second principle, equal opportunity trumps the difference principle. Still, the two principles together are the guiding light for where the representatives of all individuals, that is to say, all citizens of a political state, would come to an agreement in setting up a fair political structure.

We have finally arrived at the question of basic rights. (Rawls seems to be using liberties and rights interchangeably.) The most fundamental principle morally underpinning a just political constitution is that individuals must have a set of basic liberties (provided that that set is compatible with the basic liberties of all other individuals). Hobbes had said that in the state of nature we all have rights to everything. Locke had posited life, liberty, and property. Mill had talked of three categories of basic liberties. Rawls, on his part, is at once both unequivocal and elusive. Unequivocal, since it is the first principle of justice, rather than the second relating to social and economic equality, which prescribes the rights that are absolutely inalienable for a just society. Elusive, since Rawls provides us with different wordings and various concepts in the numerous places where he elaborates on these basic liberties (*A Theory of Justice*, "Justice as Fairness," and *Political Liberalism*). We can roughly amalgamate all of these, however, and adduce the following list of basic political rights and liberties: the rights to vote and be eligible for public office; freedom of speech and freedom of assembly; freedom of thought and conscience; freedom of the person along with personal property; and freedom from arbitrary arrest (or rights covered by the rule of law).

Hence, we can see Rawls as providing us with a basic framework for a just society which adheres to a moral notion of justice as fairness and prescribes the political constitution which abides by that morality. Rawlsian citizens are assumed to be rational and reasonable. Just as importantly, they are steered by two moral proclivities: a sense of justice and a conception of the good. That also comes into play when their representatives in the original position deliberate on the fair political system and arrive at a framework which accommodates the principles of justice. Still, beyond the basic liberties above, Rawls does not ignore the *primary goods* which free and equal citizens have as their basic interests. Freedom of movement; freedom of choice of occupation, income, and wealth; social recognition and self-confidence; and other such necessary aspects of a decent human life – all must be considered and supplied by political institutions.

There is, then, in Rawls a formidable political system of thought that is all too conscious of rights. He is a central player in the liberal tradition of highlighting individual rights and deriving the political institutions that can be both principled enough and practical enough to make the whole structure just yet still viable, viable yet still just. Two final notes on Rawls are worthy of our attention. First, although he holds to an ethics (the two principles of justice as opposed to, for instance, utilitarianism), we cannot say that his politics is derived from his ethics. Rather, his political system and his ethical theory are theoretically and practically entwined. If anything, his ethical concept of justice arises from an intimate acquaintance with and consideration of both liberal political thought and liberal constitutions already in existence. The latter may be justified or explicated after the fact by a theory of justice as fairness but they are not inferred from it. Second – and this is of great significance – the basic political rights (liberties) of which Rawls speaks are not the kind of natural rights, or their progeny, that Locke or Hobbes advanced as accruing to man before the social contract and before the constitution of a sovereign or a commonwealth. Quite the contrary: It is only after the conversation of the representatives in the original position has "occurred" that these liberties are posited as a requirement of the first principle of justice. There is no conceptual or factual precedence of these liberties (in the sense of human nature or some such posit) to the political discussion which yields the subsequent social contract. These are basic rights, or political liberties, that result from a just political system.

Notes

1 The usual, infamous antagonists of natural rights are Edmund Burke, who viewed natural rights as dangerous "abstract rights," asking "What is the use of discussing a man's abstract right to food or medicine? The question is upon the method of procuring and administering them" (*Reflections on the Revolution in France*, 1993 [1790]); and Jeremy Bentham, whose depiction of natural rights in 1838 as "simple nonsense: natural and imprescriptible rights, rhetorical nonsense, – nonsense upon stilts" is legendary (*Rights, Representation, and Reform: Nonsense upon Stilts and other Writings on the French Revolution*, 2002 [1838], 330).

2   Use of "man" here rather than the less discriminatory "human being" is loyal to the text.

3   See Hobbes, *Leviathan*, chapter 18 (Hobbes, 2010 [1651]. A fortifying depiction of the "essential rights of sovereignty" as legislation, adjudication, enforcement, taxation, war-making and right of control of normative doctrine, is found in Ian Shapiro (1986), chapter 2.

4   There are, however, many noticeable attempts to locate his political philosophy re liberalism as, for example, at a panel at the 1998 World Congress of Philosophy – "Hobbes: Conservative or Liberal?" and A. P. Martinich (1992).

5   This is from Jeremy Bentham's *A Fragment on Government* (1776). Bentham uses the word "utilitarian," but it is John Stuart Mill who brings "utilitarianism" into general use in *Utilitarianism* (1985 [1861]), giving credit to Galt (in chapter 2, footnote *).

6   Some have pointed out that this entails Mill's troubling internal contradictions. See especially Ted Honderich (2003).

7   See Chapter 10.

5   Theories of Rights

No template of a question is more quintessentially philosophical than "What is X?" We can, in a sense, view this book in its entirety as attempting to answer the question "What are human rights?" But if human rights are a certain subset of the set of rights, then it behooves us to first ask "What are rights?" One type of – again, quintessential – answer to that question would be a definition of rights. But definitions are notoriously elusive: There even are, in the philosophical literature, debates about how to define "definition"! So we begin this chapter with a divergent type of explication sometimes provided for the concept of rights, using a dissimilar route.

In the previous chapter we encountered, as background to our discussion on human rights, political liberalism, usually considered to have grounded both the philosophical concept of rights in general and the more currently popular notion of human rights. Before we continue to explore the former (and going on from there, in the next chapter, to human rights) it may be wise to probe, yet again, the status of the three disciplines that have taxed us – politics (or political science and thought), law, and philosophy – in the very explicit matter of that one term: right. In our perusal of liberalism as the natural historical and intellectual context for speaking of rights we emphasized the political and philosophical interests that motivated four philosophers who were tagged as crucial thinkers in the discussion of (liberal) rights. We must not forget, however, that all of them acknowledged the natural and necessary placement of rights within the context of the law. So, in parallel to our obligatory stroll through the legal documents that have established the contemporary human rights regime and community, it is beneficial here to introduce the legal language of rights, for which we find the most well-known and consensually accepted semantic and legal basis in Wesley Hohfeld's 1913 formulation.

Detour: Rights in Legalese – Wesley Hohfeld

In philosophy, as we will see in subsequent chapters, we do not shy away from a myriad of questions concerning a term or a concept, wanting to be clear about the meanings of our words. In the legal arena, even more emphatically, it is precisely the multi-variance of terms that hinders the agenda of legal practice. Wesley Hohfeld puts this strongly: "[I]n any closely reasoned problem, whether legal or non-legal, chameleon-hued words are a peril both to clear thought and to lucid expression." "Rights" is one of the terms that is most used, and most suspect of being indecisively used, in legal thought and expression. So much so that Hohfeld, who was one of the most prestigious authorities in the study of law and whose two tracts constituted seminal work in legal studies (Hohfeld, 1913, 1917), tarries with the idea that all legal relations have been considered as either rights or duties. In order to make sense of this assertion and in order to be able to continue to use the word "rights" – or perhaps its warranted alternatives – without involving ourselves in misunderstandings, Hohfeld proceeded to delineate a set of legal terms and relations that are all members of the family of "rights."

The four terms that occur in our language and in our talk about rights that Hohfeld is interested in disambiguating are *right, privilege, power*, and *immunity*. But thinking that looking for simple definitions of these four is likely to be unsatisfactory, Hohfeld turns instead to pairing this list with two other lists made up of these terms' opposites and correlatives. That is to say, each of the items in the original list – of right-like words – has an opposite and a correlative. So we ask, what would be the opposite situation for the holder of a right and what would correlate to his right in the situation of another person? If we can make sense of each of our terms and understand what its opposite is and what it correlates to, then we might well be on the way to explaining what rights are in general.

Let us set up the Hohfeldian duos:

Opposites	right	privilege	power	immunity
	no-right	duty	disability	liability
Correlatives	right	privilege	power	immunity
	duty	no-right	liability	disability

In the original 1913 presentation of these terms, and then again in 1917, Hohfeld presents an astounding number of instances where legal and judicial decisions, commentaries, articles, and debates make use of all of these rights-concepts – and some others which we will soon mention – with various infelicities of inexact meanings. His goal is to put order into this use by looking for the precise legal and logical relations that these concepts entail. His work was, indeed, so finely tuned that many later followers of and writers on Hohfeld have defined these terms in almost mathematical rigor. We won't go down that path, but let us see how Hohfeld can enlighten us on the meaning of "right" that is most relevant on our trail to human rights.

Obviously, in all the cases in which a person is said to have a right, or a privilege, or power, or immunity, we might, in ordinary parlance, say that the person has a right. But when we espouse exactness, we look specifically and explicitly at the term "right" and try to distinguish it from its other "cousins." Very simply put, my having a right is the opposite of my not having that right or, as Hohfeld awkwardly labels it, my having a no-right. (Whereas, in most of this discussion, words like "privilege," "power," "liability," and others seem natural and commonplace, "no-right" is somewhat artificial.) More important than its opposite, however, is its correlate: my having a right means that I have a claim against someone or some institution, and that correlates to a duty of that person or institution towards me. In Hohfeld's clear words: "A duty or a legal obligation is that which one ought or ought not to do. 'Duty' and 'right' are correlative terms. When a right is invaded, a duty is violated." And he goes on to explain that, for example, "if X has a right against Y that he shall stay off the former's land, the correlative (and equivalent) is that Y is under a duty toward X to stay off the place." If we want to even better understand this precise use of "right," a fitting synonym would indeed be the word "claim," which Hohfeld describes, perhaps tongue in cheek, as having "the advantage of being a monosyllable" (Hohfeld, 1913, 32). (The common use of the term "claim-right" in the literature on rights is a follow-up to that close link.)

How, then, would privilege be different from right? The two seem intimately connected, yet they are not the same. First again is the question of opposites – What is the opposite of having a privilege? If one has a privilege to something or to do something, then one has no duty not to do it. This may sound convoluted, but it is very naturally explicated. If I have the privilege of picking a certain fruit off a tree I am, clearly, under no duty not to pick it. Somewhat in contrast to the earlier idea of right (or claim), the concept of privilege is more oriented to the owner of the privilege, and to her not having a duty not to do something, than to the correlative about someone else. The only thing that Hohfeld initially says about the latter is that my privilege to do something means merely that you have a no-right concerning that doing on my part. But that will soon change, since "the closest synonym of legal 'privilege' seems to be legal 'liberty'," says Hohfeld. In both legal and political contexts, an individual's liberties play an important role in limiting the options of what others – an institution or a state – can legally do. Still, legal and philosophical scholars have deliberated about the interchangeability of privilege and liberty, and Hohfeld himself opts for privilege (this time with the syntactical comment that "privilege" has the added value that it can be used adjectivally, as "privileged").

Hohfeld goes on to discuss, with much attention to detailed examples of ordinary and legal use of the terms (but modestly saying that he is merely providing an "approximate explanation"), the concepts of power and immunity. Since power is the ability to change things, most specifically to change legal relations, its opposite is the inability to do so. More interesting, again, is the correlative to power. My power to do something relating to someone else makes that person liable to my exercising my power. Put differently, as long as I have a certain power, I can exercise it, or not. You are liable to my power – either to my authority to do something or to my doing it in actuality. Now, notice the move to immunity: if one is not liable to another's power or authority, then one is immune. So liability is the opposite of immunity. But what is immunity's correlative? Clearly if I am immune to your power then you have "no-power"; but having no power is tantamount to lacking the ability to change or do anything to me. And then:

> it will also be plain ... that a power bears the same general contrast to an immunity that a right does to a privilege. A right is one's affirmative claim against another, and a privilege is one's freedom from the right or claim of another. Similarly, a power is one's affirmative "control" over a given legal relation as against another; whereas an immunity is one's freedom from the legal power or "control" of another as regards some legal relation.
>
> (Hohfeld, 1913, 55)

So yes, we use the term "rights" somewhat indiscriminately in many contexts – sometimes meaning to talk about privilege, sometimes about power, sometimes about immunity. Other parallels and synonyms such as liberty, license, and claim, can also be a part of rights discourse. And, indeed, Hohfeld has shown us that all these terms are not unrelated – but if we want to use our words carefully, if we care about our semantics, and if, as in the legal context, our words can have extreme consequences, their precise meaning, and difference or correspondence, must be made as unequivocal as possible. When we say "rights" and use the term "in the strict sense," it is a right as claim that is the object of our conversation, and its correlative is duty.

Back to Philosophy

The conversation can now travel many paths. While Hohfeld, coming from the discipline of law, presented an analysis that was practical, even necessary, for legal discourse and practice, philosophical analysis requires conceptual sophistication while trying to avoid conceptual convolution. How do we organize this analysis? We can go down some typical analytic roads: definitions, categories, and distinctions. That is to say, we can attempt to understand the term "rights" by defining it; or we can group rights into several sets which appear significant; or we can distinguish rights by their relevant and essential traits. These roads – and there may be others – are not mutually exclusive; importantly, they are always accompanied by the resounding question "what justifies rights?" So, given the agenda of an organized presentation of rights (not yet at the point of *human* rights), we begin with a fairly brief introduction of the contemporary, yet all the same reasonably traditional and definitely common, vocabulary of some theories of rights.

If we ask what rights are for, or differently put – what their function is, or still differently – what they do for their holders, we encounter the distinction between the interest theory and the will theory of rights. Each of these theories may allude to various features that we have encountered in the Hohfeldian scheme, but they clearly see rights as claims; more so, they attempt to explain what these rights-claims are based on. The will theorist of rights views the holder of rights as an autonomous agent who, by having a right, can control the correlative duty of another. This agency goes hand in hand with the agent's will. The interest theorist is interest-oriented, seeing rights as being in the service of one's interests, indeed as arising out of our interests, which alone can explain them. Both theories have moral philosophers of great stature who have formulated their versions of rights (i. e., their definitions of rights) within and as deriving from the context of their ethical theories – Kant is a will theorist, Bentham is an interest theorist. And the debate between these two basic perspectives on rights is very much with us as they both show intuitive strengths and yet suffer from challenging shortcomings. The will theory, being based on a conception of the holder of rights as an autonomous controller, in general falls short of admitting into the pantheon of rights the rights against being killed or the rights for minimum wages. Most extremely (and relevant to our move to human rights), it is hard to see how the will theory can demand un-waivable – that is to say inalienable – basic rights, since so much weight is put upon the agent's will and decision. It is also questionable how it can accommodate beings who do not have an identifiable will, such as babies or harshly disabled adults, with having rights. The interest theory does make room for these lacunae, but it is problematic when we realize that not all interests give rise to rights and it is not even clear that all rights are literally interest-laden. Be that as it may, this bifurcation between will and interest is widely accepted as the theoretical underpinning of two fundamental, moral grounds for rights.

Just as widespread in the analytic rights conversation is the dichotomy between positive and negative rights. Corresponding with the rights-duties correlation that we have inherited from Hohfeld, we can straightforwardly view the character of positive and negative rights as deciding the different type of duty imposed on the duty-bearer. Positive rights demand a doing or an action on the part of the duty-bearer; negative rights require that the duty-bearer refrain from so doing or acting. If we perceive the duty-bearer as not necessarily a certain individual or even group of individuals, but also possibly an institution or the state itself, we can describe negative rights as those that preclude interference in the right-holder's activities or existence; positive rights are then claims to receive goods or services (material or otherwise) from the duty-bearer. Not only is this negative/positive contrast reminiscent of the negative and positive freedoms that we know from political thought,[1] but it is easily associated with the distinction we have seen above, in Chapter 1, between civil-political human rights and economic-social-cultural human rights. The former are usually considered negative rights (to non-interference by, for example, the government) and the latter are usually seen as positive rights (to, for instance, minimal subsistence provisions). Clearly, however, this is a superficial parallelism: The minute we entertain the question of the enforcement of rights, negativity may turn into a very positive need of resources to enable the system to uphold its non-interference; and positive rights seem no less "political" when the alleviation of poverty and sub-human conditions is recognized as a right. Indeed, complicating the easy bifurcation of rights into positive and negative is the position which takes liberalism to the extreme of libertarianism – the maximization of *individual* autonomy and freedom and the correlative minimization of government – where we meet the insistence on negative rights as the sole legitimate meaning of the real concept of rights.

Widely used in the classification of rights in general is another division – that between general rights and special rights. We can, again, look at this opposition through the eyes of rights or through those of duties. General rights would be the rights afforded to all; alternatively, general rights confer duties or make claims upon all people or institutions. Special rights are rights that are recognized as being held only by some persons or by specific groups of people; alternatively, special rights can also be conceived as placing duties upon certain people or institutions, in certain contexts or circumstances. Any contract, for example, can be translated into a right of and a duty upon the particular persons who are parties to that contract, and is therefore a case of a special right (and correlative duty). The general law – be it a moral or a legal rule – that directs us to honor contracts pertains to a general right and duty. There is, in the debates on rights, an invigorating interrogation whether this distinction is really substantive or essential. Some philosophers take the positive view – that only general rights are authentic rights – to be one of the founding pillars of libertarianism. We will return to this question in the next part of this chapter when we encounter H. L. A. Hart's deep appraisal of the concept of "right."

We have not yet explicitly asked the very crucial question from Chapter 3: How can we justify having rights? A parallel question will be critical for our understanding of human rights in particular – what justifies our, or anyone's, having human rights? But the earlier philosophical question has to do with rights in general and posits the moral problem of the justification of rights as such. Several philosophical "isms," many ethical theories, and various terminologies have been conscripted to answer this question, but we adumbrate here three common positions that permit us to justify rights – philosophically – in a relatively uncomplicated vocabulary. These are the natural rights tradition (also labelled deontological or status theories), the consequentialist or instrumentalist theories, and the view of rights as contract-dependent. Each of these has garnered an immense volume of discussion and dissection; we will meet some later in this chapter and in upcoming ones, when the issue of justification of human rights becomes relevant to other topics. Suffice for now to describe these three in principle.

Deontological theories, among which the most obvious are the natural rights theories, view human beings as naturally constituted with moral duties and rights. The description of the natural human being who holds such rights and duties, and, indeed, the identification of which rights and which duties are then "natural," might differ – think of the range of deontologists from Hobbes to Locke to Kant to Nozick – but this foundational position concerning rights has carried the day for hundreds of years. No less robust are instrumentalist theories; these view rights as the means by which a greater good (of the general good, of an optimal distribution of interests, of well-being, and of similar moral objectives) can be achieved. Utilitarian, consequentialist, egalitarian and other moral theories are all called upon to provide the justification for rights as being the right kind of instrument for the respective goals that different philosophers – starting with John Stuart Mill and going all the way to Dworkin and Sen – see them as providing. Finally, contractual theories justify rights by the consent or social contract struck between agents who agree to the principles that mandate those rights. Rights are not naturally there for humans; neither do they just function as tools for moral human ends. They "exist" as a consequence of the social contract through which we define our common, rational principles of living together decently.

These conceptual quandaries, regarding different functions of rights (will/interests), different classifications (general/special, negative/positive), and diverse justifications for rights (deontological/instrumentalist/contractual) are also inter-related. Deciding, for instance, on a deontological foundation for rights may impact one's view of their function, of their capabilities for generality, or of our acceptance of certain positive rights as truly rights. Instead of going into a combinatorial map-laying of the various games we can play with these terms (and these are, of course, not simply terminological decisions), we now introduce some theorists who swim the deep waters of defining, characterizing, and elaborating on the consequent impact of rights.

One Right Is Enough

H. L. A. Hart is considered by many to be the greatest legal philosopher of the twentieth century; his book *The Concept of Law* (1961) gave us the most astute conceptual, that is to say – philosophical, analysis of law. It is not surprising, therefore, that his work on rights, which we can identify (perhaps following Hohfeld) as the most important construct in the moral discussion of law, is thought of as a legal landmark; still, Hart's gift to us in this discussion is a philosophical, rather than legal, examination of the concept of right. And even though Hart is often presented as a legal positivist, i.e., viewing rights as deriving from man-made law, we attend to him here in a different, morally-focused light. His article "Are There Any Natural Rights?" (1955) supplies the basic investigation of what it means to have a right and, more startlingly, an argument for natural rights that proceeds to claim that we may make do with only one well-defined natural right.

Hart departs from traditional natural rights theorists, who had embarked on a depiction of the natural human being or the moral basics of natural law, by speaking more tenuously and perhaps more modestly about our common commitments in human discourse. The point is that we might be obliged to believe in natural rights given our moral beliefs and, although there is nowhere a philosophical proof of the existence of natural rights, this does give succor to the term "natural rights." Hart also positions his thesis about natural rights as a choice (i.e., will) theory of rights. And he explicitly and blatantly proclaims his thesis: "if there are any moral rights at all, it follows that there is at least one natural right, the equal right of all men to be free" (Hart, 1955, 175).

Let us elaborate on this. What does it mean to have a right? What does having a right give the person who has it that makes her different from someone who does not have a right? Hart suggests that having a right gives one control over someone else's duties or, what amounts to the same thing, over someone else's freedom. This parallelism between duties and limits on freedom is an important moral intuition: Duties are limits on what one is morally free to do. Still, there is a fascinating round-about here. We each have the right to be free, but why and how does that entail our control over others' freedom? And what makes this right – to controlling someone else's freedom and duties – a natural right? The second question is the easier one. The right to be free is not "natural" in the sense of arising from natural law or inhering in the natural features of the human being. The equal right of all persons to be free is a natural right insofar as it is held by everyone and anyone naturally, with no regard to any agreements or contracts between us. But limiting the freedom of another requires justification and – here is the clever rub – that requirement makes sense only if other people have the same right to be free. So, the equal right to be free actually *limits freedom*. In fact, all rights limit freedom; they give the person with the right the power to control other people's freedom by giving that person control over other people's duties. Since everyone has the same basic rights, however, everyone has equal freedom, including equal limits to controlling others' freedom!

This is an astounding conceptual maneuver and, if one accepts its pre-suppositions (concerning the human capacity for choice or the quirks of the meaning of "natural"), it rises to the level of a valid and sound argument for exactly one natural moral right. It also provides us with a clear view as to how a particular definition of right is interwoven with our other terms of categorization. We can see this at work in two other arguments that Hart propounds – both arising from his definition of the one natural right, the equal right of all men to be free. First, although rights and duties are clearly related, their relationship is not the superficial one of a simple correlative. Having a right does not consist merely of being the beneficiary of someone else's duty. A promise made to someone, for example, to take care of a third person, separates the beneficiary of the promise (the third person) from the right-holder (he to whom the promise was made). More unsettling is that babies or animals, concerning whom we have duties not to harm, do not have rights not to be harmed. The discussion about those duties is separate from rights discussions. Second, the argument concerning one natural right deals with general rights, i.e., rights we all hold. Special rights, i.e., specific rights resulting from certain circumstances and agreements between certain people, are trickier. A person with a special right (let's say, the right conferred by a specific promise) has special control over another person's freedom and that seems to make the distribution of freedom unequal: It reduces the freedom of the duty-holder to less freedom than the freedom of all others. How then can we bring back equal freedom here, in the case of special rights? The justifications required for special rights involve showing that they do not really make the distribution of freedom unequal; rights like those under a promise, for instance, are justified because the promiser made the promise voluntarily. More generally, in a fair society the rule-follower has the right that others comply with rules that benefit everyone in order to rectify any inequality.

Not only is the one natural right that we all have to be free inferred from the basic belief that we hold any moral rights at all, but there is an ensuing relationship between the right to be free and other rights. We will abstain from enumerating these links and remain with the focal intuition gained by Hart: recognition of the depth of our commitment to the general, indeed universal, right to be free, which shores up all other rights.

Rights as Trumps

We have mentioned earlier, in Chapter 2, Ronald Dworkin's claim to fame in the rights conversation: his characterization of rights as trumps (Dworkin, 1984), i.e., as the knock-down argument that carries the day over all other arguments for political decisions and policies having to do with the goals for a community as a whole. There is something enticing in that expression – "rights trump" – since it gives the idea of rights a priority that functions axiomatically in our political thought about the justification for our choices of action. Beyond that proclamation-like positioning of rights, Dworkin, like Hart before him, embarks on the articulation not only of the primacy of rights in general, but also of one basic right that can ground all others. It is interesting to note that, although Dworkin sees himself as "defending a liberal theory of law," at the same time he accosts other versions of liberalism having to do with rights, namely legal positivism (which he attributes to Hart) and utilitarianism (which always aims at a general good). For him, as for most traditional liberal theorists of rights, the centerpiece of liberalism is individual rights. But, as against many liberals (and certainly libertarians) who insist on the concept of liberty as the most important kernel of political rights, it is equality which rules the rights realm for Dworkin. We know of the supposed contradiction, or at least tension, between freedom and equality that is a cornerstone of liberal thought;[2] but for Dworkin it is only a supposed contradiction. In truth, "there is no right to liberty as such," and the list of specific freedoms (freedom of speech, freedom of movement, and the like) actually stems from the right to equality. In his seminal book called *Taking Rights Seriously*, Dworkin says: "This most fundamental of rights is a distinct conception of the right to equality, which I call the right to equal concern and respect" (Dworkin, 1977, 7).

But what does it mean – to take rights seriously? Differently put, who is it that must be serious about rights; or who, in the parallel terminology of duties, has the duty to provide equal concern and respect to all? It is here that we finally meet the main duty-holder in the discussion of rights: the government. We also immediately find ourselves in the midst of another familiar distinction, the one between legal and moral rights. And that leads Dworkin to the fundamental question whether there are any moral rights that citizens have against their governments that may fly in the face of the law. Do citizens have a duty to obey the law even if it invades their moral rights, or does the government have the duty to respect citizens' moral rights, no matter what? The answer, which shortly leads to a certain vertiginous incoherence, is that *government* must take rights seriously; that is to say, it must follow a consistent theory of rights. This, however, happens to be a tall order. Take, for instance, freedom of conscience and conscientious objection to legal military draft.

> If a man has a right to do what his conscience tells him he must, then how can the State be justified in discouraging him from doing it? Is it not wicked for a state to forbid and punish what it acknowledges that men have a right to do?
>
> (ibid.,187)

Where does that leave the general, legal, and political construct of the "rule of law"?

This "monstrous contradiction" between rights that the State recognizes and the punishment that it metes out to those who insist on those rights is wonderfully expressed in a very simple question: "Does a man ever have a right to break the law?" (ibid.,189).[3] Or again: "Does an American ever have the right ... to do something which is against the law?" (ibid.,190). If we examine the idea of fundamental rights, we realize that such rights are rights against the government in a very strong sense. These are rights that cannot be abrogated for reasons of the common good, of the majority will, or of any other type of "community" benefit. And here is where we get into a vicious, but necessary, circle. A person has the right to disobey a law if that law turns out to be exactly and explicitly against his right against the government. Saying that the law was democratically decided upon by a majority is precisely what jeopardizes the basic idea of having such essential rights against government. Strikingly, then, we reach a skeptical gaze at the idea of a "general duty" to obey the law. In fact, "this general duty is almost incoherent in a society that recognizes rights" (ibid.,192)!

This extraordinary declaration is not at all simplistic. It does not negate the obligation to ask, for example, about competing individual rights, on which the government must deliberate and decide according to legal and moral judgment. It leaves open the discussion about which moral rights are of this family of fundamental rights that one has against the government and that must therefore be written into a constitution. It still inquires about how government can balance the general good and individual rights. It wonders about the concept of "emergency" – and how a state of emergency can ever lead to a negation of (certain) fundamental rights.[4] In other words, it recognizes that having basic moral rights against government does not excuse us from the duty to query these rights, their unconditional acceptance, and their identification and elaboration.

Yet – if we must continue to engage in all of these explorations, how does the idea of such an institution of rights against government help us in the practice of governing? It is here that the philosophical basis of the idea of rights can help us, since it is based on two concepts: dignity and equality. Espousing dignity is the thought which "supposes that there are ways of treating a man that are inconsistent with recognizing him as a full member of the human community, and holds that such treatment is profoundly unjust." Advocating for equality brings us back to where we started, since it insists "that the weaker members of a political community are entitled to the same concern and respect of their government as the more powerful members" (ibid., 198–199). That is what it means to insist on rights. That is what it means to take rights seriously. That is how rights trump all other considerations.

Rights, Duties, and Interests

We have been looking at legal scholars whose work on rights – that is to say, their definitions, identifications, and characterizations of basic, fundamental rights – is explicitly philosophical. By emphasizing the philosophical, however, we are not leaving aside either the political or legal contexts in which talk about rights has been so abundant. On the contrary, we now bring into the conversation another philosopher – one who has, indeed, offered a definition of rights which "follows ... the usage of writers on law, politics and morality." This is Joseph Raz ("On the Nature of Rights," Raz, 1984, 194), who candidly explains that the point of a philosophical definition of rights is to position the author in the traditional discourse of rights and to make progress, one might say, by focusing on those characteristics of rights that are especially pertinent for moral, political and legal discussion. That is exactly what Raz purports to do in his widely cited definition:

Definition: "x has a right" if and only if x can have rights, and other things being equal, an aspect of x's well-being (his interest) is a sufficient reason for holding some other person(s) to be under a duty.

(ibid., 195)

Since the most surprising aspect of this wording is the idea that "x can have rights," this is understandably followed by the related formulation of:

The Principle of Capacity to have Rights: An individual is capable of having rights if and only if either his well-being is of ultimate value or he is an "artificial person" (e.g. a corporation).

(ibid.)

Reading this definition of rights, and its supplementary add-on, we see three important vertices – rights, interests, and duties. But perhaps this metaphor is misleading; perhaps these are not three elements of a rights theory that happen to be connected like the three points of a triangle. Rather, there is a central progression here, leading from interests, to rights, to duties, that explains what rights are or, as Raz puts it, explain "the common core of all rights" (ibid., 196). In short: "the interests are part of the justification of the rights which are part of the justification of the duties. Rights are intermediate conclusions in arguments from ultimate values [grounding our interests] to duties" (ibid., 208). That is to say, rights connect our interests (which, in this definition, cohere with our well-being) with the duties that others have due to those interests; they are the conceptual bridge that leads from one's interests to another's duties, resulting from the interests (which ground them) and grounding the duties (which arise from them).

Evidently, our earlier correlativity of rights and duties, coming originally from Hohfeld's legal definitions and re-emerging in most analytic discussions about rights, is here made more complex. If correlation is usually understood as a symmetric relationship, then now, since rights ground duties and not the other way around, the relationship between them is unidirectional. This means that there is no absolute (numerical) correspondence between one right and one duty; sometimes a right may lead to more than one duty, or it might be vague or even futile in securing any duty. Furthermore, rights exist in particular circumstances with changing conditions. This means that the same right may bring us to recognition of different duties in different times and places. Think, here, of the right to political participation. We are witnessing a much more dynamic aspect of the concept of a right than we would find in a simple, one-to-one correlation with a duty.

Just as noteworthy as this intricate relation between rights and duties, which Raz's novel definition has given rise to, is the second part of the definition – that part which insists on who it is that can actually hold rights.[5] Recall that the first part was tri-angled, talking about rights, duties, and interests. It is here, in the supplement, that interests come in – also in an intricate, one could almost say convoluted, way. For who, or what, is it that has ultimate value? Only someone (or something?) whose well-being has ultimate value can have rights, and if we investigate this claim we see that plants, animals, and the like – although we might have duties towards them – might not necessarily have rights. This is not because plants and animals are not members of a moral community with us.[6] It is rather because the existence and well-being of plants and animals might not be of ultimate value. Importantly, the interests – of people, plants, or animals – which ground rights are not always of ultimate value; their interests might, indeed, be instrumental. Think, for instance, of the rights of journalists not to disclose their sources; these are clearly based on instrumental interests. But it is the owners of such interests, whose well-being is considered of self-standing value, who are the ones who can have rights.

We do well to return now to one more feature of this characterization of rights. Since interests are a *part* of the justification of rights and rights are a *part* of the justification of duties, we have room for maneuver in our moral and political discourse (about rights, at the very least). Rights are a way-station, then, between the ultimate values of the members of a society (which, among other things, explain their interests) and the duties that are imposed on them. But that means that rights can function as the common currency of a society even if there is variance and even disagreement about the ultimate values. Rights are reasons, maybe even very good reasons, for certain societal and political regulations – but they are not ultimate reasons. Other considerations can always intrude and change our reasoning when we move to duties. In fact, rights can bid us to levy certain obligations on some people, but not on others, or at some times, but not at others. And the rights conversation is dynamic, involving conflicts between different rights and even between rights and other considerations. In other words, rights might not always trump.

* * *

So we see that defining rights, characterizing them, analyzing their traits, and even identifying those that are more basic than others is a potent enterprise indeed. Although we are involved in philosophical analysis, our work becomes holistic in the sense that the parts of the investigation relate, correlate, and inter-relate to one another. Any essential claim about rights may unintentionally – or perhaps very intentionally – lead to questions about duties, to the division between general and special rights, to the difference between legal and moral rights, to the issue of their absoluteness, to the burden of who holds rights, to the gulf between persons, institutions, and states, and finally to the necessary entanglement of politics, law, and philosophy in our discussion. That tangle will continue to be our constant attendant.

Notes

1 Although traceable to earlier philosophers, Isaiah Berlin is usually credited with the establishment (and, of course, the contemporary development) of the concepts of negative and positive liberty in "Two Concepts of Liberty" (from 1958), in *Four Essays on Liberty* (1969).
2 Absolute freedom opens the door to inequality, while absolute equality closes it on freedom.
3 We do not go into the related and wonderfully intricate discussion that Dworkin conducts concerning the ambiguity in the word "right" itself – an ambiguity between having a right to do something and doing the right thing.
4 Recall this problem regarding absolute rights in Chapter 3.
5 We will not go into the question of "artificial person" here.
6 Such a viewpoint is called the reciprocity thesis, and is not antithetical to our definition, yet neither is it necessary.

6   Theories of Human Rights

We move on, now, from rights to human rights. That is to say, we realize that human rights are members in the family of rights, but they are not random or coincidental members. Rather, they make up a sub-family, a group of rights that have become, in the twentieth century, the most vocalized, analyzed, debated, discussed, and questioned set of rights. Whereas in the case of rights in general we were intent on defining the concept of rights in both legal and moral – and sometimes even political – terminology, in the case of human rights we have already outlined their legal framework in the documents of international law (the UDHR, the two Covenants, and several treaties and conventions). Now we must pose the philosophical questions that arise from the ostensibly circular definition that delineates human rights as the rights human beings are entitled to by virtue of being human. Even if we suppose that we have already deciphered the meaning of "rights," it is incumbent upon us, as has been mentioned before, to ask about being human, to inquire about this type of entitlement, and, strange as it may seem, to fathom the link between the two – to understand, that is, what is meant by "by virtue of."

Very concretely, we can now say that we are searching for the foundation or justification of human rights; and that this can be found in several theories of human rights that have been proffered by moral philosophers. Surveying the massive roster of writings on human rights now with us, it becomes a challenge to report on them or even to categorize them. We will, to begin with however, first return to the principled distinction mentioned in Chapter 1 between two types of foundational theories that ground human rights – the religious and the secular – and then delve more deeply into the latter, attempting to see how philosophy can help us in validating rights that are due to us simply because we are human.

As we saw in Chapter 3, there is one concept which runs thread-like through the human rights conversation: dignity. We must return to it, yet again. It is often perceived to be the essential quality that typifies human beings, distinguishing humans from all other beings (alive or not) in the world and therefore serving as the explanatory hinge upon which to hang human rights. Human dignity, it is said, is the meaningful core of human existence; its violation is a grievous offense; and human rights are predicated, therefore, on dignity, serving to protect and maintain it. Recall the beginning of the Universal Declaration of Human Rights: "Whereas recognition of the inherent dignity and of the equal and inalienable rights of all members of the human family is the foundation of freedom, justice and peace in the world ..."; and then the first words of Article 1 in the Declaration: "All human beings are born free and equal in dignity and rights." Dignity appears to be serving as a justification, as an explanation, almost as a synonym for human rights. Dignity is the axiomatic presupposition concerning human beings that entitles them to (human) rights.

We seem to have kicked the ball down one more justificational step by asking what it is that endows human beings with human rights, and replying: dignity. We have asked before "What is dignity?" and "Why or how do humans acquire it?" Kant delivered the iconic, philosophical, secular grounding of dignity that fit so well with the move to human rights by positing a being who is a member of the realm of ends. Let us now inquire more fully about the religious version of this foundation of human rights. We will subsequently return to secular groundings in a variety of theories of human rights.

Religion as the (Sole) Basis for Human Rights

In Genesis 1:27 we find the following words: "So God created man in his *own* image, in the image of God created he him."[1] It is that mysterious verse – what does it mean to create someone in the image of God? – that has given rise to the religious posit of dignity. Indeed, biblical commentators have engaged in interpreting the meaning of "the image of God," turning to holiness, righteousness, greatness, or uprightness; and it is in Corinthians 11:7 that we find the more explicit rendering: "in the image of God created he him; ... as showing man's superior glory and dignity to the rest of the creatures." In other words, in overt biblical words, Scripture positions the human being on a higher plane than all other beings, as comprehending the God-like attribute of dignity. That is, of course, the rub: man, with his dignity, is God's creation. Now, the talk of inherent dignity that we find in the Universal Declaration of Human Rights is not, or is not necessarily, a godly construct, since it is inherent to the human being as a *human* being. But the religious view of such inherence maintains that, since the dignity-bearing human being is created by God, inherent dignity itself and consequent human rights are founded in a God-based religion. In that case, the inherence of dignity in a God-created human being appears to be almost moot.

Another manner of speaking about the dignity of man that may substantiate the idea of human rights is to say that human beings are sacred. Ronald Dworkin, whom we have seen in the analytical mode of establishing the one basic right to equality, which is the right to equal concern and respect,[2] is not loath to speak in such grandiose terms and say that "human life in all its forms is *sacred* – ... it has intrinsic and objective value quite apart from any value it might have to the person whose life it is" (Dworkin, 1993). What we are seeing here is, on the one hand, a very astute explication of the integral, non-utilitarian value of human life and, on the other hand, the use of a religious word – "sacred" – to identify that type of value. It seems, however, that by using the word "sacred" the game is given up: Sacredness is a religious attribute, akin to holiness and sanctity, to be distinguished from the secular world of the mundane and profane. Is Dworkin placing dignity in the religious realm as well? Perhaps he is not speaking religiously; perhaps he is borrowing the religiously-laden word to emphasize the uniqueness, religious or secular, of the human being. Indeed, he does explicitly say that this can be a point of religious faith or secular belief. So one needs to go a step further to insist that such a belief in human dignity is, and must be, a religious position. This is aptly voiced in 1914, for example, by R. H. Tawney:

> The essence of all morality is this: to believe that every human being is of infinite importance, and therefore that no consideration of expediency can justify the oppression of one by another. But to believe this it is necessary to believe in God.
>
> (Tawney, 1972, 67–68)

At first glance, this seems straightforward, even if – by secular lights – misguided. It is reasonable to think that only by postulating a divine creator of everything (including human beings) can we give a satisfactory account of the sacredness, that is to say, the presumed sacred dignity, of human beings and of why they "deserve" or "are entitled" to something that derives from being just that – sacred human beings. The religious worldview that presents a comprehensive world created by God, and a consequent meaning to life that is born of and in that extensiveness, can facilely entertain the idea of a human being whose needs, wants, interests, and goals have been placed at the highest level of value in that world. That is what God meant when he created, first, the world and, then, man in it in his own image. It is a short step from here to the stricture directed to all human beings – that they must recognize humans, themselves and others, as God's creations in his own image. It is an even shorter step, now, to demanding the respect and concern due to these humans, and calling that human rights.

This is conceptually straightforward; if that were all there is to the religious foundation of human rights, it could be seen as one alternative, among many, of grounding human rights – the religious alternative. There is, though, an additional, somewhat more sophisticated but perhaps trickier aspect to the claim of a religious underpinning of human rights that raises vital questions. This is best seen in the work of Michael Perry, who not only elucidates the basics of religious beliefs that lead to the sanctity of human life grounding human rights, but claims, more adamantly, that "there is, finally, no intelligible (much less persuasive) secular version of the conviction that every human being is sacred; the only intelligible versions are religious" (Perry, 1998, 5). Even if we accept that Perry is using the word "sacred" with the looser connotations noted above, still this additional, compelling step in the adherence to religion as a basis and justification for human rights is a daring argument. For what Perry goes on to explain is that a metaphysical world-view which is comprehensive enough to include a foundational explanation of the world and, more so, to advance an articulation of the meaning of life within that worldview, is and must be a religious worldview. Think, for example, of conspicuous elements in the vocabulary of human rights, the notions of "dignity," "inviolable," "end in himself," and the like. Although we try to give them meaning and standing without a turn to religious essence, these terms, says Perry, hold no secular water. There can be no human dignity, no inviolable person, no end in herself, without the supposition of the human as sacred, and this can only be offered in a religious framework. So justifying human rights can only be a religious endeavor; any other supposedly secular justification is either incoherent or garbed in irreligious vocabulary; any justification, according to Perry, is, in fact, actually godly.

Two comments about this unequivocal turn to religion in the attempt to find the foundation of human rights are in order. The first, sounding almost trite, is the oft-cited philosophical query: What is religion? We have been assuming here that the dignity or sanctity of the human being which gives a basis to human rights is a godly gift; we went as far as to correlate this godly action with the explicit biblical rendition that God created man "in his image." Could we admit different forms of religion, such as those that hold a less explicit reference to God, or indeed disavow a divine being altogether, and still contemplate the religiosity of the grounds of human rights? To be fair, although Tawney admonished that in order to make sense of human rights we must believe in God, Perry asserts the opposite. His conception of religion encompasses any worldview that is wide enough to deal with a cosmological vision of the world and deep enough to address the meaningfulness of that world and of our life in it (ibid., 13–16). But what, then, can be the criterion for distinguishing between a religious and a metaphysical Weltanschauung? Doesn't such an extensive idea of religion lay to waste not only the distinction between religion and (secular) metaphysics but even the common linguistic intuition we have concerning "religion" on its own? It almost seems as if such an inclusive understanding of religion makes any metaphysical grounding of human rights tautologically, but trivially, religious. Perhaps this is merely a semantic insight regarding the meaning of "religion," but it is no less self-defeating for that.

A second (semantic) puzzle arises when we speak of religion and human rights – but its impact is far more profound than mere semantics. It has to do with the meaning of the word "right" – with a facet of rights that is even more primary than the philosophical analysis of the term that we encountered in Chapter 5. The question here is not the quintessential "what are rights?" but rather how we can speak of rights in the same context in which we speak of God, of God's commands, or of God's laws. Admittedly, we know the historical progression from natural law to natural rights to human rights; we are also privy to early philosophers like Hobbes or Locke grappling with the place of God in their mostly secular political musings. But it is precisely the humanist tradition which emerged in the Enlightenment that turned to the human being rather than to the divine to provide both the authority and the criteria for ethical argument (and political policy). And it is exactly the concept of rights which arose in humanism that presents a contra to the notion of divine commands, divine law and divine authority. In a religious context, on the other hand, even if God mandates human eligibility to a prize, that eligibility flies in the face of rights when it is commanded and controlled by God. It is, perhaps, this deep cleavage between the divine in religion and the human in secularism that has moved most writers on human rights to refuse a place at the table of religious foundations for human rights.[3]

Two Basic Moral Human Rights

We have encountered Kant's Categorical Imperative, the moral law which is universally applicable to all rational beings, and we have seen how morality and moral theories are invoked to undergird the ethical concept of rights in general. The reasonable next step moves us onwards to the moral hinges upon which we can anchor human rights. One of the explicit and analytic paradigms of such a view to human rights is Alan Gewirth, who formulates, akin to Kant, a fundamental moral principle, the Principle of Generic Consistency: "Act in accord with the generic rights of your recipients as well as of yourself" (Gewirth, 1982, 52). Morality and rights – we will soon see that these are human rights – are, for Gewirth, inextricably connected. More to the point, human rights are based in morality. How?

If human beings have rights "simply insofar as they are human," the profound question we must ask is "whether or why A is entitled to X and hence whether or why the other person or persons have such a correlative duty to A" (ibid., 41). Very importantly, this is not a factual question that can be answered by a turn to legal or conventional facts; it is a normative question that must address universal, moral rights.[4] Furthermore, looking for a valid moral criterion which will justify a moral human right means understanding, first, what it means to be moral, and that means, second, asking for a definition of a morality. Unsurprisingly, this is answered by linking morality with action: "a morality is a set of categorically obligatory requirements for action ..." (ibid., 45), leading to the logical insight that the necessary conditions of human actions have to be something that humans have a right to. More so, since every one of us – that is to say, every rational human agent – can make this claim, it holds universally. And that entails, logically, that since we think of the purposes that we aspire to in our actions as good, the conditions for our actions are necessary goods.

What are these conditions? Analytically, starting from the rudimentary question of what grounds our rights – i.e., what makes us entitled to something, anything – and going through a definition of morality based on human action, one arrives at a basic identification and then categorization of the most foundational conditions for these rights: freedom and well-being. This is a sophisticated, highly complex philosophical exercise, but it leads to an explicit formulation of the necessary conditions for human rights based on morality. In Gewirth's words:

> ... it is possible and indeed logically necessary to infer, from the fact that certain objects are the proximate necessary conditions of human action, that all rational agents logically must hold or claim ... that they have rights to such objects ... [T]his provides a sufficient criterion for the existence of human rights, because the claim must be made or accepted by every rational human agent on his own behalf, so that it holds universally within the context of action, which is the context within which all moral rights ultimately have application.
>
> (ibid., 46)

Importantly, then, these necessary conditions, also called necessary goods, when claimed by any and all rational human agents themselves, for themselves, become human rights. "The agent is now envisaged as saying 'My freedom and well-being are necessary goods.' From this there does logically follow his further judgement, 'I have rights to freedom and well-being'" (ibid., 49). These are, consequently, our two basic human rights.

In an interesting progression, in order to make this judgment of one's own rights into a universal, moral injunction, each agent must admit that all humans have this same right. And this is what, finally, brings us to the Principle of Generic Consistency, which we do not hesitate to repeat: "Act in accord with the generic rights of your recipients as well as of yourself" (ibid., 52). We get to it by recognizing that the rights to freedom and well-being are generic moral rights – they are generic since one cannot understand the concept of action without admitting these features; and they are moral since one cannot claim them without admitting their application to all other humans. The whole idea is consistent, since one risks contradicting oneself if one does not realize both one's own, and every other human's, need for freedom and well-being in order to act.

Several related questions arise once we have thus located the grounds for human rights and the two basic families of human rights that derive from those grounds. First and foremost is the elaboration and real specification of what freedom and well-being consist in. The formal definitions that Gewirth articulates – freedom consists in "controlling one's behavior by one's unforced choice while having knowledge of relevant circumstances" and well-being consists in "having the other general abilities and conditions required for agency" (ibid., 47) – are intuitively clear, but going into the details of these formulations is truly instructive. Respecting someone's right to freedom means desisting from coercion, violence, deception; it means having regard for his autonomy and privacy. Legally and politically it involves the correct procedural applications and the appropriate measure of consent, ensuring the implementation of civil liberties. Looking out for someone's well-being is grounded in not harming, or maintaining, or even increasing the preconditions of her life situation. This includes consideration of so many elements of one's life: life itself, physical integrity, mental health, ability to plan, use of resources, self-esteem, education, and so many others. And it, like freedom, applies to institutions (usually but not always legal) that reflect and represent social rules that pertain to criminal law and others that address inequality.

Two additional issues relating to human rights and their interesting resolutions also stand to profit from this moral theory of human rights. One has to do with who holds human rights or, differently stated, are there any exceptions to the posit of universality of human rights? As we saw previously, the assumption of such universality is variously confronted by the difficulty of facilely affording human rights to children, to fetuses, to those who have suffered brain damage, to paraplegics, and others. In the context of a moral principle underwriting action we may, perhaps, consider these exceptions as less capable of action and thereby apply varying degrees of rights to them. This immediately raises another issue – the absoluteness of human rights and, more practically, the conflicts between rights. We must concede that the Principle of Generic Consistency is, itself, an absolute moral principle, but its absoluteness resides precisely in our ability to use it as a criterion for adjudicating between human rights. So, again, we turn to the central role of action in our moral judgment, and apply the principle while attempting to refrain from inconsistency (for instance, in mutual or competing transactions) and while evaluating different rights comparatively for degrees of necessity for action.

Before continuing our review of comprehensive and illuminating philosophical theories of human rights – that is to say, philosophical justifications of human rights – let us look at Gewirth's summary of what it is that he has "tried to show":

> [A]ll the human rights have a rational foundation in the necessary conditions or needs of human action [i.e., freedom and well-being], so that no human agent can deny or violate them except on pain of self-contradiction. Thus, the demands that human rights make on persons are justified by the Principle of Generic Consistency as the supreme principle of morality. It is also through the moral requirements set by this principle that the political and legal order receives its central justification as providing for the protection of human rights ... Thus, the rationally grounded requirements of

human action provide the basis and content of all human rights, both those that apply in individual transactions and those that must be protected by social rules and institutions.

(ibid., 66)

As before, as always, our involvement in morality will be seen to lead to "the political and legal order." Differently put, human rights are based on morality even when they function in the political and legal arenas.

The Capability Approach

Freedom and well-being supply the moral building blocks of Gewirth's theory of human rights. They do not disappear but, adjoined with the idea of dignity, continue to function in a different but still basic way in another perspective on human rights – the capability approach,[5] giving us, on the one hand, a description of a human life worth living, and, on the other hand, a normative account of what must be demanded for that life to exist as such and endure. Mostly presented by philosophers Amartya Sen and Martha Nussbaum,[6] the capability approach sees the primary freedom to achieve well-being as a fundamental moral requirement. Notably, it is this freedom that can be assessed through the opportunities that human beings have to achieve their goals – and these opportunities can be better expressed and explicated as capabilities. In parallel to human rights, which we have seen as applying to individuals and provided – or violated – by state institutions, the capability approach is about persons (whose well-being is at issue) and the policies of social and political institutions (which must protect and promote such well-being). Furthermore, in the context of our investigation of human rights, beyond just pointing at the concept of "capabilities," it is important to formulate more comprehensively the conceptual relationship between capabilities and human rights so as to identify its practical ramifications.

As early as 1979, engaging in political philosophy through economic lenses, Sen – in his Tanner Lecture on Human Values at Stanford University – began the discussion on equality of capabilities, arguing against other criteria of equality (such as resources, goods, opportunity, and the like).[7] This terminology of capabilities and functionings caught on well in public and political discourse, which is not necessarily philosophical; in philosophy we can point to Nussbaum as supplying the further elaboration and development of the capabilities approach, going all the way back to Aristotle's notions of human capability and moving forward, with Sen, to an emphasis on rights and a connection to (Rawlsian) liberalism. But already in 1997 we encounter Nussbaum differentiating between Sen, "who prefers to allow the account of the basic capabilities to remain largely implicit in his statements," and her own work, which "[has] produced an explicit account of the most central capabilities ..." (Nussbaum, 1997, 277). It is this list, and the reasoning that leads to it, that we shall now examine.

A fascinating aspect of the capabilities approach has to do with a topic that was addressed earlier, when we interrogated the "human" in "human rights." The capability approach offers a conception of the human being that is based on human capabilities! It clearly poses the question: What are the things that human beings can be and do that are so central to their life that their absence would make it less than a truly human life? Nussbaum complements this conceptual analysis in her clarification that the list of human capabilities is not a-historical or *a priori*, but arises from empirical results of "a broad and ongoing cross-cultural inquiry" (Nussbaum, 1999, 40). This is vital: It allows us, on the one hand, to recognize biological commonalities that are relevant to human capabilities while, on the other, to acknowledge the significance of local cultural and societal factors regarding different capabilities.[8] This, of course, also makes the list – any list – of human capabilities open to discussion and change.

We shall now enumerate and examine the capabilities that Nussbaum presented almost 20 years ago; it is an enlightening exhibition of what goes into living a decent human life and therefore what may subsequently ground any list of human rights.[9] The first three capabilities appear intuitively consensual: 1) life, 2) bodily health, and 3) bodily integrity. Already here, we can see nuances and thoughtful details that make this record of capabilities so profound. The capability to live life to its normal end is not only limited to "not dying prematurely" but also "[not dying] before one's life is so reduced as to be not worth living." Bodily health not unexpectedly includes reproductive health, nourishment, and shelter. Bodily integrity, with more complexity, includes freedom of movement but also security against violent (including sexual and domestic) assault, opportunities for sexual satisfaction, and reproduction choices. These first three capabilities exhibit the type of attentive distinctions that will continue throughout the list.

The next three capabilities are 4) senses, imagination, and thought, 5) emotions, and 6) practical reason. No less vital than the physical conditions of a worthy human life are those aspects of it that have to do with our mind and feelings. These capabilities include the abilities to use our senses, imagination, and thought in ways that are supported by education (mathematical and scientific training), by artistic expression, by several freedoms (of speech and religion), and by pleasurable (i.e., not painful) experiences. They also consist of emotional capabilities – to love, grieve, experience gratitude and anger – that must be supported, definitely not hindered. Finally, and perhaps most substantially, practical reasoning, which enables our determination of what is good (for us and others) and our planning of appropriate moves to achieve that good, is also a necessary condition for a worthwhile human life.

The seventh capability in the list is "affiliation," and it is explicitly about one's capability to engage with others. This is not to say that the first six capabilities we have adumbrated involve an essentially solitary person, but it is to highlight our unequivocal human status as social and communal beings and our capability for such a status as a rudimentary requirement of human life. Affiliation is subdivided into friendship and respect – and both of these capabilities admirably express the essential depth of human social existence. Being capable of friendship means being able "to live for and to others," showing concern and compassion, and understanding justice. Respect entails a social foundation that cherishes self-respect, non-humiliation, and our old friend – dignity. The capability of friendship and respect also demands social and political rules and institutions that protect freedoms of assembly, freedoms of political speech, and non-discrimination of any type.

The last three capabilities are not easily put under a category. They are 8) other species, 9) play, and 10) control over one's environment. Less obvious than the seven preceding capabilities (and perhaps less amenable to subsequent renditions of well-formulated human rights), these emerge as essential afterthoughts about additional facets of a worthwhile human life that must be preserved and protected. Humans must be "able to live with concern for and in relation to animals, plants, and the world of nature" in order to thrive. Humans must similarly "enjoy" their life and not just muddle through, if theirs is to be a valuable life. And finally, humans must be capable of controlling – at some level – their material and political surroundings and actions.

These ten capabilities – and remember, they are not offered as a final, never-to-be-debated-or-modified list – are distinct from one another, but not unrelated. They do not obey any hierarchy of more or less importance since each of them is crucial; one cannot be balanced or replaced by another,[10] but realization or violation of one can certainly impact another. Two questions that arise here, though, are primarily significant for our understanding of human rights. One has to do with the difference between capability and functioning; the other between capability and human rights. The first is straightforwardly resolved. Capability is the ability to function, and human beings perform central human functions in various ways and at various levels. Functions of eating, sex, and work, among others, are accomplished differently by different humans, according to their individual desires, their social contexts, and their cultural traditions. Functioning is variable, but the capability to function, on the other hand, must be there in an absolute sense, permitting the flexibility of functionings. For example, religious motivations might enjoin one to fast or to be celibate; but the capability to decide on these functionings is present, no matter what one's personal preference is. According to the capability approach, public policy is not responsible for people's functionings, only for their capability to function and to perform the central human functions described in the list. That is why the capability of practical reason thereby becomes ultra-significant, since it is "used" in the manifestation of all other functions. But, "for political purposes it is appropriate for us to shoot for capabilities ... Citizens must be left free to determine their course after that" (Nussbaum, 1997, 289).

And what is the relationship between capability and human rights? In what way is the capability approach helpful for our understanding of human rights? Has what we have said thus far about human capabilities made them an explanatory hinge for the concept of human rights, perhaps in the sense that we have, as humans, the right to fulfill our capabilities? Or is it the other way around – and human rights are the elements that actually ground the availability of our capabilities, so that having a certain right is what makes us capable of a certain function? Perhaps, finally, these are just synonymous concepts that can be substituted for each other? Nussbaum indeed investigates all these options and provides instances to illustrate how we might encounter each of them. So, for example,

> [t]he right to political participation, the right to religious free exercise, the freedom of speech, the freedom to seek employment outside the home, and the freedom from unwarranted search and seizure are all best thought of as human capacities to function in ways that we then go on to specify.
>
> (ibid., 293)

Clearly, here it is the idea of capability that provides the foundation for a human right. Contrariwise, though, we can speak of basic human rights, like the right to work outside the home, as the more fundamental notion, and recognize that in certain circumstances a person who has that right does or does not have that capability secured. That is to say, a human right is conceived as prior to the capability and, in fact, as what justifies the demand for the capability to be available and safeguarded. And, of course, capabilities and human rights are voiced as equivalent when we say that "citizens in country C 'have the right of free religious exercise'" (ibid.).

Just the same, we can appreciate Nussbaum when she prescribes the capability approach as a beneficial way of understanding human rights, since rights then become more than merely a legal construct. Furthermore, we can show that this applies both to civil-political rights and to economic-social-cultural rights, since in both cases, in all cases, the capability approach is built on the basic idea that a citizen is a free and dignified human being precisely because she is capable of functioning and making choices concerning those functions, i.e., because she is an owner of capabilities. Thus are human rights humanly conceived.

Institutional Duties (to Respect Human Rights)

Looking at theories and conceptions of human rights in secular garb, i.e., not accepting the religious foundations of human rights as exclusive or definitive, has shown us that we are concentrating on notions of morality. We have seen an example identifying two fundamental moral rights (to freedom and well-being) at the base of all others, as Gewirth does; or we can turn to a universal construct, like capability, as Sen and Nussbaum choose to do, and forage for its actualization in specific capabilities that then result in greater list of even more specific human rights. We will now entertain one more theorization – an attempt to question the concept of human rights from a different, though still moral, perspective. This is the institutional conception of human rights, adopted and introduced lucidly by Thomas Pogge ("How Should Human Rights be Conceived?", 2002). It posits that before we ask what human rights there are, we must ask what human rights are; differently put – before we attempt to provide a catalogue, or even a less concrete but still specific identification of definite human rights, we must make it clearer to ourselves how we conceive of human rights. And one innovative conception is the institutional conception, which sees human rights as moral claims on the organization of the society in which a person is a member.

The novelty lies not in the rights which are specified as human rights – indeed, no list of rights needs to be given at this conceptual stage, though some clear examples are proffered – but in the theoretical basis on which such lists can be predicated. Early on, we saw that the (historical, ideational) move from natural law to natural rights to human rights involved a development of ideas, even though all three grand conceptions dealt in weighty, unrestricted, and broadly sharable moral concerns. Whether a philosopher (or theologian, or psychologist, or political thinker) speaks about natural law or natural rights or human rights – they are speaking about important moral demands, applying them as independent of time or place or tradition or culture, and claiming that (hopefully) these demands can be shared across times and places and traditions and cultures.[11] The discursive move from natural law to natural rights involves greater attention to others' interests than to one's own; it also carries a secularizing move, and – even granting that rights are correlated with duties – it does not necessarily address religious duties, duties towards oneself, or duties towards animals. Still more pivotal is the passage from natural rights to human rights. Now the secularization becomes explicit – the human is the be-all and end-all of these rights; the orientation is political, not metaphysical; and the bearers of (human) rights are all and only humans. This last point is unreservedly significant: all humans have the same rights and all humans matter equally. And all of this relates to our previously discussed, individualistically centered, theories of human rights. What makes this novel theory unique is its insistence that institutions, rather than persons, have a duty towards individuals, regarding their human rights. Human rights laws and demands are addressed to the structural forms of those in power, i.e., human rights violations must be "official"!

That term – "official" – seems easy to understand, but needs unpacking. We can easily identify the paradigm official institution in the world state system as the government; so government officials are ... official. This includes the legislative, administrative, judicial branches of government, of course, but also the lower echelons of government – such as the police, the mail services, the educational authorities (where these are public, not private), health officials (ditto), and others. These are official in the sense that interests us for human rights since they can show *"official disrespect."* Obviously, when the higher authorities enact a law which is clearly a moral wrong – such as interning all persons of a certain ethnic group in concentration camps – or violate a law forbidding such a wrong, they are more blameworthy than a private person violating a (criminal or civil) law, since they are offending a deep idea of justice. They are, just as clearly, violating human rights. But others in official capacity can be just as culpable and, again, their responsibility is different from that of an individual criminal. Torture by a policeman is a violation of human rights; murder by a mailman is not. This is so precisely because the policeman is perpetrating his action in the context of his official capacity. It is, accordingly, official disrespect of human rights that anchors our conception of institutional human rights. It is institutions, and more precisely our social and political institutions, that are called on to not violate human rights. Obviously, in different societies and different political systems, institutions differ. They can be economic, political, legal, familial, military, health, and educational institutions, and their mode of organization is obviously relevant to their official behavior. But, no matter their structural differences, these are the bodies that should be held accountable for our human rights.

Two important extensions of this straightforward institutional variety of human rights violation are needed to make the institutional theory comprehensive and persuasive. First, we must also tend to indirect official disrespect. Official disrespect is easy to identify when it involves blatant, active violation of justice and is voiced or enacted openly, by statutes and regulations, or by actions "on the job." There is a no less insidious version of it, however, that can be ascertained in more elusive circumstances. This happens when the government fails to protect citizens from violations committed by others who are under its jurisdiction, whether they be individuals or organizations. This can happen through lackluster enforcement of laws, by bias as to who is apprehended and judged for crimes, by governmental disregard of blatant contempt of the law, or, most significantly, by allowing interference in protected conduct (according to human rights articles and laws). The government is implicated in official disrespect when it allows "outraged citizens" or death squads or any other kind of government supporters to behave as they will. And even though government might seem to be less responsible in cases where, for example, it passively accepts discriminatory speech or emboldened sanctions against unpopular opinions, these are no less insufferable cases of official disrespect for human rights; they are consequently, institutional violations of human rights.

There is a second widening of the institutional sphere that deserves special mention. We have broadened official authority to include not just government but other social and political institutions, and to be responsible not just for active attacks on human rights, but for passive official indifference to them. In explaining institutional authority, however, Pogge turns to an "active citizenry that is deeply committed" to rights and "disposed to work for [their] political realization" (Pogge, 2002, 62), without whom the respect – official or otherwise – for human rights cannot exist or be sustained. Does this contradict the insistence on institutions alone as being responsible for human rights, by letting in individuals through the back door, so to speak?[12] Not necessarily. In speaking of democratic societies, where citizens are represented and taken into consideration by government and policy makers, one can view "the citizenry," and not particular individuals, as a social-economic (perhaps somewhat abstract) institution that is called upon to respect human rights.

> Such cases, too, exemplify official disrespect when the people, who bear the ultimate responsibility for what happens on their society's territory, do not care enough about the objects of human rights to enable, encourage, and (if need be) replace or reorganize their government so as to safeguard secure access to these objects for all.
>
> (ibid., 62)

So, for example, societies which accept mistreatment of servants are violating those persons' human rights (not to be subjected to inhuman or degrading treatment); their citizenry is just as responsible as their government.

This insistence on (social and political) institutions, along with recognition of a citizenry that is committed to human rights, has an important effect on another issue – how wide is the circle of those who are duty bound to protect human rights? "Responsibility for a person's human rights falls on all and only those who participate with this person in the same social system" (ibid., 66). This is remarkably restrictive. Contrary to the oft-expressed, somewhat naïve idealization and universality of human rights, that calls on all human beings to be responsible for the human rights of all other human beings, the institutional theory is precise about who might be taken to task for violations of human rights. Since human rights are actually the moral claims made upon the structural facets of a society that are realized in its institutions, and since citizens are the ones who are responsible for the organization of their society, it is those same citizens who share accountability for their own society's institutions and for those institutions' protection or violation of human rights. Obviously, this obligation to support the human rights of one's co-partners in a social-political structure is more explicit and binding in democratic societies; in more coercive institutional orders, this shared responsibility is harder to articulate. Just as obviously, more influential or powerful citizens are more evident targets of human rights demands.

A concluding, intriguing outcome of this internal-societal feature of the institutional theory of human rights is its subsequent attitude towards minimalist vs. maximalist perceptions of the duties that rights entail; this is intimately related to the issue of negative vs. positive duties; and this, in turn, impacts our acceptance and then prioritization of civil-political rights or economic-social-cultural rights. Now, ostensibly, rights entail duties (call this the interactional understanding of human rights), and these duties may be viewed minimalistically as negative duties (to refrain from violating rights) or maximalistically as positive duties (to help, support and protect).[13] But once the institutional theory is put into play regarding who or what it is that is called upon as responsible for one's human rights – and that is one's own society's organization – we can transcend the minimalism/maximalism quandary. Instead of being called upon not to violate (anyone's) human rights (anywhere), governments' and their citizens' responsibility is "to work for an institutional order and public culture that ensure that all members of society have secure access to the objects of their human rights" (ibid., 65). This, then, strikingly leads to, on the one hand, a middle ground between minimalism and maximalism (we are not completely disconnected from what we do not directly effect, but we are also not responsible for every human rights deprivation), and, on the other hand, a possibility of still thinking of all of our (human rights) duties as negative duties to "not uphold and impose upon [others] coercive social institutions under which they do not have secure access to the objects of their human rights" (ibid., 66). Thus, negative and positive duties cohere. More so, the supposed divide between civil-political rights and economic-social-cultural rights is also outdone. By emphasizing the negative duty above, we see that all rights are controlled and impacted by social and political institutions and our duties are to never restrict people's freedom to access their basic necessities – political or economic – in a society's institutional structure. Pogge resurrects Charles Darwin to drive the point through: "If the misery of our poor be caused not by laws of nature, but by our own institutions, great is our sin" (ibid., 67).

* * *

The search for philosophical foundations, justifications, or even merely "explanations" for human rights takes a number of roads. Its findings can be categorized as a diversity of trails – the religious justification, the path through human agency, the capability approach, the institutional version – which we have presented as distinctive central understandings of the philosophical substance of human rights. This is not to say, however, that these are exclusive or uniquely exceptional. Indeed, in the past two decades, philosophers have been fortunate, while engaging and debating with these (relatively fundamental) theoretical building blocks of human rights, to be enriched by conceptual additions. Several of these will be discussed in later chapters devoted to particular subjects and contexts.[14]

Notes

1 This is the place to remark that in Scripture it is man, not woman, who is created in God's image. In fact, the end of that same verse only adds "… male and female created he them." God created only man in his own image; there is no mention of his image in the creation of woman.

2 Chapter 5.

3 This is almost naïvely expressed by Brian Orend: "Far from uniting us all behind the ideal of respect for human rights, religious appeals might serve only to exaggerate differences of opinion regarding who has equal moral status and why" (2002), 45.

4 Soon, in Chapter 7, we will ask about the relativism that is thought by some to be a necessary accompaniment to moral talk.

5 Following the leading protagonists – Amartya Sen and Martha Nussbaum – of the fit between human rights and human capabilities, we sometimes use "approach," other times "perspective," and rarely "theory."

6 See especially Amartya Sen, "Equality of What?" (1979), and "Human Rights and Capabilities" (2005); Martha Nussbaum, "Capabilities and Human Rights" (1997) and "Women and Cultural Universals" (1999).

7 Sen, "Equality of What?" (1979).

8 This corresponds with the question of universalism and cultural relativity, to be dealt with more comprehensively in Chapter 7.

9 This particular listing is taken from Nussbaum, "Capabilities and Human Rights," (1997, 287–88).

10 Nussbaum does view practical reason and affiliation as having particular importance since they give a special, human meaning to all the other capabilities (1999, 288).

11 The specific questions of such universal applicability and shareability will be dealt with explicitly in Chapter 7.

12 See Orend (2002, 129–136) for a critique of the idea that duties that correlate to human rights can be exclusively institutional.

13 The former perceptions are usually viewed as libertarian theories, the latter as utilitarian.

14 Important actors in the current conversation relate to the early theoretical contenders and provide invigorating novel ways of approaching the subject. These include Griffin, *On Human Rights* (2008); Beitz, *The Idea of Human Rights* (2009); Buchanan, *The Heart of Human Rights* (2013); and Tasioulas's articles, "Towards a Philosophy of Human Rights" (2012), "On the Nature of Human Rights" (2012), and "On the Foundations of Human Rights" (2015).

Part III

Issues in Human Rights

7 The Universalism of Human Rights

The founding document of modern human rights is the Universal Declaration of Human Rights. The origin of the concept of modern human rights inheres in the idea of a universality that applies to all human beings. The essential characteristics of human beings that are called upon to ground the thought that they all are entitled to something basic and necessary are universal traits. The rights that are then perceived as, indeed, justified demands are universally recognized rights. How are we to think, then, of human rights as anything but universal? We have seen earlier in our discussion that the interrogation of the concept of human rights is brought up against absolutism in the context of both the philosophical and even the practical questioning – whether human rights are absolute, which of them are absolute, and whether or not there is a scale of absoluteness among them (which almost sounds like a contradiction in terms). Universalism sets us up against a greater quandary, for questioning universalism sometimes seems like questioning the very essence of human rights!

What would it mean to say that human rights are, and should be, relatively rather than universally conceived, understood, interpreted, and applied? Note that the question itself is both a descriptive and normative query. One can begin by inquiring about the ethical and cultural values and norms that human beings hold and attend to – and then insist on replying with the descriptive truth that reports on deep variability, i.e., relativity, among human beings in their perception and realization of human rights. Individuals can disagree on the propriety of certain actions and have differing opinions as to their moral worth. (I might believe that a mother killing for her child is a saint; you may view her as a murderer.) Different societies view the same behavior in a diametrically opposed manner and judge it as good or bad. (Eating with one's hands is considered gauche in most Western societies; it is the natural way to eat in Ethiopia.) Religions are notoriously divided as to the permissible things to do in certain circumstances. (Judaism and Christianity prohibit polygamy; Islam and Mormonism accept it as appropriate to married life.) So it would be foolhardy to deny that cultural relativity exists in all corners of the earth, with observed actions, behavior, and regulations refuting the supposition that there is a *de facto* universalism that applies to all human beings in all known societies.

The normative question about relativism is a far cry from the descriptive portrayal of cultural relativity – for, rather than asking about the truthful portrayal of human (individual or group) conduct, it inquires whether we can even speak or think of morality in universalistic terms. Remember that in Chapter 3 we tied together universalism, absolutism, objectivism, and realism. This family of philosophical positions maintains that, in some way, moral laws are absolute, objective, and "really there." Calling them universal is another way of perceiving what is common to this group: Moral laws are objectively there, applying to all human beings, and discoverable by all as well. This is a normative position in that it assumes a universal morality that could and should be discovered, examined, and optimally followed; just as normative is the opposed viewpoint – moral relativism. There is, of course, being mindful of cultural relativity – the recognition that values depend on culture (or tradition, or family, or society, or community). Acknowledging that different cultures have different moral codes, however, can be understood as a merely descriptive recognition. Going one step further and insisting on the normative essence of moral relativism means asserting that fundamental values – i.e., our deepest ethical beliefs – cannot but be culture-bound. The true relativist holds that there is no universal good or bad, right or wrong; there is only good or right for someone in a certain culture and bad or wrong for someone in another culture. We could, if need be, simply distinguish between cultural relativism, the descriptive cognizance of cultural moral differences, and moral relativism – the normative assertion that beyond cultural differences there is no system of values that does, or should, apply in all cultures. The sincere moral relativist is a relativist all the way down.

How does this relate to human rights? In variously establishing human rights and in looking for their justification, we have entertained the options of legal (positivistic) justification, religious justification, and philosophical justifications of several sorts. That last possibility is of most interest to us here – and it usually contends that human rights are based on moral demands. The philosophical discussion of human rights is, and must be, a conversation about morals. Of course different moral theories, like utilitarianism or Kantianism, will produce different theories (of justification) of human rights. Unsurprisingly also, moral relativism – or moral realism, for that matter – will lead to human rights relativism (or realism). In fact, in the case of human rights, given the diverse cultural contexts in which they are perceived to play a role, it seems more than natural to think of human rights – their existence, their manifestation, their articulation, and their justification – as being relativistic rather than universalistic. So the very idea of universal human rights appears to be truly compromised. Differently put – one seems to be able to choose whether to be a moral relativist or a moral universalist; but, whichever way one goes, one is hard-put not to acknowledge the relativism of human rights. How, then, can one remain a universalist regarding human rights?

Unambiguous Relativism and Unmistakable Universalism

We have seen that first there was the Universal Declaration of Human Rights – in which there was nary an allowance for cultural difference or for the variability of cultural values and norms in the context of human rights. True, cultural rights are mentioned – once – but only as a type of right, along with economic and social rights, that is indispensable for one's dignity and the free development of their personality. In other words, in the UDHR, even mention of cultural rights is an instance of universal human rights; there is no hint there that these rights may be substantially different from culture to culture or, more egregiously, that they may conflict with rights that are universally conceived. But this conflictual situation – between universal rights and culturally relative rights – was astoundingly first faced even before the UDHR was fully formulated and propagated. Already in 1947, while the process of drafting the Universal Declaration by the UN Commission on Human Rights was unfolding with several well-known disagreements, and while the main agenda of all involved was to find a common document to be agreed upon and accepted by all members of the UN – that is, while universalism was the icon of the envisioned declaration – the executive board of the American Anthropological Association (AAA) published a statement that, read today in retrospect, seems to belie the dreamed-of possibility of ever producing a truly universal declaration of human rights.

The AAA statement (1947) was specifically submitted to the Commission on Human Rights, but it was published in the *American Anthropologist*, becoming thereby a public comment, supposedly in support of, but much more emphatically a critique of, the universalism that is presupposed by the project of producing a universal declaration. It begins with a double *credo* that immediately lays to waste the essential individualistic tenor of traditional, liberal human rights. Adding to any such declaration's "respect for the personality of the individual as such," it counters with the claim that "respect for the cultures of differing human groups is equally important" (AAA, 1947, 539). But these two fulcrums, individual and culture, although proclaimed to be equally important, are not symmetrically related. Groups are made up of individuals, of course – that is almost a tautology – but there is far more stress placed, from the very beginning of the AAA statement, on the insight that "human beings do not function outside the societies of which they form a part" (ibid., 539). The consequences of such a cultural and communitarian perception of human nature lead to strictures, provided by the anthropologists, on what a universal declaration of human rights must grant. First, "[t]he individual realizes his personality through his culture, hence respect for individual differences entails a respect for cultural differences" (ibid., 541). Second, this respect for differences between cultures also derives from the fact that science has refuted the possibility of any comparative, qualitative evaluation of variant cultures. Third, and arguably most charged, not only individual proclivities, but also standards and values are relative to the cultures in which they exist. Importantly, and almost paradoxically then, any attempt to formulate universal moral codes must resist adapting to any particular moral code coming from any particular culture, since so doing would detract from their universality.

The AAA's own respect for cultural difference, and its demand that the universal declaration being worked on show the same level of respect, lead to an extreme cultural relativism. And this heads on to a tenuous, just as relativistic, expression of human rights. "What is held to be a human right in one society may be regarded as anti-social by another people, or by the same people in a different period of their history. The saint of one epoch would at a later time be confined as a man not fitted to cope with reality" (ibid., 542). Since earlier proclamations of human rights, although purportedly universal, were actually localized political tracts, we fell upon slave owners writing the American Bill of Rights or slave-owning colonies accepting the slogans of the French Revolution. Today's internationally connected and recognized world of nations and cultures and ways of life (or already that of 1947) makes the application of any universal declaration far more complicated. So complicated, in fact, that the statement by the AAA seems to be caught up in an irreconcilable tension. Although it talks about "world-wide standards of freedom and justice," it is hard-put to tell us how one can identify such universal standards of freedom and justice. Instead, it chooses to espouse a relativism, not only of human rights, but also of moral constructs. Indeed, those world-wide standards of freedom and justice are "based on the principle that man is free only when he lives as his society defines freedom" (ibid., 543)! And this, if accepted by the commission drawing up the Universal Declaration of Human Rights, will provide for a truly universal declaration only when they incorporate into their declaration "the right of men to live in terms of their own traditions" (ibid.). The AAA's statement is an exclamation for inclusiveness and tolerance of various traditions; it is a veritable *cri du relativisme.*[1]

The AAA statement espouses regularly observed cultural relativity as a descriptive reason to accept the normative relativism of human rights, even in the unlikely service of a universal declaration. But that same type of cultural bias has often been used, by states and governments, to justify their own traditional (or sometimes even less traditional but certainly local) practices and beliefs, and thus to explain and excuse policies and behaviors that seem (to some, at least) to fly in the face of a conventional, even universal, idea of human rights. The same tension just mentioned, between local relativity and global universality, can then be seen to be opening the door not to the inclusiveness that results from tolerance of numerous systems of mores, as the AAA recommends, but actually to an opportunistic abuse of human rights.

A paradigmatic case of such an adoption of particular norms and standards in governmental practices that are in contradiction to, even violation of, the orthodox conception of human rights is encountered in the flagrant use of the label "Asian values." Voiced by China and several other East and Southeast Asian authorities, the main point of their position on human rights is that Asian traditions have included moral and cultural values that are based on conceptions – of human nature, of communal obligation, and, subsequently, of human rights – different from Western ones. That Asian values might be, and actually are, at variance from Western values is almost a truism – as is the descriptive cultural relativity we have already identified. The interesting ascent here goes from that descriptive awareness to the normative Asian view of human rights, and that is where we must engage more earnestly with cultural relativism.[2]

There are two levels of discussion that must be distinguished from each other. Call one the content-level: certain issues that pertain to human rights – concerning, for instance, individual vs. community, political rights vs. economic rights, or the question of interventionism – may be viewed differently by Western human-rights eyes and by those of Asian persuasion. These have to do with the content of our human rights beliefs. Call the other the philosophical-level: human rights are strictly perceived by (some in) the West as universally common to all humans; they are viewed by (some) Asians as culturally specific. This is, evidently, the more problematic stage – it is the question of the relativism or the universalism of human rights, and neither "ideology" is necessarily Western or Asian. In other words, claiming that there are certain Asian values – such as communitarian mores, valued above the individual *per se* – that characterize the content-level Asian view of human rights might be correct, but that is substantively different from holding a relativistic view on human rights in order to inevitably justify such communitarianism. This needs some more unpacking.

We are presently following the universalism-relativism debate as it pertains to human rights. Issues of community rights, economic rights, and the question of interventionism – all of which will garner specific attention in future chapters – now play a role in our discussion of universalism and relativism. These topics are oft-cited examples of Asian values that are in supposed conflict with Western values, which are perceived as those that underlie generally accepted universal human rights. So, for instance, it is claimed – by defenders of Asian values – that in Asian societies, the value of community is prioritized over that of the individual. This is also seen as an asset for both personal and group survival, functioning as a defense against the individualism that is seen to be culpable for the deterioration of Western societies. Somewhat related to this view of communal precedence is the insistence on national sovereignty, and the ensuing rejection of any kind of interference by other mostly Western countries in the management or evaluation of human rights issues within, for example, China (or any other Asian country). Finally, in the matter of "rivalry" between social-economic-cultural rights and civil-political rights, we have seen that it has long been an axiom that Eastern societies (and that includes not only Asian countries, but Eastern European states as well) favor economic well-being over political freedoms. Indeed, the Chinese White Paper (1991)[3] positions the "fundamental demands of the Chinese people ... who had long suffered cold and hunger" as eating properly and dressing warmly. The common platitude is that one cannot worry about or engage in achieving political goals such as freedom if one is starving.

How does the question of relativism relate to these Asian values that are ostensibly dissimilar to Western values? Regimes that we might consider overly authoritarian and non-democratic and governments that are obviously in violation of a slew of common human rights have repeatedly claimed that their understanding of human rights is different from the pre-dictable, orthodox reading of the UDHR. At various meetings of Asian countries dealing with issues of human rights, articulated statements emphasize the historical, societal, economic, and cultural differences between different areas of the world; these, it is asserted, must be recognized as legitimate backgrounds and contexts for their specific, exclusive human rights practices. Human rights, it is said, must be viewed relative to where they are "born" and live. But – counters the universalist – there are both concrete and theoretical fallacies in this stance. Most obvious are the inconsistencies in the way governments decide on their values of choice. When it suits them they adopt, for example, market values from the West to further their economic interests; when their absolute power is threatened, they deny individualistic rights. Their determination of "Asian values" does not stem from a different worldview. It is merely an excuse for not adhering to universally agreed-upon human rights. More academic is the "genetic fallacy" that is committed in this assumption of cultural specificity (Li, 1996, 20). The geographical or cultural origin of a moral norm, such as any that motivates a specific human right, says nothing about its significance or applicability to another place or culture. Freedom of expression, the right not to be tortured, equality before the law, and all the other norms expres-sed by numerous human rights declarations are not dependent on their place of origin. It is precisely by turning to them that human beings, universally, can evaluate the decency and justice of their regimes. In fact, it is in places where "Asian values" are present that we examine the relevance of universal human rights and try to implement them.

This universalist – that is, she who accepts the concept of human rights as one that can be both seen as relevant and implemented in other societies, including Asian societies – is not unaware of cultural relativity. But her universalism trumps the acceptance of cultural relativism. She insists that an intercultural conversation can ensue – a conversation in which there are minimal basic norms, "minimal shared beliefs: for example, that genocide, slavery, and racism are wrong" (ibid., 23). Furthermore, there are agreed upon rules of conversation based on public reasoning, including proper argumentation, demands for evidence, and requirement of coherence and consistency, that can move the conversation forward among different cul-tural assumptions and habits – all having to do with human rights – until we reach an established universal validity for listings of human rights. Importantly, these do not have to be final, and our acceptance or rejection of certain human rights and their justification may be revised. But that does not speak for relativism; it only admits that universalism is based on a reasonable, non-relativistic public conversation.

A (Universalism-Relativism) Continuum?

The American Anthropological Association's statement from 1947 and the paradigmatic standpoint taken by Xiaorong Li represent, respectively, the unequivocal relativistic and universalistic positions on human rights. Can we alternatively look at the relativism-universalism divide as less of a debate and more of a continuum model? Can we think of universalism (or relativism) as a general, philosophical ideology that admits to relativistic (or universalistic) limitations on its single-mindedness? Can we be moderate universalists and relativists? Can we use philosophy to adjudicate with nuance on the universalism or relativism of human rights? Two philosophers, Jeremy Waldron and Charles Taylor, show us how to do this, not in the purely theoretical towers of philosophical universalism and relativism, but exactly where such theoretical positions should matter – in the context of human rights.[4]

The question that is now posed is – How do we, or should we, argue for universal human rights? According to Jeremy Waldron, in "How to Argue for a Universal Claim" (1999), three strategies can be ascertained in the practices of those who defend the universalist position. Two of them, which are, in a sense, less philosophical – or, at the very least, seem initially more oriented to real life – involve using argument by example. In the first, one chooses an egregious instance of evil – like torture – and shows that employing it cannot but be considered a human rights violation. That the practice of torture is carried out by some authorities or powers cannot make it any less evil. *Ergo*, there must be a universal prohibition on torture, and even those who engage in torture recognize it as a human rights violation.[5] Using the second strategy, one points out a cultural practice that is truly horrific – say, female genital mutilation – and builds on universal abhorrence to claim its universal inadmissibility. This case is immediately seen to be problematic since it is unerringly an example of a practice that is not abhorred by all – as torture is – and is rather accepted as positive behavior in societies that perform it. Still, this strategy of arguing for universal human rights is basic: The universalist is so certain of his intuitions concerning the evil involved in this ritual that he uses the example as a fail-safe argument for universalism, not realizing that it is merely an argument for his particular stand.

It is the third strategy for defending the universalist position which is philosophically robust, without losing its pertinence to the real-life phenomenon of cultural diversity in morals and in human rights. It suggests that we attempt to articulate truly universal, i.e., "culturally transcendent," moral arguments that undergird human rights. Although the relativist position tries to locate our examples and our arguments – and, of course, those of other cultures – in certain surroundings that are particular to us, claiming that they are surroundings-dependent, that position cannot ground a general relativism – it can only point to case-by-case differences. And then "[t]he universalist will say: There is nothing about the way in which [my] moral judgments are formed or generated or nurtured which restricts the range of their appropriate application" (Waldron, 1999, 307). So, even if the relativist shows how certain human rights (like equality before the law) or wrongs (like murder, or theft) are a function of social and cultural backgrounds (that have legal systems, or value human life and property in general), we can continue to argue about and morally evaluate those very backgrounds. And this is a universal conversation! Indeed, moral claims are usually not made in reference to a certain culture. People do not usually say "Pornography is bad ... for us," or "Slavery is a good way of arranging society ... in our society." Moral discourse is not culture-dependent; it is a deep, abiding exchange of moral beliefs that are presumed to apply to all.

Where does that leave us – if we insist on universalism yet still admit that there is cultural diversity and relativity concerning human rights norms? The upshot is quite startling. Those from other cultures who disagree with us about human rights are not, or should not be seen as, voicing relativist positions. Similar to the Chinese who try to justify local customs that do not uphold human rights by pointing to their locality, Iranian clerics who outlaw pornography citing merely the difference between our societies are "silly." Rather, in both cases, these others are claiming that what they do is right and what we do is wrong – even for us. They are expressing a universalist position, not a relativist one. In fact, many of the disagreements we sustain with other cultures about moral norms – witness pornography and capital punishment, though not female genital mutilation – are prevalent within our own culture. So the debate is not between relativism and universalism, but rather about the specific content of each of our universal moralities. "Precisely because relativism is for the most part silly and misconceived as a philosophical position" (ibid., 312) we should realize, says Waldron, that our argument is with other universalists about the content, i.e., the substance, of our universal systems of human rights, not with relativists.

Finally, then, that means that other cultures living according to other value systems, and their justifications for their subsequent conceptions of human rights, should be taken seriously. Note the subtle difference between saying that all value systems are equally good, or, even more flippantly, that there is no standard by which to comparatively evaluate different cultural values – the tenets of relativism – and realizing that our norms, if they are to be adhered to universally, demand their own critical moral and political assessment. Because moral relativism is wrong, we must treat other moral beliefs seriously. This is not a philosophical dispute between relativism and universalism; this is an attempt to address the real objections against our selection of human rights and the substantial moral basis we have for them. Seen differently, this is a move away from dogmatic, self-centric universalism, but not to relativism; rather to a different universalism, a cosmopolitanism that believes "some human rights standards can be arrived at and ought to be upheld everywhere in the world" (ibid., 313), but only by honestly engaging with various cultures' perspectives on human rights.

Charles Taylor, a fabled philosopher of moral and political thought who also struggles with the give-and-take between universalism and relativism in "A World Consensus on Human Rights?" (1996), offers a way of looking at the idea of an international human rights regime through both more, and less, universalistic lenses, and so through both more, and less, relativistic ones.[6] Like Waldron and other realistic viewers of cultural diversity, he too knows we must grapple with the presence of different communities and societies that hold profoundly different worldviews, while we steadfastly aim to reach a workable consensus on human rights. How can this possibly be done?

First, while investigating the ideas and conduct of human rights throughout the world, in various traditions and cultures, there is reason to make an analytic, principled distinction between the norms that govern human behavior and the philosophical justifications that we require for those norms. If we attempt to arrive at a consensus on human rights, we must ask what that consensus is about: Do we want to agree – globally and consensually – about a certain catalogue of human rights, about rules of conduct concerning those rights, or about the deeply held philosophical and moral explanations for why those should be our agreed upon human rights? In other words, looking at our goal of achieving a worldwide harmony in issues of human rights, we must decide if we demand agreement in our foundational beliefs or in – what might seem a little less overbearing – our rules of conduct.

Think for a moment about the very concept of "rights" itself. Not only is this a Western concept – it is, as we have seen, a fairly modern idea. Rights were acceded to in the European enlightenment when human agency was recognized as a uniquely human facility and when the individual human was thought to have a natural, inherent agency that was not necessarily dependent on his (social) environment. The discursive context in which we use and make claims for human rights cannot be divorced from this philosophical, and simultaneously cultural, background. Moving forward in the discussion of rights, we also encounter the legal frameworks that deal with liberties, immunities, and even certain privileges. Such legal structures, and the specific laws that they contain (having to do with rights), can be perceived as being on a different level than the philosophical foundations that justify them. One floor houses our philosophical and cultural worldview; another consists of our legal system. But notice: Although we can analytically separate these two levels – of legal form and philosophical basis – they might not be amenable to facile detachment. Indeed, part of our grasp of modern human rights surely involves the prerequisite of certain legal arrangements and procedures in order to maintain those (now, legal) rights. More so, beyond the distinctively legal context at this level, there are also political implications that result from the modern perception of the rights-bearing human being. These occasion the prioritization of democratic systems of government as those that alone can cohere with real sensitivity to human rights; so much so, that there is an explicit conjoining of human rights law and democracy in most of our human rights documents.

Now, different areas of the world, different regimes, different cultures, different religions, and different traditions differ on both levels – that of the worldview that consists of their metaphysics, their morals, and their view of human nature; and that of the legal norms that are expressed by their (usually enforceable) explicit, legal system. Theoretically, we can imagine two legal systems that are based on the same justificatory worldview (think of constitutional law vs. precedence law – both in democratic regimes); and we can imagine one legal organization that houses divergent worldviews (think of the American legal system dependent on Republican and Democratic legislators). When we speak of achieving a world consensus on human rights, is this consensus to be an agreement on our hopefully enforceable legal norms, or on our underlying moral and philosophical justification for these norms? Clearly, the latter, which are expressed in and by the profoundly different cultures that inhabit our world, can hardly be unified without coercion. And even a fusion of legal systems all around the world is realistically almost unattainable. So there is a palpable tension between the international discourse of human rights, which purports, or cynically pretends, to engage in the global search for an agreed-upon, legal, global human rights system and the constant insistence on cultural identities – be they Western, Confucian, Buddhist, and oh-so-many others – which merit acknowledgment of their own unique worldviews. Yet still, we witness intercourse – both cultural and legal – across borders; it must be harnessed somehow.

Having familiarized us with this two-tiered analysis of the possible disagreements that communities all over the world can fall into, Taylor suggests a "tripartite distinction" that can ground a rapprochement on human rights. In fact, having been made aware of the bipartite character of our discussions on human rights – dividing between deep cultural foundations of human rights and their (perhaps not so deep) legal mechanisms – we can now turn to a third level, the place of the human rights norms themselves, on which we might be able to settle. In other words, our search must be for norms of conduct – human rights conduct, of course – which can be based on various dissimilar worldviews and might also be enforced by different legal structures. In still other words, we may be able to reach a world consensus on human rights even if we differ on their foundations and in their legal mechanisms. For example, the Buddhist or Confucian emphasis on communitarian and inter-relational values may be just as conducive to support for human persons as individualistic value-systems. Or think of certain reform streams of Buddhism where there are revolutionary visions of change that are based on compassion and non-violence. Although these are all distant from the humanism *cum* democracy that underlie the Western human rights conceptualization, they can still be seen to buttress human rights norms, sometimes even doing so more robustly than our Western egocentric, individualistic agendas do.[7] These latter worldviews are thought to have come out of a Christian tradition, but also out of a humanism that now conceptually involves a disenchantment with the world and even a disaffected bitterness. The Buddhist and Confucian alternatives are, on the other hand, oriented away from anger and acrimony. So the question of ultimate human rights is answered differently, but answered all the same. And being aware of these differences – in Taylor's words being open to a "fusion of horizons" (1996, 20)[8] and working towards it – may well bring us to a world consensus on human rights.

Intuitively, assuming that universalism and relativism are at odds with each other, thinking of both as philosophically robust theories (about truth, about reality, about knowledge, or about morals), and conceding that there is an acceptable cultural relativity which, barring exceptional cases (such as genocide or slavery – and even those might find succor in some worldviews), characterizes our global humanity, it seems that the traditional, posturing, universalism vs. relativism debate on human rights has evolved into a nuanced deliberation. We can certainly point to the American Anthropological Association's statement of 1947 as a relativistic tract that bids us view the cultural effect on humans and on their perceptions of their rights as bearing incontrovertible weight against a pipe-dream of universalism. We can likewise appreciate how philosophers like Xiaorong Li submit solid philosophical grounds – without ignoring the twists and turns of real-life political argumentation – for a needed universalism of human rights. But on the continuum between universalism and relativism one can move to a moderate universalism, like Waldron does, which does not renege on universalism but still attempts to concurrently accord pronounced respect to the variable powers of differing cultures. And, in the opposite direction, one can embrace those cultural differences as essential, rather than circumstantial, and still strive for a universalism that is no more, but no less, than a functional, civilized consensus on human rights.

Imperialistic Universalism

Universalism and relativism, we have seen, are philosophical "isms" that have been put to work in the conversation of human rights; that is to say, beginning with the axiomatic, universal assertion that human beings are all equally entitled to human rights by virtue of being human, we cannot but go on to realize that different societies understand that axiom, and then act upon it, in various different ways. Beyond this general observation, however, there is an aspect of the universalism-relativism dispute that threatens to weigh heavily and far more consequentially upon the abstractions that are at the center of this exchange. It appears that the philosophers and texts that we have encountered thus far in this context cannot but be aware of it. Note, for instance, an innocent-sounding question that is posed at the beginning of the American Anthropological Association's statement: "How can the proposed Declaration be applicable to all human beings, and not be a statement of rights conceived only in terms of the values prevalent in the countries of Western Europe and America?" (AAA, 1947, 539). Or take in Xiaorong Li's awareness of a strong accusation made by proponents of the "Asian values" view of human rights: "The West's attempt to apply universal standards of human rights to developing countries is disguised cultural imperialism ..." (Li, 1996, 20). What comes to light here is not only the tension, both theoretical and practical, between universalistic and relativistic views of human rights, but rather the onerous consequence of our idea of universalism itself: a Western human rights "imperialism," voiced in the jargon of universalism. Waldron puts it vividly:

> [W]e should stand accused of the stupidest, most arrogant form of moral imperialism if we were to swagger around trying to impose our way of life without sensitively confronting the basis of other people's and other cultures' resistance to it.
>
> (Waldron, 1999, 314)

In other words, we are not really engaged here in a purely philosophical dispute between universalism and relativism, but have actually been awakened to the historical, political, and legal phenomenon of a Western imperialism and colonialism that is seen to be hiding behind the supposedly universal concept of "human rights." Although we attempted to compromise between the two extremes of universalism and relativism by creating a continuum stretching between cosmopolitan universalism and cultural relativism, and thereby recognizing a relatively oriented universalism or a universally sensitive relativism, we are now brought face to face with a historical, political allegation: The whole edifice of universal human rights is accused of being a Western construct. As such, it becomes a cover, a tool, or a useful concept of and for Western imperialism. Looked at more neutrally, the argument can be formulated thus: Universalism mandates equal rights for all, arising from equal dignity and equal entitlement that reside in all human beings. But if we recognize that such universalism is itself a Western paradigm, we arrive at a moral conundrum. We can either claim that the Western origin of human rights does not make the Western concept of universalism on which they are based any less legitimate; other cultural values and norms might play important roles in other ethical systems, but these do not undermine the deep significance of universalism and its global application. Or we can insist on the particularism that is inherent in the very concept of (Western) universalism and give equal or greater credit to other values and norms that might challenge our own universalist ones. How is this fork in the road to be taken?

It must be admitted that we have, until now, travelled the first road above. Telling the liberal story of rights leading right up to the Universal Declaration of Human Rights has meant following the Western narrative. Taking the Western side, so to speak, of the tale does not instruct us to ignore cultural differences; it simply contends that universalism, even when critiqued, must not ever be invalidated in the context of human rights. However, one then wonders why and how the cultural relativist arguments continue to persist, given the clarity of the universal demands that do adhere to human rights. It is here that the political rears its head, along with the destructive legacy of colonialism. That legacy, and the attendant resistance to any kind of external pressure, can explain the current bias towards local, rather than universal, values. Just as firm is the desire, by formerly colonized non-Western parties, to express their own cultural, traditional, national, local pride. Furthermore, given that these particularities of diverse cultures are socially and communally dominant, there is a certain efficacy in turning to local norms in order to achieve political aims, rather than embracing universalized, but foreign, ideas. Indeed, looking at all these factors that prefer particular local values over supposed universal ones, we can discern their use, by the powers that be and by native elites, in repressive policies that are certainly opposed to those promoting human rights.

This is all very reminiscent of the "Asian values" issues that we saw above, in the standardized debate between universalism and cultural relativism. The additional factor now before us is the imperialism that is imputed to the West in its calculated dissemination of its own value-system under the guise of universal human rights. We have already mentioned the arguments that are used by Asian authorities to explain and justify their insistence on their own, different-from-the-West's, interpretations of human rights. These include adamant defense of national sovereignty vs. any international interference; prioritization of social and economic rights over classical political and civil rights; the need for economic development; the ultimate respect for community over individual; and, as always, the preference for traditional mores, even when these fly in the face of modern human rights norms. Granted, these are weighty considerations that cannot be disregarded or flippantly swept away. But how can one continue to embrace Western ideas of human rights without falling prey to a Western imperialism that can be construed as, at the very least, a case of conceptual domination?

What would it mean to give up on Western universalism? That is to say, what would it mean to take the second road above and sincerely reject the particular, Western idea of human rights, now conceived as an imperialistic maneuver? More explicitly, other than "going relativistic," which is to say adopting a stance that accepts any and all cultural values as equally respectable in the human rights arena, how can one stay universalistic yet cast off universalism as we know it, that is, standard Western universalism?

How can we assent to the imperialist accusation yet still treat seriously the notion of one humankind?

This consequential view of the human rights system as we know it will be addressed later in the book, built into two frameworks that do not directly involve the philosophical universalism-relativism quandary. Since the question of how societies make progress from traditional, mostly-hierarchical regimes to democratic, rights-respecting forms of governance has been translated, in current global human rights parlance, into the terms of "Development" and "Democratization," we will ask about the connection between Western (capitalist) hegemony and (usually Third World) development when we present and investigate the place of economic development in a human rights itinerary (Chapter 10). Perhaps more abstract, but in other ways more substantially practical, will be the deep critique of human rights discourse as it has evolved to become a *lingua franca* of current global politics. Here the question of Western authority will be instrumental in the skeptical evaluation of the whole human rights story and its liberal, conceptual foundations (Chapters 12 and 13).

For the moment, let us see an example of this type of criticism – criticism which views universal human rights as a univocally Western construct – that tells a striking modernity *cum* empire story in the context of law. Balakrishnan Rajagopal, in *International Law from Below* (2003), invites us to look at the development of international law itself and the concept and discourse of human rights which originally grounded it, not as an instance of the universalism vs. relativism problem in its standard philosophical formulation, but rather as a far deeper and more insidious historical colonialism. Rajagopal guides us through the evolution of development ideology, as it gained stature in international law, by pointing out the trenchant ideas – born of Western notions yet presented as internationally valid – that established a decidedly biased conception of human rights when they are legislated, and sometimes enforced, in international law. In fact, he views international law as the concrete manifestation of human rights concepts and ideas; it is easier to analyze, understand, and then hopefully change legal structures and tools than to alter the more abstract discursive ones of human rights in general.

Rajagopal traces a conceptual history: Importantly, the idea of development in its deepest sense rests on the cultural transition from "primitive" societies to those that can be viewed as more advanced modes of civilization; and in the material sense it follows the move from "backward" societies to those in which humans achieve well-being. Common, well-known development ideology as it is expressed in international law assumes historical value-judgments clothed as facts. These include, for example, the persistent axiom of a "cultural divide" between Christians and infidels, and of a "civilizational divide" between people of commerce and all others, thus putting advanced civilization on a footing with capitalism. Colonialism needs both of these to justify its violation of other societies' sovereignty (they do not really merit such) and economic independence (they do not really engage in the market). Most arresting, though, is his discernment of the response, by colonial powers, to twentieth-century anticolonial resistance (to these suppositions). That response became an "apparatus of management," that, among other things, organized the interplay between domestic and international authorities; and that is what became explicit in international law – which, we now clearly see, is at the hands of those colonial powers.

Strong claims are entailed by this view of human rights as they are exhibited in and through international law. Most fundamental is the realization that there is a two-way influence at work here between the concrete modes of law – "rules, doctrines, institutions, and practices" – and "development ideology" (made up of the beliefs spelled out above) (Rajagopal, 2003, 27). So international lawyers and theoreticians have been effectively interacting with each other without realizing it; consequently, the idea that the law is objective, neutral, and non-biased is mistaken and superficial. No less significant is the understanding that human rights and development have a complex, even convoluted, relationship since they would seem to be cursorily contrary to each other (development agendas might require a certain indifference to human rights), even while human rights discourse "remains too deeply mired within the progressivist and teleological imperatives set by the development discourse" (ibid., 28). Finally, and ultimately most portentously, it is the social movements of the Third World that have posed challenges to development ideology and policy. It is incumbent on both the human rights community and those involved in international legal scholarship to recognize this, if they – and we – are to understand the meaning of the "struggles waged by subaltern groups such as women, peasants, and indigenous people" (ibid.).

Notes

1 This is also wryly reminiscent of the classical paradox or self-refutation of relativism: if our acceptance of a certain standard (of truth, or freedom, or justice) is relative (to our language, or culture, or tradition), then the claim that these are relative standards must be universal.
2 An instructive discussion that guides us now through this morass is Xiaorong Li's presentation in "'Asian Values' and the Universality of Human Rights" (1996). Her analysis is not independent of her own moral viewpoint, which adamantly embraces a universalist perspective. Li cogently argues for universalism against the "Asian values" position, which is undeniably a defense of relativism.
3 See "Human Rights in China," State Council of the People's Republic of China (1991).
4 See also Donnelly, *Universal Human Rights* (2013), whose concept of "relative universality," expounded upon in Donnelly (2007), is a thoughtful development of the earlier more one-sided universalism in previous editions (1989, 2003) of the book.
5 Note that this does not address the internal human rights debate on the absoluteness of the torture prohibition and the arguments for its exceptions. See Chapter 11.
6 We do not here engage with the question of Taylor's general stance for or against moral relativism. It is important, though, to note that his professed anti-relativism

is fascinating and nuanced. Relativism is thought to be, in a sense, self-delusion, since individuals all believe in the rightness of their own moral convictions. A relativist is, therefore, unintentionally self-contradicting, since the ideas that he proclaims to be equal in value must have different values for each individual and therefore each must win out universally for that individual. This is somewhat similar to the philosophical paradox of relativism (see Note 1), whereby the relativist is accused of insisting on the universal truth of the relativist position itself.

7 There is always, of course, still the risk of descending into versions of "benevolent dictatorships," and then the question re-arises, whether these can reasonably be accepted as human rights regimes, in a real sense of "human rights."

8 The construct "fusion of horizons" is attributed to Hans-Georg Gadamer, *Truth and Method* (1960). It is distinguished from cosmopolitanism in that the cosmopolitan stands nowhere, seeing no culture as particularly his own. In contrast, in aiming for a fusion of horizons one talks to others from within one's own culture, embracing them nevertheless.

8   Groups and Other Collections

The questions of human rights that are currently with us have been topically bounded in an effort to identify particular issues that relate to particular situations. In fact, it is not necessarily the deep philosophical questions – what are rights; what are human rights; are human rights universal or relative; and so on – but rather the very concrete and pressing issues of the day that have populated the intense human rights conversation of the past few decades. The well-rehearsed labels – group rights, women's rights, minority rights, children's rights, LGBTQ rights, indigenous rights, disability rights, refugee rights, and environmental rights – each refer to a subject of human rights that is worthy of a philosophical discussion to ground their multiple justifications or, sometimes, to critique their actual human rights statuses.

Now, the overarching title of these distinctions could have been "group rights," but that term itself – group – will have to be examined closely, and its link to human rights analyzed also. Intuitively, of course, we think of women, children, minorities, people of different sexual orientations, those who are indigenous, disabled, or refugees, as groups. Some of these groups are so commonly accepted as distinctive, with unique human rights associated with them, that there are treaties in the panoply of international human rights instruments and documents "owned" by them. So, for example, one need look only as far as the United Nations treaties and conventions to encounter the International Convention on the Elimination of All Forms of Racial Discrimination, the Convention on the Elimination of All Forms of Discrimination against Women, the Convention on the Rights of the Child, the International Convention on the Protection of the Rights of All Migrant Workers and Member of Their Families, and the Convention on the Rights of Persons with Disabilities. But before we inquire about the human rights of such groups, we must first clarify the more generic term – group rights. Only after we have explained if and how groups in general can have human rights will we be able to move on to the human rights of specific groups like those above, that is to say, like those who have been formally and legally acknowledged in the human rights conversation.

Group Rights

We have seen in several previous chapters that the idea of the individual human being is foundational in the modern conception of human rights. In fact, we sketched a likeness of a pyramid, rising from innumerable individuals to the many states of which they are citizens and from there to an idea of a global authority that is in charge of ensuring that the states do indeed respect the rights of those individuals. The autonomous, dignified, solitary human being is the individual who holds human rights, and it is the discovery of, and respect for, this individual that typifies the philosophical ideas which arose in modernity and the Enlightenment. More specifically, it is the liberalism of that age that gave birth to the kind of individualism that is necessary for the concept of rights as we know it – a concept of rights that then becomes more explicitly specified as human rights held by individuals.

But do human rights apply to individuals alone, or to groups as well? Our schema of individuals → state → world does not make room for groups – be they families, tribes, communities, societies, ethnic groups, clubs, nations – as a self-standing set of people that have human rights *as a group*. Notice that we are not talking here about the human rights of individuals who happen to make up a group, but rather of human rights of the group itself. Does such a concept even make sense? Can a group, as a group, have human rights? In those several covenants of international law – like those which deal with the rights of women, the rights of children, the rights of disabled persons – we encounter groups (of women, of children, of the disabled), but it is important to see that the rights spoken of in most, if not all, of these examples are the individual rights of persons who happen to make up a certain identifiable set of people, a certain group. Can we think of a group that has rights *as* a group? And what exactly would that mean?

If we think back on the Universal Declaration of Human Rights (1948) we recall that every single one of the rights expounded in that venerable document is a right of individuals, not of groups. It is intriguing, then, to note, again, that in both of the more elaborate documents that evolved out of the UDHR – the International Covenant on Civil and Political Rights (1966) and the International Covenant on Economic, Social and Cultural Rights (1966) – we encounter *in both*, after the predictable Preamble, the following arresting formulation that we saw in Chapter 2:

Article 1:
1) All peoples have the right of self-determination. By virtue of that right they freely determine their political status and freely pursue their economic, social and cultural development.
2) All peoples may, for their own ends, freely dispose of their natural wealth and resources without prejudice to any obligations arising out of international economic co-operation, based upon

the principle of mutual benefit, and international law. In no case may a people[1] be deprived of its own means of subsistence.

3) The States Parties to the present Covenant, including those having responsibility for the administration of Non-Self-Governing and Trust Territories, shall promote the realization of the right of self-determination, and shall respect that right, in conformity with the provisions of the Charter of the United Nations.

Quite surprisingly, prior to the anticipated list of human rights of individuals, the drafters of both covenants, whether dealing with civil-political rights or with economic-social-cultural rights, found it obligatory to set out two basic rights of peoples[2] – the right to self-determination and the right to control the group's natural resources. Are these, then, the only rights we can imagine groups having *as* groups? Are all other group rights actually the human rights of the individuals who make up the group, but now in agglomeration? Might there be a conflict between the human rights of individuals in the group and the group's rights as a group? Is it always clear, when we talk about group rights, whether we are referring to group rights or the rights of all the individuals in the group? In other words, and given the individualistic underpinnings of the idea of human rights, we must dwell on the question whether human rights include group rights, or not; differently put, are group rights – supposing there are such things – really human rights?

Interestingly enough, we can sense a temporal progression in the development of the discourse of human rights precisely in this question of group human rights. The UDHR, in 1948, made nary a mention of group rights. The two covenants of human rights, the ICCPR and the ICESCR finally drawn up in 1966, gave pride of first place to the article on group rights yet, at the same time, limited their mention to one article and two – very basic, very general, and not very detailed – rights. But with the passing of time, and very explicitly in the new century, group rights have advanced to frontstage, most obviously in the discussion on indigenous rights.[3] Here, as in the case of cultural relativism, the play between theory and present-day practice merits additional investigation. Theory – since the very definitional question of human rights must be explored if we are to decide on group rights as human rights (assuming that we have already determined that individual rights carry principal weight); practice – since burning issues of several mostly indigenous groups (but some minority groups as well) and their rights are now part and parcel of political policy-making and activism.

Put bluntly, if human rights are the rights to which humans are entitled as humans, group rights are not human rights. A group of humans is not a human; the group as a group cannot, therefore, be viewed as an entity deserving of human rights. Yes, every human who makes up the group is, by definition, a possessor of human rights and, if viewed as a grouping of humans, the group can be seen, facilely, as a group of humans each having human rights.

But, in truth, we are hardly able to claim that that new being, the group, has human rights. It may have other rights – but not human rights.

In effect, there are groups, or conglomerations, or collaborations, or associations and the like, that are legally recognized as holding various rights. This is usually conceived as the "corporation view" of groups; and corporations are certainly self-standing legal bodies that can claim rights and inhibit violations of those rights. So, for example, a historical right of a group to receive compensation for violations perpetrated by another group may be considered binding upon the present members of both groups, even though the past individuals who were involved in the atrocities – on both sides – are long gone. I am here speaking, of course, of a familiar demand made by successor generations of slaves against successor generations of slave-owners. That claim, and others like it, perceives the groups as holding rights and attendant duties – of, for example, compensation – *as groups*. The groups, as corporations, are the holders of rights. But it makes sense to ask: Are these the rights of the group or of the individuals who make up the group? Are they full-blown human rights?

An interesting attempt to find a middle-way between a full-fledged denial of group rights as human rights – insisting on only the exclusive rights of the individuals who make up the group as human rights – and an acceptance of corporation rights as somehow akin to human rights is the collective version of group rights. This says that a group is made up of individuals who have human rights and, in some nebulous manner, that the group holds these human rights in collective fashion. Less lenient than the corporation view, in which the group *as a group*, has its own moral and legal existence and thereby its (human) rights, the collective view recognizes that human rights are due to humans alone. But less stringent than the single-minded individualism of classical human rights, it acknowledges the relevance of human rights to groups of individuals as well. That is to say, it recognizes the possibility of a group of humans collectively holding human rights that depend, in essence, on the individual rights of the group's members, but that somehow seep into the group's identity as well. Such would be the rights to religious practice, the rights to linguistic and cultural traditions, and the rights of minority practices.

Still, there is an essential conceptual and practical difficulty that accompanies the very idea of group rights, in both the corporate and collective versions of its formulation. When we recognize group rights – for whatever historical or political reason – as binding upon both the members of a group and the outside world, one might say, we must seriously entertain the possibility that those group rights that now acquire legitimacy may, in some way, intrude upon the human rights of (some of the) individuals who make up that group. It almost goes without saying that group rights protect a group against violations of its, and its members', rights committed by persons, institutions, and states that are not part of that group. These are seen as externally focused; that is, motivated by a group's need to defend itself and its members against external limitations, harms, and abuses, executed by both governments and societies at large. But it is almost as obvious that group rights are also internally oriented; that is, leaning towards imposing restrictions on the group's members with the goal of preserving and maintaining group traditions, customs, and values. And these restrictions may, indeed, violate recognized human rights of the individuals who are members of the group!

Think, for example, of groups in which social hierarchies are genuinely respected and enforced. These may involve a clear subjugation of women by men, or of a certain class by another, or of one religious group by a different one – leading to an explicit renunciation of the equality assumed in human rights fundamentals. Or consider the (in)famous cases of female genital mutilation, or male circumcision, or child marriage, or even slavery. A group that abides by traditions that dictate these norms and practices may claim its group's right to persist in them. The challenge now surfaces: How are we to attend to such conflicts between the group's rights and the human rights of the individuals who make up the group? In Will Kymlicka's words (Kymlicka, 1996), when do these "bad" group rights, which restrict basic liberties of group members, become "intolerable"?

Not for naught, then, are group rights, the rights of a group *as a group* rather than as a sincere representative of the individual rights of its members, treated – by some, perhaps most, in the human rights scholarly community – suspiciously. While group rights, and the rights of its members to believe in and practice their chosen mores, are seen as worthy of protection from any external coercion, the danger of internal coercion of that group's members (by the group or its in-house authorities) to believe and practice in a way that contradicts their individual human rights is negatively perceived. This precarious balance between individual rights and group rights can be seen, indeed, to be at the center of both liberal thought and liberal action. The classical enigma of toleration – can liberalism conceptually tolerate forms of life that are, themselves, intolerant? – is translated, in our apparent clash between individual rights and group rights, to the question: Can liberal thought that ostensibly respects the way of life of other groups that are not liberal uphold that respect when it entails a violation of individual human rights? It is interesting to note, also, that in liberal policy and practice, both domestic and international, the adherents to a liberal human rights worldview are less reluctant to impose their principles on illiberal groups in their own society than on regimes far and wide that are gross human rights violators (ibid., 26).

We see, then, that the matter of group rights is fraught with conceptual questions that unsettle the liberal basis of human rights; it is also, in the twenty-first century of diversity and of hyper-connected populations both within and outside particular polities, at the center of a myriad of human rights concerns. The human rights of local minorities, migrants and refugees, women and children, and a host of other classifiable "groups" must be addressed through our principled understanding of human rights but even more so in our daily human rights-related imbroglios. Furthermore, the perceived tension between individual rights and group rights impacts policy decisions regarding domestic and international regulations, political and military intervention in other countries' affairs, and the admission of some groups as legitimate rights holding bodies (and others not!). All of these inter- and intra-related topics spring from the primary concept of group rights and will continue to be dealt with when relevant.

Minority Rights

It is usually thought that human beings can be identified as belonging to certain groups in virtue of their nationalities (e.g., French, American, German, Indian), their religions (Buddhist, Jewish, Catholic, Muslim), their gender (male, female, trans), their sexual orientation (gay, heterosexual, bisexual), their ethnic roots (Latino, Roma), their race (Caucasian, Asian), etc.[4] They might also belong to groups that espouse a certain ideology (e.g., Capitalists, Marxists, Liberals), that have a certain profession (doctors, electricians, actors), that engage in certain activities (athletes, Red Cross volunteers, book club members), etc. And we can naturally collect people according to their height, their weight, their hair color, the length of their finger-nails ... All of this is pertinent to the factors that have a bearing on a human being's identity and to the universal *cri de coeur* of human rights – that all human beings are equally entitled to human rights, irrespective of any of the above identifying features. Still, certain particular groupings have, during the history of humankind, been more vulnerable than others to a type of discrimination that can be articulated, in modern times, as an explicit violation of human rights. We shall term these groups, for the sake of generality, "minorities" and focus on three familiar minorities – racial minorities, religious minorities, and minorities of sexual orientation.

Before the adoption of the ICCPR (1966) and the ICESCR (1966), already in 1965, the United Nations adopted the International Convention on the Elimination of All Forms of Racial Discrimination (based on a similar Declaration from 1963). Tellingly, in explicating the word "racial," in the title and in the ensuing document, we read that "the term 'racial discrimination' shall mean any distinction, exclusion, restriction or preference based on race, color, descent, or national or ethnic origin." In other words, groupings of different sorts, that is, those referring to race,[5] color, descent, and national or ethnic origin, are all seen as equally pernicious in their potential for discrimination and can all be labeled as "racial discrimination." This five-aspect attribution is stimulating, but also challenging. Are these groupings based on biological traits, as race and color seem to imply? Are they historically motivated, as might appear to be the case with descent and ethnic origin? Or are they perhaps based on political association, as hinted at by "nation"? Beyond an intuitive acceptance of these markers as commonly used in cases of discrimination, there appears to be no obligating rationale for precisely these labels of identification. Still, it is easy to see that the human rights of individuals in the groups that carry these labels have been, throughout the ages, trampled upon and desecrated. Racial discrimination, by this or any other name, has become a paradigm of human rights violations.

Interestingly, the convention against racial discrimination, while widening its scope to what it views as synonymous discriminations, does not explicitly include religious groups as vulnerable to the same type of violation (of their human rights). Yet history shows that religious persons have been the object of discrimination – and worse – due to religious group association. Ancient tribes engaged in religious wars before any others The Inquisition was an institutional persecution carried out against all non-believers by the Roman Catholic Church, using imprisonment, banishment, torture and execution against people of other religions. Anti-Semitism, according to some[6] the epitome of religious intolerance, culminated in the horrific manifestation of genocide and the crimes against humanity of the Holocaust. The Hindu caste system, well-established in India, is dependent on a religion – Hinduism. And, in this case, it is not a matter of discrimination of the worshippers of one religion by those of another, but actually of abominable internal discrimination and attendant violations of human rights by members of the Hindu religion against other members of the same religion, who happen to be of the Dalit caste.[7] Just as (in)famous are the religious wars between Hindu and Muslim populations in India.[8] All of these conflicts and violent altercations are familiar in human history; how do they become, so explicitly, players in the human rights arena? The answer – that is, the posit of religion – is more nuanced than just isolating a religious minority and insisting on its fundamental right to non-discrimination.

We have already seen that the UDHR, in espousing its universality of reach, mentions religion along with other distinctions of human groupings.

Article 2:
Everyone is entitled to all the rights and freedoms set forth in this Declaration, without distinction of any kind, such as race, color, sex, language, religion, political or other opinion, national or social origin, property, birth or other status.

One's religion, as a group identity, is not to have any bearing on one's human rights. But the UDHR goes on to single out religion in articulation of other rights. So we meet, for example,

Article 16.
1) Men and women of full age, without any limitation due to race, nationality or religion, have the right to marry and to found a family.

This is somewhat more than just an instance of the general claim in Article 2 that human rights, and in this case the human right to marry, are to be accorded to all regardless of differential identities, including race, nationality, and religion. Indeed, beyond speculating on identity, it presents a defense of human rights against the proclivities of certain national or religious institutions. But it is in Article 18 that religion seems to pivot to a different station:

Article 18.

Everyone has the right to freedom of thought, conscience and religion; this right includes freedom to change his religion or belief, and freedom, either alone or in community with others and in public or private, to manifest his religion or belief in teaching, practice, worship and observance.

Whereas in Article 2 of the UDHR religion is one among many distinctions that must not lessen our recognition of the universality of human rights, and whereas in Article 16 religion itself must not interfere with the universality of human rights, we here encounter the right to religion – not a right *from* religion – as a human right in and of itself. The right to religion is the right to religious belief and religious practice – in private, in public, in education, in association with others, and in any manner of performative or reflection. In other words, one's "membership" in a certain religion must not hinder one's eligibility to universal human rights, but neither may any authority hinder one's human right to thought and practice that are entailed by that membership. We have moved here beyond the mere discrimination issue and our focus has traveled beyond the general question of minorities.

Similar to the conundrum of the rights of a group that act in contradiction to the human rights of individuals who are members of that group, the rights that originate in a religious belief, or group, or culture are liable in many cases to run against some of our conventional human rights originating in the customary documents. As mentioned above, there are religious groups that engage in traditional customs (like female genital mutilation or circumcision) that are antithetical to human rights; but believers may call upon their religious rights, rather than on group rights, to ground such traditions. Several other notorious examples abide: Religious cultural mores that treat women as a subordinate gender are accepted and enforced in communities all over the world. Can their adherents claim their rights to religion as justification for such violations of the acknowledged human rights of women? The debate about abortion can be seen as pitting a woman's human right (to have control over her body) against a fetus's right to life. But it can just as convincingly be understood as a secular human right opposing religious beliefs that are based upon religious commands against abortion; still, those holding these latter beliefs may be no less deserving of their human right to practice their religion. An owner of a firm who is required by law to provide healthcare for his employees (with such requirement being based on the human right to "a standard of living adequate for ... health and well-being" (UDHR, Article 25)[9]) may cite his religious beliefs and his human right to act upon them as the explanation for his refusal to provide funding for contraception. And the oft-heard argument in favor of teaching Creationism in schools, both private and public, can be – though is not always – based on the right to religious education.

The issue of religious rights – both the rights from religious coercion and the rights to religion – is doubly fascinating because it challenges, in essence, the tenets of liberalism itself. Since it recognizes and respects, almost absolutely, the individual who makes up the collective (society, community, state), liberalism must tolerate the different values held by different individuals. Yet what is liberalism to do with the values of illiberal individuals and institutions? This is often couched in the semantics of tolerance: Can liberalism tolerate those who are not tolerant? In the case of religious values, liberalism must deal with a specific obstruction to tolerance, running up against its own provenance. Liberalism is a secular world-view which recognizes the existence and legitimacy of religious world-views. But how is liberalism, a world-view that prioritizes human rights, able to relate to and engage with a religious value-system that not only does not highlight such rights but also accepts their violation by a non-human authority?

A paradigm of such rights that are vehemently negated by Western religious authorities, be they the Church, Jewish Orthodoxy, or Islamic Sharia law, is the contemporary, pertinent and much-discussed subject of LGBT rights.[10] But beyond this or that religious attitude, it is the general discrimination against sexual minorities that raises painful dilemmas of human rights. Indeed, the only mention of sex – "gender" was not yet a common term in 1948 – in the UDHR is that list of identifying modifiers of human beings that we have encountered several times before: human rights are accorded universally, to all human beings, with no distinctions "such as race, color, sex ... etc." This mention of sex does not, however, seem to touch upon the matter of gender identity or sexual orientation. There is, in fact, no allusion at all in the prominent rights documents to gender identity and sexual orientation. The only place in the UDHR that gestures, unintentionally it seems, to what would become, in due time, a heralding though problematic cry of gay rights is Article 16:

1) Men and women of full age, without any limitation due to race, nationality or religion, have the right to marry and to found a family. They are entitled to equal rights as to marriage, during marriage and at its dissolution.
2) Marriage shall be entered into only with the free and full consent of the intending spouses.
3) The family is the natural and fundamental group unit of society and is entitled to protection by society and the State.

It almost goes without saying that the phrase "men and women" of this articulation was intended to be read as pertaining to the union between heterosexual men and women. If we anchor our discussion of human rights in international human rights law that is based on the earlier UN documents (and some other official papers), it is no surprise that we find nary a reference to gay rights. So one must first ask about the discrimination against a minority which is identified by its sexual self-identification and orientation, and then also inquire about the rights to that orientation and all that those rights entail. A curious difference between religious groups and gay (and other sexual orienta-tion) groups arises out of their characterization as minorities. In the case of religion we cannot but recognize the overwhelming presence of religion in human life. Although the insistence on human rights irrespective of religion may sometimes gesture at religious minorities, the challenge to human rights from religion is hardly a matter of minority rights. On the other hand, in the case of gay rights, not only are we squarely in line with minority rights but, even more striking, the very idea of sexual identities and of sexual unions as different from the norm is considered in almost all communities, formulated in almost all state legal systems, and determined by all religions as illegitimate. From where, then, do gay rights spring?

Admittedly, the treaties that we accept as the cornerstones of interna-tional human rights law, i.e., the UDHR and its two elaborations, the ICCPR and the ICESCR, along with the conventions formulated to deal with the specific human rights of particular vulnerable populations (like the Convention on the Rights of the Child, or the Convention on the Elimina-tion of All Forms of Discrimination against Women), do not make any reference to sexual orientation and identity. It is also undeniable that in the great majority of states in the world there is scant toleration for a gay way of life; gay marriage, in particular, is deemed illegal in all but 25 countries (as of 2018).

Still, and quite remarkably, it is in the UN itself, specifically in its Office of the High Commissioner for Human Rights (OHCHR), that the recognition of gay people's human rights has inched towards the light. The steps taken towards some new documents are themselves conceptually thought-provoking and exhibit strands of both hesitation and daring. Beginning in 2011, the UN's Human Rights Council attempted to explain the impulse to engage in gay human rights. In a very short document titled "Human rights, sexual orien-tation and gender identity" (Human Rights Council, 2011), the council reports incrementally on its motivations: First, it recalls the universality of human rights; second, it recalls that the UDHR is adamant that rights hold "without distinction of any kind, such as race, color, sex, language, religion, political or other opinion, national or social origin, property, birth or other status"; and finally, it recalls a General Assembly resolution from 2006 that protects human rights "without distinction of any kind and in a fair and equal manner." This somewhat feeble resolution merely requests more information and promises to discuss the issues that arise from the forthcoming study. But the connection between the unequivocal rejection of any distinction between humans and these more practical decisions is established via the "*grave concern* at acts of violence and discrimination, in all regions of the world, committed against individuals because of their sexual orientation and gender identity." It is finally explicit!

Let us emphasize, again, that the main impetus logically relating gay rights to human rights – contending that gay rights *are* human rights – is the point of discrimination. People of differing sexual identities and orientations are entitled to the same rights as all other people; in fact, they are doubly worthy of protection against the discrimination and violence that are their usual lot (because they are doubly vulnerable in most countries, religions, and traditions). Indeed, in its 2016 full-fledged resolution "Protection against violence and discrimination based on sexual orientation and gender identity," going beyond reportage and acknowledgment of a human rights challenge, the UN Human Rights Council appointed an Independent Expert

(a) To assess the implementation of existing international human rights instruments with regard to ways to overcome violence and dis- crimination against persons on the basis of their sexual orientation or gender identity, while identifying both best practices and gaps;

(b) To raise awareness of violence and discrimination against persons on the basis of their sexual orientation or gender identity, and to identify and address the root causes of violence and discrimination;

(c) To engage in dialogue and to consult with States and other relevant stakeholders, including United Nations agencies, programmes and funds, regional human rights mechanisms, national human rights institutions, civil society organizations and academic institutions;

(d) To work in cooperation with States in order to foster the imple- mentation of measures that contribute to the protection of all persons against violence and discrimination based on sexual orientation and gender identity;

(e) To address the multiple, intersecting and aggravated forms of violence and discrimination faced by persons on the basis of their sexual orientation and gender identity;

(f) To conduct, facilitate and support the provision of advisory services, technical assistance, capacity-building and international cooperation in support of national efforts to combat violence and discrimination against persons on the basis of their sexual orientation or gender identity.

This is a full agenda for a full-fledged object of human rights attention.

UN bodies, originally trailing behind but now working in step with several international organizations, national movements, local communities of civil society, and many celebrities and VIPs, have joined a worldwide campaign devoted to issues of gay human rights. Organizations like Human Rights Watch or Amnesty International locate the attitudes and actions that can be documented as outright discrimination and, more so, as unambiguous violations of the human rights of gay individuals, gay groups, and gay communities. Cases of unequal treatment, abuses against gay children and adults, denial of family rights, medical abuse, unjust arrests, torture, executions – all directed against gays for the explicit liability of being gay – are exposed all over the world precisely for reasons of discrimination and violation of human rights.

There are two aspects of this "awakening" to the human rights dimension of gay rights that must be addressed. First, note that in the UN document above there is mention made, though not necessarily stressed, of dialogue and cooperation with States in implementing and persuading of the needed protection against discrimination and violence. We cannot discount the immense antipathy to gay life in so many parts of the world, ranging from societal antagonism to institutional intolerance to legal criminalization. Second, we must tackle the positive demand for gay rights beyond the usual, defensive petition for protection, most especially the call for gay marriage. Both of these perspectives – the turn to anti-gay societies at large and the appeal for gay marriage – are a matter of advocacy. Here again we are witness to the UN's positioning with regard to gay human rights: In 2013, the Office of the High Commissioner for Human Rights at the UN launched a global campaign against homophobia and transphobia called UN FREE & EQUAL, with the purpose of advocating for "equal rights and fair treatment of LGBTI people." In more recent years, several countries have joined UN bodies in promoting the legalization of gay marriage in the domestic laws of other countries. And in the U.S., which was not the first country to legalize gay marriage but is surely the one looked to for leadership and impact, the *Obergefell vs. Hodges Supreme Court* decision in June 2015 determined that marriage is a fundamental right that all couples, straight or gay, are entitled to. This decision was not predicated on international human rights law but rather on the Fourteenth Amendment of the Constitution, but it was voiced, nevertheless, in the language of rights.

The three arenas of minority rights that we have probed in passing are mainstays of the human rights conversation. In fact, one can say that questions of human rights that have to do with race, with religion, and with LGBT issues are, periodically, at the front-line of contemporary human rights advocacy and activism. All three sectionalities of human identity have suffered, through the ages, from bias and prejudice against them – usually, but not always as minorities – that have perpetrated attitudes and actions leading to great inequity. In other words, persons thought to be of certain races, certain religions, and certain sexual orientations have suffered grave violations of their human rights. In the case of racial discrimination, the posit of human rights has become so obvious that it now merits the vernacular of very concrete and practical civil rights (despite the oft-rehearsed assertion that "race" does not exist biologically or essentially). But even after years of analysis and debate, it is clear that racism has not yet exited the social and political stage. Whether we speak of the offensively high rate of incarceration of African Americans in the U.S., of the preponderance of anti-Islamic conduct in Europe, of the low education rates of First Nation children in Canada, or of the poverty-stricken Maya in central America and Mexico, it is racial distinctions that give rise to the human rights concerns facing us. The violations of human rights that accompany religious groups and persons of various gender and sexual identities are similarly atrocious. These groupings, and some others like them which are viewed as numerical or conceptual minorities, are the well-known sites of human rights abuses of the individuals who populate them.

Indigenous Rights

We have seen that group rights – the rights of a group of people *as a group* – are considered suspect when in the realm of human rights, since these latter are considered the rights of individual persons by default. The principled argument against recognizing group rights as human rights is based on the essential tension between group rights and individual rights: Respect and support for a group's rights to engage in its customs, to stay faithful to its traditions, to stay true to its values, and to answer only to its internal authority may, whether intentionally or not, violate the universal human rights of that group's members. Indeed, Will Kymlicka ponders the impact that group rights have on the individual rights of members in that group (Kymlicka, 1996): In some cases, when the individual rights of group members are systematically derided – as in the cases we mentioned above – the internal strength of that group may supply protection from external violations. In other cases, such internal strength may, on the contrary, bring about bad or even intolerable damage to the individual human rights of certain members of the group. How are we, then, to adjudicate between these possible outcomes of recognizing group rights? How are we to decide which groups merit recognition as groups with their own independently recognized rights, and which must adapt precisely to the conventional model of individual human rights? How can we distinguish between the "good" that group rights bestow on group members, the "bad" that might ensue from the respect given to the group's internal impact, and the "intolerable" harm that the group can cause to its own individuals? It is not surprising that group rights are usually thought to be distant from and in conflict with universal, individual human rights. Yet even Jack Donnelly, a consistent opponent of group rights, when replying straightforwardly to these questions, tells us that "[i]ndigenous peoples probably present an exception to the individual rights approach" (Donnelly, 2013, 51). But why?

In the list of commonly acknowledged international human rights instruments established by the UN, which we have made reference to before, there is no official treaty regarding indigenous peoples. As opposed to children, women, races, migrants, the disabled – all groups of people who are seen to warrant explicit protection – the international community has not succeeded in drawing up a contractual, legally binding document regarding indigenous peoples. That is not to say that there is no public awareness of the specific predicament of indigenous groups that has, nevertheless, infiltrated into the consciousness of global actors. Responsiveness to the plight of indigenous peoples has resulted in a superbly voiced declaration. In September 2007, the UN General Assembly resolved to adopt the United Nations Declaration on the Rights of Indigenous Peoples. Recall that a declaration is not a treaty, covenant, or contract; and yet, like the UDHR, public declarations, signed by several countries and promulgated widely, present a moral and political stance that cannot be ignored. It is important to also notice that the declaration was up for consideration since 1982 in different UN bodies, finally being formulated by the Commission on Human Rights, adopted in 2006 by the Human Rights Council, and then referred to the General Assembly. The voting results at the General Assembly are also intriguing: 143 countries voted in favor, 11 countries abstained, 34 countries were absent from the vote, and, remarkably, only four countries – Australia, Canada, New Zealand, and the United States – voted against. This is remarkable, but predictable, since these are four countries that originated as colonies of the U.K. whose immigrant, non-indigenous populations have by and large thrived at the expense of the indigenous populations. Interestingly, in the years since the declaration was adopted by the General Assembly, all four nay-sayers have made statements explicitly accepting and supporting the declaration.

It is by perusing the objects of resistance to the declaration and its own explication of its reasoning that we can grasp the main thorny issues confronting the idea of political or economic group rights and, importantly, the exceptional counterpoint made by and about indigenous group rights. As we have seen, the two notable group rights that appeared in the ICCPR and the ICESCR were those of self-determination and access to (with consequent use of) natural resources. It is obvious that both of these claims present deep challenges against states, their sovereignty, and their authority over their territory. That was, indeed, the point of dissimilarity between individual rights – that do not threaten the state's legitimate sovereignty and authority – and group rights, whose acceptance as human rights is questioned for precisely that reason. But it is in the case of indigenous groups that those rights are thought to somehow be legitimated. Indigenous groups' claims to self-determination and to some authority to compete with the state are more persuasive than other groups' privileges, due to their indigeneity. But what does that mean?

One need only glance at the Declaration on the Rights of Indigenous Peoples to discover how indigenous groups are different from other groups. Beyond the insistence on the non-discrimination owing to any person of any group, some outstanding rights, which seem novel in essence and in style of formulation, catch the eye. Article 3, speaking of self-determination, is identical to Article 1 of the ICCPR. Where the latter insisted that "[a]ll people have the right of self-determination" (and that "[b]y virtue of that right they freely determine their political status and freely pursue their economic, social and cultural development"), in the new declaration it is explicitly "indigenous peoples" who have this right and its consequent entailments. Not being satisfied, however, with this small move of a general, somewhat problematic group right of all peoples now applying specifically to indigenous peoples, the new declaration elaborates: "Indigenous peoples, in exercising their right to self-determination, have the right to autonomy or self-government in matters relating to their internal and local affairs, as well as ways and means for financing their autonomous functions" (Article 4). And it goes on to expound:

> Indigenous peoples have the right to maintain and strengthen their distinct political, legal, economic, social and cultural institutions, while retaining their right to participate fully, if they so choose, in the political, economic, social and cultural life of the State.
>
> (Article 5)

The knotty issue of self-determination of all peoples is here made not only unambiguous but also stronger and clearer. More patently, the rights of indigenous groups are formulated to protect those groups' rights against what might befall them as a group. For example, they must not be subjected to genocide and their children must not be removed (Article 7.2); their culture must not be destroyed (Article 8.1);[11] they must not undergo population transfer or be forced to assimilate or integrate (Article 8.2); no propaganda against them is permitted (Article 8.2); and they must not be forcibly removed from their lands (Article 10). Looking forward, and given that they have, in the past, undergone some of these egregious atrocities, they now also have the right "to practice and revitalize their cultural traditions and customs," and this also means they may transmit their traditions to future generations, control their own group's education, language, and media, and be supported, encouraged, and funded in doing all of this by the states in which they dwell. This is a mesmerizing document of reinforcement of the political, economic, and cultural rights of indigenous groups.

In order to understand on the one hand the strange divide between the almost laconic mention of group rights in the ICCPR and the ICESCR, a mention reduced to just two somewhat vague and very general rights (self-determination and access to natural resources), and the fully-expressed and very detailed rights in the Declaration on the Rights of Indigenous Peoples on the other, one need only examine the thorough and reflective first part of the declaration, i.e., the preparatory conditions of indigenous rights. Even more striking than the articles dealing with these indigenous group rights themselves, the preliminary sections of the declaration provide us with a profound justification for the exception to the rule that is applied to indigenous peoples amongst all other groups. It is there that we read, first, of the rights of peoples to be equal but different and to be respected in that difference; we also encounter the affirmation that "all peoples contribute to the diversity and richness of civilizations and cultures, which constitute the common heritage of mankind." Reminiscent of the statement of the American Anthropological Association from 1947, it seems that the insistent universalism that characterized the decades since the UDHR was written (1948), and even since the two main covenants were instituted (1966), has finally given way to the recognition of cultural variety that must impact human rights. Another object of explicit recognition is the painful history of colonialism: Indigenous peoples "have suffered from historic injustices as a result of, inter alia, their colonization and dispossession of their lands, territories and resources." Their rights must, therefore, be protected in some retroactive sense, to the point of compensation for past infringements and violations. Finally, the current political, economic, social, and cultural activist consciousness of indigenous peoples is celebrated in the declaration – for it occasions cooperative relations between them and the states in which they reside. Indeed, that consciousness has certainly seeped into the global awareness of indigenous rights and, more so, into the workings of state institutions all over the world.

The three fulcra of justification for indigenous group rights – the positivity of diversity, the wretched history of indigenous peoples, and the current responsiveness to indigenous issues – can explain the exceptionalism accorded to indigenous rights versus other group rights. Looking at the rights of indigenous peoples, one cannot but be struck by the seeming priority given to group rights, i.e., to the collective rights of the group when that group is an indigenous one. Beyond the cultural rights to control their education, their language, their customs, or their media, indigenous peoples are explicitly recognized as owning the rights to their own economic institutions, their development and subsistence programs, and their traditional means to health and medicine. Even more arresting are the rights to their traditionally owned or used "lands, territories and resources," and the right to redress and compensation for those they have lost; furthermore, those lands must be conserved and may not be used for military activities – rather, their development and use must be determined by the indigenous peoples themselves. Finally, indigenous groups have their own prerogative to determine their conditions of membership, the responsibilities of members to the group, and their institutions of justice.

This highlights, yet again, the core problem we have encountered: the familiar tensions between group rights and individual rights are those that arise when we recognize that a group's rights to its non-liberal mores and traditions are likely to contradict universal, individual human rights. The declaration does not set the problem aside but rather seems to ping-pong between the two. Its 46 articles, which include 76 points of rights, are generally punctuated with "... indigenous peoples have the right of ..." but also with a few unequivocal mentions of "... indigenous individuals." One could say that it advances the preliminary dual condition that "indigenous individuals are entitled without discrimination to all human rights recognized in international law," *and* that "indigenous peoples possess collective rights which are indispensable for their existence, well-being and integral development as peoples." One could also stress the double pertinence of Article 1:

> Indigenous peoples have the right to the full enjoyment, *as a collective or as individuals*, of all human rights and fundamental freedoms as recognized in the Charter of the United Nations, the Universal Declaration of Human Rights, and international human rights law.
>
> (Emphasis added)

And we do, in the ensuing gestures to indigenous individuals, find repetition of "routine" individual human rights; these (e.g., the same right to life, physical and mental integrity, liberty, security of person, education, labor rights, physical and mental health, and so on) are here underscored as a consequence of common discrimination against indigenous people.

It is, however, the question of the indigenous individual's rights against his own group that still concerns us here. And that question is skirted only once in this momentous declaration. Having first announced that indigenous peoples and individuals "have the right to belong to an indigenous community or nation," the drafters of the declaration hint at only one mark of possible discord: Yes, "indigenous peoples have the right to determine their own identity or membership in accordance with their customs and traditions," but "[t]his does not impair the right of indigenous individuals to obtain citizenship of the States in which they live" (Article 33.1). This posits the group against the individual in no uncertain terms and insists that the human rights of indigenous individuals are still protected by international human rights law and the civil law of the state. Given the indigenous group's rights, the indigenous individual's rights are still up for deliberation.

Notes

1 Note the grammatical distinction: A person is singular; many persons are people. But a different version of "people" considers the singular people, "a people," as a group, with "peoples," in the plural, referring to groups. These are the peoples/groups that are referenced in both Articles 1 of the covenants.

2 There is a political quandary that we will not investigate here: what is a "people"? The notion is a somewhat amorphous indicator of a group, attempting to distance itself from the more politically charged "nation." It is unclear how it relates to "community," "society," "sect," and the like, and whether these might, in certain circumstances, be recognized as peoples as well. This is obviously crucial, especially in the question of self-determination: Do we agree to any group's aspiration to self-determination? Furthermore, note the covenants' hesitancy in not formulating explicitly how self-determination manifests itself. Does a people always have the right to self-determination as a state? Are there other forms of self-determination, such as autonomy, self-rule, cultural independence, and the like?

3 This chronological development has led some to call group rights third generation rights. As we saw above (Chapter 1), that sort of nomenclature has also
   served for first generation (civil, political) rights and second generation (social,
   economic, and cultural) rights.

4 All of these labels may be debated – both as regarding their categorization and as
   pertains to the real existence of such categories. One of the predominant debates
   now with us concerns the naturalness or essentialism of these categories, as
   opposed to their identification as social constructions. We do not enter this
   debate here but note that it is germane to this discussion.

5 The construct of race, already in 1965, is considered problematic, since, as the
   convention says, "… any doctrine of superiority based on racial differentiation is
   scientifically false." Even before superiority, the idea that biological race is an
   essential, identifiable human characteristic is considered obsolete in scientific circles.
   For that reason, it seems that "racial discrimination" is used here as a *mode de
   parler* for the general phenomenon of discrimination against groups characterized by
   all the above categories (descent, ethnicity, etc.).

6 Anti-Semitism has been the object of innumerable historical, political, and
   philosophical studies. One especially influential contribution is the chapter
   "Elements of Anti-Semitism: Limits of Enlightenment" in Max Horkheimer and
   Theodor Adorno's *Dialectic of Enlightenment*, originally published in German
   in 1944, revised in 1947, and first translated into English in 1972.

7 Stressing the human rights angle of these atrocities is the report by Human Rights
   Watch, *Broken People: Caste Violence against India's "Untouchables"* (1999).

8 See the Human Rights Watch report: *"We have no orders to save you": State
   participation and complicity in communal violence in Gujarat* (2002).

9 We will presently address the intricacies of the right to healthcare as an instance
   of the more general question concerning social, economic, and cultural rights.

10 LGBT – Lesbian, Gay, Bisexual, Transgender. In more recent times, we have
   been witness to an expansion of this label to LGBTQ (Queer), all the way to
   LGBTQIAPK (Intersex, Asexual, Polygamous, Kink), sometimes generalized to
   the inclusive LGBTQIA+. I will continue to use the shorter label, usually
   speaking of "gay rights" and sexual minorities; but note also, and especially, the
   philosophical aspects of queer thought. A founding text is Judith Butler's *Gender
   Trouble* (1990).

11 For a moving philosopher's appraisal of cultural devastation, see Jonathan Lear,
   Radical Hope: Ethics in the Face of Cultural Devastation (2006).

9 Rights on Our Mind

The question of group rights was philosophically constituted as a fundamental issue in human rights, since human rights are crucially conceived as being individual rights. For reasons having to do with their histories and identities, indigenous peoples are the quintessential paradigm of groups that are thought to be entitled to a type of right different from individual rights. Minority rights are, also as a matter of principle, the marker for the general occurrence of discrimination against individuals who are members of certain groups, because they are members of those groups.

Yet when we scan the declarations and covenants – both official and informal – pertaining to human rights, we come across oh-so-many groupings that are seen to merit particular mention, such as children, migrant workers and their families, persons with disabilities, Women, LGBTQ persons, workers, and refugees, among others. Rather than either list them all cursorily, with some related data, or pose very wide-ranging queries relating to them all, we will concentrate on three topics that are at the center of contemporary interest. One might say that they are, at this time, burning issues: women's rights, the rights of disabled persons, and refugee rights.

Women's Rights

"Women's rights are human rights!" has become the mantra heard locally, nationally, and globally in any and all conversations about women's rights. Its literal, textual provenance is somewhat in doubt, but it cannot be denied that it achieved historical and feminist renown in Hillary Clinton's speech at the United Nations Fourth World Congress on Women, that took place in Beijing, China in 1995. Like other hypothetical tautologies, it swings between truism and deep significance. If human rights are owed to all human beings, and if women are human beings, then there is no denying that women are entitled to the same human rights as all other human beings. One wants to exclaim that it goes without saying that women's rights are human rights. But if so, if these are points that seemingly do not need to be made, then why is it so important to insist on that explicit denotation of women's rights as human rights? Is it not enough to note that the UDHR underscores all the "equal rights of men *and* women"? Would it not suffice to take account of the UDHR's oft-quoted instructions against discrimination born of sex – along with race, color, language, religion, etc. – in Article 2?

It has long been noted by analysts of that definitive document that its default reference is to the male human; from the beginning of the text, where "it is essential, if *man* is not to be compelled to have recourse ... to rebellion," on through "the fundamental rights granted *him*," "in the determination of *his* rights," "... at which *he* has had all the guarantees," and to the deliberate wording of Article 12: "No one shall be subjected to arbitrary interference with *his* privacy, family, home or correspondence, nor to attacks upon *his* honor and reputation." This automatic, instinctive, and unthinking use of the male pronoun is ceremoniously heralded in Article 1: "All human beings are born free and equal in dignity and rights. They are endowed with reason and conscience and should act towards one another in a spirit of *brotherhood*" (all instances of emphasis added). Two related casual rejoinders to this grievance indicate social-linguistic quirks. Yes, they say, the use of male pronouns is indeed an automatic, linguistic reflex, but that is all it is and it carries no intentional meaning. And yes, they add, the use of male pronouns was a conventional way of expressing any generalization at the time the UDHR was formulated. We are – socially, linguistically, conventionally – older and wiser now.

Without delving into the intricacies of the philosophy of language and questions of meaning and sense, intention, and convention – that is to say, without dealing with the semantics and pragmatics[1] of the words of the UDHR – we can ascertain that, although these might seem to be only the external, linguistic manifestations of its "vision of humanity," this vision does not substantively consist in any way of "a woman's face" (MacKinnon, 2006, 42). Although the conceptualization of universal human rights purports to include all humans, in practice women's human rights are violated to a degree that is almost unfathomable. Catharine MacKinnon's celebrated description of these violations is impossible to discount:

> If women were human, would we be a cash crop shipped from Thailand in containers into New York's brothels? Would we be sexual and reproductive slaves? Would we be bred, worked without pay our whole lives, burned when our dowry money wasn't enough or when men tired of us, starved as widows when our husbands died (if we survived his funeral pyre), sold for sex because we are not valued for anything else? Would we be sold into marriage to priests to atone for our family's sins or to improve our family's earthly prospects? Would we, when allowed to work for pay, be made to work at the most menial jobs and exploited at barely starvation level? Would our genitals be sliced out to "cleanse" us (our body parts are dirt?), to control us, to mark us and define our cultures? Would we be trafficked as things for sexual use and

entertainment worldwide in whatever form current technology makes possible? Would we be kept from learning to read and write?

If women were human, would we have so little voice in public deliberations and in government in the countries where we live? Would we be hidden behind veils and imprisoned in houses and stoned and shot for refusing? Would we be beaten nearly to death, and to death, by men with whom we are close? Would we be sexually molested in our families? Would we be raped in genocide to terrorize and eject and destroy our ethnic communities, and raped again in that undeclared war that goes on every day in every country in the world in what is called peacetime? If women were human, would our violation be enjoyed by our violators? And, if we were human, when these things happened, would virtually nothing be done about it?

(ibid., 41)

MacKinnon's lament is usually placed in the space of feminism, that is, in the ideological stance that cries out for equality (of rights) of women to (those of) men. Yet the philosophically nuanced argument here is deeper than an easily typecast feminism that might assume universal human rights and bemoan their withholding from women. MacKinnon is highlighting the fact that the very concept of "human" is so gendered that women are not really seen as human; and, correspondingly, the very concept of "human rights" astoundingly does not include women's rights. All the well-known violations of rights that are specifically the violations of the human rights of women – trafficking, sexual slavery, work that is akin to slavery, workplace exploitation, female genital mutilation, prohibition of political and public representation, rape, familial harassment and abuse, and so many others – are forbidden in international human rights treaties but are rampant and unenforced in social, communal, and political practice. It is no surprise, then, that the human rights conversation, both colloquial and legal, includes special treaties and conventions for women's rights. And it is, nevertheless, thought-provoking that the awareness of this essential lacuna comes on the heels of the UDHR's attempt to talk about humanity at large. Thus, the Convention on the Elimination of All Forms of Discrimination against Women, in 1979, noting that erstwhile covenants of human rights assumed equal rights for men and women, was "[c]oncerned … that despite these various instruments extensive discrimination against women continues to exist," and was "[a]ware that a change in the traditional role of men as well as the role of women in society and in the family is needed to achieve full equality between men and women." Women's rights, then, in the conventional arena of legal human rights, are to be especially recognized like other expressly specified human rights and are therefore to be spelled out in singular treaties. Whether this answers to MacKinnon's (and others') deep challenges is an ongoing – philosophical – question.[2]

Let us take a few steps back from MacKinnon's (and others') radical subversion of the orthodox presuppositions of liberal human rights and note how a classical view of human rights might address the particular plight of women, yet still get entangled in problems arising from liberalism that we have met before. Let us think back on the capabilities approach, promulgated by Amartya Sen and Martha Nussbaum, as offering a conception of being human that concentrates on human capabilities and uses those capabilities as the basis for our demands on human rights. Recall the list of capabilities: 1) life; 2) bodily health; 3) bodily integrity; 4) senses, imagination, and thought; 5) emotions; 6) practical reason; 7) affiliation; 8) other species; 9) play; and 10) control over one's environment (Nussbaum, 1999, 41–42). It is interesting to note that from these capabilities one can infer both civil-political and economic-social-cultural rights, that is, both negative and positive rights (or freedoms, in Berlin's terminology). It is also important to note that the basic intuition motivating the capabilities approach when we turn to social and mostly political contexts is that our recognition of human capabilities exerts a moral claim that must be developed by political actors and institutions. And this is, finally, where the claims of women come in – and differently from perceived simplistic universal claims of all.

The capabilities approach, which broaches the fundamental question of what people can actually do and be, sees capabilities as politically inflected according to the customs, arrangements, institutions, laws, and governments in different countries. In other words, the political surroundings in and through which we must assess human capabilities are relevant to the happiness and success or to the misery and failure of humans. These settings are therefore the causes, in Nussbaum's terms, of women's negative circumstances; they are also connected to our demand for justice and to our application of ideas of justice to these same legal-political arrangements. Of course – and here is the rub – "there are universal obligations to protect human functioning and its dignity, and ... the dignity of women is equal to that of men." The fact that social-political structures and systems all over the world do not acquiesce to that equality between women and men cannot provide a defense for reneging on those obligations.[3] "If that involves assault on many local traditions, both Western and non-Western, so much the better, because any tradition that denies these things is unjust" (ibid., 30).

The capabilities approach offers us a conception of the human being that both presupposes and avers the equality of men and women; it is, most perceptibly, a universalist conception. We have previously encountered (in Chapter 7) the philosophical puzzles that accompany universalism and the practical strains put upon it by the cultural relativity of differing conceptions of human rights. Nussbaum is not oblivious to these challenges and indeed recognizes the more serious assaults on universalism that signal awareness of historical and cultural differences, the contest of autonomy – that is, one's right to choose freely (irrespective of some transcendent universal rights), and our inevitable prejudicial application of the label "human." She is, however, single-minded in her belief that focusing on human capabilities provides a conception of the human being that is universal, in the sense of being neither ahistorical nor *a priori* and of engaging with the empirical findings of cross-cultural inquiry. The strength of her argument then allows her to insist on the "profoundly liberal idea ...: the idea of the citizen as a free and dignified human being, a maker of choices" (ibid., 46). Importantly, oh-so-importantly, women cannot be excepted from this idea. A society in which priority is given to cultural norms based on preferences of males (for example, lack of freedom for women to choose work, restrictions on women's life plans, vulnerability to particular ailments, menstruation taboos, no choices for women to education, no possibility of political participation for women, etc.) cannot be a just society. According to the capabilities approach, "a woman's affiliation with a certain group or culture should not be taken as normative for her unless, on due consideration, with all the capabilities at her disposal, she makes that norm her own" (ibid.). When we acknowledge the impermissible treatment of women in these different cultures and societies, the relativistic admonition that we must take into account and indeed respect social and cultural values that are at variance with our own "Western" and therefore imperialistic normative scales is seen to collapse. To be sure, "[w]hy should women cling to a tradition ... when it is usually not their voice that speaks or their interests that are served" (ibid., 47)? Furthermore, the supposed contrast between the relativist's accepted (usually traditional) communities and the universalist's perceived individuals (usually holding human rights) is somewhat crude. The common goals of women can impart a glue of community – different, perhaps, from the old, conventional structure, but no less providing of affiliation and friendship. So this is a sophisticated version of universalism, cognizant of other cultures but antipathetic to their inevitable injustices, especially in the case of women's rights. The inability of women to realize their "most central human functions" precisely because they are women is an essential, political "problem of justice."

The examination of women's rights in the conversation and practice of universal human rights, with the attendant mindfulness that our society and history have been forever controlled by men, lead to an incremental optimism: With time, with effort, with awareness, and with political action, the circle of human rights which, at present, excludes a large segment of humanity – that is, women – will widen to embrace them. Such hopefulness is noncommittal regarding whether this will be achieved by the clarification of conceptual and legal meanings (of "human rights"), by a change in social and community consciousness, or by on-the-ground political evolution and revolution. But perhaps such confidence is misplaced; perhaps the ultimate status of women's rights as a necessary sub-class of liberal human rights in masculine society as we know it – and as it has always been – is inherently problematic. It is in Wendy Brown's work that we meet the more critical and eventually disheartening view of women's rights in liberal society.[4] And it is from her quote of Gayatri Spivak's (in)famous characterization of liberalism as "that which we cannot not want" (1993, 45–46) that we will finally arrive with her at "what liberalism cannot deliver, what its hidden cruelties are, what unemancipatory relations of power it conceals in its sunny formulations of freedom and equality" regarding women's rights (Brown, 2002, 421).

We can, of course, highlight the progress women have made in liberal societies, in places where human rights are valued, by listing those rights that have been achieved in the twentieth century:

> ... to vote, work, and divorce; to keep our children when we deviate from sexual norms; to not be sexually harassed at work and school; to have equal access to jobs and be paid equal sums for the work we do side by side with men; to prosecute sexual violence without putting our own sexual lives on trial; to decide whether, when, and how we will have children; to be free of violence in our homes.
>
> (ibid., 421)

Yet not only are these accomplishments apparent in very few places in the world – the "liberal" places – but even in those, we cannot overlook "our relative reproductive unfreedom; our sexual violability and objectification; the highly exploitable character of much of our paid and unpaid labor; our vulnerability to losing our children, means of subsistence, and social standing when we resist compulsory heterosexuality" (ibid.).

Brown is adamantly clear that the difference between men and women is constructed as a matter of subordination. More so, the list of rights that seem to have been attained only mitigates the list of inequities; the problem of subordination is structural and deep and has not really been resolved. This is because there is a deep paradox in the issue of women's rights, one that we cannot escape by insisting that women's rights are human rights. The paradox is double-sided. On the one hand, the more that rights are specified *as* women's rights, the more they reinforce the definition of women as different, in both legal and "ordinary" language. For example, the rights to abortion or to prosecute sexual harassers are considered to be rights of women – not universal human rights – and are controlled and regulated as such. On the other hand, the more a right is accepted as gender-neutral, the more it will enhance the structural, deep-seated privilege of men (and of heterosexuality). Indeed, the rights procured for women consolidate the heterosexual, regulatory norms of gender. And like in any case of rights-competition between actors on the rights-stage, those who are already powerful have a head start on empowerment resulting from more or new rights.

> The paradox, then, is that rights that entail some specification of our suffering, injury, or inequality lock us into the identity defined by our subordination, and rights that eschew this specificity not only sustain the invisibility of our subordination but potentially even enhance it.
>
> (ibid., 423)

Almost tragically, then, the work of feminists – those who maintain that women's rights are human rights – is focused on the thought that women as individuals are entitled to rights both exclusively for women and identical to those of men. This self-contradicting struggle becomes especially unsustainable since it is carried out in the language of universal, male-dominated discourse; the very idea of an autonomous individual is based on a history of male autonomy and individuality. The hope of changing that age-old conceptual, social, political environment seems slim indeed.

We cannot deny that, in the last century or so, the condition of women in several parts of the world has improved and the suffering of women ameliorated. Neither can we refute the assessment that women are still the objects of discrimination, violation, inequity, and prejudice in most, if not all, human societies. When speaking of concrete human rights, we may be able to detail the data that confirms both of these evaluations. As a matter of philosophical critique, however, we are faced with deep queries that correspond to our principled challenges to the fundamentals of human rights. Are women to be treated as a group, with the corresponding claims to group rights? Are cultures that accept the essential subordination of women to be tolerated, supported by our repugnance towards the imperialistic attitude of western human rights considerations? Is the now well-established discussion of identities – especially in the case of minorities – relevant to a woman's identity? And does this not bring into our arguments the topic of intersectionality, subsequently differentiating between women of different origins, sexual orientation, religions, and the like? It appears that in talking about women's rights we cannot but talk about all other substantive issues having to do with human rights. But perhaps it makes sense to evoke Hannah Arendt's orientation to human rights as "the right to have rights" (1966, 298)[5] and to reconsider her insistence that human rights are embedded in politics; that they are what we have called civil-political rights – since without the fundamental, formal status of a citizen with rights, one cannot really be a human with rights. The fight for women's human rights is then clearly perceived as a struggle to change the political-legal systems in which we live. It is, consequently, also a fight for women's civil rights.

Disability Rights

Looking at the core human rights instruments – conventions that function formally and functionally as legally binding treaties with the bodies that monitor and, optimally, are responsible for gauging enforcement[6] – that have been established since the UDHR was broadcast in 1948 and its elaborations, the ICCPR and the ICESCR, both in 1966, we see, far apart during the ensuing decades, specific treaties dedicated to the human rights of particular populations. Racial discrimination earns pride of place in 1965, the rights of women in 1979, victims of torture, explicitly, in 1984, the rights of the child in 1989, migrants in 1990, and protections from enforced disappearance in 2006. Also at that late date (2006) we meet the Convention on the Rights of Persons with Disabilities (the "Disabilities Convention"). As we have seen, there are issues concerning universal human rights that task our insights, which emerge as soon as we choose to focus on specified sets of humans: Are group rights human rights? Is a group's identity an essence that can be recognized in any and all contexts? Are these contexts always, never, or only sometimes relevant to the human rights conversation? Do the special circumstances of different societies and communities permit us to renege on the demand for universal equal rights for all members of all groups? Does the articulation of (specific) rights for only some people rein-force difference or eradicate acknowledgment of discrimination? It appears that these questions, and others that probe those concepts we have been highlighting, "human" and "rights," receive a sharp and explicit demon-stration in the case of disability rights.[7] Let us investigate them again.

Human rights are those rights that all humans own. We have, in earlier chapters, noted the problems that attach to that claim since we know, all too well, that there are too many humans who are not thought worthy of human rights by several societies and states. Our philosophical theories of human rights run the gamut of essential characteristics that are appreciated as necessary traits of a human being if one is to be considered eligible for human rights. Whether these be rationality or autonomy or choice-making capabilities or a holding of interests, their fundamental inherence in all human beings is a presupposition of human rights claims. Why, then, do the human rights of certain groups of humans merit special mention, even to the point of special treaties and conventions relating to them? Why do we need to single out children, women, racial groups, or the disabled for their own treatment? Why does it not suffice to insist on rights for everyone? Or to simply underscore anti-discrimination? The most obvious and perhaps too facile answer is that certain groups have been, throughout history (and even today), methodically and continuously deprived of their human rights; thus, their human rights must be openly and unambiguously claimed. The basic non-discrimination assertion that is present in so many of the opening credos or, indeed, in the unconditional statements of the central human rights declarations does not achieve the task of stopping widespread inequity, neither legally nor in practice. So – goes this explanation – we must explicitly point out the special vulnerabilities of special populations that must be protected.

A more intricate view of human rights makes note of the important var-iances between human beings and of their essential identities as having an impact on the specificities of their human rights. Moreover, it is precisely items of identity – racial, religious, gendered, etc. – that are responsible for society's disparate treatment of distinct groups of people. It makes sense, then, to relate to those groups and to ensure the security of their human rights. Human rights instruments that are established for that exact purpose can begin, straightforwardly, with emphasis on those human rights that are already well-formulated in the established documents and treaties but that are more liable to be violated in the case of particular groups. Such is, for instance, the insistence on the detailed reference to equal work conditions, equal political representation, or equal education in the Convention on the Elimination of All Forms of Discrimination against Women. More pointed is the elaboration of accepted human rights through the specific presentation they acquire in these special populations. In the case of women, again, we encounter the requirement to "suppress all forms of traffic in women and exploitation of prostitution of women" (Article 6). Although trafficking and prostitution are not exclusively centered on women (and girls, of course), the vulnerability of females to these atrocities is, factually and historically, more conspicuous.

The thought of allocating a well-defined portion of our human rights agenda to a certain category of human beings is therefore justified by their circumstances and by aspects of their identity. A further step, which becomes acute in the case of the rights of the disabled (though it is theoretically pertinent to the other groups we have mentioned), entertains the idea that for certain groups of humans we need to create new and different human rights. We will shortly address the deep, enigmatic nature of this suggestion – that different groups might be entitled to different rights – in the context of universal human rights. Let us first, however, acquaint ourselves with the Convention on the Rights of Persons with Disabilities and accept, for the moment, its distinct position as a treaty that might be seen as offering new, unfamiliar rights in the coterie of human rights instruments. Termed "pluralism" by Frédéric Mégret, this perspective views the Disabilities Convention as "a very subtle mix of the old and the new, which confirms existing rights even as it amplifies upon, evolves from and even departs from them in the sort of creative ways required by the issue of disability" (Mégret, 2008, 498). Indeed, it is often claimed that the Disabilities Convention is the most obvious case of such an awareness of difference leading to new human rights.

In the continuum that goes from, early on, accepting the original, conventional lists of human rights and simply applying them to persons with disabilities to, later, the absolutely novel offering of rights relevant to these persons, we can identify four stations: affirmation of the "old" human rights, reformulation of these rights in language that applies to the disabled, extension of the old rights to new categories of rights, and innovation relying on the creation of new rights pertaining to the disabled (ibid., 498). Quite clearly, that first stop – affirmation of human rights in general as applying to the disabled – is almost a given. So the list of rights in the UDHR, the ICCPR, and the ICESCR, which includes the right to life, the right to be recognized as a person before the law, freedom of movement, the right to education, the right to an adequate standard of living, freedom of opinion, the right to privacy, and other proverbial rights, are all there in the Convention, explicitly recognized and reaffirmed. It is, however, the additional steps taken concerning disability rights that make this document exceptional. Well-known rights are rearticulated to expressly pertain to the situation of the disabled. So, for example, the right to recognition before the law is enriched with the requirement that the disabled must receive "the support they may require in exercising their legal capacity" (Article 12.3). In the context of disability, the critical issue of freedom of expression and opinion is enhanced by "accepting and facilitating the use of sign languages, Braille, augmentative and alternative communication, and all other accessible means, modes and formats of communication of their choice by persons with disabilities in official interactions" (Article 21). And the obligations meted out to the state to enable the disabled to partake of their rights is telling as well: special infrastructures, training of personnel, public awareness campaigns, and specialized services. Beyond all of these, anchoring a general attitude that recognizes these rights as obligatory, is the duty to enact and repeal laws that have to do with the hampered condition of the disabled.

A striking addition to the familiar rights in the UDHR, the ICCPR, and the ICESCR that appears in the Disabilities Convention is Article 16: Freedom from exploitation, violence, and abuse. It is almost poignant to discover that this freedom is not voiced in any of the basic documents of human rights that we have been quoting and using for several decades. It would seem that there is nothing more evident than this freedom – almost as a notable, axiomatic right; or perhaps it can be viewed as one more way of grounding several other rights, like that of life, liberty, security of person, freedom from torture, and freedom from slavery. Why, then, does it appear so unequivocally and openly in this particular convention, and not in others? The palpable, yet intricate answer is that the disabled are almost by definition exposed to exploitation, violence, and abuse. Moreover, such violations of the rights of the disabled are usually perpetrated by other individuals and members of society, not necessarily by the official state; still, it is the state's duty to ensure that these fundamental protections against exploitation, violence, and abuse are implemented in the case of disabled persons because of their heightened vulnerability, borne of their disability.

Perusing the Disabilities Convention and examining its complex articles is an exercise in newly awakening to the "irreducibility of the experience of certain group members in terms of their human rights" (Mégret, 2008, 496). The articles of the Convention tell the story. As we have seen, some are to be expected in any inventory of human rights, but are here applied exceptionally to disabled persons. Others primarily target more particular situations having to do with disability, such as women with disabilities, children with disabilities, accessibility, personal mobility, habilitation and rehabilitation, etc. But it is in articles that are startlingly principled about the context of disability that we realize that the Convention either addresses "old" human rights in an entirely changed way or even invents "new" human rights of the disabled. These include "Equality and non-discrimination" (Article 5), "Awareness-raising" (Article 8), "Access to justice" (Article 13), "Freedom from exploitation, violence and abuse"

(Article 16), "Living independently and being included in the community" (Article 19), "Adequate standard of living and social protection" (Article 28), "Participation in political and public live" (Article 29), and "Participation in cultural life, recreation, leisure and sport" (Article 30).

It is in the formulation of articles such as these last, and it is in the moral credos of the Convention spelled out in its Preamble, that one finds the deep insights that pertain to a singular type of human rights or, at the least, to a distinctive way of viewing human rights when they concern various categories of humans – in this case, disabled persons. Think, first, of the issue of participation in one's community, in one's society, in one's cultural surroundings, or in one's political institutions and bodies. The UDHR mentions cultural participation only once (Article 27.1): "Everyone has the right freely to participate in the cultural life of the community, to enjoy the arts and to share in scientific advancement and its benefits." Interestingly, in Nussbaum's list of capabilities there is mention of political participation as a part of the capability of control over one's environment. It consists of "[b]eing able to participate effectively in political choices that govern one's life; having the right of political participation ..." (Nussbaum, 1997, 288). For disabled persons, however, participation in various aspects of life is far knottier and more troubling. So much so that the Convention takes pains to discuss it at length and in detail, precisely while expounding on the very meaning and consequences of disability. "[D]isability is an evolving concept and ... disability results from the interaction between persons with impairments and attitudinal and environmental barriers that hinders their full and effective participation in society on an equal basis with others" (Preamble, e). There is, then, dire need for this Convention. "[A] comprehensive and integral international convention ... will ... promote participation [of persons with disabilities] in the civil, political, economic, social and cultural spheres" (Preamble, y). Such participation is crucial for meaningful human experience and "full participation by persons with disabilities will result in their enhanced sense of belonging" (Preamble, m). Accordingly, in an important sense, participation is on a par with human rights. "[P]ersons with disabilities continue to face barriers in their participation as equal members of society and violations of their human rights in all parts of the world" (Preamble, k).

In our conceptual, and even terminological, quandaries about human rights, one can ask whether participation (in political life, or in social-cultural life) is a right or a necessary condition for enjoying other rights. In the case of the disabled, the question is more than a matter of semantics: The inability to participate in various aspects of life is constitutive of this special condition, and therefore must be seen as a crucial hindrance to the enjoyment of universally available human rights (at least in theory). "Full and effective participation and inclusion in society" is therefore a *principle* laid out in the Convention (Article 3) – not just in the Preamble, and not in this or that particular right. Whether the explicit elaboration of the principle in various rights, such as the right to accessibility (Article 9), to independent living and being included in the community (Article 19), to education (Article 24), to habilitation and rehabilitation (Article 26), makes it a right on its own is debatable. But, in any case, its essence is crucial and essential in the conception of the human rights of disabled persons.[8]

Previously, in attempting to locate the philosophical foundations of human rights, we came across concepts and ideas that function both as basic renderings of a human being and as justification for his entitlement to human rights. (The former was sometimes given as such justification.) We have mentioned, among others, dignity, autonomy, independence, and equality. These are, contrary to common belief, the presuppositions of human rights, not human rights in themselves. The human being who is the main actor in our drama does not have a right to dignity, a right to autonomy, a right to independence, or a right to equality. He is, rather, assumed to have dignity, described as autonomous (see Kant, in Chapter 3), perceived as independent in making his own choices, and said to be entitled to equal rights (as an explanatory hinge for the universalism of human rights). In other words, those essential human qualities – dignity, autonomy, independence and equality – are presuppositions of the claims for all human rights. "All human beings are born free and equal in dignity and rights." Thus begins the first article of the UDHR, and subsequent talk of equality is a modifier of rights ("all are entitled to equal protection …", "they are entitled to equal rights …", "the right of equal access …", "equal suffrage," "equal pay for equal work," etc.); the human being does not have a right to equality but is assumed to be equal to all others. Dignity is similarly not a right; rather it acts as the basis of rights, which are, in turn, "indispensable for his dignity" (Article 22). Strikingly, autonomy and independence (of the individual, as opposed to state independence) are never mentioned in the basic documents that spell out universal human rights; they are, we can admit, simply assumed as an explanatory, philosophical basis for all human rights.

This is where the human rights of disabled persons become different, in principle, from allegedly universal human rights. These presumptions of what it is that makes one a human being worthy of human rights are not a given in the case of persons with disabilities. In great contrast with the standard treaties and conventions, the Disabilities Convention mentions autonomy, independence, and dignity no less than twenty times; there are seventy occurrences of "equality"! Clearly, these assumed portrayals of the human being are, in the case of disabled persons, far from presumed; they must be bluntly heralded in order to stress not the distinct rights of which disabled persons might be worthy, but rather their equal worthiness of human rights. That basic requirement of non-discrimination, which we have recognized as axiomatic and seen as more relevant to some groups than to others, here becomes crucial. Not only is non-discrimination posited as one principle of the Convention (Article 3), and not only is discrimination prohibited explicitly in the elaboration of many – most – of the specific rights in it (home and family, education, health, work, standard of living, participation in political life, participation in cultural life – all topics that do not warrant mention of discrimination in the universal human rights instruments), but also the duty of states to ensure non-discrimination is connected to the axiom of equality that must ground human rights for a population that is more often than not deemed less equal. In the article on "Equality and non-discrimination" it is mandated that "States Parties shall prohibit all discrimination on the basis of disability and guarantee to persons with disabilities equal and effective legal protection against discrimination on all grounds" (Article 5.2). Even more principled is the connection to dignity: "[D]iscrimination against any person on the basis of disability is a violation of the inherent dignity and worth of the human person" (Preamble, f). The conceptual tie between such dignity of the human person in general and her autonomy and independence is obvious, demanding "[r]espect for inherent dignity, individual autonomy including the freedom to make one's own choices, and independence of persons" (Article 3a). But in the case of disabled persons, that direct relation between dignity, autonomy, and independence must be clearly voiced. We must recognize "the importance for persons of disabilities of their individual autonomy and independence, including the freedom to make their own choices" (Preamble, n) precisely because of the discrimination that is regularly, sometimes unthinkingly and oft-times as the norm, carried out against them. The Convention highlights, in no uncertain terms, the need – in the case of persons with disabilities – for explicit claims concerning those moral and normative principles that are the (usually implicit) suppositions of human rights.

This finally returns us to the question of substance (about the pluralism that underlies the idea that different groups are entitled to different human rights, and its attendant difficulty): Do pluralism and the specificity of certain rights for certain people not negate the universalism and equality that are at the core of human rights? The condition of persons with disabilities throughout history has been one of a constant negation of their recognition as autonomous, independent, dignity-bearing, participating members of society. This denial of existential and experiential status goes hand in hand, integrally, with the constant violation of their human rights. We can choose to view the remedies for this horrific situation proposed in the Convention on the Rights of Persons with Disabilities in two fundamental ways. Either the Convention is perceived as no more – but definitely no less – than an overt reiteration of the "usual" human rights, as they must be articulated and applied in the case of the disabled. In this case, the rights of the disabled are seen as no more – but definitely no less – than universal human rights as they are perceived in human rights practice, with the focus of our interest then naturally centered on non-discrimination. Alternatively, the Convention is accepted as an instrument which legitimately creates a body of rights that is apposite and correct for a certain group of people. The questions that subsequently cannot be evaded are: Are these rights different from former human rights? Are they really human rights? As Mégret so perfectly puts it, are they the human rights of persons with disabilities or disability rights? Since "difference and pluralism are obviously in tension with the ideas of equality and universality" (Mégret, 2008, 496), navigating between these two options means reflecting deeply on the essence of human rights.

Refugee Rights

In the wake of World War II, there were over 11 million displaced persons in Europe; by 1951, when the United Nations decided to devote its efforts to articulating a fundamental document on the human rights of refugees, there were still 1 million European refugees. Today, that is, in 2018, there are over 68 million forcibly displaced persons all over the world; over 25 million of them are refugees; 40 million are internally displaced; and 10 million are stateless. Since the subject of migration is intensively discussed in Europe – with its dire political consequences – it is apt to ask whether this is a global condition or a European, Western crisis? Europe actually hosts only 6% of the world's displaced people, with 19% in the Middle East and North Africa, 29% in Africa, 14% in Asia and the Pacific, and 12% in the Americas. The top five countries from which refugees come are Syria, Afghanistan, South Sudan, Myanmar, and Somalia. The top hosting countries in the world are Turkey, Uganda, Pakistan, Lebanon, Iran, Ethiopia, and Jordan.[9] There is, however, reason to submit that although the very high numbers seem exceptional, massive migration is a commonplace of the modern era. But would we call it a modern, or perhaps even a postmodern, crisis? Zygmunt Bauman, to whom we will presently return, tells us that "humanity is in crisis" (Evans and Bauman, 2016).

It pays to turn to the UDHR and the ICCPR to ascertain the preliminary considerations that will subsequently anchor the status and rights of refugees and migrants in the context of human rights. These are the first locales of explanation for the rights of the human who moves physically and geographically within and between sovereign states.

Three articles in the UDHR of 1948 speak to some aspect of this movement, but at that early stage they seem somewhat disorganized.

> Article 13: (1) Everyone has the right to freedom of movement and residence within the borders of each state. (2) Everyone has the right to leave any country, including his own, and to return to his country.
>
> Article 14: (1) Everyone has the right to seek and to enjoy in other countries asylum from persecution. (2) This right may not be invoked in the case of prosecutions genuinely arising from non-political crimes or from acts contrary to the purposes and principles of the United Nations.
>
> Article 15: (1) Everyone has the right to a nationality. (2) No one shall be arbitrarily deprived of his nationality nor denied the right to change his nationality.

It is in the ICCPR of 1966, which, we recall, is the legally binding document of civil and political human rights, that we find the more accurate formulation of the rights that prescribe refugee status.

> Article 12. – 1. Everyone lawfully within the territory of a State shall, within that territory, have the right to liberty of movement and freedom to choose his residence. 2. Everyone shall be free to leave any country, including his own. 3. The above-mentioned rights shall not be subject to any restrictions except those which are provided by law, are necessary to protect national security, public order (ordre public), public health or morals or the rights and freedoms of others, and are consistent with the other rights recognized in the present Covenant. 4. No one shall be arbitrarily deprived of the right to enter his own country.
>
> Article 13 – An alien lawfully in the territory of a State Party to the present Covenant may be expelled therefrom only in pursuance of a decision reached in accordance with law and shall, except where compelling reasons of national security otherwise require, be allowed to submit the reasons against his expulsion and to have his case reviewed by, and be represented for the purpose before, the competent authority or a person or persons especially designated by the competent authority.

Note, however, that neither of these documents speaks directly of refugees; but it would appear that the first definitional question one asks, when speaking of refugee rights, is "who is a refugee?" Indeed, in 1950, the General Assembly convened a conference in which members of the UN drafted and signed the Convention Relating to the Status of Refugees (1951). Also in 1950, the UN established the office of the High Commissioner for Refugees (UNHCR) – charged with aiding the millions of post-World War II refugees. The UNHCR was envisioned as a three-year project that would fulfill its charge; it is still in place, working in both emergency and long-term operations to protect the rights of refugees.

The first point on the agenda of the Refugee Convention was to provide an explicit, precise, and substantive designation of "refugee":

> Article 1: Definition of the Term "Refugee"
> A. ... the term "refugee" shall apply to any person who: ...
> 2. ... owing to well-founded fear of being persecuted for reasons of race, religion, nationality, membership of a particular social group or political opinion, is outside the country of his nationality and is unable or, owing to such fear, is unwilling to avail himself of the protection of that country; or who, not having a nationality and being outside the country of his former habitual residence as a result of such events, is unable or, owing to such fear, is unwilling to return to it ...[10]

Clearly this definition rests upon Article 14 of the UDHR, which acknowledges the basic human right of individuals to seek asylum in another country from persecution in their own country. Now, our current conversation about refugees, although seriously engaged with this Convention, begins by interrogating and critiquing the definition itself. First, note that the refugee is assumed to be a part of a group, and that belonging to the group is what makes her vulnerable to persecution. Second, note that the groups are well defined: race, religion, nationality, membership in a particular social group and political opinion. A dual question here arises: Does all persecution derive only from group identity, and are these the only group identities that precipitate persecution?[11] Regarding the latter, and given the sharp realization of sources of discrimination outlawed by human rights law, persecution due to other factors (such as sex, age, disability, and sexual orientation, among others) must also be accepted as pertaining to refugees. But this leads to another quandary. Does one become a refugee only in the occurrence of persecution? Is the status of forced displacement always the result of persecution? What about unbearable poverty? Or medical epidemics and plagues? Or the ravages of war? Would a person fleeing such circumstances really be denied the status of a refugee? Finally, the firmness of this definition on the refugee's abode "outside the country of his nationality" is blind to the situation of internal displacement, which has now become the scourge of millions of human beings. This limitation seems unrealistic and impractical, perhaps even unethical; it was originally, of course, a consequence of the discourse of 1951, ruled by an international structure made up of nation states demarcated by borders and their fixed political interrelationships.

How does the Convention conceive of that key term, "asylum"? Two obvious points that support the idea of a country providing asylum to someone who uses that country as a haven from persecution (or other dire maltreatment) concern the duties of the state to which the refugee has escaped. First, the Convention recognizes the shaky legal status of refugees, their entrance into a country through illegal methods, and their presence in the country, at least initially, as an undefined standing. This is precisely the meaning of being a refugee; and it must not be penalized (Article 31). Just as critical and, again, constitutive of the meaning of "refugee," is the principle of *non-refoulement*: The country of asylum is prohibited from expelling or returning the refugee to the country from which he escaped or, for that matter, any country "where his life or freedom would be threatened" (Article 33).[12] But lest we infer that the refugee is thus prohibited from travel both inside and outside the country of his asylum, the Convention addresses a third issue – the freedom of movement of a person, notwithstanding her refugee status, to travel within and out of that territory. Accordingly, the state in which the refugee has found asylum is obliged to issue identity papers that can function as her travel documents.

What are, however, the human rights of a refugee in his new abode? Which of the rights that populate the conventional documents – the UDHR, the ICPPR, and the ICESCR – apply to a refugee? One would want to suggest that since human rights are the rights of all humans, irrespective of their location or citizenship status in that location, refugees are entitled to the same rights that the "locals" of the asylum state enjoy. If we peruse the Convention Relating to the Status of Refugees we do, indeed, find a fair representation of familiar human rights, both civil-political rights and economic-social-cultural rights. In contrast to the familiar documents, the Convention deals early on with freedom of religion and religious education (Article 4). One surmises that that precedence is a consequence of the circumstances of refugees that so often result from religious wars and religious persecution. The Convention then addresses several other rights, including the following: the (political) right of access to the courts (Article 16); the right to work, as a wage-earner, in self-employment, and in diploma-dependent professions (Articles 17, 18, 19); the right to housing (Article 21); the right to education (Article 22); the right to public relief and assistance (Article 23); and the right to labor privileges and social security (Article 24). Since the refugee is not a citizen,[13] but neither is he an "ordinary" alien or foreigner, the legal and practical specifics of the rights discussed in the Convention often refer to "the same treatment as a national," or treatment "not less favorable than that accorded to aliens generally in the same circumstances," and, in all cases, "treatment as favorable as possible."

Like in the matter of rights of persons with disabilities, the rights of refugees are a complex amalgam both of human rights that are accorded to all human beings and of the rights that pertain only to refugees. Unsurprisingly, addressing the philosophical, ethical questions of the treatment of refugees is closely related to examining the concept of migration, especially since, as we have noted, the definition of "refugee" in legal contexts sometimes falls short of our intuitions concerning legitimate reasons for the movement of groups or individuals. And this, again unsurprisingly, raises the associated questions of borders, sovereignty, the world order (usually of nation states), and even cosmopolitanism. The most basic of these concerns are the borders of the nation-state. The rights of "locals" and the duties of a state derive from the status of citizenship; the idea of sovereignty is based on the state existing to safeguard the welfare of its citizens, and only them. It is from this idea that we infer, rightly or wrongly, that the state can bar others from its frontiers, while its citizens can move within them and enter them if and as they choose. But there is an interesting tension here: On the one hand, at the basis of the separation of states lies the concept of borders; but on the other hand, perhaps somewhat counter-intuitively (and counter to what we have all experienced in our border crossings), there is the cosmopolitan thought that borders should be free and open. So we arrive at an inconsistent border-ideology: States can retain control over their borders but must recognize the principle of open borders allowing all to freely enter and reside in any country they like. A striking example of this is Pope John XXIII's encyclical Pacem, invoking the moral principle behind open borders: Every human being, when there are just reasons in favour of it, ... must be permitted to emigrate to other countries and take up residence there. The fact that he is a citizen of a particular state does not debar him from membership of the human family, or from citizenship of that universal society, the common, worldwide fellowship of men.

(Dummett, 2001, 49)

An additional, important conceptualization of refugee rights in the context of human rights comes from the well-known structural conflict between, on one side, an individual's universal human rights and, on the other, state sovereignty. This infamous question deals with the issue of authority – who has the authority to secure an individual's human rights other than the state, and what happens when that authority threatens state sovereignty (as, for example, when the state violates its own citizens' human rights)?[14] Now, in the case of refugees these questions reach the level of convolution. Refugees, who by definition are not citizens of the state in which they (temporarily or not) reside, do not have civil rights in that state; being humans, however, they are entitled to human rights that are not state-specific. What, then, are the rights and duties of a state regarding the refugees residing in it? Are they derivable from the roster of acknowledged human rights (from the UDHR, the ICCPR, and the ICESCR)? The 1951 Convention does, indeed, seem to take further steps, spelling out particular rights (such as *non-defoulement*) owed to refugees by the state in which they have found haven. But what is the moral-political reasoning supporting these legalities?

Both of these quandaries (the state as defined by its borders and state sovereignty vs. the universalism of individual human rights) lead to the most fundamental question concerning both migrants in general and refugees (who are a sub-species of migrants) in particular. Why do we owe anything to migrants or refugees? Another way of putting this is: Do they have rights, and, if they do, are these human rights? Our compassion[15] for them as a conceivable moral duty does not necessarily entail recognition of their rights. In a sense, their citizen status, that is, their membership in a political space, is suspended. Going one step further (with Arendt, to whom we will return shortly), and given the world structure of nation-states, civil rights in the nation-state have become more fundamental and prominent than human rights. The departure of the migrant or refugee from the state in which she is – or was – a citizen puts her in a precarious stateless, and therefore rights-less, space. And this leads to practical, yet still principled, questions: What are the refugees' options? Should they surrender and leave? Where to? Should they attempt to assimilate, to become citizens entitled to civil rights? Should they create a new political community to substitute for the old community which has denied them a legitimate space within it? And if we have arrived at the realm of real political ideology and policy, how should we look at the cohesiveness of traditional societies now faced with the influx of refugees? Is such cohesiveness to be treated with understanding, acquiescence and tolerance; or can we think of it as a source of racism, a flower-bed of poisonous weeds?

Current awareness of great global migrations and, more so, present avowal of a refugee crisis are the result of the contemporary political condition. These political, often practical, questions, buttressed by the legal documents we have seen, are at times philosophically tilted. Indeed, there are philosophical conversations that address these issues from the compound perspectives of political ethics, which certainly have a bearing upon human rights, but do not put them at the center of the investigation. One can turn to utilitarianism or Marxism, for example, to clothe the question of refugees in terms of political analysis. Peter Singer, for one, provides a classic rendition of utilitarian thought – to minimize suffering and maximize wellbeing – in the case of refugees as in all other cases (Singer, 2015). He has very tangible recommendations for how to "solve" – literally – the refugee crisis, by increasing the number of refugees taken in by affluent countries or by supporting poorer countries (in which refugees more often find themselves, though they intend to go on to better-off lands). He formulates his discussion as a rational utilitarian solution, but it is based, importantly, on the ethical idea that we have the same moral obligations towards foreigners as we do towards compatriots (or even family). This is quintessential Singer! Very differently, the Slovenian philosopher, Slavoj Žižek, speaking from a Marxist perspective, sees the contemporary refugee situation as a product not only of wars (like in Syria) and military interventions (like in Iraq or Afghanistan), but also of far-reaching and horrendously influential global capitalism. Political impositions by powerful economic players have led to extreme violations of workers' rights everywhere. The resulting social divisions, according to Žižek, have brought us to the present refugee crisis, which can only be ameliorated through radical economic changes. That said, however, Žižek does also bring forth a different value which underscores policies of refugee acceptance and rehabilitation: solidarity. Somewhat contemptuous even of liberal humanitarian performance, which he views as hypocritical, he insists on recognizing differences – between host populations and refugee or migrant cultures – rather than facilely succumbing to a supposed universalism. Refugees' rights are not based on an equalizing, universalist value-system, but rather on the acknowledgment of difference. "No, we are not [all the same people] – we have fundamental differences, and true solidarity is in spite of these differences." It is, then "on behalf of a higher ethical standard [that] we should accept refugees and take care of them even if the majority of the population is against migrants" (Žižek, "Interview," 2016).[16]

Let us, nevertheless, return to refugees precisely in the context of human rights, and problematize the point in that setting. Whereas our paradoxical question in previous sections about the human rights of several categories of persons focused on the issue of generality vs. specification – why identify certain people dissimilarly from the universal human being when ascertaining their human rights? – the case of refugees (and even migrants at large) raises a novel tension: it asks about the existence of their human rights *per se*. Our earlier query had to do with the special rights that might be applicable – as human rights – to women, indigenous people, individuals with disabilities, or any groups of special standing. In the matter of minorities, we did test the waters of their oft-denied universal human rights – and could, in general, point to discrimination as the social, political, and cultural culprit, thereby maintaining universalism. The situation of refugees, however, holds a complication that is differently problematic, that is problematic in essence.

We can see a version of this in Michael Dummett's ruminations (Dummett, 2001). A superb philosopher of language whose dealings in ethics and politics were little known, Dummett writes about the political straits of migrants and refugees, delving into both ethics and realistic policy-making. Concerning the latter, more practical level, Dummett explains the refugee predicament as exclusively a manifestation of xenophobia; its resolution is then, unsurprisingly, a matter of anti-racist, anti-discrimination education, and regulations. Change will come "only if the amelioration of immigration and asylum policies is accompanied by a determined effort to eradicate racism and its sibling, xenophobia" (ibid., 77). That is all well and good – anti-racism is to be commended and implemented. But Dummett is just as cognizant of the conceptual and terminological quandaries that accompany the idea of human rights in the modern nation-state system. He goes into great detail discussing the rights – if they are rights, and if they are human rights – of individuals to not be expelled from their country, the right to live *somewhere*, the right to asylum, the right to leave one's country, the right to return to it, and the right to citizenship, i.e., "the right to have somewhere where one is incontestably entitled to live" (ibid., 27–29). Different countries have different basic or constitutional laws prescribing these rights; international law also engages with these questions.[17] But Dummett interrogates the matter of open borders with trenchant analytical argument (adducing that, except in rare cases, it is "one of the human rights of each individual to go wherever in the world he chooses" (ibid., 73) and concludes that "[o]nce within a country, anyone, whether citizen or not, puts himself under the protection of its government, and is entitled to receive it" (ibid., 85). The human rights of migrants and refugees are, then, no different than those of a country's citizens.

Whereas Dummett believes that painstaking work within a country and among countries (such as in the European Union) may lead to policies that respect the rights of migrants and refugees and, more so, encourage the creation and development of attitudes that respect their absolute and equal human rights, it is in two other philosophers' work – Zygmunt Bauman and Hannah Arendt – that we meet the impenetrability of this idea. We have met them both before. Bauman stands for the thoughtful, humanistic, yet postmodern thinker, for whom the modern way of life has produced "redundant people" who must go elsewhere from their original abode to find tolerable living circumstances, and, more recently, refugees who are escaping civil wars and horrific conflicts. Importantly, these people are not only stateless, they are "worldless in a world that is spliced into sovereign territorial states, and that demands identifying the possession of human rights with state citizenship" (Evans and Bauman, 2016). Distressingly also, refugees are not only considered bare of rights, they are perceived as a threat to the human rights of locals. The immense numbers of such people have produced "migration panic," while the tides of globalization have created interdependence among states that obfuscate the clear identities of citizens, without providing for cosmopolitan awareness. Nationality is passé for postmodernists such as Bauman, but internationalism is not yet equipped to attend to refugees. Such complexities lead Bauman to proclaim: "I don't believe there is a shortcut solution to the current refugee problem. Humanity is in crisis – and there is no exit from that crisis other than the solidarity of humans" (ibid.).

Hannah Arendt is the progenitor of the "worldlessness" we have just mentioned.[18] "Political questions are far too serious to be left to the politicians," she says (Arendt, 1968). It is philosophical, conceptual analyses that might – that must – guide us in these painful matters. It is from Arendt that we learn that human rights are only civil rights;[19] differently put, the human who is not a citizen, that is to say, the human who does not merit civil rights, cannot have stateless human rights. He actually embodies worldlessness, not just statelessness. In the *Origins of Totalitarianism* she goes further, explaining what this means for migrants and refugees:

> The prolongation of [forced migrants'] lives is *due to charity* and not to right, for no law exists which could force the nations to feed them; their freedom of movement, if they have it at all, gives them *no right to residence* which even the jailed criminal enjoys as a matter of course; and their freedom of opinion is a fool's freedom, for *nothing they think matters anyhow*.
>
> (Arendt, 1966 [1951], 296)

Bluntly but far from simplistically, Arendt sees that refugees have no human rights because, not being citizens of the state to which they have come seeking asylum, but also not having the protection of their rights in the state from which they have been exiled (by compulsion, personal or other, physical or social, natural or artificial) – in other words, because they have no civil rights as citizens – they are also bereft of human rights.

It is poignant to note Arendt's depiction of the Jew as refugee; it is, indeed, pertinent to our discussion of all refugees. This serves to elucidate a deep understanding of the refugee experience, since, for Arendt, the Jew was, by definition, a refugee.

> ... [B]eing a Jew does not give any legal status in this world. If we should start telling the truth that we are nothing but Jews, it would mean that we expose ourselves to the fate of human beings who,

unprotected by any specific law or political convention, are nothing but human beings ... we actually live in a world in which human beings as such have ceased to exist for quite a while; since society has discovered discrimination as the great social weapon by which one may kill men without any bloodshed ...

(Arendt, "We Refugees" (2007 [1943]), 273)

A Case Study: The Palestinian Refugees

Almost by default, our discussion of refugee rights has revolved around the human rights of refugees in the countries to which they have escaped from their own country. Not only have we centered on the human rights to live, work, study, or practice one's religion in the "new" country, but we have noted the essential status of *non-refoulement* – the principle that the refugee is entitled to stay in the country of refuge without being compelled to leave it; indeed, according to Article 32 in the Refugee Convention of 1951, it is the duty of the country to which the refugee has come to "welcome" him – it must not compel him to return to his country of origin.

We have not, however, remarked on a very different aspect of refugee rights – the right to return to one's country after having been a refugee. Recall Article 13(2) of the UDHR: "Everyone has the right to leave any country, including his own, and *to return to his country*" (my emphasis). It presages the ICCPR's Article 12(4): "No one shall be arbitrarily deprived of the right to enter his own country." Both of these articles of human rights are also complemented by humanitarian law, in particular the Geneva Conventions, where we encounter the situations where transfers and evacuations of populations may happen: "Persons thus evacuated shall be transferred back to their homes as soon as hostilities in the area in question have ceased" (Fourth Geneva Convention, Article 49).[20] Coupled with the principle of *non-refoulement*, these rights of the refugee to return to the country from which he fled are fertile ground for deliberation from two different perspectives – as a negatively perceived origin point and as a positive goal of re-attainment. It is the latter that invigorates the Palestinian claim to a Right of Return.

Without delving into a detailed telling of the historical background to this claim, we may still pinpoint the year 1947 as its opening.[21] It was after the UN General Assembly's Resolution 181 (usually called the Partition Plan), adopted in November 1947, in which the area of Palestine under the British Mandate was slated to be partitioned into a Jewish state and an Arab state, that military and civil conflict broke out between the two parties – Jews and Palestinians. From that time until 1949 (when hostilities officially ended), between 700,000 and 800,000 – of a total of about 1,250,000 – Palestinians had fled or been expelled from their homes, leaving behind their property and finding shelter in refugee camps in the surrounding countries. Almost 20 years later, in the war of 1967 between Israel and (almost) the same surrounding countries, another 300,000 Palestinians escaped from the West Bank (which had been under Jordanian rule), the Gaza Strip (under Egyptian rule), and the Golan Heights (in Syria). The reasons for their flight, especially in 1947–1949, are variously recounted: the Israeli version, holding that the "Arabs" were enticed by their leaders to leave and then return with triumphant Arab victors, has been shown to be a myth.[22] The Palestinian version relates a Nakba, a catastrophe, in which over 500 villages were destroyed and emptied of their inhabitants, with the land appropriated for Jewish settlers. But whether these Palestinians fled due to fear (having been witness to scathing battles and horrific massacres) or were intentionally expelled by Jewish forces – indeed, even if they were cajoled to leave by Arab leaders – their status as refugees is legally undeniable. These almost one million original refugees, with their descendants now four generations on, are currently estimated to number anywhere between five and seven million persons – all of whom hold claims to being Palestinian refugees and therefore entitled to a right of return.[23]

In the context of this historical narrative, some legal points pertaining to international law – mostly constituted by the UN – are pertinent to the human rights of the Palestinian refugees. Differently from the status accorded to other refugees in the Refugee Convention of 1951 and the care and protection rendered them by the United Nations High Commissioner for Refugees (UNHCR) since then, the Palestinian refugees were singularly addressed via the United Nations Conciliation Commission on Palestine (UNCCP), established in December 1948, and the United Nations Relief and Works Agency for Palestine Refugees (UNRWA), created in December 1949. The first was entrusted with protecting the refugees and advancing a political solution to their plight; the second was made responsible for aid and work possibilities. Making very little headway *vis à vis* the Israeli authorities in the matter of solutions – and in particular the refugees' return – the UNCCP ceased its operations by 1952 (other than continuing to amass data on refugee property). More troubling, however, was the Palestinian refugees' status as articulated by the UNCHR, effectively excluding them from protection and care regarding human rights that are afforded to other refugees around the world. For all intents and purposes, besides the work of several NGOs, UNRWA is the only body currently catering to any of the Palestinian refugees' needs. That body, though, providing avenues of assistance that center on labor, health, and education, is not able or expected to protect the Palestinians' refugee rights in the countries of their dispersal, least of all their right of return. This general situation is termed, by Susan Akram, the "protection gap":

> Although [Palestinian refugees] were to be beneficiaries of a special regime to ensure their protection, when the main prongs of that regime failed, they were left without even the minimal protections afforded all other refugees under the international burden-sharing system.
>
> (Akram, 2002, 42)[24]

Human rights, as we have seen, travel between legal and political considerations in variegated ways that impact both their protection and their violation. The history of the Palestinian refugees is a flagrant case in point. Consider the following illustrations, which do not only represent a play between the legal and the political, but also exemplify the conceptual convolutions that – sometimes – cannot be avoided. One is the tension between individual and collective rights. According to the Refugee Convention of 1951, refugee rights are the rights of individuals. Although this is a staple of refugee human rights, the Palestinian case brings to bear a particular form of the tension between individual and collective rights, born of the sad circumstances of Palestinian history. The current discussion – if such there be – of the right of return is conducted with the Palestinian Authority (PA), which claims to represent the Palestinian "nation." As such, it treats the right of return as a collective right, which can be negotiated and bargained in the name of the Palestinian people, rather than as a right owned by individual Palestinians. Is this not, then, detrimental to Palestinian individuals and their inalienable rights, including the right of return?

Similarly tricky is the status that has been affixed to UN General Assembly Resolution 194, reached near the end of the military hostilities in December 1948, especially in the context of the issue of Palestinian refugees. Seemingly unequivocal – and therefore considered pivotal for the Palestinian right of return – the resolution states that the General Assembly:

> [r]esolves that the refugees wishing to return to their homes and live at peace with their neighbours should be permitted to do so at the earliest practicable date, and that compensation should be paid for the property of those choosing not to return and for loss of or damage to property which, under principles of international law or in equity, should be made good by the Governments or authorities responsible.

It also instructs the CCP (which, as we have seen, was to all intents and purposes dismantled early on) "to facilitate the repatriation, resettlement and economic and social rehabilitation of the refugees and the payment of compensation ..." (UNGA Resolution 194(11)). Still, although seen by Palestinians and other champions of human rights as the definitive document grounding the right of return,[25] the resolution has been interpreted as non-binding (since being a General Assembly rather than a Security Council document) and as non-general (since qualifying recipients of the right to "those wishing to live in peace with their neighbors").

The history of the Palestinian refugees is nothing less than tragic. For a moment, during the CCP's active attempts to negotiate a resolution of the refugees' predicament, Israel offered to accept 100,000 refugees back; not long after, in 1951, it rescinded its offer. Consistently since that time, Israel – both officially and in consensual Israeli discourse – has denied the right of return as a (Palestinian) human right while only seldom agreeing to discuss a "just solution" to the refugee problem that does not bow before the right of return. In customary refugee discussions, not pertaining solely to the Palestinian case, the solutions to refugee problems can take one or more of three paths: repatriation, absorption (in the country of refuge), and resettlement (in a third country). The right of return is predicated on repatriation, but once recognized, it might also be in tandem with ideas of reparations and compensation.[26] These are all legal exercises resting upon international law – of refugees – but their resolution is in the political field. That dependence, of human rights, their theories, and mostly their realization, on the political showground undercuts legal purity and niceties. We will return to it more substantively in Chapter 13.

Notes

1 Pragmatics is that area of language study that prioritizes the users of a language in the investigation of the meaning of its words.
2 For a vibrant discussion of these issues, see "Are Women Human?" by Catherine MacKinnon (2011), and comments by Heidi Howkins Lockwood, Mindy Jane Roseman, Lani Roberts, Rae Langton, Linda Zerilli, Nancy J. Hirschmann, and Anat Biletzki. Online at: On the Human, http://nationalhumanitiescenter.org/on-the-human/2011/03/are-women-human/
3 Nussbaum details the horrendous statistics, as of 1999, arising from these structures and systems in the global south. Employment participation rates of women in South Asia were 50% those of men; female literacy rates were 50% of men with two-thirds of the world's illiterate people being women; 10% of the world's parliamentary representatives were women. Current numbers, though better, are no less disheartening. Employment participation rates of women are 67% those of men; female literacy rates have risen impressively around the world, but women still make up two-thirds of the world's illiterate people, with no change in the last 20 years; and only about 24% of parliamentary representatives around the world are women.
4 Wendy Brown, "Suffering the Paradoxes of Rights" (2002). In Chapter 12, where we will present the variety of systematic, multi-faceted, philosophical critiques of liberal human rights, we will return to Brown.
5 See Chapter 1.
6 See www.ohchr.org/EN/ProfessionalInterest/Pages/CoreInstruments.aspx
7 See the instructive article by Frédéric Mégret (2008) that asks explicitly if these are "human rights of persons with disabilities, or disability rights?"
8 See Mégret (2008, 508–510) for more discussion on participation as a right in itself.
9 The numbers and data are from UNHCR – the UN Refugee Agency: www.unhcr.org/figures-at-a-glance.html. Please note that they are liable to change in short periods of time.
10 Given the context – place and time – of this decision and this articulation, it is no wonder that the Convention also restricted the recognition of "refugee" to persons whose status was due to conditions in Europe before January 1951. Importantly, the additional Protocol to the Convention, established in 1967, removed that restriction.
11 Political opinion may, perhaps, be less obviously a group label; one may certainly hold an individual political opinion and have nothing to do with others of the same opinion.

12 The principle of *non-refoulement* can also be seen to mandate that countries to which refugees come may not refuse them entrance. Furthermore, this is considered a part of customary international law, that is, it pertains to all countries, not only those that have signed or ratified the Convention.

13 The weighty question about the disparity between the civil rights of a citizen and the human rights of all persons, discussed in Chapter 1, is central also to the issue of refugees and will be discussed shortly.

14 We will return to this topic at length in Chapter 11.

15 This may also be ascribed to hospitality, rather than compassion. See Seyla Benhabib, *The Rights of Others* (2004), chapter 1. Julia Kristeva tells us that "[t]he minimal definition of humanity, the zero degree of humanity, to borrow an expression from Barthes, is precisely hospitality" (*Hatred and Forgiveness*, 2010, 9).

16 For Žižek's comprehensive treatment of the subject, see *Refugees, Terror and Other Troubles with the Neighbors* (2016).

17 Beyond the documents that we have already encountered, a very significant addition is the Convention Relating to the Status of Stateless Persons (1954).

18 Hannah Arendt first used "wordlessness" to define conditions of not mattering as a human being. See Arendt, *Between Past and Future* (1961), p. 53.

19 See Chapter 1.

20 This right of return has been claimed by several groups, such as Circassians, Georgians, and Greek-Cypriots. In parallel, several states have enacted laws that, explicitly or by innuendo, recognize a right of return for their national or ethnic compatriots.

21 Any telling of the history of the "Arab-Israeli conflict" involves a bias, a taking of sides. We will concentrate, here, predominantly on the human rights perspective.

22 This unmasking of the Israeli version as factually questionable is attributed to the "New Historians," most prominent of whom are: Benny Morris, *The Birth of the Palestinian Refugee Problem, 1947–1949* (1988); Avi Shlaim, "The Debate about 1948" (1995); and Ilan Pappé, *The Ethnic Cleansing of Palestine* (2006).

23 Although the Refugee Convention defines refugees as only those persons who flee to another country – not future generations of these "direct" refugees – the Palestinian case answers to different criteria, as set out by the UNRWA instructions from 1950. This will be discussed shortly.

24 Susan Akram's "Palestinian Refugees and Their Legal Status: Rights, Politics, and Implications for a Just Solution" (2002) provides the most trenchant analysis available of the legal complexities of the Palestinian refugees' situation.

25 Equally strong is the UN General Assembly's Resolution 3236 (1974) that "[r]eaffirms ... the inalienable right of the Palestinians to return to their homes and property from which they have been displaced and uprooted, and calls for their return ..."

26 Repatriation and other options of restitution and compensation populate several resolutions and peace agreements of the last few decades. See Akram (2002, 46).

10 Global Economic Rights

Poverty as a Human Rights Issue

Here are some arresting facts and numbers. About 700 million people, about 10% of the world, live in extreme poverty – less than $1.90 a day; 1.3 billion live in multidimensional poverty,[1] and half of those are under the age of 18. Consider also that 821 million do not have enough food; 844 million do not have clean drinking water. Every year 3.1 million children die of under-nutrition. Also, every year, 1.4 million children, living among the world's poorest populations, die of preventable diseases like pneumonia or diarrhoea. As many as 57 million primary school-aged children are not in school, with 60% of them not achieving a minimum level of proficiency in reading and math; in "developing" countries, one out of four girls does not attend school. And between 15,000 to 20,000 children die every day due to poverty.[2]

Were we to try to relate the above data – and so many others – to human rights, we would very naturally, almost automatically, be reminded of some articles in the UDHR, most obvious of which is

> Article 25 (1) – Everyone has the right to a standard of living adequate for the health and well-being of himself and of his family, including food, clothing, housing and medical care and necessary social services.

Perhaps we would also add

> Article 26 (1) – Everyone has the right to education.

In other words, we can easily determine the rights to an adequate standard of living – adequate, that is, for sustenance, health, housing, and education – as explicit human rights that have earned a place of significance in the conventional list of human rights and, more particularly, in the category of economic-social-cultural rights. It is painfully clear that lack of a basic, satisfactory income denies food, clothing, housing, and medical care to large parts of the world's population. It is also easy to show the connection between the level of earnings or otherwise received income of households around the world and the education afforded to the children of those households. But we can also attend to additional facts that pertain to the rights we have listed in previous chapters. People with a low income have scant access to legal services. Children raised in underprivileged areas are less likely to participate in cultural activities or engage in political institutions. Indeed, the basic threesome of Article 3 in the UDHR – life, liberty, and security of person – are consistently threatened by the conditions and circumstances of poverty.

Poverty – that is the essential label that we may give to all the above phenomena. Lack of food, health, housing, education; the absence of viable paths to legal remedies, to political activity, to institutional services; the threat of violence, harassment, discrimination; the constant, unnerving existence of precarious living circumstances. All of these are intimately connected with issues of human rights, since it is in a life of poverty that human beings are substantially deprived of the products that accompany civil, political, social, economic, and cultural human rights. It is not that one has the right not to be poor; it is rather that poverty is the human condition in which human rights are theoretically threatened, practically unachieved, and essentially unattainable.

Let us elaborate a little further the idea of poverty as a violation of human rights. The conventional yet substantial distinction between social, economic, and cultural rights, civil and political rights, and even group and collective rights might seem to locate the violations that poverty entails as naturally belonging to the first grouping – social, economic and cultural rights in general, and economic rights in particular. However, the all-encompassing dysfunctionality brought about by a life of poverty and by the systematic and communal structures of poor societies and states points to a far more sweeping set of human rights deficiencies contingent on poverty. The somewhat superficial conflict between economic rights and political rights that we encountered when reading about China's claim that the former must be prioritized over the latter ("someone who is starving does not worry about freedom"), and about its Western counter-idea ("without freedom one's food is meaningless"), is seen to be moot in the case of poverty, not to mention extreme poverty. Economic rights – to sustenance, to work, to a standard of living, to respectable levels of health and education – cannot be divorced from those rights we usually consider as civil and political rights, since the enmeshment of social, economic, and political rights is unavoidable in the context of poverty. Is there really a comprehensible difference between saying that "non-poverty" is a human right and recognizing that human rights detractions – be they economic, social, civil, political, or cultural – are a clear result of a life of poverty?

No less problematic in this same framework is the question of *who* is the addressee of the claim to human rights of the poor.[3] The simplistic answer is in line with the liberal presupposition of human rights accruing to the individual and demanded from the state; it becomes, in environments of poverty, far more complex. Although we can continue to view the poor individual person as being the target, so to speak, of human rights violations, it is not clear that that individual can always address her own state or government with claims to human rights pertaining to poverty. Such claims are immensely multifaceted, being dependent on the political structures in place in a particular country and on the specific community to which that individual belongs. Moreover, the individualistic basis of the liberal conception of human rights, which posits the poor individual's situation in poverty as being resolvable by the state, also assumes the state's capability to eliminate individual cases of scarcity, and perhaps even the poverty of certain groups. But what about poor states? What about poverty as a societal, communal phenomenon and, more so, a condition of some states as opposed to others in the global economy?

It appears, then, that in attending to poverty through the perspective of human rights, we cannot escape two essential moves. First, we need to deal with quantitative economic realities substantively, recognizing their interlocking relations with social and political sites of engagement that are just as critical for the attainment of human rights. Second, we must explicitly transfer our attention not only to domestic institutional framings of human rights (as discussed in Chapter 6) but, even more challenging, to the global economic relationships between states, rather than to those between citizens and their states that we have advanced as basic to human rights. Let us start with that.

Rawls – From Domestic Social Justice to Justice in International Relations

In Chapter 4 we presented John Rawls as one of the important theorists whose rendition and revision of liberalism provided – along with Thomas Hobbes, John Locke, and John Stuart Mill – a basic political Weltanschauung, or world-view, that could ground theories of rights and, more overtly, human rights. Rawls laid out in orderly, explicit detail a theory of justice – in his book of the same title – that imagined an *original position* of persons behind a *veil of ignorance* engaging in discussion, and used that thought experiment to arrive at the fundamental mainstays of a just society. Recall, this system of justice is based on the *principle of liberty* – enjoining the maximum amount of freedom for each member of this society that is compatible with the same degree of liberty for all; and on a principle of equality – insisting on *equal opportunity* and even a certain degree of inequality, but allowing – through the *difference principle* – only those social inequalities that benefit all, including especially those members of society who are least advantaged. In complex fashion, this system of justice entails certain rights, that is, basic warranties for all and expressly for those least well off, so that their dire position will not maim the equality required of a just society. Obviously, this version of internal justice, that is to say, justice within a social and political system, makes room for and indeed values social, economic, and cultural rights – those rights that we have (in Chapter 5) called positive rights – in the framework of domestic politics. These are the rights that act as bedrock guarantees of a just society.

Almost 30 years after *A Theory of Justice* (1971), Rawls extended his aforementioned thought experiment and the theory that it grounded to questions of a just global system in *The Law of Peoples* (1999).[4] Beyond the relationships among individuals and between individuals and their government, Rawls recognized that a comprehensive treatment of political justice could not disregard international relations between different states, different nations, or different peoples. So while *A Theory of Justice* deals with domestic justice, *The Law of Peoples* has to do with justice in the context of international relations – that is, international law and practice. Interestingly, it is clear to Rawls that human "evils" follow from political injustice and that, therefore, if politically just "or at least decent" societies and institutions can be established, the great evils will "eventually disappear." But it will still be incumbent upon societies, even if they are just, to engage with other societies if we are to escape "unjust war and oppression, religious persecution and the denial of liberty of conscience, starvation and poverty, not to mention genocide and mass murder" (Rawls, 1999, 7).

What now arises is a critical question regarding the just world-order which underlies a law of peoples: which are the peoples that we must consider when we include the world's societies in that just global system? Rawls recognizes two types of peoples that can legitimately participate in this discussion – just ones and decent ones. Just societies are those that abide by his earlier articulated liberal structure – those that have devised constitutions, that have initiated and supported democratic governments, and that legislate the principles of liberalism. But other peoples have established different social, economic, and political systems that are ruled by non-liberal and undemocratic governments; these are systems that do not abide by all stipulations of Rawls's just societies. Their members live in conditions of injustice, according to the requirements of liberal justice that involve the familiar aspects of liberal societies. Still, we may be hard put to deny to those societies that do not live up to this minimal concept of justice any participation in the community of nations that make up the global society. Using a terminology different from "liberal" and "non-liberal," or even "just" and "unjust," we may say that we need societies to be, at the very least, decent. These peoples, while not liberal, and therefore not really just, may perhaps be discriminatory towards certain religions; they may subjugate women or deny them rights of political participation; they may be institutionally hierarchical; indeed, not all of their citizens may be free and equal, and perhaps even not all of their residents may be citizens. Very significantly, decent societies adhere to certain human rights – not the liberal human rights which we have reiterated again and again, not even the fundamental human rights which Rawls expounded in his elaboration of a just society, but rather a different list of rights which, nevertheless, bespeaks decency: subsistence, security, personal property, equality before the law, freedom from slavery, protection from genocide, and a modicum of freedom of conscience.

That stalwart icon of *A Theory of Justice*, the original position, is made to do similar work in *The Law of Peoples*. Again, a group of peoples (rather than persons) needs to be brought together, in an imaginary, analytical, hypothetical situation, to decide on a practicable system of international law that commits all of them. Again, Rawls puts representatives of these peoples behind a veil of ignorance (concerning certain information about the particular people represented – their number, political strength, living area, etc.) and sees them as attempting to further the interests of their (represented) people. We will soon return to this very essential question – what are the interests of a people? And, again, Rawls articulates principles that this meeting in the original position of peoples would generate. "I contend that the eight principles of the Law of Peoples ... are superior to any others," he says. These are:

1   Peoples are free and independent, and their freedom and independence are to be respected by other peoples.
2   Peoples are to observe treaties and undertakings.
3   Peoples are equal and are parties to the agreements that bind them.
4   Peoples are to observe a duty of non-intervention.
5   Peoples have the right of self-defense but no right to instigate war for reasons other than self-defense.
6   Peoples are to honor human rights.
7   Peoples are to observe certain specified restrictions in the conduct of war.
8   Peoples have a duty to assist other peoples living under unfavorable conditions that prevent their having a just or decent political and social regime.

(Rawls, 1999, 41)

It is worth noting that, in the move from one society and its requirement of justice to an international arena of states, Rawls has extended his favored, liberal society – with its liberal tolerance of a pluralism of political world-views joined to a vigorous conception of human rights – to a world-community of both liberal and non-liberal, yet still decent societies, now tolerant of non-liberal peoples and making do with a minimal list of human rights. This is obviously necessary for any sustainable international cooperation among a plethora of states and their various internal legal and governmental structures. But such cooperation is limited to just and decent societies; in a way, one can say that just societies espouse liberal egalitarianism while decent societies may be hierarchical, yet still well-ordered and cognizant of their members' core human rights. Indecent states are those that do not live up to this minimum; they are, consequently, not tolerated by the international community pictured here as able to conduct cooperative legal, international relations. Within the society of societies, that is to say, in the community of liberal and decent peoples, there is a positive principle of "honor[ing] human rights" (without further elaboration, here in the list of principles, of which human rights are absolutely required). We shall soon see that the question of "which human rights?" impacts the essential capacity of an international legal order among liberal and decent societies to be just. Surprisingly, perhaps, this arises from the problem of poverty as a condition which exists in some countries of the world, but not in others. This seemingly coincidental situation is the pivot upon which we will address our interrogation of poverty as a human rights issue.

Criticism of Rawls's Move from Domestic Justice to World (In)Justice

It is in the work of Thomas Pogge,[5] a leading exponent of Rawls, that we encounter an investigation of Rawls's idea of international justice, as expressed in *The Law of Peoples*, that exposes its shortcomings concerning human rights in general and poverty as a human condition bespeaking a series of violations of human rights in particular. Although *A Theory of Justice* (1971) addressed domestic justice with an eye, especially, to questions of equality, Rawls's move to the international context in the second book falls short of a satisfactory political view of right and justice (Pogge, 1994, 196). Specifically, it seems to disregard the inequality that is inherent in the current world order – where persons who are members of the peoples who constitute that order do not really have an equal say in international political decisions; where education and professional positions are far from evenly distributed; and where social and economic inequalities certainly do not benefit those who are the worst off (as Rawls's domestic difference principle required). Nonetheless, according to Pogge, "[a] plausible conception of global justice must be sensitive to international social and economic inequalities" (ibid.), and only a critical redoing of Rawls's "law of peoples" can provide attention to such inequalities. In other words, that last invention of a second session of original position – amongst representatives of peoples rather than representatives of persons – must be adapted to the real-world situation of dire inequalities.

Looking in detail of form and content at Rawls's stipulations regarding this meeting of representatives of liberal and non-liberal but still decent societies, we can ascertain that there are two basic assumptions made about these representatives that must be accepted if we are to entertain a workable law of peoples. First, the representatives of peoples who are functioning at the second session, meeting behind a veil of ignorance similar to that of the first meeting, do represent their societies, that is, their peoples, in the matter of their interests. But recall that, given the diversity and pluralism accepted by liberal societies – and it is not yet clear if also by all decent societies, such as, for example, hierarchical ones – and their various structures of domestic justice, we cannot identify in real detail the particular interests of different societies. Suffice it then to realize that each people must have one fundamental interest: that their institutions, and subsequently any international institutions they ascribe to, satisfy their own conception of justice; and the representative of a people in the second session of the original position represents this interest when discussing the law of peoples. This leads immediately to Rawls's second conjectural claim: The delegates of different peoples, although representing somewhat different conceptions of justice, will, however, since they represent liberal and decent (even if hierarchical) peoples, all agree on the law of peoples with its eight principles above.

This is, admittedly, a thought experiment. The original positions, where representatives of persons meet in the case of domestic justice and delegates of peoples meet in the case of international justice, can be variously experimented on. Although Rawls's double-invention of a two-stage original position is a method of reasoning used to identify both domestic and international basics of justice, one can surely argue with his assumptions concerning the latter. And, indeed, Pogge takes issue with them. No, he says, it is not reasonable to presume that delegates of peoples can only attend to that one interest – that of the law of peoples only satisfying the institutional adherence to a people's conception of justice. We must also add on to our list of (peoples') interests the well-being of individuals, that is to say, the well-being of the persons who are members of a people. Delegates of a people cannot be viewed as representing only an abstract, structural stance of a people in relation to their institutions and conceptions of justice. Delegates of a people, although they are now in a second session of the original position, do not really ever lose the function of representing the individuals who make up a people. And it is the well-being of those persons which necessarily leads to the well-being of a people. So peoples have an additional interest, beyond promoting and guarding their conception of justice in the international context: the well-being of their members.

Even more intuitively beckoning is Pogge's dismissal of Rawls's sanguine stipulation that, since people's interests are of that formal, institutional type, all participants in the second session would agree in the adoption of the law of peoples. Recall that the delegates in this meeting are representatives of all decent societies, including both liberal and hierarchical societies, whose conceptions of justice are thus, in general, alike. And recall that, according to Rawls, they are all thereby assumed to accept the same law of peoples, knowing that they have only the interests of their peoples – as targeting their own domestic conception of justice – in mind. But remarkably now, the egalitarian bent of Rawls's domestic theory of justice – in which the difference principle was called upon to ensure that gross inequality between persons would not prevail – is now missing from the world order in the law of peoples so solidly accepted. Whereas inequality had been denied and the difference principle posited as a fundamental condition of justice in *A Theory of Justice*, inequality among peoples is, for Rawls, dissimilar. Indeed, the fact that certain societies happen to be better endowed with natural resources, or happen to have profited from the vagaries of certain historical circumstances, is not seen as detrimental to the equal acceptance of the law of peoples. Indeed, Rawls places the "blame" for the dire conditions of poor societies on internal cultural and political traditions, or corrupt government and elites (Rawls, 1999, 77). Pogge, contrariwise, notes the fallacy adhering to Rawls's assumption that ownership of natural resources is "natural," whereas any other distribution of wealth between peoples is contrived. Just like such "natural" distribution was denied in the case of individual inequality and difference in the context of domestic justice, so the inequality between societies must be repudiated in the case of international justice systems.

> Yes, egalitarian institutions are demanding upon naturally and historically favored societies, as they would do better in a scheme with unlimited ownership rights. But then, symmetrically, a scheme with unlimited ownership rights is at least equally demanding upon naturally and historically disfavored societies, since they and their members would do much better under a more egalitarian global basic structure.
>
> (Pogge, 1994, 213)

This way of viewing the issue of just distribution regarding natural, even historical privilege holds an intriguing insight. There is a basic – though not necessarily correct – intuition that the "natural" circumstances of a society give rise to that society's unlimited ownership of its resources. Such an intuition also views limited ownership of resources, not to mention distribution of the profits accruing to that ownership, as non-natural and therefore artificial. Pogge's alternative perception does away with any correlation between "natural" and "just" as they relate to ownership of resources. The scheme of unlimited ownership of the resources in one's circumstantial surroundings is no more natural than an alternative scheme of egalitarian distribution of all of our resources. Both are human social and political decisions regarding ownership of the resources of the earth; unlimited ownership is a humanly created construction which is just as non-natural as any deliberative, sharing dispersal of resources. As such, the quest for just ownership is coherently justified when it refuses to forfeit the priority of equal distribution. Indeed, it turns back to the equal status of all human beings in their entitlement to human rights.

The Second Session Original Position – and Back to Liberalism

Let us return, then, to that second session of the original position in which representatives of different peoples attempt to arrive at an international system of laws that applies to them all. The question of their consensual agreement is arguable: If each people has only the fundamental interests of creating institutions satisfying their conception of justice, they might coincide; if they also have the interests of persons' well-being, then liberal and hierarchical societies might well diverge from one another. Put differently, delegates of liberal societies represent their societies precisely by representing the interests of the persons in those societies; they also insist on their egalitarian concerns; and, consequently, they are devoted to a full catalogue of human rights, including democratic political rights, freedom of speech, liberty of conscience, and freedom of thought – which Rawls has omitted from his list of basic human rights. That nominal Rawlsian list is doubly problematic. First, it is indeed basic and minimal, answering to what Rawls believes is absolutely necessary for decent societies to in fact be decent. Second, however, as Pogge notes, there is no reason to assume that hierarchical societies – which are decent but explicitly non-liberal – would accept even those basic human rights into the supposedly consensual international system. There is, subsequently, no reason to think that Rawls's "politically neutral" (Rawls, 1999, 69) law of peoples would be accepted by and serve all decent societies.

These infelicities accompanying the very idea of a second session of the original position, holding delegates of both liberal and hierarchical communities, can be explicated forcefully if we think, yet again, of the place of human rights in a domestic, legal liberal system as contrasted with their position in the arena of international law. We immediately arrive at the classical conundrums of liberal thought: How does the liberal treat the non-liberal? More practically: How is a liberal society to deal with non-liberal value communities? And going even further, how do liberal nations accommodate or engage with states that adopt illiberal regimes? Therein lies the celebrated question of the liberal tolerance of non-liberal individuals, societies, and states. Now, it has become conventional wisdom that the essence of a liberal society lies in its acceptance of any non-liberals – individuals or communities – within it. This has a limit, however, and that limit resides in a liberal society's insistence on its liberal structures and institutions. In other words, the liberal society cannot go as far as reneging on its liberalism, that is, accepting non-liberalism, for liberalism's sake. To impose liberal institutions is not a case of illiberalism. That imposition – on non-liberals – must be accepted in the name of liberalism. Liberalism cannot follow in its own footsteps to the extreme point of complying with illiberalism.

All of this pertains, of course, to the domestic systems in liberal states. But what would be the international parallel to this reasoning? Instead of speaking about domestic liberalism and a domestic liberal system of laws and institutions, we now move to the case of a liberal world order, that is, an international legal and institutional structure which proffers liberalism as the just basis of our choosing. Parallel to the acknowledgment above, we may claim that a liberal world order can and must accept the existence of non-liberal states. Yet in exactly the same way, we may also differentiate between that concession and the more troubling claim that enforcing a liberal world order on illiberal national regimes constitutes, in itself, a case of illiberalism. Again, as in the domestic case, liberalism must protect itself from illiberal competitors; doing so does not make it illiberal.

Again in subtle manner, Pogge takes Rawls to task for compromising international liberalism for the sake of accommodating international non-liberals. Rawls does not see the parallelism between domestic liberalism and global liberalism when he proceeds to limit international liberals in their (hypothetical, imaginary) would-be insistence on a liberal world order. Just like there is a legitimate move from the domestic, liberal tolerance of illiberal communities to the domestic imposition of liberal institutions on illiberal persons (and communities) – which Rawls recognizes – so there is a desirable concurrence between a world order that recognizes non-liberal, albeit still decent states and one that would still insist on a liberal global order – which Rawls relinquishes. Put differently, Rawls cedes certain parts of liberalism, and in particular certain human rights, in order to placate the representatives of illiberal, hierarchical societies in the second session. He does so for the sake of an (imagined) agreement, between all societies and states, on the law of peoples. But Pogge sees this as lacking in "assertiveness":

> We should ... work toward a global order that ... is itself decidedly liberal in character, for example by conceiving of individual persons and of them alone as ultimate units of equal moral concern. This quest will put us at odds with many hierarchical societies whose ideal of a fully just world order will be different from ours.
>
> (Pogge, 1994, 218)[6]

Clearly, then, the disharmony between liberal states and hierarchical states, especially in the matter of human rights, is a significant hindrance to the idea of global justice based on an international law of peoples. If human rights are posited at the base of a just world-order, just as we have advanced them at the foundation of domestic justice, then it is difficult to imagine a well-functioning international legal system when between different societies and states there is real disagreement on those human rights. It is, in fact, challenging to imagine a "compromise" between states whose very political and legal substance is so basically unalike. Let us now also add to this divergence our earlier distinction between civil-political rights and economic-social-cultural rights. In our exposition of Rawls's basic rights as opposed to other, liberal rights, we were delimiting the conversation to the former category. Now, however, when speaking of poverty and its attendant rights, we are squarely in the realm of social and economic rights, such as the rights to sustenance, well-being, health, and education, among others. It is here that the concept of equality, so central to human rights,[7] emphatically reappears. And it is here that Rawls's inconsistency, between the domestic and international contexts, becomes blatant: *A Theory of Justice* explicitly focused on inequality as the most potent threat to domestic justice; therein lay the daring difference principle. *The Law of Peoples* falls short precisely there.

A Suggestion for a Solution

How can we rethink global inequality in a way that ensures our attention both to the individuals who are holders of human rights and to the wealth of the states which are globally linked through international law? How can we consistently talk of human rights – the rights of individuals *vis à vis* the state of which they are citizens – and of the relative riches of states and (geographical) societies? In other words, how can we adjudicate between states the relationship that addresses inequality between individuals? This is the goal that Pogge advances with his idea of a Global Resources Tax (GRT), levied upon prosperous states with the explicit purpose of improving the lot of persons in poorer states. Going back to his earlier, philosophically astute insight that the "natural" division of the world's resources (and even utilization of those resources) is not inherently just, whereas an egalitarian division should be pursued in principle, Pogge suggests a global tax, "[whose] basic idea is that, while each people owns and fully controls all resources within its national territory, it must pay a tax on any resources it chooses to extract" (Pogge, 1994, 200). This is not an economic version of a world government, but it does address the interconnected workings of the global political economy. Without going into the intricate complications of the relationship between tax rates and economic activity, the relative simplicity or complexity of any tax law and practice, or the convolutions of taxes on land used for basic commodities (all dealt with by Pogge in detail), we must note the principled and ethical aspects, that is, the human rights facets, of such a creative idea. The ownership, appropriation, and use by nations of their natural resources – be they land, oil, air, water, or diamonds – are qualified by a "kind of a minority stake" of "humankind at large" (ibid.) in these treasures.

Notably, the overt objective that fuels the GRT is that its proceeds

> are to be used toward the emancipation of the present and future global poor: toward assuring that all have access to education, health care, means of production (land) and/or jobs to a sufficient extent to be able to meet their own basic needs with dignity and to represent their rights and interests effectively against the rest of humankind: compatriots and foreigners.
> (ibid., 201)

Rich countries pay into the GRT; poor countries receive well-calculated GRT amounts. Since the global poor are citizens of poor countries, and since we are assuming an entitlement to human rights claimed by individuals towards their own states, these governments may use the funds for lowering taxes or raising the levels of funding for those needs which are specified by our standard economic human rights: education, healthcare, well-being effected by infrastructure, and other services. But the double emphasis on human rights and on mitigation of inequality, as the grounds upon which the GRT is established conceptualizes the movement of funds from rich countries to poor ones as "a matter of entitlement rather than charity and ... would not be conditional upon rendering political or economic favors to a donor or upon adopting a donor's favored political or economic institutions" (ibid., 202). In keeping with the institutional rendering of human rights that we have encountered (Chapter 6), the GRT is a global institution that operates on an international level; but it is an institution nevertheless, established to protect and further individuals' needs arising from the dire condition of poverty and addressed in the language of human rights.

In thinking about the idea of a GRT, we cannot but consider the relationship between rich countries of the world and poor countries – rather than between the members of poor countries and their rulers and states. Moreover, in demanding that rich nations "pay out" for poor nations, we may be presupposing the responsibility and even blame of the rich states for the poverty rampant in the poor ones. Indeed, the systematic structure that is advocated by solutions like the GRT focuses on the interdependence among various societies in the global economic system; and it repudiates the thought that these societies are, or have ever been, truly independent. "[T]oday's most unfortunate societies ... are still reeling from the effects of slavery and colonial oppression and exploitation and are also highly vulnerable to global market forces and destabilization from abroad" (ibid., 221). The recognition of such interdependence and mutual accountability is a moral realization. And liberalism, once viewed as a political impetus for domestic justice, can be put to work in the international arena for global justice; but only, according to Pogge, if egalitarian values play a crucial part in the law of peoples. This may be a challenge for diplomats, rulers, and statesmen. But,

> our task as philosophers requires that we try to imagine new, better political structures and different, better moral sentiments. Yes, we must be realistic, but not to the point of presenting to the parties in the original position the essentials of the status quo as unalterable facts.
>
> (ibid., 224)

Counting, Measuring, and Assessing Poverty

What could be alterable or unalterable facts in the story of poverty and hunger? Whether we deal with states and their interrelations, citizens and their interactions with their own states, individuals engaging in worldwide philanthropy, or global institutions that purport to ameliorate hunger and poverty, there are basic definitional questions that must be answered if we are to assess the state of the world's poor and, even more knottily, weigh the moves that must be made if we are to eradicate poverty.

A first basic quandary has to do with "counting the poor." Without devoting too much space and time to economic details – of measuring and comparing income and consumption of individuals and states – we should note the overt numbers that have been bandied about and generally accepted by the world at large when counting the poor. For many years what played the role of defining poverty was the World Bank's determination of an income of less than $1 a day. Remember that the World Bank is the body "appointed" in 1944 at the Bretton Woods Conference (along with the IMF – the International Monetary Fund) and closely integrated with the UN to provide, monitor, and manage loans to countries around the world for their capital projects. It is the World Bank's data and assessments that are almost consensually accepted as providing the determination of and facts about the world's poor populations. Beyond the question regarding the uncertainty of that poverty line – Why $1? Why not $2? Or $1.50? – there have been sharp criticisms of the methodology used in these orthodox evaluations of the poor.[8] These have to do with the inadequacy of the Bank's use of PPP (purchasing power parity) to compare prices in different times and places according to national CPIs (consumer price indexes) – leading to a complicated, perhaps even convoluted, and suspiciously arbitrary IPL (international poverty line). Beyond troublesome and poorly grounded calculations, the Bank's decisions as to what is to count as poverty are based on additional problematic pivots. For one, income and even consumption do not necessarily point to people's real needs and requirements, so do not address the real vagaries of poverty. For another, the Bank infers general conditions and trends from limited and sometimes irrelevant data, giving rise to grandiose estimates of wide-ranging facts that are far-removed from the real life of poor communities all over the world.

Sanjay Reddy and Thomas Pogge (*How Not to Count the Poor*, 2009), who have investigated the ideological background, the economic frameworks, and the computational details of the World Bank's contribution to counting the poor and describing poverty, have termed this the "money-metric" approach: it is based on financial quantification of poverty and poor people that does not really penetrate the qualitative situation that bespeaks poverty. Just as significantly, the World Bank is so enamored of its own supposed ability to encompass global descriptions that it flattens out the particularities and context-dependencies of different societies' and different countries' specific problems. Most importantly, however, the money-metric approach enveloping the Bank's determinations does not really address the question of what is needed for the achievement of basic human requirements – that is to say, the resources to fulfill the human capabilities which we have posited[9] as necessary criteria for human rights satisfaction in the matter of a sustainable life.

How else, then, can we count the world's poor or precisely define "poverty"? It continues to be Reddy and Pogge's analysis through which we can look to a different perspective. "Income poverty is," they write, "only one aspect of poverty, and other poverty estimates, based on under-nutrition, infant mortality, access to health services, and other indicators can continue to inform us even in the absence of usable figures concerning global income poverty" (Reddy and Pogge, 2009, 45). In other words, not only are the World Bank's estimates of income poverty awkwardly skewed and perhaps invalid, but we must go beyond income if we are to grasp the real meaning of world poverty. To allay these doubts and to make real progress – first – in our understanding of the state of world poverty, we need an "alternative procedure [of counting the poor]" that

> would construct poverty lines in each country that possess a *common* achievement interpretation. Each poverty line would refer to the local cost requirements of achieving a *specific set of ends* [my emphasis]. These ends should be specified at the global level and can include elementary human capabilities ... Each poverty line should reflect the cost of purchasing commodities containing relevant characteristics ... that enable individuals to achieve the desired ends ... Poverty lines defined in this way would have a common meaning across space and time, offering a consistent framework for identifying the poor. As a result, they would permit meaningful and consistent inter-country comparison and aggregation. The proposed procedure focuses not on whether the incomes of poor people are sufficient in relation to an abstract IPL but rather on whether they are sufficient to achieve a set of elementary requirements.
>
> (ibid., 46–47)

Such an approach to assessing poverty and counting the poor is, indeed, a human-rights (as capabilities) based approach.

In the year 2000, at the Millennium Summit of the United Nations, a declaration setting out goals for the nations of the world to achieve by 2015 elaborated on several areas of human existence that called for international conscription.[10] One of these was formulated as a general goal whose heading was "development and poverty eradication,"[11] spelling out elements of governance, resources, special needs of underdeveloped countries, national debt, etc., which established the tight connection between poverty and its "cure" – development. Obviously, such a family of goals had need of different types of estimates: how bad poverty had been in earlier times, where it stood at the date of this formulation, and how it would develop, negatively or positively, in the future. Exhibiting an almost childish trust in our ability to quantify, measure, and temporally compare the extent of poverty, the United Nations went on to say that "[w]e resolve further ... to halve, by the year 2015, the proportion of the world's people whose income is less than one dollar a day and the proportion of people who suffer from hunger ..." (UN Millennium Declaration, 2000).

So there is now the assessment of the *trends* in world poverty that we must ascertain if we are to say that we have eradicated poverty or are, at the very least, on a sure path to doing so. Unsurprisingly, it continues to be the World Bank that supplies the data according to which it then claims that poverty has in fact decreased mightily in the last few decades (sometimes referring to the period between 1990 and today, sometimes to the 15 years since the 2000 Declaration). Again, and without going into intricate mathematical equations and calculations, we need to decipher how it is that we calculate proportions and ratios such as, for example, "halving" poverty. When we attempt to show that we have halved the world's poor populations, are we saying that the absolute number of poor people has declined by exactly half? Or are we dealing with the percentage of poor people out of the entire population of the world? Clearly, the proportion of the poor on earth may decrease even while their absolute numbers increase (since the world population has also increased) – and we might still be faced with grotesque numbers (millions) of poor people who are undernourished, irrevocably ill, lack housing, or suffer any number of the motley plagues of poverty.

The point of intentionally playing with numbers in order to present a desired end is made by Thomas Pogge in several of his writings. A striking example consists of showing that not only do the World Bank's reports at different times seem to change using identical data,[12] but that the bank, the Committee on World Food Security (CFS), and the Food and Agriculture Organization of the United Nations (FAO, reporting on the state of undernourishment around the world) put effort into aligning all of their numbers so as to present a coherent and consistent view of their predicted world trends. Indeed, in one case, while working over their reports, these groups changed the mathematical methods they employed for certain measurements just before the final dates of the Millennium Development Goals (MDG), leading

> not to minor changes but to a dramatic reversal in the reported trend data … [converting] a 9% increase in the number of undernourished people into a 13% decrease and thereby [bringing] the FAO's reporting into closer alignment with the World Bank's.
>
> (Pogge, 2016, 7)

Somewhat more dramatic were two outstanding pieces of information promulgated by the World Bank in 2015 at the end of the stated period for the MDGs. In one, the president of the Bank, Jim Yong Kim, announced that the percentage of people living in the world who can be labeled "poor" was down to 9.6%, that is, less than 10%. Just as ceremoniously, the bank also changed its IPL, the International Poverty Line, from $1.25 (to which it had risen from $1 in 2008) to $1.90, that is, almost $2. This rise was explained, as before, by calculations of PPPs and other familiar steps, but mostly by the increase in prices around the world in the previous decade. As before, however, the questions at issue continue to engage with what it is that is being measured. Can $1.90 today buy – all comparisons being taken into consideration – what $1 bought in 2000? Who is doing the buying? What are their needs? What do they require for a decent level of nourishment, education, health? Despite the myriad of impressive calculations, as long as questions about the needs and requirements that must be met so as to provide the capabilities for a decent human life remain elusive, the criticism that revolves around the World Bank's methodology regarding the poor will not abate.

Freedom from Poverty as a Fundamental Human Right

Measurement of poverty is complex and is not exclusively a function of a household's income or its levels of consumption. Verily, since individuals in a household may be distinctly different, providing the resources to satisfy a person's rather than a household's needs in achieving their capability for all aspects of a sustainable life is dependent on factors far more complex than only monetary income. And a sustainable life is to be understood as a meaningful life in all of its aspects, be they straightforwardly economic, or social and cultural, or a matter of civil engagement, participation, or political entitlements.

In philosophical terms, the definitions of rights we have encountered cater to an understanding of how poverty indeed impacts economic-social-cultural rights, on the one hand, and civil-political rights on the other. We have also seen that poverty can be attributed both to individuals and to states, thus answering to the very insistent, liberal idea of human rights as the rights of an individual in and against his state, and the subsequent (Rawls-inspired, but more stringent than Rawls's) idea of the rights of some states facing other states. And we can also mention the determination, by the UN Office of the High Commissioner for Human Rights, that the human rights we recognize as fundamental entitlements can only be acknowledged and understood holistically; in other words, human rights are neither each posited to stand on its own, nor are they easily categorized into distinct groups. Even when they are so pigeonholed, both their justification and their applicability are, nevertheless, a function of their ultimate inter-relatedness.[13] So the right or group of rights that we may call "freedom from poverty" is, thence, instructive. In fact, there is no mention of poverty, *per se*, in the Universal "Bill of Rights" (that is, the UDHR, the ICCPR, and the ICESCR). Although we encounter the explicit mention of food, clothing, housing, medical care, social services, and education, there is no general reference to freedom from poverty as a human right. Still, the UN has long recognized the problem of poverty *as a human rights problem* and has articulated it as such.

> [P]overty may be defined as a human condition characterized by sustained or chronic deprivation of the resources, capabilities, choices,

security and power necessary for the enjoyment of an adequate standard of living and other civil, cultural, economic, political and social rights. While acknowledging that there is no universally accepted definition, the Committee [on Economic, Social and Cultural Rights] endorses this multi-dimensional understanding of poverty, which reflects the indivisible and interdependent nature of all human rights.[14]

The UN's Millennium Development Goals (MDGs), spelled out in 2000 (UN General Assembly, Millennium Declaration 2000) and obligating all members of the UN to strive for them until 2015, and the subsequent Sustainable Development Goals (SDGs), enumerated in 2015 targeting the year 2030 (UN General Assembly, Agenda for Sustainable Development 2015), are a manifestation of the new catchword, "development," that has in a sense replaced previous grand ambitions – such as peace or democracy – of the international community. In both idealistic lists of objectives, the eradication of poverty appears as the first (of eight in the MDGs and of 17 in the SDGs) explicit aim. In both lists, several additional targets relate to phenomena that we automatically identify as directly implicated in poverty: hunger, health, education, sanitation, work, environmental factors, and the like. Development is conceived as either a means or a parallel goal to the goals of poverty elimination; the two are intimately connected. Resolving to "create an environment – at the national and global levels alike – which is conducive to development and to the elimination of poverty," the MDG Declaration of 2000 talked about finance and resource mobilization which would require international institutions and, in particular, the developed countries to adopt substantive steps of debt relief, duty- and quota-free access for exports, development assistance and the like, with a view to ending poverty. Interestingly, development is not thought to be a replacement for that other catchphrase, "human rights." On the contrary: development, and poverty as its contrarian mainstay, can only be truly comprehended and conjointly dealt with in a conceptual or practical human rights framework.

The explicit inventory of requisites in the UDHR that made up the human right to an adequate standard of life began with "food." It is a direct implication of that enumeration that hunger and undernourishment are, in some palpable way, almost synonymous with poverty as violations of human rights.[15] "To banish severe poverty and hunger from this planet, we need to recognize them as massive human rights violations that we must stop at once" (Pogge, 2016, 19). This conceptual positioning of hunger alongside poverty is easily seen as a gesture towards that keynote of human rights – dignity. Indeed, the most obvious tie between poverty and human rights lies in that original, definitional attempt to conjoin human rights with dignity. It remains to us only to emphasize that freedom from poverty can be most straightforwardly seen to implicate human dignity, since life in the throes of scarcity is precariously undignified. Yes, we have been seduced to accept – mostly in literary works by the likes of Charles Dickens and Victor Hugo, by fairy tales and religious parables – that respect and dignity are not a function of one's material situation, but rather of some amorphous inner self-respect. But in the here and now of legal, political, economic, and cultural conditions that pertain to human rights, we must recognize that poverty is very nearly a definitive context of lack of dignity. It bespeaks "the critical vulnerability and subjective daily assaults on human dignity" that cannot be seen as anything other than a "comprehensive assault on human rights."[16]

Notes

1 Multidimensional poverty relates to aspects and factors of poverty that go beyond the income-based approach to poverty, which ruled the global (e.g., UN or World Bank) discussion previously.
2 These data are culled from several UN reports between 2015–2018: *United Nations Development Programme – Human Development Reports* (http://hdr. undp.org/en/global-reports), *UNICEF and WHO – Progress on Drinking Water, Sanitation and Hygiene: 2017 Update and SDG Baselines* (www.unicef.org/p ublications/index_96611.html), *UNICEF – One is too many: Ending child deaths from pneumonia and diarrhoea* (www.unicef.org/publications/index_93020.html).
3 For a philosophical rendering of the questions on responsibility to help those in need, see Tomalty (2017).
4 *The Law of Peoples*, published in 1999, was published in 1993 as an article (Rawls, 1993), and joined with another essay for the later publication as a book (Rawls, 1999).
5 Our rendition of the aspects of *The Law of Peoples* that are relevant to human rights and poverty are based on Pogge's reading (Pogge, 1994) of Rawls's (1993) article.
6 The question of the consequences of such "putting at odds," and in particular the topic of our intervention in other societies where human rights are egregiously violated, will be dealt with in Chapter 11.
7 Recall Chapter 1 and Chapter 3, where equality and freedom were counter-posed and joined together in the discussion of the liberal basis of human rights.
8 Interestingly, there was also criticism of the World Bank's *inflation* of the numbers of the poor. We are focusing here, however, on the counter-position, which asserts that the Bank was intentionally minimizing the problem.
9 See Chapter 6.
10 UN General Assembly, United Nations Millennium Declaration 2000.
11 Some others were: to achieve universal primary education, to promote gender equality and empower women, to reduce child and maternal mortality, to combat HIV/AIDS, malaria and other diseases, to ensure environmental sustainability, to develop a global partnership for development, to promote democracy and the rule of law, and on and on. Needless to say, many of these goals have a direct bearing on, and are directly impacted by, poverty.
12 For a humbling rendition of how the World Bank, the FAO (Food and Agriculture Organization of the United Nations), and other international organizations misuse mathematical and statistical date, see especially Pogge, "Fighting Global Poverty" (2017).
13 See, especially, UN Office of the High Commissioner for Human Rights, "What are Human Rights?" (n.d.).

14 United Nations Committee on Economic, Social and Cultural Rights, *Statement on Poverty and the ICESCR* (2001, para 8).
15 In Chapter 11, dealing with international crimes (rather than violations of human rights), we will see the related issue of willful, intentional starvation.
16 UN Office of the High Commissioner for Human Rights, "Human Rights Dimension of Poverty," (n.d.).

11 Security, Sovereignty, and Humanitarian Intervention

From Personal Security to National Security

"Everyone has the right to life, liberty and security of person." Thus we meet "security of person" as a human right in the Universal Declaration of Human Rights, in Article 3, which is – after Articles 1 and 2 that give us the lay of the land with axioms for all human rights – the first article elaborating specific human rights. Where Locke taught us that our *basic* rights consist of life, liberty, and property,[1] and the American Declaration of Independence pointed to the inalienable rights to "Life, Liberty and the pursuit of Happiness" (1776), it is already in the French Declaration of the Rights of Man and Citizen (1789) that we encounter security as one of "the natural and imprescriptible rights of man ... liberty, property, security and resistance to oppression."

The personal security of a human being is a right that must be secured by the state. In fact, starting from the libertarian position that sees the state's legitimacy as deriving from the need for individuals' security that it satisfies, and moving to the state-oriented views of the goals and objectives of communities that create governments, security has always been recognized as a paramount interest of the citizen of a state, for which the state is responsible. More so, if the state is constituted by its obligation to protect the security of its citizens, then the token of "state security" might be no more, but no less, than the amalgamation of a myriad of individual, personal securities. If we then restrict security to the same level as other human rights that the state must respect and protect, we arrive at the well-travelled terrain of conflicting rights or prioritization of some rights over others. Protecting its citizens' human right to security, the state might well use that claim to human rights as justification for its violation of other human rights, perhaps of other human beings. However, as we have previously seen (Chapter 3), in the elaboration of human rights some rights have been branded more "absolute" than others. Thus, in the International Covenant on Civil and Political Rights (ICCPR) we witness the admonition to never derogate from a very particular set of human rights – not even in the situation described as a "public emergency which threatens the life of the nation"

(ICCPR, Article 4). The human right to life or the right to never endure torture or slavery, among others, are absolute in the sense that extreme circumstances of public emergencies cannot be used as a reason for their annulment, even if it be temporary. Not only does the right to personal security not seem to play a similar, absolute role, but its amalgamation into public security appears to explicitly place it second to those specific, unimpeachable individual human rights of the ICCPR.

Still, we cannot avoid the unique value constantly given to state security in the context of the human rights of individuals. When considering the more mundane meaning of "state security," indeed, even when viewing state security as a mass incorporation of individual personal securities, this construct does affect our appraisal of human rights, making them seemingly contingent on it. Freedom of movement, the right to exit a country, rights to asylum, open courtrooms, freedom of expression, the right to peaceful assembly, and freedom of association – dealing with all these human rights, the ICCPR fixes restrictions that are due to "the interests of national security" (ICCPR, Articles 12, 13, 14, 19, 21, and 22). There is conceptual convolution here: individual personal security – a basic human right – when grouped to become state or national security, ceases to function as just another human right and enters a distinct arena of considerations. Different from the other human rights which were labeled absolute and not-to-be-derogated from, personal security, now morphed into national security, becomes an opponent of human rights. In ordinary, popular parlance, security is not a human right; instead, it spars with human rights.

The Dilemma of Security vs. Human Rights

Ask the person on the street – about security and human rights – and, with a high degree of probability, the reply will be familiar:

> Of course there is a dilemma. The more we worry and deal with security, the less attendant are we to human rights; and the more we protect human rights the less will we be able to guarantee a reasonable level of security.

The two terms, "security" and "human rights," have become comingled and habitually juxtaposed in political science and politics, in security studies and the military, in legal thought and the courts. This is a descriptive assessment that is validated simply by the enormous number of their co-mentions encountered in current (political, security, and legal) discourse. A few representative – albeit almost haphazard – exemplars usually suffice in order to highlight the ubiquity of this consensus. Ironically predictable, for example, is the U.S. State Department's reference to the initiative of "Voluntary Principles on Security and Human Rights," drawn up on the occasion of cooperation between government agencies, companies, and NGOs, and purporting to (be able to) explicitly formulate the challenges faced by all of these when addressing the "safety and security of [the companies'] operations" (US Department of State, 2000). The opening presentation of the motivation for such cooperation is worded with guileless simplicity:

> Acknowledging that security is a fundamental need, shared by individuals, communities, businesses, and governments alike, and acknowledging the difficult security issues faced by Companies operating globally, we recognize that security and respect for human rights can and should be consistent.
>
> (ibid.)

The presumption motivating such formulations appears to be a mutual, common interest in putting to work a cooperative synthesis between security and human rights. The perspective of governments (and, of course, companies) is, however, skewed in favor of security, putting human rights in the position of a factor to be considered while safety and security are the natural priority.

The almost-diametrically opposed position at the other side of the divide – between governments and companies touting security, on the one hand, and human rights organizations expounding the preference for human rights considerations on the other – is also populated by countless bodies and manifestos. Here the presupposition of the possibility of human rights and security co-existing is sometimes literally questioned, pitting the individual's human rights as something to be balanced *against* the state's security interests. Indeed, several organizations, institutions and movements that are engaged with questions of not only human rights, but the conduct and status of civil society and community, deem it necessary to explicitly address the question of security vs. human rights. Often noted, in fact, is the ongoing panic, resulting from irrational fear, that has given rise to the assumed binary divide between security and human rights and its detrimental effects. A turn to rational discourse is often called upon to help us realize that it is violations of human rights that beget terrorism and that protection of human rights is beneficial for security itself. Countless statements published by Human Rights Watch, People's Union for Civil Liberties, the American Civil Liberties Union, and others, address these problematics.

More scholarly, but no less predictable, are the innumerable books and articles dealing with the pair of security and human rights. Beyond the explicit recognition of the familiar tension (such as the explicitly titled *Security and Human Rights* (Goold and Lazarus, 2007) or *Humanitarian Intervention and the Responsibility to Protect: Security and Human Rights* (Badescu, 2010)[2]), other books, even while speaking of security *or* human rights, exhibit that same awareness by (almost routinely) presenting the other part of the duo as an oppositional factor. An illustrative instance can be found in the book *Arab-Israeli Military Forces in an Era of Asymmetric Wars*

(Cordesman, 2008), where, amidst chapters dealing with military resources, army forces, capital, air-prowess, ground tactics, terrorism, counter-terrorism and so on, one comes upon a sub-chapter entitled "Internal Security vs. Human Rights and Political Impact." Similarly localized, expounding on one country's national security is *Strategic US Foreign Assistance: The Battle Between Human Rights and National Security* (Callaway and Matthews, 2008). Also, one cannot but be struck by the innumerable titles of dissertations submitted on the subject, such as the following, representative list at the Human Rights Centre at the University of Essex: "Does the nature and scale of threat posed by Islamist terrorism to liberal Western states sufficiently legitimize a reformulation of the relationship between liberty, security and risk?"; "What limitations does international human rights law put on the creation of criminal offences that are meant to fight 'terrorism'?"; "The private security company (PSC) based in the United Kingdom and human rights: Is the PSC capable of promoting human rights?"; "State of Emergency and Human Rights: The War on Terror in the UK"; "Counter-terrorism Measures Post 9/11; Security requirements or Human Rights Sacrificed? An Analysis of the Interface of Security Concerns and Immigration Law Adjustments"; "By Any Means Necessary? Human Rights, Regime Change and the Use of Force."

Accordingly, it is warranted to assert that there is a "security vs. human rights" dilemma with us today. In the terms of ordinary-language philosophy, this is corroborated as a "real" dilemma, having been made one in regular parlance and common practice. We are all constantly inundated by the conversation going on in the public arena, positing a conflict between security and human rights, presenting it as an unbridgeable impasse, or, more often than not, insisting on the moral, political, or legal priority of security. What is, then, the case for human rights?

Dilemma or Pseudo-Dilemma?

To reiterate: Since the advent of modernity and the concept of the modern state bequeathed us by Thomas Hobbes and John Locke, we have been well aware of the idea of the state-as-providing-security, from its most libertarian excesses which reduce it to this goal alone, via the classical liberal, contractarian construct which recognizes security as the main or first motivation for state-building, to more communitarian viewpoints which minimize that aspect of the state to one statist objective among others. The equally fundamental idea of rights in most liberal viewpoints then provides the scaffolding for the state framework, but, just as surely, problematizes the state's obligation and ability to provide the bulwark of security. Dynamic discussion of this predicament is rampant in political philosophy; its relevance to real politics is part of our question when we focus on human rights.

The philosophical analysis with which we can now engage is straightforwardly analytic, maintaining that security and human rights are not born of comparable conceptual categories and therefore cannot be posited in the "X as Y," "X or Y," or "X vs. Y" rubric. But this preliminary step in analysis does not release us from investigation of their differences. Security, on the one hand, and human rights, on the other, must be placed in their respective domains of discourse if we are to uphold a categorical distinction fruitfully. In other words, in order to explore the possibility of dilemma, we must examine the supposition that the two constructs are on equal grounds for entertaining that possibility.

Perhaps they are not. Human rights, it could be said, inhabit the moral arena; the question of their foundations, their justification, their significance, their range, and their applicability is rooted in the realms of ethics and moral theory. Security, on the other hand, lives in the very professional field of military (or police) theory and action. Security – that is to say, its analysis, construction and investigation – is a vibrant and heavily funded, richly populated, and highly valued subject of study, research, and activity concerning concrete methods and tools in the day-to-day management of our private and public life. Although suspiciously superficial, this first try at contextual categorization places the construct of human rights – the very idea – "high" in the academic discipline of philosophy (or political thought), while positioning security – with far less thought to the *idea* of security – "low" on the ladder, engaging us in the milieu of "real life." But this threatens to be, at best, sophistic and, at worst, question-begging, since we are looking to philosophy itself to inform real life (with no scare-quotes). So let us leave behind sophism and question-begging, and take the risk of sliding into complexities. Let us attend to two settings where security and human rights are seen to merit mutual and common examination: the legal and the political arenas. Both house complex, sometimes even convoluted, approaches precisely by their joining and disjoining of human rights and security.

Human rights are a well-defined term under the purview of international law. It is in both legal theory and legal practice that human rights get a hearing: International human rights law, made up of treaties and conventions that are acknowledged by the global community and, not always but more often than not, ratified by local jurisdictions, is also the basis upon which human rights organizations center their activity. After establishing institutional bodies and increasing public engagement, we are recently also witness to (mostly international) human rights courts where alleged violators encounter indictment, opinion, and conviction or acquittal, all orchestrated by legal institutions. In other words, human rights have become common actors on the active stage of legal thought and action.

Now, is there a sense in which one can speak of security under an analogous umbrella of law? Here we must ask about conscription of the law, in the shape of legal instruction and injunction, to guard and sustain security itself. And we easily find a plurality of answers in the various security apparatuses that are legally established in local – that is, municipal, regional, provincial, and state – regulations.

Looking at human rights and security through these legal lenses then reveals conceptual complications, since the legal conversation about human rights is grounded in individual rights and international law while the parallel legal turn to security is built upon the vertices of individual or state security and national interest. Attempting a shared discussion requires a high-powered conceptual-legal exercise, linking national interests with international law without letting go of the individual (that is, their needs and rights). This is not impossible or even unfeasible; but it is a complicated exercise nevertheless. It is what human rights lawyers do; it is also what state and government lawyers do. Together they perpetuate the problematics of the juxtaposition and the assumption that there is real rivalry here.

Understandably, it is in the fiery arena of real-life politics that human rights and security have been lined up together precisely in order to place them in contrary positions. It is there, in the realm of politics along with its unique political discourse, that talk of security and human rights is manipulated in such a way as to implant, in the ears of (perhaps non-reflective) listeners, an apparent dilemma between the two, bestowing it with the aura of a real dilemma. For it is in the mouths of political advocates, always on the lookout for personal, partisan, or national interests, that this duo has been used and abused. Used – in the straightforward (but as will shortly be illustrated, sometimes malign) agendas for which security is the be-all and end-all of feats that must somehow be explained and justified when it is recognized as violating human rights. Abused – in rhetorical mode, when such politicians aspire to be seen as putting human rights at the apex of their objectives.

We shall, in a moment, illustrate this conundrum with a case study, showing how the security-human rights clash is brought into play by powers that be in their own interests. But we first ask the more universal question: Can a generalization be made – referring to cases and issues in several locations around the globe in which security and human rights appear to be at loggerheads – that identifies a common behavior exhibited by authorities that use and abuse the security-human rights duo in the service of political interests? Before making such a sweeping accusatory claim, we must still contemplate an analysis that can do justice to contemporary world-dealings around security and human rights. It is the philosophical concern about the relationship between security and human rights that sets it up as either a theoretically grounded dilemma or an analytically exposed pseudo-dilemma. The real-life problem, though, is posed to practitioners of politics, law, human rights and security: which should we prioritize, security or human rights? As a real political problem it may therefore constitute a real dilemma. That predicament, however, has been appropriated by the "security panic" of the current, predominant political conversation. It is, in fact, the rhetorical-political use of this duo by dealers in panic that returns it – and us – to a pseudo-dilemma: the very explicit pair, security and human rights, is now being presented as a dilemma by actors who are manipulating the question itself for their own benefit. When performed in the interests of security, even against human rights, such uses merit a serious confrontation – both theoretical and practical. When perpetrated with other pernicious ambitions in mind, these uses must be seen as abuses and the dilemma they advertise must be exposed as a pseudo-dilemma. Is there a functional, well-based criterion for distinguishing between the two? We cannot offer a solution for this challenge, except to recommend and even advocate for absolute support of human rights as the only guard against use, misuse and abuse of such pseudo-dilemmas. Less dogmatically, an even more convincing relationship between security and human rights can be found in the statement made in 2003 by the UN High Commissioner for Human Rights, Bertrand Ramcharan: "... human rights define human security ... you cannot have security without the protection of human rights."[3]

A Case Study: The Security Wall

The substance of this investigation is ably illustrated by a chronicle of a case study and an attendant argument that arise from the "real world" – not in philosophy but rather in human rights practice. It will shortly be utilized to ground the thesis being suggested here: The security-human rights puzzle is a philosophical dilemma that has become – in a way not usually adumbrated – a political problem *cum* pseudo-dilemma.

We have insinuated that talk of human rights and security is manipulated; more explicitly, the security-human rights dilemma is a case of rhetoric in the service of politics. An iconographic exemplar of such exploitation is the "Wall" being built in Israel-Palestine for several years now by Israeli authorities. Note, first, its name: sometimes it is termed a wall, sometimes a fence, sometimes a barrier; sometimes its modifier speaks of separation, sometimes of security. So one sometimes encounters mention of the "Separation Barrier," at other times of the "Security Wall," at still other times simply of the "Fence."[4] The ostensible and ubiquitously formulated reason for the Wall, from its initiation to the ongoing and current debate about it, is "Security." The Wall, we are told, is there, is needed, has proven its mettle, and will continue to be built until completed because it can and will provide the security that Israelis need against Palestinian terrorist threats. Note the obvious argument: The Wall plays a role in the security that the state provides in order to satisfy the human right to personal security of its citizens. This is what Israeli citizens are told by state authorities, and this is what one hears as consensual agreement in the media, on the street, in academia, in the courts, in the military, in Israel and abroad. That the Wall also violates human rights – Palestinian human rights – is usually shrugged off as the price one must pay for security. The zero-sum game of security and human rights is perfectly managed and propagated by all actors in the political game and on the political stage.

Witness, however, the work done by *B'Tselem* – the Israeli Information Center for Human Rights in the Occupied Territories. As a human rights organization committed to detailed and trustworthy data amassment, it has monitored, documented and written about the construction of the Wall since its inception in 2002, as a possible, and then actual, infringement of human rights. In December 2005, *B'Tselem* put out a report called "Under the Guise of Security: Routing the Separation Barrier to Enable the Expansion of Israeli Settlements in the West Bank" (*B'Tselem*, 2005). In the vein of standard human rights reports, this one outlines the details of human rights violations that are triggered by the Wall: violation of freedom of movement; impairment of the ability to earn a living; infringement of health, education, family and social ties; and impingement of the right of property, among others.[5] Perusing this list of breaches of International Human Rights Law, one might conclude that this is, in fact, a case in point of the dilemma between security and human rights. Indeed, one might be brought to think that security and human rights, in the context of the Israeli control over occupied Palestinian territories, must be posited contra each other and someone – the military authorities, the legal authorities, the bureaucratic authorities, perhaps outside forces, maybe even international courts – must balance and weigh the contraposition in order to make, explain and justify a resultant decision on one side or the other. The Wall, its construction, and location, one may finally claim, all reflect such a decision – prioritizing security.

But now the rub! *B'Tselem*'s thorough report of 2005 did not merely expose the price of human rights violations exacted for the cause of security. It went on to claim, and to ground the claim with evidence and argument, that the use of the term "security," that is, the turn to security as the *raison d'être* for the Wall, was a rhetorical political ruse. The allegation postulated by the human rights organization was that security's role here was that of a mask, behind which other interests lay – tangible interests that have nothing to do with security (be they legitimate national interests, or not).

> The barrier's penetration into the West Bank is the root cause of barrier-related human rights violations. How does Israel justify the deviation of the barrier's routes from the Green Line [the internationally recognized Israeli border]? In particular, what does Israel contend is the connection between the barrier and the settlements? To what degree do the state's reasons and explanations reflect the real reasons for the barrier's route?
>
> (*B'Tselem*, 2005, 9)

These questions guide the organization's investigation into the actual considerations determining the route that the Wall takes. A comparative analysis is afforded of the official version usually presented in public and always based on "security" considerations, as opposed to settlement considerations, that is to say, ideology, expansion and real estate. The latter win out. *B'Tselem*'s report concludes:

It goes without saying that, because many sections of the barrier's route were not based on security considerations – not even according to Israel's definition of the term – but on the settlements' expansion plans, the argument that human rights violations resulting from the route chosen are proportionate automatically collapses. Had settlement expansion not played a role in dictating the route, Israel would have been able to achieve its purported principal security objectives (preventing the infiltration of terrorists into Israel and protection of the settlers) without causing nearly as much harm as the chosen route has caused.

(ibid., 18)

It is interesting to note that, although *B'Tselem*, like most human rights organizations, usually maintains its apolitical status, preferring to focus on the legal aspect of its discussions, the political – and more so, the rhetorical – agendas related to the Wall had become so overpowering that this report, surprisingly and unambiguously, could not but express its misgivings concerning these political trickeries. Assessing that "Israel's public-relations efforts regarding the barrier have improved," the penultimate words of the report still adamantly insist that "central aspects of the planning and construction of the barrier" are a case of the government trying to "mislead the public" (ibid., 81).

Torture

One of the topics that plays a grand role in discussions of security vs. human rights is torture. We are all apprised of and well-versed in the tales and arguments regarding torture, rendition, surveillance, drone-warfare, and other tools and accoutrements of security that clearly involve violations of human rights. These have been documented and dissected ably and professionally by the relevant qualified experts, be they from the legal profession or the security establishment. In some cases, concerning some human rights issues, we cannot but venture into very realistic quagmires that involve the purveyors of security in moral and legal debates. Nowhere is this more obvious than in the case of torture.

Recall the prohibition on torture. The UDHR brings it up early, following only the fundamental rights of life, liberty, security of person and the just as fundamental veto against slavery. In Article 5 we read: "No one shall be subjected to torture or to cruel, inhuman or degrading treatment or punishment." And this is repeated, word for word, in Article 7 of the International Covenant on Civil and Political Rights. Importantly, though, in the ICCPR, there is an additional feature of the human right to be free from torture: it is absolute. In other words, according to Article 4 in the ICCPR, no derogation from Article 7 is allowed, not even in a time of "public emergency." It seems that torture, or more explicitly the right to be free of torture anywhere, anytime, and in any circumstances, should not be open to any deliberations. That right, according to the ICCPR, cannot be subject to any negotiations in regard to other rights, in any extenuating circumstances, or for any exceptional reasons. How has torture become, nonetheless, an object of debate? And how is it that torture is debated in the context of human rights, precisely where it had seemed to attain an unqualified veto?

Before we can examine its twists and turns, we are called on, first, to know what torture is. There are several "definitions" on hand, along with substantive accounts of its workings and descriptions of what it is, focusing on its essential aspects. A detailed formal and legal characterization is found in the UN Convention against Torture (1984), where torture is:

> any act by which severe pain or suffering, whether physical or mental, is intentionally inflicted on a person for such purposes as obtaining from him or a third person information or a confession, punishing him for an act he or a third person has committed or is suspected of having committed, or intimidating or coercing him or a third person, or for any reason based on discrimination of any kind, when such pain or suffering is inflicted by or at the instigation of or with the consent or acquiescence of a public official or other person acting in an official capacity.

Legally more succinct is the Tokyo Declaration (1975), addressed to physicians, where torture is:

> the deliberate, systematic or wanton infliction of physical or mental suffering by one or more persons acting alone or on the orders of any authority, to force another person to yield information, to make a confession, or for any other reason.

Other renditions (chronologically ordered) posit torture as:

1 "the systematic and deliberate infliction of acute pain in any form by one person on another" (Paskins, 1976, 138).
2 "the deliberate infliction of pain in order to destroy the victim's normative world and capacity to create shared realities" (Cover, 1986, 1602).
3 "any act by which severe pain or suffering, whether physical or mental, is intentionally inflicted on a person for such purposes as obtaining from that person or a third person information or confession, punishing that person for an act committed or suspected to have been committed, or intimidating or dehumanizing that person or other persons" (Tindale, 1996, 355).
4 "a crime of specific intent: It involves the use of pain deliberately and specifically to *break the will* of the subject" (Waldron, 2005, 1703).

These articulations and others all point to torture as involving an act inflicting severe pain or suffering (physical and/or mental), unambiguous intent, an overt purpose, and, in some definitions, though not all, the involvement of an official who is related to the seats of power. In the context of human rights that last aspect is clearly pivotal, since there the individual's relationship with the state is definitional of human rights as well.

How, then, can freedom from torture, even if variously defined, have attained the status of a debated human right? Looking for a pertinently contextual explanation, some see the advent of the heated engagement with torture as coming on the heels of the "war on terror" that began after 9/11. That may be a convenient explanation for the popularization of the debate, which certainly became an integral part of the daily media conversation in those years. However, the interrogation of the "absoluteness" of the injunction against torture, wondering if there are or could be any exceptions to this categorical ban, has long been present in both legal and philosophical questioning. As Bob Brecher (2007) relates,[6] there is a sizable number of thinkers who have toyed with scenarios that might make torture not only necessary but even reasonable. One well-known champion of this possibility is, of course, the illustrious attorney Alan Dershowitz, whose position regarding the legalization of torture is infamous; others are Jean Elshtain (2004), Martha Nussbaum,[7] and even human rights champion, Henry Shue (1978). All of them claim to abhor the idea of torture; but all admit that there are feasible exceptions to the rule of prohibition. Famously, the thought experiment that sums up their arguments is *the ticking bomb scenario*.

Very similar to the famous trolley problem – where one is asked to choose between two morally painful options – the ticking bomb scenario presents an imagined situation which is perceived as presenting a moral quandary. In (one version of) the trolley story, we either let a runaway train continue on its path and kill a number of people who are tied to the tracks, or pull a lever and divert the train to another track where "only" one person is lying immovably. The question posed is, quite clearly, a question of ethics that is graphically illustrated by the trolley story.[8] Correspondingly, the ticking bomb scenario imagines, in various configurations, a terrorist who knows the place of a bomb that is slated to explode at a given time. Here the question is whether it is morally justified to torture the terrorist in order to obtain information about the location of the bomb, saving tens, hundreds, thousands, or even millions of people. Again, this is touted as a moral dilemma.

How can we secure the absolute renunciation of torture, as it is presented in human rights vocabulary, given such a set of circumstances? It is not surprising that most people, when asked about the ticking bomb scenario and exceptions to the rule, reply in the affirmative: yes, there are some situations in which it would be moral and legitimate to torture. Thoughtful counter-arguments, held by those who insist that torture is non-negotiable, sometimes turn to descriptive skepticism about the imagined situation. It is not reasonable, they say, to believe that we could or would know what a terrorist knows (or doesn't know) in most circumstances. In other circumstances, if there is some time to spare before the imagined bomb's explosion, why not use that time to evacuate people, secure the area, or prepare preventive measures, rather than torture someone who might, but also might not, know what he is claiming to know. Furthermore, given the training that terrorists receive and, more so, given the ideological fanaticism of many terrorists, what reason do we have to believe that torture will always work? These down-to-earth appraisals of the ticking bomb scenario simply cast doubt on the supposed givens of the imagined state of affairs.

A different fact-based argument is expressed by Dershowitz and other "realists." Given that torture does invariably happen and knowing that it is commonly used by governments and security forces, our moral position against it should be buttressed by legal directives that qualify it. In other words, the acknowledgment that torture is here to stay is at the center of an argument that permits its happening – even if only in exceptional situations – but calls for its official, legal control.

Notwithstanding these positions on the practice of torture that are predicated on "facts," most damaging to their assumed veracity is the artless awareness that, as most security experts know, there has never been a real ticking bomb situation. "Realists pay surprisingly little attention to reality," quips Michael Davis (2005, 170). The ticking bomb scenario is really a *scenario*, merely a thought experiment – thought up by those who are willing to accept the imaginable option of torture, or even relish the prospect.

Beyond the pseudo-factual dispute concerning the applicability of the ticking bomb scenario, there loom other substantial hardships for the idea of torture. First, we must be able to encircle the types of pain and suffering that can earn the epithet of torture. Is tearing off a suspect's nails torture? Is sleep deprivation? Is water-boarding? Is there a continuum of pain, from lesser to intolerable, upon which we can draw the line that borders off torturous pain? What would be outside that line? These psychological, medical, and even conceptual questions make the definition of torture, which is to be used in our moral and legal decision-making regarding its practice, hardly applicable universally. Just as profound, and perhaps even more philosophically knotty, is the problem of regularization. If we are to regulate the use of torture by defining the exception to the rule (of its prohibition), we run the risk of making exceptions all too regular. The point here is not only quantitative – so many more instances of torture will now become acceptable – but downright essential: the exception has become a rule. Many other critiques of both the idea and the exercise of torture address the distinction between physical and mental torture, the fit (or mis-fit) between its moral and legal status, and the jeopardy we put ourselves into by even permitting it to be debated. Taking this final step, we realize that the legitimacy of torture is made respectable by our discussion itself. "Even to raise the issue … is to give publicity to what is so abhorrent as to be beyond discussion" (Brecher, 2007, 2).

Let us return, again, to that axis of human rights that has not yet made an appearance in our analysis of torture: dignity. In evaluating and adjudicating the impermissibility of torture as a blatant violation of human rights, it is the death (of others, or of many others) that is considered on balance with torture (of, for example, a terrorist). We have, in fact, been tempted into placing torture at the penultimate end of a continuum that runs from weak (physical or mental) pain, to moderate pain, to strong pain, to intolerable pain, to death. But what if this continuum itself is also fabricated? What if torture, that is, intolerable pain, is worse than death? Or what if torture is not on a spectrum predicated on pain, but is nevertheless intolerable? To substantiate this insight – that torture causes a greater devastation of human life than even death itself – we turn (with Brecher) to the story of Jean Améry (1980). Améry, who was a prisoner in Nazi concentration camps (Auschwitz, Buchenwald, and Bergen-Belsen), reported on the torture he underwent in unspeakably vivid terms. He described in detail physical and mental pain that cannot ever be forgotten or overcome. But beyond the reports and the descriptions, there is an anguished assessment:

> Whoever has succumbed to torture can no longer feel at home in the world. The shame of destruction cannot be erased. Trust in the world, which already collapsed in part at the first blow, but in the end, under torture, fully, will not be regained.

Torture destroys the dignity of the human being and dignity is definitive of a meaningful human life. In that sense, torture is the greatest imaginable violator of human rights. It is therefore not to be wondered at that Améry, some 30 years after suffering torture, committed suicide.

Sovereignty and Humanitarian Intervention

As we have seen, the issue of security and human rights is a vexed one, pitting individual human rights – of, for example, personal security, freedom from torture, freedom of movement, the right to privacy, and others – against one another and forcing us to query the special status that our security has among these rights. Moving from individual security to state security, we ascertained that the peculiar nature of the idea of national security sometimes tells us to question whether the term "security," when used by the state's authorities, is as straightforward and pristine as rulers and politicians would have us believe. This returns us, full circle, to the original structure of the relationship that abides, in the context of human rights, between the individual, the state (of which he is a citizen, but also in which he might be a visitor, or migrant, or refugee), and the international arena. The human rights of the individual are to be respected and protected by the state; but the violation of those rights by the state can be monitored and adjudicated by the international bodies – the UN and international courts – that are "above" the state system. It is with the issue of security, however, that this clear structure is foiled. Not only might the state be violating the human rights of its citizens; those violations may appear as a direct result of the state's claim to be protecting the citizens whose rights it is impairing. And the state does this while engaging with other states – as in the case of wars and international mayhem – or with other individuals – as in the searing matter of terrorism.

It is appropriate, at this point of our analysis, to engage (again) with the concept of sovereignty. The linchpin of modern political thought is the sovereignty of national groups in the form of states – that is, the self-determination and self-rule of political communities that have been recognized by the international community as worthy of being self-governing and of relating properly to other such communities. This standing of nation-states[9] provides the axiomatic form of current discourse in international relations, most clearly seen in the language, rules, treaties, and workings of the UN.[10] The sovereignty of each state – which is to say, the independence, autonomy, self-government, rights to land, military, self-defense, and rule over its people – is an explicit presupposition of the kind of global system which is accepted by the legal and political structures of twentieth- and twenty-first-century world organization. Indeed, the priority of the idea of sovereignty in the way we think of states, in both their internal and international relations, has been noticed in some of our previous discussions. Recall the puzzle of group rights (Chapter 8): We noted that while liberal thinkers may come up with explanations and excuses for interference when groups' treatment of their members bespeaks a violation of human rights, they are less disposed to do so in the case of foreign states that engage in such behavior. The question of poverty (Chapter 10) supplied us with a similar dilemma. Although Pogge presented us with a creative "solution" to world poverty that involved a type of global control over countries' economic responsibilities, we are painfully aware of how remote that solution is from the conventional perception of state independence regarding domestic economic decisions. And now, leaving the context of state security and moving on to state sovereignty, we are faced with the question: what are the limits of what we allow sovereign states to do in the matter of the human rights of their own inhabitants? Put differently – when may we intervene in the affairs of sovereign states?

Knowing that states may not be sufficiently protective of their inhabitants' human rights, knowing that they may even violate those human rights, it is sometimes up to the foreign policies and actions of other states, alone or in cooperation, to attempt to rectify these situations. We are familiar with different types of "soft" intervention – pressure put upon states through negotiations, public relations campaigns, boycotts, sanctions, divestments – that are the standard playlists of international relations. These moves, taken by sovereign states or groups of states against other sovereign states, may be viewed as literally "interventionist," but they are not abusively problematic for sovereignty. The real clash, between human rights and sovereignty, arises in cases of "hard" intervention, that is to say – military intervention. Often designated as humanitarian military intervention, this presents problems of legality, morality, and – always – politics.

Now, viewing the questions of humanitarian intervention through the lens of conventional "realist" political thought, one can point to realist arguments that stress states' interests and are disdainful of any ethical reasons for intervention. Of course, if intervention can be shown to be beneficial for the intervening state, then it merits a different rationalization that has nothing to do with human rights. Or we can claim, with due honesty and integrity, that humanitarianism itself is a national interest for the state; indeed, we must then also explain, in realistic terms, the value of an international system that is based on humanitarian norms (Smith, 1999). As opposed to the realist, liberal arguments for and against intervention bring us back to the tensions between the universally conceived individual whose rights are being violated, and group self-determination which constitutes the sovereignty of the state violating those rights, both of which were crucial in the founding documents of human rights.[11] Based on this classic liberal tension, we find a gamut of positions from interventionist to non-interventionist extremes, each prioritizing distinct facets of liberal human rights ideas. Thus, there are universal vs. communitarian arguments, there are questions of toleration (between different cultural mores), and there is the difference between unilateral intervention and collective intervention. The liberal is, as usual, conflicted; so the question of humanitarian deeds and its answer are, for the liberal, complex. In general, we observe that unilateral intervention is suspiciously interest-ridden while collective intervention can be more visibly and uniformly justified, especially when it has the basis of formal UN regulation. But the liberal is destined to weigh the scale of evils and priorities, take into consideration the feasibility of success, and rule about each case on its own.[12]

Still, several events of the decades after World War II and, more so, of the end of the twentieth century and turn of the twenty-first century, have altered the discourse and practice of humanitarian intervention. Important signposts are Rwanda, Kosovo, Darfur, Syria, and others. Mass killings, mass starvation, dictatorial abuse, authoritarian mistreatment, systematic torture, and other atrocities have tragically become a mainstay of contemporary politics. Consequently, humanitarian intervention has become a central issue in international relations and world politics. It is interesting that the focus of military intervention has grown to revolve less around archetypal human rights violations than around total, egregious violations. Even more significantly, the international community has recognized in sovereignty not only the state's right to control its affairs autonomously, but also its responsibility to protect its people. These conceptual factors have been instrumental in changing the general view towards the question of legitimacy in humanitarian intervention.

In 2000 the UN Secretary-General, Kofi Annan, posed the challenging question: "If humanitarian intervention is, indeed, an unacceptable assault on sovereignty, how should we respond to a Rwanda, to a Srebrenica – to gross and systematic violations of human rights that offend every precept of our common humanity?"[13] Soon after the posing of the question, the Canadian government gathered the International Commission on Intervention and State Sovereignty (ICISS), which put out the report "The Responsibility to Protect" (2001). In the exposition of its basic principles in the Synopsis, the document includes the following answer to Annan's question:

BASIC PRINCIPLES
  A. State sovereignty implies responsibility, and the primary responsibility for the protection of its people lies with the state itself.
  B. Where a population is suffering serious harm, as a result of internal war, insurgency, repression or state failure, and the state in question is unwilling or unable to halt or avert it, the principle of non-intervention yields to the international responsibility to protect.
                    (ICISS, 2001, "The Responsibility to Protect," XI)

It was in the 2005 World Summit that all the members of the UN General Assembly adopted the norm of Responsibility to Protect (also called R2P), agreeing on the following:

Each individual State has the responsibility to protect its populations from genocide, war crimes, ethnic cleansing and crimes against humanity ... The international community, through the United Nations, also has the responsibility to use appropriate diplomatic, humanitarian and other peaceful means ... to help protect populations ... In this context, we are prepared to take collective action, in a timely and decisive manner, through the Security Council, in accordance with the Charter, including Chapter VII, on a case-by-case basis and in cooperation with relevant regional organizations as appropriate, *should peaceful means be inadequate and national authorities manifestly fail to protect their populations from genocide, war crimes, ethnic cleansing and crimes against humanity.* [my emphasis][14]

There are four points to notice in this espousal of Responsibility to Protect. First, as we have stressed, the state itself has a duty – a responsibility – to protect its inhabitants. Second, the international community has the same responsibility for another state's inhabitants when the state reneges, intentionally or through incapability, on its own duty. Third, international responsibility begins with "peaceful means," but can progress on to other "collective action" – that is to say, humanitarian military intervention. Finally, the reasons for such action are not any run-of-the-mill violation of human rights by a state towards its inhabitants. The violations must be of a certain extreme kind: genocide, war crimes, ethnic cleansing or crimes against humanity.[15]

It is worth noting that the horrendous wrongdoings that count as grounds for humanitarian military intervention are mass atrocities.[16] Except for ethnic cleansing, they have been defined and accepted in international law and all are in common use in legal contexts. *Genocide*, the first to be explicitly defined in the UN Convention on the Prevention and Punishment of the Crime of Genocide in 1948,

> means any of the following acts committed with intent to destroy, in whole or in part, a national, ethnical, racial or religious group, as such: Killing members of the group; Causing serious bodily or mental harm to members of the group; Deliberately inflicting on the group conditions of life calculated to bring about its physical destruction in whole or in part; Imposing measures intended to prevent births within the group; Forcibly transferring children of the group to another group.[17]

War crimes are obviously violations of humanitarian law (the law of armed conflict), that is, of the Hague and Geneva Conventions, but not all violations are war crimes. In fact, there are several locales for lists of war crimes, the most current of which is in the Rome Statute of the International Criminal Court, where war crimes are "grave breaches of the Geneva Conventions … against persons or property protected under the provisions of the relevant Geneva Convention … [and] other serious violations of the laws and customs applicable in international armed conflict."[18] The accompanying list elaborates over 50 acts that are to be persecuted as war crimes, including willful killing, torture or inhuman treatment, extensive destruction, taking of hostages, intentionally directing attacks against the civilian population, and on and on. *Crimes against humanity* have also been variously defined, with the Rome Statute providing the latest consensus. Again, the general attribution is of actions "committed as part of a widespread or systematic attack directed against any civilian population, with knowledge of the attack,"[19] followed by eleven such acts, including murder, extermination, enslavement, torture, rape, sexual slavery, persecution against a group, and apartheid. Finally, *ethnic cleansing*, which has not been clearly accepted in international law as an identifiable crime, receives various related definitions such as "a purposeful policy designed by one ethnic or religious group to remove by violent and terror-inspiring means the civilian population of another ethnic or religious group from certain geographic areas."[20] Unremarkably, it has been suggested that ethnic cleansing can be seen to constitute crimes against humanity, war crimes, or even genocide.[21]

Does Annan's question still stand? Are we to continue to deliberate between a state's autonomy and forceful intervention or, more to the point, between the values of sovereignty and those of human rights? Has the legal-political move to an acceptance of a universal responsibility to protect gained purchase in the perception of human rights and in the policy-making of both independent countries and international bodies? Or is the global nation-state system still predicated on the axiom of states whose autonomy – that is to say, their sovereignty – is their fundamental validation? These queries return us to the original building we constructed, with the liberal idea of individuals owning human rights on the ground level, demanding them from states on the next level, and being looked out for by international authorities on the highest level. A human rights perspective requires the top level, such as UN or non-governmental bodies, to dictate human rights considerations that trump other priorities of the second level, relating to the rights of the individuals on the first level. In the case of humanitarian intervention, that same human rights perspective becomes more explicit and concrete but also more convoluted: States do not only contract with one another in treaties that protect human rights; they can, in extreme cases, collectively negate the autonomous status of other states. But such a strong moral position is still questionable in political contexts and undecided in legal action. While international human rights law and international humanitarian law are made up of legally binding treaties and conventions (along with customary law), the Responsibility to Protect has not yet reached the point of being legally binding. It is still an open question whether it is "dead, dying, or thriving" (Powers, 2015).

Notes

1 Recall (Chapter 4) that the precise quote from Locke speaks of either "life, health, liberty, or possessions," or a little later of "the life, the liberty, health, limb, or goods" (Locke, 1689, *Two Treatises of Civil Government*, Book II, chapter II, §6); Further on he mentions "his property, that is, his life, liberty and estate" (ibid., Book II, chapter VII, §87).

2 We will return to the issue of "responsibility to protect" shortly.

3 "Security and Human Rights," www.un.org/ruleoflaw/files/Ramcharan.pdf

4 Unsurprisingly, the choice of name for the eyesore being erected in Israel-Palestine is usually a good mark of the political orientation of the speaker using that name.

5 As will be elaborated, this particular report serves admirably for our examination of the security-human rights relationship. *B'Tselem* has published several other reports that spell out the detailed human rights violations effected by the Wall. Beyond numerous reports that attend to specific localities and specific human rights, of general note are also "The Separation Barrier" (September, 2002), www.btselem.org/sites/default/files/sites/default/files2/200209_separation_barrier_eng.pdf; "Behind the Barrier: Human Rights Violations as a Result of Israel's Separation Barrier" (March, 2003), www.btselem.org/sites/default/files/sites/default/files2/publication/200304_behind_the_barrier_eng.pdf; and "Arrested Development: The Long Term Impact of Israel's Separation Barrier in the West Bank" (October, 2012), www.btselem.org/sites/default/files/sites/default/files2/201210_arrested_development_eng.pdf

6 Bob Brecher, in *Torture and the Ticking Bomb* (2007) provides us with the most sensitive and astute rendering of the quandary of torture. Many of the following insights follow his lead.

7 Nussbaum is quoted by Eyal Press, writing in *The Nation* (2003), as saying: "I don't think any sensible moral position would deny that there might be some imaginable situations in which torture is justified."

8 The trolley problem in its modern form was posed by Philippa Foot (1967). It has become a staple of studies in ethics. Notable contributions are Judith Jarvis Thomson (1976), Frances Kamm (1989), and many others.

9 In political thought there is wide engagement with the concept of "nation" and with the historical phenomenon of nation-states, that is, of modern states having developed out of the acknowledgment of national identities. Indeed, in the UDHR, nations, rather than states, are often posited as the principal players in the international arena. We do not have the space here to challenge this traditional – and perhaps no longer as prominent – perception of international relations. See also Chapter 8, Note 2.

10 Note: "United *Nations*," not "United States" or even "United Nation-States."

11 Recall the addition of Articles 1 in the ICCPR and the ICESCR, regarding self-determination, that were absent in the UDHR.

12 See Smith, "Humanitarian Intervention: An Overview of the Ethical Issues" (1999, 287–293). Smith brings up the fascinating suggestion that state sovereignty is not an *a priori* value but rather contingent. In the struggle between state sovereignty and individual rights, from a liberal perspective the latter should trump because the justification for the former cannot automatically assume its legitimacy.

13 http://unpan1.un.org/intradoc/groups/public/documents/un/unpan000923.pdf

14 2005 World Summit Outcome Document, sections 138–139. This is General Assembly resolution 60/1 (2005), reaffirmed by the Security Council in Resolution 1674 (2006), www.un.org/en/development/desa/population/migration/generalassem bly/docs/globalcompact/A_RES_60_1.pdf

15 In the original ICISS's R2P report, the criterion of "just cause" for military intervention includes "overwhelming natural or environmental catastrophes, where the state concerned is either unwilling or unable to cope, or call for assistance, and significant loss of life is occurring or threatened." This situation was not accepted by the United Nations as an acceptable reason for military intervention.

16 See Conley-Zilkic, *How Mass Atrocities End* (2016).

17 Convention on the Prevention and Punishment of the Crime of Genocide (1948), Article II.

18 Rome Statute of the International Criminal Court (1998), Article 8, War Crimes.

19 Rome Statute of the International Criminal Court (1998), Article 7, Crimes Against Humanity.

20 Final Report of Commission of Experts on former Yugoslavia, S/1994/674.

21 It has recently been suggested that famine or mass starvation should be seen as an instance of mass atrocities – that is, war crimes or crimes against humanity or genocides (as opposed to hunger, which is treated under the auspices of violations of human rights). See especially de Waal's *Mass Starvation: The History and Future of Famine* (2018).

Part IV
Critique

12 Philosophical Critique of Human Rights

Philosophy is the activity of asking critical, conceptual questions. The philosophy of human rights is, then, the activity of asking critical, conceptual questions about human rights. We have meandered, to and fro, around the historical, political, economic, and social facets of the field called "human rights," telling of its purported beginnings in the twentieth century (with some earlier, philosophical harbingers), its legal wrappings, and its political effects. We have emphasized the conceptual centers of this conversation, attempting to comprehensively attend to both the theoretical issues and the concrete manifestations of the idea of human rights. Our basic presupposition was historically and, admittedly, conventionally based: human rights is an area of legal and political practice that is founded upon the ideology of liberalism, borne of and perpetrated in modern, Western society.[1] So the critique of human rights would involve, first, an internal questioning – both of liberalism and foundationalism. Accepting the basics of human rights discourse, the critic may decry liberalism itself in the very concept of human rights, or even the need for foundations – liberal or otherwise. Going beyond liberalism, or perhaps ignoring it, the critic might harbor misgivings about the modern nomenclature that provides the engine for human rights engagement. These are all uniquely philosophical appraisals.

Perhaps less purely conceptual, but not less strident, are the challenges posed to human rights practice; conceptualism can be surrendered for the down-to-earth ethical dilemmas that accompany the doing of human rights with questions of moral weight that must not be disregarded. In fact, it is this conversation about ethical quandaries that may put a skeptic's cog in the human rights wheel, infusing us with different measures of hopelessness or, worse, cynicism concerning human rights. A subsequently more fruitful type of critique, then, guides us to think, and talk, differently about human rights – different perhaps from the customary discussion that has ruled the conventional human rights stage, but just as steadfast in the essential, moral obligations we take upon ourselves when we commit to human rights. In this chapter we will traverse these varying critiques of human rights – as theory and practice – allowing them to open doors of questioning that test our relaxed and seemingly unequivocal acceptance of the field. Subsequently, we will see what can, nevertheless, be salvaged.

The Paradoxes of Liberalism – From Marx to Brown

We use the word "paradox" seriously, even while not precisely adhering to the classical, logical definitions that emphasize the contradictory and therefore resolution-less aspects of paradoxes. Going with Joan Scott's political predilection, we adopt the literal translation of para-dox – against popular opinion – as "put[ting] into circulation a set of truths that challenge but don't displace orthodox beliefs" (Scott, 1996, 5–6). The tension that arises between a new set of "truths" and the old, un-displaced beliefs is similar to that which is created by a contradiction in logical paradoxes. Liberalism, writ large, is the orthodox belief; Marx presents one of its most paradoxical critiques. To be precise, Karl Marx's devastating, yet still sympathetic analysis is of natural rights and the concept of right in general, rather than of the object of the term "human rights" as we have been using it. That is to say, given the historical context of Marx's life and the issues that animated his political thought, his engagement with rights preceded our current use of "human rights." Still, as we shall see, it is, indeed, the human-oriented aspect of rights that will play a central part in Marx's words.

Of note is the fact that Marx's famous attack on rights is to be found in his infamous "On the Jewish Question" (Marx, 1978 [1844]). Oft-times perceived as an anti-Semitic tome, its involvement with "the Jewish Question" is worthy of independent analysis. For example, Isaiah Berlin's emotional response is telling:

> It is a dull and shallow composition, but it shows Marx in a typical mood: he was determined that the sarcasms and insults, to which some of the notable Jews of his generation were all their lives a target, should, so far as he could effect it, never be used to plague him. Consequently, he decided to kill the Jewish problem once and for all so far as he was concerned, declaring it to be an unreal subject, invented as a screen for other more pressing questions: a problem which offered no special difficulty, but arose from the general social chaos which demanded to be put in order.
>
> (Berlin, 1996 [1939], 82)

As surprising as it might seem to the discerning reader, our interest in Marx's critique of human rights will not venture into his actual misgivings about Jews, or about the anti-Semitism sometimes attributed to his treatment of the Jewish Question. We – paradoxically perhaps – maintain that in this context of rights and human rights. that is immaterial. Even Marx's analysis of the particular question of Jewish emancipation will not play a relevant part in our engagement with Marx on human rights.

What is relevant, then? To understand Marx's invective against rights, we must place him in the milieu of liberalism and the Lockean (and Hobbesian) axioms of natural rights. We must also locate his thought in the more concrete setting of the end of feudalism, the Industrial Revolution, and the rise of the *bourgeoisie*. It is this ideational and social-economic environment that gives the clear impetus to Marx's critique from the left, so to speak, of liberalism in general and of the liberal concept of rights in particular. What Marx brings to the fore is the insight that rights, in their liberal provenance, are an abstract construct that was erected with the very particular interests of a certain class of people – those who constructed it – in mind. More basic than that socio-economic political claim, however, is the type of human being that Marx describes as the necessary foundation for the idea of natural rights. Quoting the French Declaration of the Rights of Man and Citizen, emphasizing that "natural and imprescriptible rights are: equality, liberty, security, property" (Article 2), Marx prompts the realization that these are "the rights of egoistic man, of man separated from other men and the community" (Marx, 1978, 42)! Liberally citing the *Declaration*, he elaborates on each of these rights, for example, "Liberty is the power which man has to do everything that does not harm the rights of others" (Article 6) or "Security consists of the protection afforded by society to each of its members for the preservation of his person, his rights, and his property" (Article 8). The point he makes categorically, though, is striking in its starkness.

> None of the supposed rights of man … go beyond the egoistic man … that is, an individual separated from the community, withdrawn into himself, wholly preoccupied with his private interest and acting in accordance with his private caprice … The only bond between men is natural necessity, need and private interest, the preservation of their property and their egoistic persons.
>
> (ibid., 43)

In other words, the natural rights of the natural human being, that is, his human rights, center on the individual person who is guided by, even controlled, only by his own egoistical interests.

There is an interesting, even paradoxical intuition here. The political emancipation which is so perfectly portrayed by the French Revolution does, indeed, represent the positive move away from feudalism, where "estates, corporations, guilds and privileges … expressed the separation of the people from community life," to a condition "which made state affairs the affairs of the people." Marx cannot but admit that this is a forward-looking change that "set free the political spirit, which had, so to speak, been dissolved, fragmented and lost in the various *culs-de-sac* of feudal society" (ibid., 45). However, this freedom is an abstract freedom which is manifested only through the abstract relationships that depend on the state's laws. The political condition that is prescribed by political emancipation presupposes a natural person who has natural rights; but these rights belong to "*political* man [who] is only abstract, artificial man, man as an *allegorical, moral* person" (ibid., 46). This divide between the natural man and the political man (the citizen) is the painful reality of political emancipation, where individual rights are the ultimate expression of an abstract, rather than real, person. So, for example, the right of liberty that is couched in terms of freedom from interference is not a real freedom; rather, for Marx, freedom is to be found in the essential bedrock of the community and in the relations between human beings, not in or for humans in isolation. Consequently, we can accept the undebatable value of rights for political emancipation while still admitting that they are context-independent, based on alienated man, and certainly a result of the bourgeois interests of propertied individuals. "Human emancipation will only be complete when the real, individual man has absorbed into himself the abstract citizen" (ibid.). In other words, the realization of abstract, civil rights must materialize in a real human being if they are to be considered as more than just formalistic, legal devices.

It should be noted and stressed that Marx's critique of the construct of rights – and especially liberal rights – is not a denial of their conceptual worth or even of their political value. Instead, Marx views the political context in which he is writing as a step on the way to human emancipation, to which he ultimately aspires. Liberalism is, consequently, an ideology which must be analyzed with great detail and nuance – for it is paradoxical precisely because, at base, it has a self-contradictory attitude towards man as both autonomous and a member of society. Not surprisingly, given the subsequent victory of capitalism in Western political theory and practice over most versions of Marxism (socialism, communism, even welfare-statism), it is the individualistic version of human rights that has been triumphant as well.[2] Just as predictable, however, is the current resurgence of "Marxist" analyses, along with other critiques of that liberal view of human rights.

Fast forward a century-and-a-half to a contemporary thinker who exposes the paradoxes within the liberal conception of human rights as they emerge today – Wendy Brown (2002), whose thought we have already encountered in the context of women's human rights (Chapter 9). In her article, Brown explicitly and forcefully traces the contradictions that arise within liberal discourse in general, and specifically in the liberal articulation of rights. As we have seen, she brings in the verbal banner that pinpoints the essence of paradox, Gayatri Spivak's mantra, "that which we cannot not want" (Spivak, 1993, 45–46). In other words, it seems as if, on the one hand, we would be foolish to refuse the yields of liberalism; yet on the other hand, we must ask about the value of espousing the rights language that is bestowed upon us by that same liberalism.

Now, obviously, the liberal edifice of rights can be credited with the progress that women and other groups have made in the twentieth century. But although "new" rights exist formally in the institutions of law, the fact that so many humans are still in a situation where they "need and want" them (Brown, 2002, 421) means that, in some way, the formal existence of rights and the discourse surrounding them belie their material mode of gratification. Precisely because we still live in a world that is so often gripped by discrimination, exploitation, and subordination, rights that exist in the legal domain and may at times alleviate extreme suffering do not really address the essential problem at hand. In fact, and similar to Marx's complaint, the existence of these formal rights may work – paradoxically – against tangible emancipation.

Paradoxes – like contradictions in logic – give rise to a show of phenomena that can hardly be grasped without attending to the illogical yet predominant discursive framework in which we are trapped. We have seen one basic paradox of liberal rights, which seems to bespeak a "damned if you do, damned if you don't" effect when we deal with women's rights. Insisting on these being *women's* rights encircles women inside a legal, semantic fence; ignoring a special status for women in the matter of rights – that is, continuing to speak in neutral, universal rights jargon – permits traditional, social, hierarchical presuppositions to continue as before.[3] Furthermore, since the rights having to do with different aspects of persons' identities – their gender, class, religion, race, sexual orientation, and so on – are treated separately in legal formulations and thereby also in our applications of those terms in different contexts, any intersection of identities might suffer from either disregard or, even worse, a contradiction in the interests of various identities. A worthwhile example brought in by Brown is the construct of privacy – where distinct identities may be expressed differently, indeed contrarily, to either welcome or abhor the results of the "right to privacy." Thus, on one side is the exclusively feminist desire to expose the violations on women that are protected by privacy laws: "reproduction, domestic assault, incest, unremunerated household labor, and compulsory emotional and sexual service to men" (Brown, 2002, 428). At a very different place, however, are the interests of the gay, or the poor, or the victims of racism, whose insistence on privacy "will be seen variously to advance or deter emancipation, to cloak inequality or procure equality" (ibid.). So the right to privacy itself, classically conceived as a valued right, becomes a paradoxical construct in the everyday contexts of intersectional identity. Or think, even, of the past "crime" of sodomy, now protected as the right to an act of sexual freedom. Is this really a right to act in a certain way, or the right to assume a certain identity – a homosexual identity – and isn't the difference between the two critical for our understanding of liberal rights? Doesn't the insistence on these types of rights in liberal rights discourse bring us up against the same paradox: the right to an act is really the right to an identity, and our talk of a right to a certain identity reinforces the presupposition of that (homosexual) identity's inferiority and subordination to the better-received, conventionally superior (heterosexual) identity. "That which we cannot not want is also that which ensnares us in the terms of our domination" (ibid., 430)!

Two points are worthy of pointed notice in the acknowledgment of paradox in the liberal conceptions of rights; both straddle the distance between theory and practice, between structural conceptual schemes and fundamental on-the-ground contexts, and – finally – between a philosophical grasp of human rights and their political essence. First, there is no escaping the enveloping, all-encompassing presuppositions in our liberal discourse of rights. As Brown emphasizes, referencing Scott (1996), when, for example, feminists engage with women's rights, in talk and action, they do this in a context where the ideas of individuality and rights, that is, liberal ideas, are "relentlessly identified with masculinity ... women's struggle for rights occurs in the context of a specifically masculinist discourse of rights, a discourse that presumes an ontologically autonomous, self-sufficient, unencumbered subject." (Brown, 2002, 431). Marx's insight, that the entire setting for liberal rights is encumbered by the *bourgeois*, property-owning basis for their rationale, contains a similar, paradox-raising tension: certainly, this political emancipation is to be welcomed, but it cannot attain the heights of an actual all-human emancipation. In other words, theories of (human) rights are born of, and therefore might be forever entrapped in, particular contexts that control our discourse – even of rights.

A second consequence of the paradoxes of liberalism is, as Brown puts it, the political question:

> How might paradox gain political richness when it is understood as affirming the impossibility of justice in the present and as articulating the conditions and contours of justice in the future? How might attention to paradox help formulate a political struggle for rights in which they are conceived neither as instruments nor as ends, but as articulating through their instantiation what equality and freedom might consist in that exceeds them? In other words, how might the paradoxical elements of the struggle for rights in an emancipatory context articulate a field of justice beyond "that which we cannot not want"? And what form of rights claims have the temerity to sacrifice an absolutist or naturalized status in order to carry this possibility?
>
> (ibid., 432)

We will return to these questions, which are actually one question, shortly, when we address the politicization of human rights. For the moment, however, let us continue critiquing the tradition of liberal human rights via other philosophical routes.

Anti-Foundationalism – A Different Conversation

We regularly speak about context-dependent "discourse," accepting the contemporary awareness that our language-use is rooted in a certain tradition, a certain culture, a certain system of thought and action; that all of these function as the setting within which our ideas – in this case, of human rights – are entrenched. And thus far we have also accepted, in some measure, the historical and philosophical supposition that liberalism was (and is) the conceptual home of human rights, providing its various postulates of human nature (man as a rational and individualistic being) and its rationale for government (guardian of that rational individual) in the animated conversation on the foundations of human rights. Liberalism, for its part, can be seen as one branch of the age-old philosophical pursuit of the question about our humanity – what is it that makes us essentially human? Before and after liberalism, we have lines of western philosophers who have inquired about the basic feature – or set of features – that makes us human. Just as edifying, moreover, is the position usually ascribed to Nietzsche that denies the value of such a search for whatever it is that is fundamentally human (positing that it is only the weaker members of the human species who indulge in these pursuits, trying to protect themselves against the stronger ones). One could then ask: Which of these paths, or even the lack of such, can enlighten us further concerning the *human* in "human rights"?

Richard Rorty, a philosopher renowned for his recalcitrant appraisal of the Western philosophical tradition,[4] offers us a diametrically different way of looking at human rights – different, that is, from the foundational liberal tradition. His agenda, spelled out in a lecture called "Human Rights, Rationality, and Sentimentality" (Rorty, 1993), involves changing the questions that we must ask when attempting to justify human rights; obviously also changing the answers; and, most importantly, changing our mode of persuasion and education for human rights – in other words, changing our discourse at large. According to Rorty, concentrating on the theoretical definition of a human being has been responsible, in fact, for the practice of dehumanizing some living beings, giving rise to some of the most egregious phenomena in human history. Rorty points to the distinctions between humans and animals, adults and children, and males and females as erstwhile examples of this type of misuse, or abuse, that was caused by the project of defining the human. And he claims that we – in the modern, Western world – have made progress and have already advanced to a point where we are no longer mesmerized by the search for definitions of the human being, or even by the Nietzschean dismissal of that search. Instead, he says, we recognize that the human is a "flexible, protean, self-shaping, animal," and we have, subsequently, transferred our interest to the question "What can we make of ourselves?" (ibid., 115). Added to this conceptual inquiry – which has gone from theoretical definition to practical normativity – is the recognition of our contingent, present-day situation, which is characterized as being a "human rights culture."

Like he had in his earlier iconoclastic book, *Philosophy and the Mirror of Nature*, Rorty is here making groundbreaking philosophical moves. He is demeaning any foundationalist and therefore universalist (liberal or other) analysis of the "human" in human rights, but this is not done by adopting a cheap brand of cultural relativism of the "anything goes" type. Our human rights culture can be explained and justified, but not by doing the kind of popular meta-ethics that turns to moral intuitions or "claims to knowledge about the nature of human beings." More so, he does not drop human rights as valueless or not worthy of realization and our utmost esteem. Rather, he wants to show us – and any detractors there might be of human rights – that there is a coherent and perspicuous way of making the human rights culture in which we participate now even more powerful. Ironically perhaps, Rorty's belief that this – our – culture is morally superior does not lead him to thereby assert the existence of a universal human nature or to base that superiority on that human nature. "[I]t is not clear why 'respect for human dignity' – our sense that the difference between Serb and Muslim, Christian and infidel, gay and straight, male and female should not matter – must presuppose the existence of [a distinctively human] attribute" (ibid., 116).

So what is to be done (according to Rorty)? First, in light of the deep question that should now guide philosophical questioning– "What can we make of ourselves?" – the examination of human rights must cease to engage with the definitional, foundational nature of human beings. Furthermore, the traditional, that is Platonist or Kantian, identification of human morality with rationality, which led to the distinction between knowing and feeling and to the additional divide between humans as knowing and animals as feeling, should be exited. "We should substitute 'We can feel *for each other* to a much greater extent than [animals] can.'" (ibid., 122). Instead, philosophers and other human rightists should be pragmatically oriented to making our human rights culture more predominant and more accepted by others who do not recognize us primarily as feeling for each other. But what does it mean to be "pragmatically oriented"? It is here that Rorty makes the radical move vacating foundational philosophy. "The best, and probably the only, argument for putting foundationalism behind us is the one I have already suggested: It would be more efficient to do so, because it would let us concentrate our energy on manipulating sentiments, on sentimental education" (ibid.) And he continues to very practical and very concrete steps:

> That sort of education sufficiently acquaints people of different kinds with one another so that they are less tempted to think of those different from themselves as only quasi-human. The goal of this manipulation of sentiment is to expand the reference of the terms "our kind of people" and "people like us."
>
> (ibid., 122–123)

In captivating manner, Rorty touches upon issues that are mainstays of the human rights conversation in a manner that seems somewhat unfamiliar and takes them to unfamiliar terrains. Most unnerving, the old conundrum of universalism vs. relativism plays its part here – but Rorty's unembarrassed culturalism, insisting on a "human rights culture," is different from the anti-Western relativism that we encountered in Chapters 3 and 7. Contrary to the conventional division between Western universalists and "other" relativists, Rorty is pro-Western, insisting that there are people "whom we should convince to join our Eurocentric human rights culture" (ibid.,

126).⁵ And, true to his own call for sentimental education, he supplies a mostly compassionate explanation for such people's remove from considerations of human rights.

> The bad people's problem is that they were not so lucky in the circumstances of their upbringing as we were ... we should treat them as deprived ... Foundationalists think of these people as deprived of truth, of moral knowledge. But it would be better – more specific, more suggestive of possible remedies – to think of them as deprived of two more concrete things: security and sympathy.
>
> (ibid., 128)

He elaborates on this strikingly, telling us that security is what one needs in order to be risk-free of losing one's self-respect facing another. Sympathy is not ever defined, but is seen as that which one acquires by being exposed – usually through art and theater – to human suffering. What lies then, at the basis of human rights, is not a rational foundation, liberal or other, for the recognition of their legitimacy or even mandatory deployment, but rather a consciousness of the sentiments – "love, friendship, trust, or social solidarity" (ibid., 122) – that make human life human. In the same basic space lies also a human rights culture that should be propagated widely.

The tired exchange, then, between theorists who need a rational justification in their dealings with human rights should be replaced by human rights education; but "education" does not mean analytic investigation into foundational questions. It is, rather, an experiential, story-telling endeavor which is based on the sentimental essence of human responsiveness to the other. It is not that the Platonic or Enlightenment ideal of rational people wanting to do good is philosophically misconstrued, but that it is outmoded and no longer relevant for our times, when "the human rights phenomenon is a 'fact of the world'" (ibid., 134). The last two centuries

> are most easily understood not as a period of deepening understanding of the nature of rationality or of morality, but rather as one in which there occurred an astonishingly rapid progress of sentiments, in which it has become much easier for us to be moved to action by sad and sentimental stories.
>
> (ibid.)

In other words, sentimental storytelling is both the point of a philosophy of human rights and the pragmatic method of human rights education. It cannot substitute for human rights organizations or activism – storytelling is hardly a site of action – but it rather replaces the incessant conversation we have been conducting in our attempt, as philosophers, to justify, explain, and validate the *idea* of human rights. It is a mode of persuasion that moves to understanding, to an epistemic commitment, and, hopefully, to action.

Alternative Discourses – Foucault and Levinas

Richard Rorty often provides the philosophical springboard from which, in American and Anglo-Saxon philosophy, or perhaps in what we have come to call analytic philosophy, the critique of modernism is explicitly staged as a move to postmodernism. The *systematic* outline of the idea of human rights that we have been surveying has, admittedly, been in the tradition of modernism, basing itself on liberal thought, which is almost automatically associated with the Enlightenment ideals of human rationality and autonomy. Rorty's *Philosophy and the Mirror of Nature* (1979) was one of the first, and certainly one of the most prodigious, subversions of that dominant tradition in Western, analytic philosophy.

That is not to say, however, that we haven't been privy to other conceptual frameworks that are both theoretically independent of standard modernism and, at the same time, critical of the hegemony accorded to that standard. Sometimes described as postmodernism, sometimes as Continental Philosophy, sometimes as structuralism and post-structuralism, sometimes as critical theory, sometimes even as post-humanist,[6] these ways of doing philosophy entail ways of thinking about human rights that are unlike the conventional story that we have been telling. The philosophers of these schools who have explicitly[7] spoken about human rights are many and variegated. We shall here take note of some of their outstanding contributions to our understanding of human rights.

The name that looms largest in an alternative reading of "human rights" is Michel Foucault (1926–1984). Credited with a post-humanism which is sometimes even considered an anti-humanism, that is, a denial of a universal human essence made up of rational agency and intentionality, Foucault gave us a new way of attending to un-generalized humanity in its social and mostly political surroundings. In his early books, especially *Madness and Civilization* (1961), *The Birth of the Clinic* (1963), *The Order of Things* (1966), and then, a little later, in *Discipline and Punish* (1975), Foucault laid out his critique of two basic ideas: the human "subject," that is, the autonomous individual who is a given, in the first place, before any external influence on her can be ascertained, and the sovereign government that is constituted, in the second place, as a function of – and perhaps later even as a function of power over – that subject. Both are fundamental to Enlightenment and liberal suppositions concerning humanity, and Foucault destroys their supposedly natural givenness and relationships in human affairs. Tritely, we may say that Foucault turns the liberal structure of individuals who make up a sovereign state on its head. It is power – of all sorts, be it governmental, or educational, or social, or legal – that determines, and even creates, the characteristics and identity, the very being, of the subjects that it rules and controls. So the individual posited in classical human rights and thought of as having natural human rights, that is to say, rights that are held by all humans possessing a natural human essence, is entirely misconceived. Can there, in fact, be any meaning to the concept of "human rights" itself, according to Foucault?

Interestingly, even poignantly, Foucault himself was an activist, in a manner of speaking, for gay rights, refugee rights, prisoners' rights, the right to suicide, and others – without ever shirking from calling them human rights. So the question naturally arises: how can we countenance the apparent inconsistency between a philosophy of human existence and politics that is explicitly anti-liberal and support for human rights that seem to be a product – both theoretically and in practice – of traditional liberal thought? This seeming discrepancy has been noted and variously explained by several Foucault scholars. Proffered explanations that are somewhat philosophically evasive tell us that the early, critical Foucault matured into a more tolerant, realistic philosopher who had to acknowledge not only the political fact of the ascendance of liberalism worldwide, but also its theoretical triumph over his own and others' windmill-tilting theoretical abundances.[8] Foucault was not unaware of this apparent incongruity, and he had his own deep reply: "I try to consider human rights in their historical reality while not admitting that there is a human nature," he said in 1981 (Foucault, 2014, 265). He could accept the factuality of human rights – their use, their contingency, their malleability, their vulnerability to cynical opportunism, their potential for progressive achievements – without reneging on his repudiation of an essential human nature that underlies humanity itself. Here, too, there is a wonderful paradox. It is clear to Foucault that human rights function in the political arena – that we can use them, neither naïvely nor cynically, for legitimate political purposes. Yet, by the same token, arguing about human rights – what they are, which they are, and especially what the "human" in them means – is at the crux of politics itself. Put differently, human rights can be advocated and fought for in our political struggles since they are something we permit ourselves to assume as a given value or interest; but those same political struggles must themselves be intent on clarifying, widening, or sometimes even narrowing, the space of human rights itself. There is no obvious or set humanistic foundation to human rights. In this sense, Foucauldian human rights remain a critique of, and perhaps even a replacement for, liberal human rights.

Emmanuel Levinas (1906–1994) is another intellectual giant whose philosophical impact is immeasurable. Different from the paradoxical tension between apparent anti-humanism and a somewhat embrace of human rights activism that one encounters in Foucault's thought and action, it is in Levinas's ethics that one discovers an unadulterated moral foundation for human rights that is anything but liberal. Interestingly, however, there are two points to note about Levinas's philosophy that make the claim above itself somewhat problematic. First, there is a scholarly discussion concerning the term "ethics" and the question whether what Levinas was engaged in was, indeed, ethics. Second, although Levinas does deliberate on human rights, there is not much scholarship devoted to his contribution in this arena.[9] Still – his engagement with human relationships as the most profound element of human existence provides us with a unique opportunity to achieve a novel perspective on human rights.

Famously, Levinas offered us an explicit and essential understanding of that now prevalent, widespread and over-used term – the "other." Importantly, Levinas insisted that the encounter with the other is at the base of human existence. But this encounter is not a simple relationship between two objects, or between a subject – I – and an object – the other, or even, to begin with, between two subjects. The relationship that any person, a subject, has with the other consists of being face-to-face with another person and recognizing that other's face as affecting me – asking me, telling me, beseeching me, commanding me. That is the most basic and impactful aspect of human existence – without which we cannot actually perceive the world or ourselves in it. Yet our recognition of the other's face as precisely the face of the other does more than just make out the other's demands upon us. It leads us immediately to the acknowledgment that we must, indeed, respond and, more than that, that our response must express that acknowledgment. More so, that direct acquaintance with our social, dialogical essence as human beings is undeniably a matter of our responsibility to and for that other. Amazingly, the very singular, direct perception of a person's self-identity as herself is attained only via that person's grasp of her responsibility to another.

We cannot here mine all the complexities and nuances of Levinas's ethics. Let us only emphasize, for the moment, a startling discernment. The "face of the other" that occupies such an essential place in Levinas's philosophy is a "naked" face. An other that one encounters could have been any other other. It does not matter that it is a particular, identified other; what matters is only that it is an other. And there are innumerable others; in fact, the other is a universal other. So, despite being a particular individual, his face is naked in the sense that all other faces that one may bump into in this interpersonal meeting are just as particular but also just as universal. Paradoxically, but oh-so-authentically, any human is an individual at the same time that she is universal.

It is this insight, along with the awareness of our monumental, primary obligation to be responsible for the other, that delivers us promptly into the field of human rights. Human rights are first and foremost the rights of the other, for which I am responsible. By admitting the first, original encounter with another as the most foundational feature of a human's conscious– or even unconscious, but still experiential – existence, yet insisting on its consequential responsiveness and responsibility for that other, Levinas has ushered in the other's needs and desires, the other's demands, as my own responsibility and therefore as the other's *rights*.

It is important to note how different this is from the liberal grounding of human rights. Remember, first, that liberalism celebrated the human's own individuality and that individual's own demands from the other as her own rights. Rights were predicated on the individual "I" that is inherent in each human being; as human rights they gave rise to the other's duties. For Levinas, the move is in the "opposite direction." It is by recognizing the other that I immediately perceive myself as being responsible for the other's rights. The duty comes before the right. Or perhaps one might say that my responsibility can only be understood as most overtly the responsibility for the other's rights. This way of looking at Levinasian human rights thereby puts to waste not only the direction of derivation of rights vs. duties (or responsibility), but, in fact, the very individualism that was so crucial in liberalism's posit of human rights. The human person, according to Levinas, intuits her own personality, her own humanity, not as an individual but rather as a partner in a relationship with an other. Finally, the *rational* individual – who is the foundation of liberal human rights (and for whom Rorty counter-offered the sentimental one) – is absent here. The consciousness of myself as a human who is responsible for the other is an affective, phenomenological condition – not a realization rationally worked out from assessment of the world around me. It is, indeed, the very primal essence of my being in the world.

We should, nevertheless, point to a certain important parallelism between Levinas's human rights, which seem to come from a world view so fundamentally different from traditional liberalism, and human rights as we have conventionally presented them. Whether rooted in liberalism or in a Levinasian ethics, human rights seem to be simultaneously both at the base of and still above all other rights. Yes, for Levinas, human rights are "before all else the rights of the other person" (Levinas, 1991, 234), rather than of the subjective individual. But this "not only makes it clear that human rights (should) surpass every social, economic, juridical and political order, but that they also (should) form their foundation" (Burggraeve, 2005, 96). The existential, phenomenological, dialogical underpinning of human rights in Levinas, as responsibility for the other's demands, posits them in the same justificational place – as a base for all other rights – that they had in classical liberalism. In another sense, however, human rights – the rights we have simply in virtue of being human – have received, in Levinas's hands, moral substance of a very different caliber.

Philosophically Political – Balibar and Arendt

We can think of Marx as the obvious progenitor of the anti-liberal attack on human rights yet continue, as we have, to inspect critical philosophical investigation of human rights that is variously engaged with the question of their foundations – more or less affected by Marx's thought. Many important names come up in this reflective exchange on human rights; what makes them philosophically pertinent is their conceptual, critical stance regarding the liberal idea of human rights. Thus, for instance, we could make note of Jacques Rancière, who – while engaging with Hannah Arendt – politicizes human rights, writing that they are "the rights of those who have not the rights that they have and have the rights that they have not" (Rancière, 2004, 302). Another notable thinker, who also reads Hannah Arendt on human rights and focuses on those of migrants and refugees, is Giorgio

Agamben. His words – "Here the paradox is that precisely the figure that should have embodied human rights more than any other – namely, the refugee – marked instead the radical crisis of the concept" (Agamben, 2008, 92) – remind us yet again of the political desperation that engulfs the rights-less in the liberal political landscape.[10]

Early on, in Chapter 1, we alluded to the notion of the "political" and the question of the political pieces in and of human rights. Before continuing with this question, though, we must make some terminological clarifications. Attaching the label "politics" or "political" to a set of ideas, a mode of action, an area of human endeavor, a group of people, an institution, or a type of discourse, is hazardous if we don't elucidate to ourselves what we mean by this attribution. We could, if we wanted, distinguish between "politics" and "the political," and somewhat superficially say that politics is the down-to-earth engagement having to do with human actions that constitute real politics in practice, while the political is that facet of those actions that is institutionalized and theorized.[11] In fact, in the next chapter we will concentrate on politics in the first sense and interrogate the concrete relationship between the phenomenon of human rights in real life, so to speak, and the practice, material institutions, and living agents that we may call "politics." For the moment, however, we shall continue to ask about the deep political role of human rights; that is to say, about the meaning and standing of human rights in our political human existence.

It is Etienne Balibar, the French philosopher, who immediately comes to mind at this juncture, for it is his striking appraisal of the political dimension of being human, along with a no less arresting articulation of the meaning of human rights, that gives the lie to the liberal axioms – of the essentially individualistic flavor of human rights and of their existence prior to any political institutionalization – that we have so often encountered. The "birth" of human rights can be ascertained, according to Balibar, in the French Declaration of the Rights of Man and Citizen of 1789. Note that, when earlier on (in Chapters 1 and 2) we noted three basic declarations of human rights – the Universal Declaration of Human Rights (1948) and its obvious harbingers, the American Declaration of Independence (with its subsequent Bill of Rights) and the French Declaration of the Rights of Man and Citizen, we credited all three with a recognized status of being essentialistic documents of *human* rights. What Balibar insists on, however, is that the French declaration is most emphatically and explicitly – note its title – a declaration of human and *citizen* rights. More so, he goes on to explicate the priority of the "Citizen" over the "Man." This is a critical change in the view of human rights: whereas in classical liberalism we recognize a human being who holds individual human rights that are his before and independent of being a citizen of any state, according to Balibar the French declaration, at the very least, does not distinguish between human and citizen rights. More profoundly, it makes human rights dependent on citizen rights. How does that happen, and why is it important?[12]

Let us recall, for a moment, our earlier note (in Chapter 4) that in classical political thought the two basic anchors of liberalism are freedom and equality. Let us also accept, for another moment, that the natural perception of these two constructs (and the word "constructs" will soon carry more weight) is that they are in competition: put blandly, the more equality one meets in a political system, the less freedom it harbors; and conversely, the more freedom one encounters in political structures, the less equality they can boast. This can be almost graphically illustrated. In a society where equality is seen as mandatory (by law, or custom, or religion, or tradition), people are not at liberty to do what they want – if what they want violates that decree of equality. And in a society where liberty is uppermost (in the law, or custom, or religion, or tradition), equality will surely suffer at the hands of free agents who do not treasure its priority. Indeed, one of the most common missions of philosophers, practitioners of political science, economists and various other ethically minded scholars has been the attempt to bridge that apparent gap of liberal tension between equality and freedom.

Yet, when we speak of human rights, the question of equality and freedom arises in different garb. Is there a human right to freedom? To equality? Are these descriptive constructs – insisting, for example, that the human being who is entitled to rights is free and equal to all other human beings by nature? Or are they normative concepts – maintaining that freedom and equality are the objects to which we aspire in our pursuit of human rights? And what *is* the relationship between them, however we articulate their essence? The American Declaration of Independence is somewhat strange in reply to these questions, with a seemingly uneven positioning of liberty and equality. "We hold these truths to be self-evident, that all men are created equal, that they are endowed ... with certain unalienable Rights ... [including] Liberty." Equality seems to be functioning within a descriptive truth which is parallel to the truth of unalienable rights, one of which is Liberty. Almost two centuries later, the UDHR places its answer to these questions in Article 1: "All human beings are born free and equal in dignity and rights." There, it seems, freedom and equality are not rights in themselves, but are rather traits that are descriptively presupposed as justificational safeguards of human rights (and dignity). Balibar, in fact, sees the seeds of this connection in the UDHR between freedom and equality, on the one hand, and human rights, on the other, in the very clear formulation of the French Declaration of the Rights of Man and Citizen, where Article 1 proclaims: "Men are born and remain free and equal in rights." This may be seen as both descriptive and normative ("born *and* remain"); it puts freedom and equality on an equal standing; and it gives succor to the idea that human and citizen rights – all of them – are grounded in freedom and equality.

Balibar's contribution, call it even invention, is found in the term "equaliberty," easily unpacked into "equal liberty"; undeniably, he gives full credit for its genesis to the French Revolution and its resultant Declaration. In fact, the political act of declaring the rights enunciated in that document is a part of its realization. "[T]he *Declaration* in fact says that equality is identical to freedom, is equal to freedom, and vice versa. Each is the exact measure of the other. This is what I propose to call ... the proposition of equaliberty ..." (Balibar, 2014, 46). But what does the claim that freedom and equality are identical and equal to each other mean? For Balibar, such an assertion is not an *a priori* analysis of their conceptual meaning, but is rather a depiction, realized by the French revolutionaries, of the historical realities that gave rise to both political freedom and political equality. "[T]he proposition of equaliberty is indeed an irreversible truth, discovered by and in the revolutionary struggle – precisely the universally true proposition on which, at the decisive moment, the different forces making up the revolutionary camp had to agree" (ibid., 48). And what they had to agree on, what they must have uncovered almost "experimentally," is that "[s]imply put, the situations in which both are present or absent are necessarily the same. Or, again, the (de facto) historical conditions of freedom are exactly the same as the (de facto) historical conditions of equality" (ibid.). Liberty and equality are not, as the liberal might have it, contradictory conditions which cancel each other out. On the contrary, the conditions that support a human being's access to freedom cohere with those that further his equality with other humans. Most significantly, this pertains to and is possible only in the situation of a social community which is legally enacted – in other words, only in the political state.

This is a far cry from a search for foundations of human rights grounded in human nature, or a human essence, or divine decree, or even positivistic legalism. Rather, it is a tense recognition of the place that the constitution of nation-state sovereignty inhabits in our quest to understand the meaning of human rights. Without the declaration, that is, the claim of rights by rights-holders, there is no ground for them to stand upon. But the declaration of rights is, itself, a political act; more so, it is simultaneously an act of claiming by the rights holders and the establishment of the sovereign body which must ensure those same rights. In precisely that sense, the rights that are claimed are the rights of citizens that are couched in the language of human rights. Crucially, they are first the former, then the latter. There is no way of grasping the essence, indeed the meaning, of human rights without their political institution. Declaring them, giving them constitutive status, and putting them in a necessary legal context is what makes human rights viable; but the crux of all those verbs – declaring, constituting, legalizing – is their civic and political essence. So Balibar, understandably, focuses not only on Article 1, which talks of freedom and equality, but also on Article 6 of the French Declaration, which proclaims that "all citizens, being equal in the eyes of the law, are equally eligible to all dignities ...". Once again, it is citizens who are presumed to be "equal in the eyes of the law": equality before the law is not a particular *human* right (as it is usually labelled in our conventional lists of human rights), but is rather the basic form of any *citizen's* eligibility for rights. Human rights are nothing if they are not political – and they are political only if they are, first and essentially, citizens' rights. That is why Balibar can say, referring to Arendt, that "[i]f the abolition of civic rights is also the destruction of human rights, it is because in reality the latter rest on the former and not the reverse" (ibid., 171).

And that, of course, brings us back full-circle to Hannah Arendt, who instilled in our conversation on human rights the onus of understanding "the right to have rights." We have, previously (in Chapter 1 and in Chapter 9) encountered Arendt's thoughts on human rights in two contexts; first, in our earlier, terminological clarification of the ordinary use of "civil" rights as opposed to "human" rights, and then in our specific discussion of the rights of stateless persons. Through Balibar's resounding espousal of Arendt's insights, we now return to the question of the foundations of human rights and re-examine her variously interpreted exclamation – sometimes, oft-times misinterpreted as an attack on human rights – that human rights have no foundations in natural moral rights outside and prior to the framework of political structures. Famously, Arendt told us that "[f]rom the beginning the paradox involved in the declaration of inalienable human rights was that it reckoned with an abstract human being who seemed to exist nowhere" (Arendt, 1958, 291). Indeed,

> The calamity of the rightless is not they are deprived of life, liberty, and the pursuit of happiness, or of equality before the law and freedom of opinion – formulas which were designed to solve problems within given communities – but that they no longer belong to any community what-soever. Their plight is not that they are not equal before the law, but that no law exists for them; not that they are oppressed but that nobody wants even to oppress them.
>
> (ibid., 295–296)

Still, Arendt's critique of the conventional, anthropological (in Balibar's terms), speculative version of the foundations of human rights is proble-matic and paradoxical, since it goes hand in hand with a bemoaning of the destructive consequences of violations of those same human rights. "How is it possible," says Balibar, "at the same time to reject the idea that there are fundamental human rights ... in theory and to place an intransigent politics of the rights of man at the very heart of the democratic construction?" (Balibar, 2014, 166). The answer lies, of course, in Arendt's reversal of the accepted movement from foundational metaphysics to active politics. For her, the *vita activa*, the active life (explicated in her *The Human Condition*) is at the core of human existence, and history is never mandated by a deterministic, theoretical form of the world but is rather always contingent. Human rights are, consequently, not grounded in any moral or metaphysical essence, but are identified with political practice. Yet the political practice that is most familiar in modernity is the institutional rubric of the nation-

state, "which served as the historical framework for the universal proclamation of certain fundamental rights of the person, but also rigorously
identified belonging to a community with possession of a nationality or the
status of a national citizen" (ibid., 170). One would have thought, accordingly, that those fundamental rights would be more basic, more universally
protected, more respected than the civic rights that go with being a
"national citizen." But, as Arendt insists, history has taught us that when
the civic rights of individuals and, more so, "masses of individuals" (Arendt,
1958, 171), are taken away – they lose their human rights. This is because
rights are not a matter of personal, individual belongings that we each have,
but are a reciprocal, relational quality that we share with others in our
community or society, that is to say, in our political systems. That is what is
meant by the "right to have rights" – the right to claim rights in general, as
a foundational aspect of our human, albeit always political, existence.

Notes

1 See Chapter 4, Note 1, for early criticism of "natural rights."
2 This harkens back to our discussion of group rights vs. individual rights in
 Chapter 8.
3 See Chapter 9, p. 130.
4 Rorty first acquired the status of such philosophical intractability in his shatter-
 ing *Philosophy and the Mirror of Nature*, 1979.
5 This was written in 1993. It is doubtful that today (2019) such unconcealed
 Eurocentrism would be condoned.
6 These are, obviously, not all synonymous, but we do not have the time or place
 here to elaborate on their differences. Furthermore, their dissimilarity does not
 detract from their common position of critique and criticism.
7 One could claim, of course, that mention of human rights does not need to be explicit
 for a certain school of thought to be relevant and applicable to our discussion. But
 addressing all the philosophical contexts – mostly of ethics and political thought – in
 which human rights may be implicated is certainly beyond our purview here.
8 A comprehensive analysis of these supposed changes in Foucault's thought and a
 systematic obliteration of their being actual deviations from his original thought
 can be found in Ben Golder, *Foucault and the Politics of Rights* (2015).
9 Scott Davidson ("The Rights of the Other: Levinas and Human Rights," 2012)
 wonders at the lack of much scholarship on Levinas's writings on human rights;
 Anya Topolski echoes the sentiment, mentioning as exceptions only Burggraeve
 (2005) and Douzinas (2000), and showing that this is strange, "given how much
 Levinas wrote about human rights" (Topolski, 2014, "Relationality as a 'Foundation' for Human Rights," 8).
10 Some other critical philosophers in the continental tradition who have con-
 tributed to the philosophical conversation on human rights are Jacques Derrida,
 Jean-Luc Nancy, and Jean-Francois Lyotard. Jürgen Habermas, in contrast to
 these thinkers, does not address the liberal state in a voice of radical opposition,
 but rather intends to enrich its somewhat naïve and straightforward acceptance of
 the basic, individualistic foundations of human rights with investigation as to how
 to consolidate political cosmopolitanism with the international, legal status of
 human rights (Habermas, 1998). All these philosophers point us in the direction of
 a more complex understanding of the concept of human rights and its foundations.

11 See Balibar, "What is a Politics of the Rights of Man?" (1994, 205).
12 The following, structured explication of Balibar's view follows J. M. Bernstein, "Rights," in *Political Concepts: A Critical Lexicon – The Balibar Edition* (n.d.), www.politicalconcepts.org/rights-bernstein/

13 Back to the Rough Ground

We have proceeded from the conventional, most predominant philosophical view of human rights – as rights that human beings are entitled to by virtue of being human – that grounds them in a natural human essence, which might be debatable and arguable but which functions as a foundational justification for their acceptance and implementation, to a perception of human rights that refuses to ignore the political framework in which they are couched and sees politics as the definitional anchor upon which we base our explanations for and expectations from human rights. We will, in this chapter, accept that political center of human rights as a given and continue, nevertheless, to question – not so much the theoretical underpinnings of human rights but rather its modern-day practice in current political life. Differently put, we shall put aside our essentialistic questions regarding either the "human" or the "right" in human rights, and engage with the actors, organizations, institutions, and communities which practice and talk human rights "in the field." Doing so serves two important purposes in our comprehensive presentation of human rights: It leads us to better understand both the deeds and the public discourse of human rights while opening up a different avenue of critique that can now focus on those deeds and that discourse.

A short detour is called for here, in the matter of the *philosophy* of human rights, since what we are about to undertake in this final chapter is, by some lights, questionably philosophical. We have not, along the way, insisted on a particular definition of "philosophy" – there are many, of course – except to stress that, as philosophers, we *question* our *concepts* in *analytic* fashion. It is that threesome – questioning, conceptualization, and analysis – that has provided the backbone of our philosophical discussion of human rights. Looking for validation of what we are about to embark on here, we mention in passing two names that inspire the type of philosophy done in this chapter: Marx and Wittgenstein.

The first is already familiar to us: Karl Marx, who posited that practice – in his terminology "praxis" – arises simultaneously, and sometimes even precedes, theory. Contrary to the modernistic, somewhat scientific, methodology for the attainment of knowledge and understanding that places theory at the beginning of our intellectual journeys and infers practice from it, Marx taught us that theory has no epistemic priority or applied import over practice; they are both necessarily intertwined. In fact, says Marx, only by beginning at a conversance with real experienced life, that is, with practice, can we move on to articulate theories. He famously says, in *The German Ideology*:

> The production of ideas, of conceptions, of consciousness, is at first directly interwoven with the material activity and the material intercourse of men, the language of real life. … The same applies to mental production as expressed in the language of the politics, laws, morality, religion, metaphysics, of a people. Men are the producers of their conceptions, ideas, etc. – real, active men, as they are conditioned by a definite development of their productive forces and of the intercourse corresponding to them … – Consciousness can never be anything else than conscious existence, and the existence of men is their actual life-process.
>
> (Marx and Engels, 1932 [1846], Part IA)

Thus, engaging with human rights in this manner, that is to say, investigating its on-the-ground manifestations, is no less a philosophical endeavor than articulating, as we have been doing, its theoretical presumptions. It is merely a different, perhaps a Marxist, exercise.

Ludwig Wittgenstein, considered by some to be the greatest philosopher of the twentieth century, provides our inquiry at this point with a fresh and unfamiliar slant on doing philosophy. Just as famously (as Marx), he is the source of a number of so-called mantras – statements that have invigorated philosophical stupefaction and multitudinous attempts at interpretation. Revolutionizing the method of philosophy by denying almost any method, he concluded his first (and only published) book, the *Tractatus Logico-Philosophicus*,[1] with the famous admonition: "Whereof one cannot speak, thereof one must be silent" (*TLP*, 7). Continuing, nevertheless, to speak about language and meaning and philosophy in general, Wittgenstein, in his later phase called "later Wittgenstein," eschewed any turn to theory, even in the doing of philosophy. In the iconic text of that period, *Philosophical Investigations*, he maintained that philosophy itself, whose goal is to provide us with understanding, is not a matter of conceptual analysis but rather a concrete activity of "perspicuously" exposing our linguistic practices and uses of words.[2] Accordingly, what we do when we do philosophy, when we want to understand ourselves and our world, is *describe*. His celebrated adages are far too many to impart here; the game of interpreting and understanding them is, in itself, an entire field of study in philosophy. Suffice only to mention some outstanding examples. "[D]on't think, but look!" (*PI*, §66); "We must do away with all *explanation*, and description alone must take its place" (*PI*, §109); "'knowing' it only means:

being able to describe it" (*PI*, p. 185); and the most striking – "Back to the rough ground!" (*PI*, §107). So we embark here on describing the deeds and discourse of human rights on the rough ground.

The Law, and Politics

As we have noted, the two noticeable areas where one encounters the deployment of human rights are politics (in the somewhat narrow meaning of politics we cited in the previous chapter), and the law. As we have seen all along, the latter plays a crucial role in formulating, regulating, synchronizing, adjudicating, and enforcing human rights. We have also seen that the problematic structure of the theoretical edifice of human rights – individuals, states, and international grounds – gives rise to the as-yet unresolved relation between domestic law and international law. Still, it is in the context of international law – particularly International Human Rights Law (IHRL) and International Humanitarian Law (IHL) – that the practice of human rights is realized. Conventionally, of course, we can profess to the status of moral rights being the theoretical justification of human rights as they are determined and brought to bear in international human rights law. That is, in point of fact, what we have mostly been doing in chasing down the elaboration of the "human" and the "right" in human rights. But why not, instead, concentrate on reality and on the undeniable circumstance that human rights are ruled, so to speak, by international human rights law? Realizing this, why not even give primacy to international human rights law as constituting the essence of human rights?

That is the novel position taken by Allen Buchanan in *The Heart of Human Rights* (2013). Calling our previous justificational method of basing legal human rights on moral human rights (which require, in turn, a philosophically robust ethical basis) the "mirroring view," Buchanan insists that there are moral human rights which do not receive legal protection in international law and there are legal human rights which cannot really appeal to moral rights as their justification. Accordingly, we cannot claim that legal human rights "mirror" moral human rights. With extraordinary candor he tells us that

> once we understand that legal rights can serve several distinct kinds of moral purposes, and that the realization of moral rights is only one of these, we should acknowledge that a sound justification for international legal human rights need not refer to moral rights at all.
>
> (Buchanan, 2013, 312)

Instead, accepting the orthodox description and explanation of the international legal structure as being made up of the continuum of individual-state-globe, he places the onus for human rights on the international legal system itself, thinking that it is called upon to "provide universal standards for regulating the behavior of states toward those under their jurisdiction, for the sake of those individuals themselves ..." (ibid., 27).

Once a moral theory of individual rights is left at the side of the road in our attempt to validate the legal body of international human rights (and once we realize that there is more than one such theory), we can be open to different ways of endorsing the law. After we recognize the different circumstances and contexts in which we turn to and use international human rights law, we cannot but accept a pluralistic justification that serves not just individuals, but also the interests of states themselves, in instrumental fashion. Thus are explained the support for and protection of social goods, institutional duties, group rights, equal rights to democracy, and human welfare. It is fascinating to follow Buchanan while rethinking – and sometimes reasserting – our basic beliefs that cohere with human rights: they are still owing to individuals "simply by virtue of their humanity" (ibid., 73–74) and we still demand that they provide the safeguards for a minimally good life. But these basic axioms pertain to international law and its uses, not to some transcendent or foundational moral theory of rights.

Subsequently, the discussion about human rights, and even its philosophical questioning, moves to the interrogation of international human rights law. We must rehearse, yet again, the relationship between domestic law and international law – especially given that three-tiered construction of the human rights system. A balance must be achieved between the adulation of international human rights law (by democratic societies) and its limitation of states' sovereignty through its emphasis on individual human rights. In order to achieve such equilibrium and, indeed, in order to make the international human rights legal system function both substantively and efficiently, the current legal human rights regime needs to address practical, rather than only theoretical, issues. One is the question of formal legal enforcement of states' duties to abide by international treaties and agreements. Another is the similar, but different in principle, roadblock of institutions with global reach – banks, corporations, trade associations, international organizations – that must somehow abide by international law even though that law, by default, only obligates states. Still another source of distress, as we have seen, is the difficulty – in practice, just as it was in theory – of intervention when states violate the human rights of their citizens and residents. The adoption of international human rights law as the essential place of human rights – since it is (in) the real world of human rights activity and conversation – transfers our conversation from searching ineffectually for the foundations of human rights to engaging fruitfully with their realistic – since legal – intents.

Just as realistic and down-to-earth are treatments by philosophers who view the substance of human rights as being unavoidably concrete, that is to say, political.[3] Where Buchanan takes legal practice for our object of inspection, thinkers such as Charles Beitz or Joseph Raz believe that investigation of the essence of human rights travels through and with political engagement and procedure. Interestingly, these analyses of the phenomenon of human rights take place at approximately the same time – at the period when, on the one hand, the discourse of and on human rights has become regular currency but, on the other hand, the project of justifying human rights in theoretical contexts seems to have overstayed its welcome. And it is Raz who provides the mantra for this move to real politics: "Human Rights without Foundations."[4]

Recall that Raz was, indeed, adept at formulating a theory of rights in general, and at showing us that "the common core of all rights" puts them as mid-posts between values (or interests) and duties.[5] In the matter of human rights, however, one must be careful, for it is a fallacy of philosophers of the "traditional" school of human rights – those that attempt to ground human rights in ethical stances that turn to values – that they "tend to take it for granted that human rights are important rights" (Raz, 2007, 3). Raz chastises these traditionalists for not understanding the relationship between values and rights (that is to say, for not doing a proper ethics), for not succeeding in the (nearly impossible) derivation of rights (that is to say, for not working logically), and – most important – for being disconnected from the way human rights is really done, that is, from political practice. Beitz, on his part in *The Idea of Human Rights* (2009), categorizes (what Raz would call) traditional theories of human rights as being either "naturalistic" – looking for the universal common factor that all humans share naturally – or "agreement theories" – looking for the Rawlsian "overlapping consensus" that all of us can agree on. Neither approach to human rights, thinks Beitz, is fruitful since neither can really explain how human rights came to exist historically and, more so, how they function. This question of how human rights function is the important query for all dealers in the politics of human rights; more explicitly, it is precisely in the field of international human rights that the issue of the functioning of human rights must arise. It is therefore not in the least surprising that John Rawls's *The Law of Peoples* (1999) – that we have already encountered as a seminal text – can serve as the springboard for this type of discussion. Rawls positions the discussion of human rights politically in proverbial "international relations," saying that "[h]uman rights are a class of rights that play a special role in a reasonable Law of Peoples: they restrict the justifying reasons for war and its conduct, and they specify limits to a regime's internal autonomy" (*The Law of Peoples*, 79). Understanding that role and how it is manifested and practiced is the goal of a political theory of human rights.

Indeed, Beitz connects the practice and the idea of human rights magnificently:

> ... we might frame our understanding of the idea of a human right by identifying the roles this idea plays within a discursive practice. We attend to the practical inferences that would be drawn by competent participants in the practice from what they regard as valid claims of human rights. An inventory of these inferences generates a view of the

discursive functions of human rights and this informs an account of the meaning of the concept. I shall call a conception of human rights arrived at by this route a "practical" conception.

(Beitz, 2009, 102)

He then expounds on this more overtly: "... international human rights is the name of a collective political enterprise – a practice – with distinctive purposes and modes of action" (ibid., 103). Raz appears to provide an even more applied version of practical engagement. Requiring of an account – not really a theory – of human rights that it identify the necessary traits of human rights as they are attributed to rights in general by human rights practice, and calling such an account a "political conception of human rights," Raz is explicit and material: "Following Rawls, I will take human rights to be rights which set limits to the sovereignty of states, in that their actual or anticipated violation is a (defeasible) reason for taking action against the violator in the international arena" (Raz, 2007, 9). In both pronouncements, though, the emphasis is on political reasoning that is expressed in the terminology of human rights for the purpose of taking international action.

Lest we be prone to flattening these political views of human rights to a simple, non-foundational, non-theoretical, only internationalist understanding of human rights, we must note that these appointments with human rights are nothing if not nuanced. Two cases should suffice to make this point. First is the meaning of foundationalism. Beitz, having repudiated the naturalist and agreement theories of human rights – which may be viewed as looking for (moral) foundations of human rights – might naturally be seen as an opponent of the search for the fundamental essence of human rights. However, his elaboration on this quandary is more sophisticated.

One need not say ... that practical views are nonfoundationalist, if by this is meant that such views deny that there are reasons to adhere to and support international human rights ... because a practical conception prescinds from taking any philosophical view about the nature or basis of human rights, it can distinguish between the problem of conceptualizing human rights and that of understanding their authority.

(Beitz, 2009, 103)

Raz is, again, more matter-of-fact, yet similarly discriminating in his explanation of the international nature of human rights.

So far states have been the main targets in international law, and I will continue to treat human rights as being rights against states. But I do not mean that human rights are rights held only against states, or only in the international arena. Human rights can be held against international organizations, and other international agents, and almost always

they will also be rights against individuals and other domestic institutions. The claim is only that being rights whose violation is a reason for
action against states in the international arena is distinctive of human
rights, according to human rights practice.

(Raz, 2007, 9–10)

In other words, we need not be ultra-finicky in attributing political
intent and practice by insisting on those three traditional stations of the
individual-state-international arena and insulating human rights in the
third level alone. The politicizing of human rights does, in a sense, make it
a player in the game of international relations between states, but putting
human rights to work politically involves it in internal, external, societal,
community, intra-state, inter-state, and yes, sometimes even personal,
individual relations. Campaigning for the indictment of individual war-
criminals, for example, is a highly political human rights agenda; yet it
does not, in any formal sense, address a sovereign state as such.

Understanding the human rights phenomena as they have emerged in
the last few decades – in other words, assessing the practice and discourse of the entire community of people and organizations that go
under the title of "human rights" – requires us, then, to look at politics
and at (usually international, sometimes domestic) law. Evidently, these
two contexts are not unrelated. Michael Ignatieff, a leading protagonist
in the human rights field, tells the historical story of this emergence by
putting politics and law together as a composite of the "juridical, advocacy, and enforcement revolutions" of human rights (Ignatieff, 2001,
Human Rights as Politics and Idolatry, 5). Human rights, as we have
seen, is constituted legally in and by the legal arena of International
Human Rights Law made up of declarations, covenants, treaties, and
contracts; it is a veritable union of human rights advocacy instruments
put together in NGOs and making up "global civil society" (ibid., 8);
and it is now making headway in international commissions, tribunals
and courts. The way to understand all of this, the way to perceive that
human rights has become such a potent and infective part of our contemporary life, is by looking at politics and the law, not by entertaining
"the illusion ... that human rights is above politics, a set of moral trump
cards whose function is to bring political disputes to closure and conclusion" (ibid., 21). The quest for moral certainty that could or might
anchor human rights in some type of universal absolutism is detrimental
to the progress we can make by using human rights, which "is nothing
other than a politics, one that must reconcile moral ends to concrete
situations and must be prepared to make painful compromises not only
between means and ends, but between ends themselves" (ibid., 21–22). So
political is this turn to and use of human rights that "there are occasions ... when human rights as politics become a fighting creed, a call to
arms" (ibid., 22)!

Talking Human Rights

Let us pivot for a moment to a somewhat different mode of criticism – that which views the proliferation of human rights discourse as a negative development. Let us accept, with these criticizers, that the vocabulary, terminology, and semantics of human rights have become forceful and all-pervading. Let us even think of human rights discourse, owned by the human rights community and bestowed upon the world at large, as strongly effectual and even powerful. How can this type of change be viewed as detrimental – to who and to what purpose?

Just as Ignatieff spoke of the juridical, advocacy and enforcement human rights revolutions, one can legitimately speak of the discursive revolution – the change in public talk and engagement that prioritizes rights in all manner of political doings. It is in Mary Ann Glendon's book of 1991, *Rights Talk: The Impoverishment of Political Discourse*, that we meet a one-sided, though factually and argumentatively reasoned, invective against the contemporary (that is, in 1990) use and, according to Glendon, overuse of "rights talk." On all sides of every debate rights are called upon to supply the hinge of every argument. They are used as trumps to defeat and sometimes even cancel out other elements of the conversation. Pervasive rights talk ranks the individual and her rights above community, society, and polity and ignores duties and responsibilities to others and to the collective. Rights are also overly legalistic, so talking about them so ubiquitously makes our law-oriented dialogue supposedly clean, formalistic, and unequivocal. But instead of engaging with our values and asking about our social commitments and obligations, we focus on our individualistic entitlements, whether they are critically relevant to the issue at hand or not.

Two related questions attach themselves to this kind of complaint against rights. The first has to do with the differentiation that we made early on in our discussion between rights in general and human rights in particular. It appears that the protest against rights and rights talk that is pitched by Glendon in *Rights Talk* can be easily adapted to the case of human rights and the human rights talk now so much with us. In a much later article, Glendon indeed worries about similar deficiencies in the proliferation of human rights talk, now asking "whether the noble post-World War II universal human-rights idea has finally been so manipulated and politicized as to justify its abandonment by men and women of good will" (Glendon, 2016, 19). Indeed she sees "human-rights" ideas as being at the core of deleterious developments like their abuse by special-interest groups (in Eastern Europe and South Africa) and their dismemberment into "scattered rights of personal autonomy" (ibid., 20). And she equally blames the court system for "judicially created rights [that] have displaced political judgments that could and should have been left to the ordinary processes of bargaining, education, persuasion, and voting" (ibid.). Objecting even to the all-encompassing international focus of human rights, she accuses, for example, the expansion of their use in the

European Union for the narrowing down of democratic decision making in national governments.

A second difficulty in such an attack on rights talk – or even human rights talk – resides in the question of substance vs. rhetoric. While Glendon's ruminations are on the human rights "idea," it is no coincidence that she titles her book *Rights Talk*, with the emphasis on "talk." One of the most strident chapters of that book is titled "Refining the Rhetoric of Rights," and it encapsulates her ire in the following words:

> Our stark, simple rights dialect puts a damper on the process of public justification, communication, and deliberation upon which the continuing vitality of a democratic regime depends. It contributes to the erosion of the habits, practices, and attitudes of respect for others that are the ultimate and surest guarantors of human rights. It impedes creative, long-range thinking about our most pressing social problems.
>
> (Glendon, 1991, 171)

Do our shortcomings, then, accompanying the ironic success of the human rights project belong to the realm of language and rhetoric, or are they more substantive, having to do with the actual practice of the human rights community? Looking through the lenses of the philosophical position called "pragmatism" (or sometimes, in the philosophy of language, "pragmatics"), we now put discourse and practice together, holding discourse to *be* practice.[6] Our questions that (with Glendon) seemed to concern human rights rhetoric alone now widen to the practice of human rights: What would it mean to say that the human rights community is *too* strong? That human rights struggles have been *too* successful? That human rights have become *too* dominant or effective? And how can we justify harboring such views? What makes them conceptually possible or factually reasonable?

The facts of the matter have to do with the way the human rights project, since 1948 but much more so since the 1970s and 1980s of the previous century, has become institutionalized, both alongside and within the powerful political bodies of domestic government and international organizations. Such institutionalization is easily seen as a socio-linguistic phenomenon – call it rhetoric – but it also rests upon the hyper-legalization of human rights norms and their consensual reception not only by society at large but even by the heretofore recalcitrant powers that be. This transformation of human rights from its oppositional, generally underdog station to being a partner in power-sharing is sometimes gingerly recognized by both thinkers and activists. But it is described most acerbically by David Kennedy, in his article "Reassessing International Humanitarianism: The Dark Sides" (2006).[7] We are troubled, as the title hints, by "humanitarianism" writ large; in other words, by the people, organizations, laws, and institutions born of both international human rights and the international laws (and management) of war. That large body puts together a collection of "humanitarian commitments" to engagement with the citizenry and

governments of the world, to multilateralism and intergovernmental institutions, to moral ideals, to a cosmopolitanism that holds respect for other
cultures and nations, and – most essentially – to a renunciation of power
politics that involve military might. Obviously, this broad but, for that
matter, no less deep collection of beliefs opens up a beehive of internal and
inter-related tensions and arguments within the humanitarian project itself.
Still, we can generally identify this set of sentiments, sometimes explicitly
and sometimes between the lines, in the workings of international human
rights bodies and international humanitarian organizations.

Public engagement that is predicated on these tenets seems to require
humanitarians to be in conflict with power politics. We must also admit that
the institutional tools at our service in this engagement – for example, the
UN bodies and the human rights NGOs themselves – reflect and house those
same conflicts. More problematical, however, is that as the human rights
community has grown and become influential, with its language ever-present
and its motions socially and politically regularized, the struggle against the
halls of power has dissipated.

> As a result, we humanitarians have a hard time acknowledging our own
> participation in rulership, preferring to think of ourselves off to one side
> speaking truth to power … But humanitarians increasingly provide the
> terms in which global power is exercised. We speak the same language
> as those who plan and fight wars, the language of humanitarian objec-
> tives and proportional, even humane means. Our legal and professional
> terminology has seeped into popular parlance … and has become the
> vocabulary of governance.
>
> (Kennedy, 2004, 132)

In other words, human rights is complicit with governments and other
authorities in designing immigration and refugee policies, in making legal
and judicial decisions concerning citizens' needs and "rights," and in discussing and determining warfare under common tags like collateral
damage, collective security, or humanitarian intervention. That is to say,
human rights is an active participant in the power wielding policies of
governments and, as such, is also responsible for the damage wrought by
attendant political actions.

It is abundantly clear that human rights has become a profession which is
justly viewed as having done a lot of good. It has given a voice to victims, it
has put on front stage the organizations of civil society that fight for justice
against abusive governments, and it has, as we noted, articulated a language
of ethics and values which is now predominant in both domestic and international legal affairs. What then are the damages that one might identify as
attaching to the human rights agenda when it becomes a tool of governance?
What might emerge as the costs of this power? How do particular negatives
accompany such a positively viewed service to humanity? Kennedy lists a

reasonable inventory of some well-known and often discussed failings: First and most bluntly, human rights, in now being so exclusively dominant, has crowded out of the conversation other players in achieving justice, including tradition, religion, movements of solidarity, organizations for economic justice, and the like. We have noted, already, that being the liberal icon that it is, human rights focuses on the individual to the detriment of groups and other social communes. Furthermore, being so closely in touch with political bodies, current human rights professionals often overlook economic and social rights, even though these were also posited axiomatically in the UDHR. Indeed, because of their affinity to the powers that be, human rights organizations are sometimes lenient towards government action that is not up to (humanitarian) par, as long as it is not grievously lower than the expected standards. Finally, such collaboration with government makes it seem that human rights is all about the state, in favor of the formally established center at the price of inattention to society, community, and mostly the periphery.

Just as we might bemoan the overreaching rhetoric of human rights language and its paradoxically harmful effects on political language, so do we thus arrive at a lament about the power that human rights practice now has through its – paradoxical again – adoption by and partnership with dominant authorities, be they governmental, financial, legal, or even cultural. According to Kennedy the onus is now on human rightists to accept the responsibility that goes with power and influence by admitting that we are part of the ruling classes. The human rights community cannot simultaneously participate in power and deny its effectiveness; political maturity involves being nuanced and seeing the various sides – good and evil – of humanitarian action. "We have met the empire, and it is us" (Kennedy, 2004, 151).

We shall immediately return to the question of "empire," imperialism, and colonialism in less metaphorical style. But let us permit the question to cast its shadow on us for a little while longer and ask incredulously – is human rights really an empire?

Universalism Reconsidered

In Chapter 7, we addressed the philosophical quandaries arising from the oft-accepted supposition of the universalism of human rights, mostly counterpoised by philosophical relativism. We saw that the universalism-relativism debate, as we encounter it in philosophy, may inquire about metaphysics (is there a universal truth or is truth relative to a language, a culture, a society?), about epistemology (are our sources and justification of knowledge universal or relative to a tradition, a context, or even a goal?), or about ethics (is there a universally grounded ethics or is our morality relative to our discourse, our history, our community?). Importantly, in the philosophical consideration of human rights, we noted that there is an almost unthinking presupposition in the concept of human rights – at least as it is conceived in the Western world – leading to an adamant insistence on universalism: how can we talk about human rights without assuming that they are common to all human beings? Is universalism not a necessary condition for any additional question we might want to ask about human rights, such as their absolutism, their categorization, their inter-relations, and so on? Is there, indeed, any way of asking anything about human rights without the prior, conceptual acceptance of their universality? Isn't the very meaning of "human rights" a consequence of the acknowledgment of the universal nature of being human?

Two noteworthy perspectives on this question have already been mentioned. One involves the anthropological awareness of cultural relativity (not necessarily a philosophical position espousing relativism) that must be dealt with if we are to do justice to the consequences of universalism. Thus, for example, an internal paradox of human rights universalism was noted[8] in the American Anthropological Association's statement of 1947, where a universal declaration of human rights was called upon to recognize the diversity and multiplicity of moral norms and values precisely for the goal of being universal. The tension involved in this double acknowledgment of both commonality and difference seems to thwart the single-minded acceptance of naïve universalism that has always accompanied the UDHR as the bible of human rights religion.

A different problematics accompanies the Western provenance of universalism in general, and the positioning and functioning of human rights particularly in international law.[9] Beyond the catchy "the West and the Rest," there is keen awareness of profound imbalance, even incoherence, between the imperialistic tradition of international law and the countries and cultures of the global South upon and in which it was brought to bear. Accepting the always biased legal grounding of human rights – biased because it was a part of the colonial masters' regime – really means propounding the gap between "advanced" states and the societies deemed more "backward" and, more so, coercing the non-West to consent to Western imperialistic, capitalist mores. "Universalism," in intended scare-quotes, is one of the values that is inevitably presumed to undergird the human rights conversation; as a result, resistance to such an automatic universalism is perceived to be a protest against "human rights" (again, in intended scare-quotes). But perhaps such dissent is not an argument against the universalism of human rights *per se*, but rather an appeal, even a demand, for a more inclusive, less imperialist version of human rights.

A notable, foundational contribution to this critical view of the supposed universalism of human rights is to be found in Makau Mutua's inspired article, "Savages, Victims, and Saviors: The Metaphor of Human Rights" (2001). Its opening words and subsequent explication point out the basic conceptual structure of the human rights project, as we know it, that has played such a substantial part in the Westernized view of human rights that is universally promulgated.

The grand narrative of human rights contains a subtext that depicts an epochal contest pitting savages, on the one hand, against victims and saviors, on the other. The savages-victims-saviors construction is a three-dimensional compound metaphor in which each dimension is a metaphor in itself. The main authors of the human rights discourse, including the United Nations, Western states, international non-governmental organizations (INGOs), and senior Western academics, constructed this three-dimensional prism. This rendering of the human rights corpus and its discourse is unidirectional and predictable, a black-and-white construction that pits good against evil.

(Mutua, 2001, 201–202)

Elaborating on the savages-victims-saviors metaphor, Mutua famously shows us the who's who of its references. The savages are the violators of human rights, most often states, and clearly these must be evil –

illiberal, anti-democratic, or other authoritarian culture. ... [S]avagery inheres in the theory and practice of the one-party state, military junta, controlled or closed state, theocracy, or even cultural practices such as the one popularly known in the West as female genital mutilation.

(ibid., 203)

What "redeems" the savage is its "submission to human rights norms" (ibid.). The victim is always a human being – in singular – "whose 'dignity and worth' have been violated by the savage" (ibid.). And the third participant of the metaphor, the savior, "protects, vindicates, civilizes, restrains, and safeguards" (ibid., 204). Outside the metaphor, the savior "is the human rights corpus itself, with the United Nations, Western governments, INGOs, and Western charities as the actual rescuers, redeemers of a benighted world" (ibid.). This metaphor, and its parallels in the real world, would not be awkward, were it not for its hidden presuppositions. For "the savior is ultimately a set of culturally based norms and practices that inhere in liberal thought and philosophy" (ibid.)!

Mutua and other critics of this Western human-rights doctrine have awoken the players in human rights to the shortcomings, indeed harms, that come out of such a consensually accepted dogma. Most often recalled is the Eurocentric colonial project, which accepts a ranking of superior and subordinate (cultures, societies, people) and which therefore belies any real universality. The human rights project is a part, or definitely an outgrowth, of that colonial enterprise, ignoring or forgetting other important campaigns against "tyranny and imperialism" (ibid., 205). Furthermore, the human rights program, predicated on such savages-victims-saviors, holds a language and a rhetoric that is oriented towards liberalism and democracy, ostracizing and, at the least, keeping out of the conversation of human rights cultures that have different political norms. Again, universalism is compromised. Even at the very concrete political level, it is a Western terminology and vocabulary that defines situations of "peace," "stability," or "equality," pretending to be neutral and universal. Similarly, and still in keeping with the metaphor, the relatively young human rights culture has been racially biased, usually painting the savages and victims in non-white colors, the saviors white. But political power itself cannot be disregarded, and the human rights culture must change into a "multicultural, inclusive, and deeply political" (ibid., 207) form that recognizes its own misplaced Eurocentric centrism that has moved other cultures to the periphery.

The point of such critique is –

> an attempt at locating – philosophically, culturally, and historically – the normative edifice of the human rights corpus. If the human rights movement is driven by ... the mission to require that all human societies transform themselves to fit a particular blueprint, then there is an acute shortage of deep reflection and a troubling abundance of zealotry in the human rights community.
>
> (ibid.)

More pertinent, and housing practical consequences, is the fact that the human rights project, with its bogus universalism, is not received in non-Western societies as the benevolent do-gooder that it purports and pretends to be. "The movement does not deeply resonate in the cultural fabrics of non-Western states, except among hypocritical elites steeped in Western ideas. In order ultimately to prevail, the human rights movement must be moored in the cultures of all peoples" (ibid., 208). We must acknowledge, then, that the seeming anchor of human rights, the obvious and simplistic belief in universalism as the lever with which human rights can fix the world, is not only a utopian – that is to say unachievable – ambition, but is in point of fact its own defeating own goal.

Back to Political Rough Grounds

Whereas in the previous chapter we dove into deep philosophical conundrums of liberalism that waylaid the conventional and almost consensual project of thinking about human rights in "traditional" modes, we have in this present discussion been embroiled in the questions of the workings of human rights, both theoretical and in practice. Our queries have led us to investigate human rights as (customary) legal and political action; its use as rhetoric and means of power; and the impossibility of living up to its ultimate vision of manifesting a universal code. When one is thus stumped by tensions that seem to drown human rights both ideationally and realistically, hopelessness about human rights seems imminent. One way of addressing these questions is clearly available – not positing replies or even suggestions for unraveling these internal-to-human-rights conflicts, but posing another looming query: Where do we go from here? Similar formulations of that question indeed make themselves heard in some recent books and articles: *Can Human Rights Survive?* (Gearty, 2006), *The Endtimes of Human Rights* (Hopgood, 2013), "Is the Human Rights Era Ending?" (Ignatieff, 2002), or the very explicit "The Future of Human Rights" (Moyn, 2014).

Looking at these (and other) ruminations reveals the theme that we have brought up diversely and often: embrace the political. In Chapter 12, we dealt with the complex meaning of the political kernel ascribed to human rights – that is to say, the conceptual question of what makes human rights fundamentally political. Here, in this chapter, we have encountered a different insistence on the somewhat narrower "political" as that aspect of human rights that is carried out in *de facto* international relations. Now, when trying to assess a future for human rights as either promising or hopeless, it behooves us to traverse those two vertices – the political as a deep core of human rights and the political as concrete international exercise of power – and perhaps even some options lying between them. That famed, infamous question, "What is to be done?"[10] will now hopefully serve to move us forward through our critiques of human rights to a constructive address where well-defined challenges of the type we have encountered – as between the individual and the community, between the global and the local, between security and human rights, between civil and economic rights – can be explicitly entertained, even if not finally resolved.

One way of advancing is somewhat reminiscent of our erstwhile discussion of the politics of human rights, which attempted to separate between descriptive "politics" – rough, down-to-earth, halls-of-power politics, and the analytic "political" – sophisticated ideas of power with its uses and balances. Here, however, in a newly articulated political human rights, we shall meld the two – practical and conceptual – together and emphasize another divide, that between the organized, institutional bodies and the informal, activist versions of human rights. Taking our cue from Hopgood's *The Endtimes of Human Rights* (2013), we realize, when looking at human rights in the twenty-first century, that there are two worlds of human rights. One is the capitalized institution of Human Rights, the "global structure of laws, courts, norms and organizations that raise money, write reports, run international campaigns, open local offices, lobby governments, and claim to speak with singular authority in the name of humanity as a whole" (Hopgood, 2013, ix). This is the institutional, international conglomerate body or norms and organizations that we have been describing; this is also the Human Rights of which Kennedy should have spoken when he called it the "empire."

There is, however, a different engagement with human rights, in small letters, that centers on the "local and transnational networks of activists who bring publicity to abuses they and their communities face and who try to exert pressure on governments and the United Nations for action" (ibid., viii). This latter manifestation of human rights is a wider swath of activism that permits itself to work in a less formalized, organizational structure and is open to discourse that is not always that of International Human Rights Law.

In combating violence and deprivation, any language is useful that helps to raise awareness, generate transnational activism, put pressure on governments, facilitate legal redress, and attracts funds for campaigning, whether it is that of human rights [conventionally understood], compassion, solidarity, freedom, brotherhood, sisterhood, justice, religion, grace, charity, kin, ethnicity, nationalism, pity, love, or equality ... It is a flexible and negotiable language.

(ibid.)

It is imperative, then, that we distinguish between Human Rights and human rights. Our many doubts concerning human rights were actually bouts against Human Rights. The thoughts of empire and collaboration with power were entertained in the context of our familiarity with the institutions of Human Rights and their articulations of Human Rights norms, laws, and regulations. And it is that grand, international, organizational, formalistic institution that suffers from illusions of grandeur rather than admitting ordinary suffering, from a desire for power rather than objection to it, and from globalized interests rather than a local interest in welfare. A related predicament that we have seen involves Human Rights accentuating the rights of individuals with less or no attention given to rights of groups or communities. And it is Human Rights, not human rights, that Hopgood is speaking of when he says "endtimes": The kind of dead ends that have arisen in the practice of Human Rights – because of their establishment as part of the Western empire and its accompanying internal conflicts and external pressures – make their viability uncertain at the least. Moving to human rights means recognizing the practicality of their tactical use "to help prevent torture, disappearances, or extrajudicial executions or to demand economic and social rights to food, water, and health care" (ibid.). And this means, again, looking at and doing human rights in actual political frameworks.

Let us recall another context, which is visibly political and in which we have seen human rights founder. In Chapter 11 we investigated the supposed clash between human rights and security, asking whether personal security and its expanded idea of state security provided a case of a clash of rights (for example, one's right to liberty, free movement, privacy, etc. vs. another's right to personal security) or were, perhaps, a tool in the state's arsenal that actually violates human rights almost by definition, being state-sponsored against the individual. The issue of national security, in general, is fertile ground upon which to query a host of state policies and procedures precisely because they work in defense of a national regime even though they are regularly presented by state authorities as protective of individual citizens. We can straightforwardly follow the popular reports and analysis of state security policies that point out how torture, surveillance, violent policing, immigration control, and similar security measures harbor great threats to human rights. Indeed, human rights activists and NGOs are seen to be

following their natural calling – of standing up to and against state authority – in matters of security that violate individual human rights. But the inner-
workings of the very idea of security, troubled as it is by the conceptual
ambiguity mentioned above regarding the human right to personal security,
have given rise to a current malaise within the conversation of human rights
that is internally devastating. Let us turn to Conor Gearty's *Can Human
Rights Survive?* (2006) to see how and why.

Of all the topical points, such as torture, profiling, gun-control, and
others that are raised when we deliberate about national security, we can
attach the label "political" most patently to the issue of terrorism, to the
political uses, misuses, and abuses of the term "terrorism" itself, and to that
constant, contemporary headline – "The War Against Terror." Interestingly,
Gearty locates the beginning of the war against terror not as we usually do,
in post-9/11 rhetoric, policy, and action, but in the Israeli-Palestinian conflict
and the attribution of "terrorism" to the Palestine Liberation Organization,
with its political violence starting in the 1960s. We have already brought up
the case of the Israeli "Security Wall"[11] as paradigmatic of the use of
"security" in rhetorically and dishonestly furthering state interests. A more
pernicious ploy is traced by Gearty in the case of the Israeli-Palestinian conflict
where, he claims, "the idea of a world-wide contagion of terror inspired by evil
forces with designs on western civilization" began (2006, 114). Following the
development of this idea – of political violence as "terrorism" – all over the
world (in the U.S.S.R., Germany, Afghanistan, Iraq, and so many others),
we realize that the governments and authorities engaging in "counter-terrorism"
and "the war on terror" have become, in the common mind, the forces of good
against evil, no matter their methods of battle against terrorism and no matter
their violent dismissal of human rights. The creation of a "Coalition of the
Willing," which encompasses powerful state powers, leaves no room for discussion or debate about the "terrorists" who happen to be "small, weak groups
that cause a fraction of the fatalities of their more powerful opponents" (ibid.,
123). And in this process, human rights becomes corrupted since "a large
number of intellectuals, politicians and non-governmental bodies promptly
[echo] this theme of a new global war" (ibid., 122). Thinking of the world of
power and politics, in both war and peace, through the "terrorism model" leads
to a sharp change in the way we, that is, people involved in and caring for
human rights, think of human rights. "Human rights law ... has largely
accommodated ... security-oriented changes, and the effect of this has been to
render them seemingly compliant with rather than inherently hostile to human
rights principles" (ibid., 125). The original idea formulated in the ICCPR, that
state power even in the case of national security ("the life of the nation") has
limits determined by absolute, non-derogable human rights, has in these times
of terror given way to security law which is incompatible with human rights.
The human rights trump is no longer a trump and even those conversant in the
field of human rights law and policy have accepted placing human rights opposite security as equal contenders in the conversation.

The details matter less than the fact of the discussions: internment, torture, coercive interrogation, covert surveillance and other manifestations of lawless state power are not any longer simple wrongs to be avoided and severely punished when they occur; rather they have become a set of proposed solutions to supposed ethical dilemmas that need now to be considered and debated, as you might consider and debate any other kind of policy proposal. The unspeakable is no longer unspoken!

(ibid., 132)

As before, such a deep crisis, internal to the human rights community itself – since it does not see itself combating the powers that be but rather conversing with them – is not easily solved, ignored, or vacated, since it is the very idea of human rights which is called upon to justify the war against terror in "selective aggression abroad and ... brutality at home" (ibid., 136). The complex redeeming path involves, yet again, an engagement with politics and political rhetoric. The language of human rights cannot, and must not, continue to be used "turning our subject into a kind of moral mask behind which lurk cruelty and oppression" (ibid., 138). The human rights community must insist on fighting the political battle against those waging the war on terror by owning its language and not letting it be abused by talk about emergencies and national security as if they were siblings of human rights. The "war on terror," that demagogical display of security interests, is a tool in the hands of powerful authorities who are the usual suspects in violation of human rights. Human rights will survive only if they are re-appropriated in the political landscape.[12]

So human rights issues – whether they concern institutional strengths and then collaboration with the powers that be or collaborative dealings with governments and world powers on questions of security – are unavoidably political. Let us revisit, in short, one more matter that has also engaged us in the question of how the political, that is – politics, impacts human rights. Very early on we encountered the conventionally accepted division between civil-political rights and economic-social-cultural rights; so conventional and basic was it, that the two foundational documents of human rights law became the independent ICCPR (International Covenant on Civil and Political Rights) and the separate but equal ICESCR (International Covenant on Economic, Social, and Cultural Rights) that make up, together with the UDHR (Universal Declaration of Human Rights), the so-called International Bill of Human Rights. Accompanying this bifurcation has been the question of priority (which "comes first" or is more central – civil-political rights or economic-social-cultural rights?) and the slew of answers that take us through several issues in attempting to ascertain the relationships between these two families of human rights. This is the context in which we discussed cultural relativity (in some cultures social-economic rights precede civil-political rights), or poverty (economic rights of individuals populate the principled discussions), or international responsibilities between states (global justice involves the rich states "owing" to the poor). Now, however, we move to inquire about the contemporary landscape, where globalization is the central player, and suggest that not only are the political and the economic patently connected but that in the matter of human rights political human rights are only fathomable if we return to the question of economic human rights. Indeed, the proposition at hand is that human rights in general can be understood, and then perhaps achieved, only by attending to today's globally managed economic world.

When thinking about economic welfare (in Chapter 10), we were faced with the notion that the very existence of poverty is tantamount to a violation of human rights. In fact, we can reasonably utter the idea that, given the current riches of the world and the availability of resources and techniques that make it possible today to feed anyone anywhere in the world, both the quantity (that is, the number of people) and quality (that is, the inhuman degradation involved) of poverty and hunger all around the globe attest to a conscious and intentional obliviousness to human rights by governments and individuals alike.[13] But now let us take the question of poverty one step further to the global context of neoliberal capitalism and the stultifying economic inequality that has resulted from the financial market policies that have overridden almost all other systems of economic conduct. Although it is true that the world is "richer" in the sense of material welfare as a whole, and although one might even claim that the international condition of poverty has been ameliorated – in other words, we can seriously now suggest that there is sufficient food and sustenance, perhaps even shelter, health care, and education, for almost everyone around the globe – it is just as evident today that the levels of inequality between rich and poor are the most obvious consequence of global market fundamentalism.[14]

Samuel Moyn, in his book *Not Enough: Human Rights in an Unequal World* (2018) posits two "imperatives" for the measure of economic distribution, in intriguing contrast to each other.

> Sufficiency concerns how far an individual is *from having nothing* and how well she is doing *in relation to some minimum of provision* of the good things in life. Equality concerns how far individuals are *from one another* in the portion of those good things they get.
>
> (Moyn, 2018, 3)

The question that needs raising is – which of these is pertinent to human rights? When we speak of economic and social rights, are we focusing on an individual's minimal needs that are sufficient for living a decent life, or are we scrutinizing her relative situation compared to others (and are these all other individuals in the world, other people in her community, or other citizens in a state)? This is the place to recall that equality, in and of itself, is not a human right: we do not have a right to equality. Rather, there is a presupposition manifestly claimed in the UDHR about "recognition of the inherent dignity and of the equal and inalienable rights of all members of the human family." Equality, like dignity, is at the basis of human rights; it is not, by itself, a human right.[15] Indeed, the insufficiency of basic resources – both material and spiritual – is properly deemed to be a violation of human rights, usually social and economic human rights. We have seen how the capabilities approach to human rights or the institutional definition of human rights gesture exactly towards a minimal demand, that is, a sufficient condition, for human functioning. Sufficiency, then, is naturally associated with human rights; insufficiency violates them. But how can we designate inequality itself as such a violation? Differently put, how does distributive inequality in the economic and social spheres cause the type of harm that we can identify as a human rights grievance? If a human being has sufficient resources for not being hungry, having a roof above his head, achieving a worthwhile education, or obtaining reasonable healthcare, how is his relative positioning in all of these relevant to his human rights?

In answering this question, Moyn takes a noteworthy step, turning to the historical and political advent of human rights to make a remarkable claim:

> The distinction between sufficiency and equality allows us to see how profoundly the age of human rights, while a good one for some of the worst off, has mainly been a golden age for the rich. The meaning of human rights has slowly transformed as egalitarian aspiration has fallen.
>
> (ibid., 5)

This assertion is not a causal one. It is not that the rise of human rights has led to the demise of equality or egalitarianism; neither can we declare that the ailment of gross inequality simplistically fostered the pantheon of human rights abuses. But something dire has happened to the equality that functioned as the conceptual basis for demanding universal human rights and this has transpired in strange parallel to the political and cultural success of human rights.

> Expanded in coverage, human rights have become a worldwide slogan in a time of downsized ambition. Across time ... the spirit of human rights and the political enterprise with which people associate them has shifted from nationally framed egalitarian citizenship to a globally scaled subsistence minimum ... They have been a banner for campaigns against discriminatory treatment on the basis of gender, race, and sexual orientation. But they have also become our language for indicating that it is enough ... for our solidarity with our fellow human being to remain weak and cheap. To a startling extent, human rights have become prisoners of the contemporary age of inequality.
>
> (ibid., 6)

This "companionship between human rights and market fundamentalism" must be investigated, and Moyn tells the historical tale of how it emerged and developed. The story he tells is a sad one – for both equality and human rights.

Part of the account that emerges has to do with what we have seen before as collaboration with governments and powerful authorities. Or, if not outright collaboration, then an acceptance of the powers that be: "Neoliberalism [that is, market fundamentalism] has changed the world, while the human rights movement has posed no threat to it" (ibid., 216). On both the state and global levels, human rights activists have not joined the fight against oppressive capitalism. In fact, the human rights movement acquiesced in moving from a state-centered to a world-centered outlook in its emphasis on the universal individual. It is true that in some cases (such as in the instances that naturally cohere with conventional human rights interests), especially in those that are amenable to the discourse of human rights law (such as in the overflow of economic migration), the human rights movement can join forces with other movements demanding economic and social justice. Thus, "... the human rights movement at its most inspiring has stigmatized governmental repression and violence," but, alas, it has not presented us with a real alternative to either the governmental or international market economy that is based on inequality and that has brought it to its staggering heights.

For Moyn, the answer to his question and the solution to his problem can only be political. Similar yet in some ways contrary to our insistence on a deep sense of political engagement that must accompany human rights, Moyn contends that only explicit political action, different from familiar human rights praxis, can change things.[16]

> [W]hen it comes to mobilizing support for economic fairness, the chief tools of the human rights movement – playing informational politics to stigmatize the repressions of states or the disasters of war – are simply not fit for use ... The truth is that local and global economic justice requires redesigning markets or at least redistributing from the rich to the rest, something that naming and shaming are never likely to achieve, even when supplemented by novel forms of legal activism.
>
> (ibid., 218)

So, again, what is to be done? Human rights must be political, says Moyn, in a vigorous sense. To stay loyal to its current milieu, it cannot take the roads of real dissidence or rebellion. Neither can it simply and peacefully collaborate with local or international authorities. In order to become a real "movement," human rights "will not look like *our* human rights movement, ... it will need to take on the task of governance, local and global, and not critique alone" (ibid., 219, my emphasis)! On the one hand, being political means being able to dissent and rebel, not just critique; on the other hand, being political means taking on the real responsibilities of government and law. These are tall orders, involving internal tensions and conflicts and external threats and dangers that human rights must engage with to earn the tag of "political." But this political essence of human rights cannot be avoided or evaded. Human rights are political all the way down.

Notes

1 Ludwig Wittgenstein, *Tractatus Logico-Philosophicus* (1922).
2 Ludwig Wittgenstein, *Philosophical Investigations* (1953).
3 This is a use of "political" that is reminiscent of the "politics" (rather than "the political") of Balibar's distinction. See Chapter 12, Note 11.
4 Joseph Raz, "Human Rights Without Foundations" (2007).
5 See Chapter 5 for Raz on rights and "On the Nature of Rights" (1984).
6 From Michel Foucault we have learned the deep meaning of "discourse," realizing that labeling a phenomenon as discourse means that we "show that to speak is to do something – something other than to express what one thinks; ... show that to add a statement to a pre-existing series of statements is to perform a complicated and costly gesture" (Foucault, 1972, *The Archaeology of Knowledge*, 209).
7 A more comprehensive treatment of these same themes appears in Kennedy's book *The Dark Sides of Virtue: Reassessing International Humanitarianism* (2004). In an earlier article, "The International Human Rights Movement: Part of the Problem?" (2001) Kennedy deals with a more principled question which we will address in the next section.
8 See Chapter 7.
9 See the discussion in Chapter 7 on Rajagopal, *International Law from Below* (2003).
10 This was the title of Vladimir Lenin's political pamphlet (1902).
11 See Chapter 11.
12 It is poignant to witness Gearty's final sentence in this chapter (on "The Crisis of National Security"), pointing to a far-fetched hope of "fighting back" against the misuse of human rights rhetoric: "And for ... these [hopeful] outcomes to be regarded even as possibilities, a just solution must first be found to the political problems in Palestine and Israel" (Gearty, 2006, 139).
13 See Chapter 10 on hunger as one manifestation of poverty, which plays a part in the concrete violations of human rights. See also mention of *Mass Starvation* (de Waal, 2018) (Chapter 11, note 21) on the intentional mode of mass starvation and famines, putting them in the rubric of war crimes and genocide.
14 Two outstanding pieces of research on the inequality derived from global market capitalism are Thomas Piketty, *Capital in the Twenty-First Century* (2014) and Branko Milanovic, *Global Inequality: A New Approach for the Age of Globalization* (2016).
15 Note that equality as a self-standing noun does not make an appearance in the UDHR. In the times that equality is referenced, it is always as the modifier of rights, such as "equal protection," "equal access," "equal suffrage," etc. In other words, it is the assumed condition of humanity that regulates all other determinations. There is no "equality-less" *a priori* human condition in which one has a right to equality, but rather our equal humanity which mandates all human rights.
16 In more ordinary political jargon, he is not averse to calling for socialism as the ultimate solution.

A Somewhat Epilogue: On the Ground

We have soared with the idea of human rights to the heights of philosophical conceptualization, casting and analyzing the body of notions and critique that make up the thinking, yet nevertheless intensely active, community called human rights. We have also engaged, sometimes gingerly, with the laws, conventions, institutions, and organizations that make up the human rights "regime," which is the material realization of those ideas. But ours is not a "theory and practice" book, attempting to understand the direct application of theory to practice. Rather, we have grappled with philosophical conundrums in themselves; or, if anything, we have gone the other way, pursuing the conceptual complications that may stem from the purportedly straightforward beliefs or well-meaning activism of human rightists, and may thence put sticks in the wheels of the supposedly smoothly running (liberal) theory of human rights. From the depths of *a priori* philosophical anti-liberalism, through the troubling knots of universalism and modernism, to quandaries that shadow contemporary issues such as national security or economic globalization, it is the political crux of human rights' essential character that, in the end, provides both the framework and the innards, the context and the content, of human rights.[1]

What about down-to-earth politics? What about the politics that we associate with the gritty halls of power? The politics that house corruption and influence? The politics that cannot shy away from funding and wrangling? What about the real work-on-the-ground of human rights activists who are human to a fault? Who must contend with local cavils while holding on to lofty ideals – all still within structures that are explicitly political? What about good intentions and dire consequences? In other words – what about the gap between reality and ideal?

Barbora Bukovská, in her pointed "Perpetrating Good" (2008), admits to the "noble and hard work" of human rights advocates and is profusely complimentary; human activists are "heroic," "helpful," "courageous," and are motivated by "altruism" and "a deep commitment to justice." Still, the methodology of human rights, which consists of reporting, advocacy, and strategic litigation, is fraught with internal contradictions – both structural and contingent – that threaten the ability of both organizations and individual activists in the human rights community to really represent the victims of human rights abuses.

A long inventory of what can go wrong, indeed has gone wrong, in the way human rights bodies put their goals to action includes, firstly, the misapplied tools of documentation and presentation of information used by international human rights organizations. The emphasis on victims who are "not responsible ... weak, submissive, pitied, defeated, and powerless" (Bukovská, 2008, 10), the dubious validity of testimonies, the misinterpretation of local struggles, and the lack of coordination between international and local human rights organizations, among other foibles, prevent human rightists from really achieving their grandiose objectives and contribute to disillusionment and even negative consequences. And the strategic litigation in which human rights groups engage – in other words, litigation which aspires to "a wider effect than simply providing a remedy for a particular plaintiff in a specific case" (ibid., 12) – is liable to ignore particularistic ethical duties "or even a basic respect for victims" (ibid., 13). "It can very easily happen that the victims are, in a sense, manipulated and abused ... when the focus of the action is not the victim but an ideology alien to them" (ibid.).

The deep explanation for why and how international human rights has gone so wrong in its on-the-ground workings is to be found in the abyss of representation and responsibility: Who do the organizations and activists represent and to whom are they responsible? "[W]ith few exceptions, most international human rights NGOs purporting to speak for the masses are clearly not representatives of larger constituencies of human rights victims; their constituencies are donors, their employees, other international organizations, and governments" (ibid., 15). Obviously related to our earlier quarrel with privileged, Western universalism, this type of reproach, addressing the concrete machinery of international human rights, also brings to mind the gap between "Human Rights" and "human rights," the question of individual vs. group rights, and the real significance of that trendy motto, "think global, act local." These semi-philosophical conundrums are manifestly expressed through Bukovská's concrete analysis; it is in her lament that philosophy needs to look for its practical confirmation.

* * *

We shall end with a story, this time a real story, a real and tragic story. It happened in 1997 in the Occupied Palestinian Territories, during the years when there seemed to be some movement in the direction of a peace agreement between Israel and the Palestinians. It is an ironic happenstance that in times of relative political quiet, when the guns are not incessantly shooting and hope is in the air, human rights organizations are welcomed into the social fold rather than despised as unsolicited censure. It was in that kind of ambience that in a village near Hebron, a Palestinian city holy to Muslims and Jews, a 4-year-old girl was raped by a mentally disabled young man while the village people were all celebrating a wedding. The little girl readily identified the rapist – she knew him from the neighborhood – who was immediately apprehended by the Palestinian Authority; just in time, it turned out, for he was about to be lynched by the enraged villagers. It seemed that both the Palestinian enforcement organs and the Palestinian judicial systems were in control.

This "control," however, was elusive. Within three days, the official figures of the Palestinian Authority – the political pseudo-government that had been charged with governing some parts of the occupied territories – had incarcerated him, indicted him, tried him, and sentenced him to life-imprisonment. This seemed to hardly be a fair and legal procedure, conversant with human rights and lawful constraints. *B'Tselem*, the Israeli Information Center for Human Rights in the Occupied Territories,[2] and the equally conscientious Palestinian Center for Human Rights (in Ramallah), in a seemingly commendable cooperative human rights project, began investigating the event, collecting evidence, receiving witnesses' reports, tallying up the various stories – all with the purpose in mind of defending the young man's human rights (to due process, at the least).

We do not, here, wish to suggest that the young man's rights were unimportant; we do not, in any way, wish to impugn them. We only wish to point to the ignorance and blindness which accompany certain well-meaning activists and advocates, while they are pursuing their "enlightened" goals. For it came to pass that, within three months, the village was in a social shambles. The little girl's father had divorced his wife for having failed to watch over her daughter during the festivities, and the men who were married to the wife's four sisters did the same – for traditional, religious reasons of family honor. The young man's family, who had watched over his and their own respect for years, were the victims of tangible ostracism. Some young people who had been responsible for keeping order throughout the wedding were shamed into withdrawing from any public activities. Long-term relationships built on familial and social trust were ripped apart. And all of this – as a result of the diligence of the human rights organizations; for these probes had exposed what would otherwise have remained hidden and silenced. Enlightenment deplores the darkness of hidden secrets; enlightenment distributes information freely; enlightenment does this with pure motives concerning the human condition. But enlightenment in the guise of human rights, in this story, brought about so many added tragedies.

We have seen, all along our way, that there are, in principle, different ways of viewing the storm with which these events surrounded human rights workers (and some attendant philosophers). Most obviously, such an appalling tale puts us in mind, once again, of the multi-pronged idea of universalism. Human rights has been described as the new "world-wide secular religion," along with its sacred text, The Universal Declaration of Human Rights, "the essential document, the touchstone, the creed of humanity that surely sums up all other creeds directing human behaviour" (Gordimer, 1999). We have seen, though, that it has become intellectually respectable to question the universalism of "universalism": The concept of "universalism" has come to be seen, at the least, as a Western, liberal, privileged construct of a certain (Western, liberal, privileged) tradition. In parallel and in accordance with this ambivalent stance towards universalism, human rights has come to be seen as less objective, less absolute, less obviously universal. Differently put, we may accept the postmodern commonplace that universalism and human rights are not, or should not be, automatically conjoined. The discussants of human rights now seem obligated to account for perspectival aspects of their analysis, such perspectives having to do with race, gender, geography, history, and religion, to name a few. And activists in human rights are now called upon to balance "universal human rights" with concrete context-dependent human circumstance. Our tale of the little girl near Hebron, and her wretched rapist, may sway some to the side of relativism: was it not the naïve universalism of human rights workers that brought about the disasters of the village? Would not a more particularistic, context-sensitive approach have been better suited to deal with that event? Perhaps; and perhaps not.

The tragic happenings of the village near Hebron can be, perhaps more effortlessly, interpreted as an instance of what John Dewey was pointing at when he said "[The individual] may be moved by sympathy to labor for the good of others, but, because of lack of deliberation and thoughtfulness, be quite ignorant of what their good really is, and do a great deal of harm ..." (Dewey, 1908, *Ethics*). This kind of psychologically oriented, very unpretentious attempt at understanding human action and intention is dissimilar to what we have been pursuing in this book. But it contains kernels, perhaps even a central anchor, of the narrative that would explain that special kind of activity termed "human rights." Indeed, the brand of philosophical systematization that we have been tracking has often been eschewed as being too alienated, too demanding, too disconnected from the real life of human rights work. Perhaps precisely the right attitude to the deep questions of human rights – thought and activism – is the Deweyian approach. Call it the pragmatic, personal approach: one should inculcate and teach human rights vocabulary, one should insist on its internalization, one should estimate real life situations, one should address real motivations and interests of politicians, and one should never lose sight of the human contexts in which we fight for human rights.

Notes

1 See the book by a corresponding title: Brian Orend, *Human Rights, Concept and Context* (2002), where concept is executed in detail while context remains somewhat external.
2 See Chapter 11 for *B'Tselem*'s part in exposing the subterfuge of Israel's "Security Wall."

Formal Documents of Human Rights

The following list includes human rights documents – declarations, covenants, and treaties – that have been referenced in the book as crucial and essential legal statements of engagement with human rights.

The International Bill of Human Rights

1) Universal Declaration of Human Rights *(1948)*

www.un.org/en/universal-declaration-human-rights/

2) International Covenant on Civil and Political Rights *(1966)*

www.ohchr.org/en/professionalinterest/pages/ccpr.aspx

3) International Covenant on Economic, Social and Cultural Rights *(1966)*

www.ohchr.org/en/professionalinterest/pages/cescr.aspx

Core Human Rights Treaties

4) International Convention on the Elimination of All Forms of Racial Discrimination *(1965)*

www.ohchr.org/EN/ProfessionalInterest/Pages/CERD.aspx

5) Convention on the Elimination of All Forms of Discrimination against Women *(1979)*

www.ohchr.org/EN/ProfessionalInterest/Pages/CEDAW.aspx

6) Convention against Torture and Other Cruel, Inhuman or Degrading Treatment or Punishment *(1984)*

www.ohchr.org/EN/ProfessionalInterest/Pages/CAT.aspx

7) Convention on the Rights of the Child *(1989)*

www.ohchr.org/EN/ProfessionalInterest/Pages/CRC.aspx

8) International Convention on the Protection of the Rights of All Migrant Workers and Members of Their Families *(1990)*

www.ohchr.org/EN/ProfessionalInterest/Pages/CMW.aspx

9) International Convention for the Protection of All Persons from Enforced Disappearance *(2006)*

www.ohchr.org/en/hrbodies/ced/pages/conventionced.aspx

10) Convention on the Rights of Persons with Disabilities *(2006)*

www.ohchr.org/EN/HRBodies/CRPD/Pages/ConventionRightsPersonsWithDisabilities.aspx

Other Human Rights Instruments

11) Convention on the Prevention and Punishment of the Crime of Genocide *(1948)*

www.ohchr.org/EN/ProfessionalInterest/Pages/CrimeOfGenocide.aspx

12) Convention Relating to the Status of Refugees *(1951)*

www.ohchr.org/EN/ProfessionalInterest/Pages/StatusOfRefugees.aspx

13) Protocol relating to the Status of Refugees *(1967)*

www.ohchr.org/EN/ProfessionalInterest/Pages/ProtocolStatusOfRefugees.aspx

14) Declaration on the Granting of Independence to Colonial Countries and Peoples *(1960)*

www.ohchr.org/EN/ProfessionalInterest/Pages/Independence.aspx

15) Principles of international co-operation in the detection, arrest, extradition and punishment of persons guilty of war crimes and crimes against humanity *(1973)*

www.ohchr.org/EN/ProfessionalInterest/Pages/PersonsGuilty.aspx

16) Universal Declaration on the Eradication of Hunger and Malnutrition *(1974)*

www.ohchr.org/EN/ProfessionalInterest/Pages/EradicationOfHungerAndMa lnutrition.aspx

17) Rome Statute of the International Criminal Court *(1998)*

www.ohchr.org/EN/ProfessionalInterest/Pages/InternationalCriminalCourt.aspx

18) UN Millennium Declaration *(2000)*

www.un.org/en/ga/search/view_doc.asp?symbol=A/RES/55/2

19) United Nations Declaration on the Rights of Indigenous Peoples *(2007)*

https://documents-dds-ny.un.org/doc/UNDOC/GEN/N06/512/07/PDF/ N0651207.pdf?OpenElement

20) The 2030 Agenda for Sustainable Development *(2015)*

www.un.org/en/development/desa/population/migration/generalassembly/ docs/globalcompact/A_RES_70_1_E.pdf

Bibliography

Agamben, Giorgio. "Beyond Human Rights." *Open*, 15 (2008): 90–95.

Akram, Susan. "Palestinian Refugees and Their Legal Status: Rights, Politics, and Implications for a Just Solution." *Journal of Palestine Studies*, 31, 3 (Spring, 2002): 36–51.

Albers, Marion, Thomas Hoffmann, and Jörn Reinhardt. *Human Rights and Human Nature*. Dordrecht, The Netherlands: Springer, 2014.

Alston, Philip, ed. *The United Nations and Human Rights: A Critical Appraisal*. Oxford: Oxford University Press, 2011.

American Anthropological Association (AAA). "Statement on Human Rights." *American Anthropologist*, 49 (1947): 539–543.

Améry, Jean. *At the Mind's Limit*. Bloomington: Indiana University Press, 1980.

Anaya, S. James. *International Human Rights and Indigenous Peoples*. New York: Aspen, 2009.

Angle, Stephen C. *Human Rights and Chinese Thought: A Cross-Cultural Inquiry*. Cambridge: Cambridge University Press, 2002.

Arendt, Hannah. *The Human Condition*. Chicago, IL: University of Chicago Press, 1958.

Arendt, Hannah. *Between Past and Future*. New York: The Viking Press, 1961.

Arendt, Hannah. *Origins of Totalitarianism*. New York: Meridian Books, 1966 [1951].

Arendt, Hannah. *Men in Dark Times*. New York: Harcourt Brace & Company, 1968.

Arendt, Hannah. "We Refugees." In Jerome Kohn and Ron H. Feldman (eds), *The Jewish Writings by Hannah Arendt*. New York: Schocken Books, 2007 [1943], 264–274.

Ashford, Elizabeth. "In What Sense Is the Right to Subsistence a Basic Right?" *Journal of Social Philosophy*, 40, 4 (December, 2009): 488–503.

Badescu, Cristina Gabriela. *Humanitarian Intervention and the Responsibility to Protect: Security and Human Rights*. New York: Routledge, 2010.

Balibar, Etienne. "What is a Politics of the Rights of Man?" In E. Balibar, *Masses Classes and Ideas*. New York: Routledge, 1994, 205–226.

Balibar, Etienne. *Equaliberty*. Durham, NC: Duke University Press, 2014.

Basch, Linda, Linda Glick Schiller, and Cristina Szanton Blanc. *Nations Unbound: Transnational Projects, Postcolonial Predicaments and Deterritorialized Nation-States*. London: Routledge, 1993.

Bauman, Zygmunt. *Culture in a Liquid Modern World*. Cambridge: Polity, 2011.

Beitz, Charles. *The Idea of Human Rights*. Oxford: Oxford University Press, 2009.

Bell, Daniel. "The East Asian Challenge to Human Rights: Reflections on an East-West Dialogue." *Human Rights Quarterly*, 18, 3 (August, 1996): 641–667.

Benhabib, Seyla. *Transformations of Citizenship: Dilemmas of the Nation State in the Era of Globalization*. Drenthe, The Netherlands: Van Gorcum, 2001.

Benhabib, Seyla. *The Rights of Others: Aliens, Residents, and Citizens*. Cambridge: Cambridge University Press, 2004.

Bentham, Jeremy. *A Fragment on Government*. Cambridge: Cambridge University Press, 1988 [1776].

Bentham, Jeremy. *Rights, Representation, and Reform: Nonsense upon Stilts and other Writings on the French Revolution*. Edited by P. Schofield, C. Pease-Watkin, & C. Blamires. Oxford: Clarendon Press, 2002 [1838].

Berlin, Isaiah. "Two Concepts of Liberty." In I. Berlin, *Four Essays on Liberty*. Oxford: Oxford University Press, 1969, 118–172.

Berlin, Isaiah. *Karl Marx: His Life and Environment*. Oxford: Oxford University Press, 1996 [1939].

Bernstein, J. M. "Rights." *Political Concepts: A Critical Lexicon*, Issue 4: The Balibar Edition, n.d., www.politicalconcepts.org/category/issue-4-the-balibar-edition/

Biletzki, Anat. "The Judicial Rhetoric of Morality: Israel's High Court of Justice on the Legality of Torture." *Occasional Papers of the School of Social Science*. Princeton, NJ: Institute for Advanced Study, 2001.

Boersema, David. *Philosophy of Human Rights: Theory and Practice*. Boulder, CO: Westview Press, 2011.

Brecher, Bob. *Torture and the Ticking Bomb*. Oxford: Blackwell Publishing, 2007.

Bricmont, Jean. *Humanitarian Imperialism: Using Human Rights to Sell War*. Translated by D. Johnstone. New York: Monthly Review Press, 2006.

Brown, Wendy. "Suffering the Paradoxes of Rights." In W. Brown, and J. Halley, *Left Legalism/Left Critique*. Durham, NC: Duke University Press, 2002, 420–434.

Brysk, Alison. *The Future of Human Rights*. Medford, MA: Polity, 2018.

B'Tselem. "Under the Guise of Security." Human Rights Report, Jerusalem: B'Tselem, December, 2005, www.btselem.org/download/200512_under_the_guise_of_security_eng.pdf.

Buchanan, Allen. *The Heart of Human Rights*. Oxford: Oxford University Press, 2013.

Bukovská, Barbora. "Perpetrating Good." *Sur: International Journal on Human Rights*, 5, 9 (January, 2008): 7–21.

Burggraeve, Roger. "The Good and Its Shadow: The View of Levinas on Human Rights as the Surpassing of Political Rationality." *Human Rights Review*, 6, 2 (June, 2005): 80–101.

Burke, Edmund. *Reflections on the Revolution in France*. Oxford: Oxford University Press, 1993, [1790].

Butler, Judith. *Gender Trouble: Feminism and the Subversion of Identity*. New York: Routledge, 1990.

Callaway, Ronda L., and Elizabeth G. Matthews. *Strategic US Foreign Assistance: The Battle Between Human Rights and National Security*. New York: Routledge, 2008.

Churchill, Robert Paul. *Human Rights and Global Diversity*. Upper Saddle River, NJ: Pearson Prentice Hall, 2005.

Cohen, Joshua. "Minimalism about Human Rights: The Most We Can Hope For?" *Journal of Political Philosophy*, 12, 2 (June, 2004): 190–213.

Conley-Zilkic, Bridget. *How Mass Atrocities End*. New York: Cambridge University Press, 2016.

Cordesman, Anthony H. *Arab-Israeli Military Forces in an Era of Asymmetric Wars.* Stanford, CA: Stanford University Press, 2008.

Corradetti, Claudio (ed.). *Philosophical Dimensions of Human Rights.* Dordrecht, The Netherlands: Springer, 2012.

Cover, Robert. "Violence and the Word." *Yale Law Journal,* 95, 8 (July, 1986): 1601–1638.

Cranston, Maurice. *What Are Human Rights?* New York: Basic Books, 1964.

Cruft, Rowan, S. Matthew Liao, and Massimo Renzo. *Philosophical Foundations of Human Rights.* Oxford: Oxford University Press, 2015.

Cunliffe, Philip (ed.). *Critical Perspectives on the Responsibility to Protect.* New York: Routledge, 2011.

Cushman, Thomas (ed.). *Handbook of Human Rights.* New York: Routledge, 2012.

Davidson, Alastair. *The Immutable Laws of Mankind: The Struggle for Universal Human Rights.* New York: Springer, 2012.

Davidson, Scott. "The rights of the other: Levinas and human rights." In S. Davidson and D. Perpich (eds), *Totality and Infinity at 50.* Pittsburgh, PA: Duquesne University Press, 2012, 171–187.

Davies, Norman. *Vanished Kingdoms: The Rise and Fall of States and Nations.* London: Allen Lane, 2011.

Davis, Michael. "The Moral Justifiability of Torture and Other Cruel, Inhuman, or Degrading Treatment." *International Journal of Applied Philosophy,* 19, 2 (Fall, 2005): 161–178.

Dayan, Colin. *The Story of Cruel & Unusual.* Cambridge, MA: MIT Press, 2007.

Dewey, John. *Ethics.* Edited by J. A. Boydston. Carbondale, IL: Southern Illinois University Press, 1908.

Donnelly, Jack. "The Relative Universality of Human Rights." *Human Rights Quarterly,* 29, 2 (May, 2007): 281–306.

Donnelly, Jack. *Universal Human Rights in Theory and Practice,* 3rd edn. Ithaca, NY and London: Cornell University Press, 2013.

Douzinas, Costas. *The End of Human Rights: Critical Legal Thought at the Turn of the Century.* Oxford and Portland, OR: Hart, 2000.

Douzinas, Costas, and Conor Gearty. *The Meanings of Rights.* Cambridge: Cambridge University Press, 2014.

Dummett, Michael. *On Immigration and Refugees.* New York: Routledge, 2001.

Düwell, Marcus, Jens Braarvig, Roger Brownsword, and Dietmar Mieth. *The Cambridge Handbook of Human Dignity: Interdisciplinary Perspectives.* Cambridge: Cambridge University Press, 2014.

Dworkin, Ronald. *Taking Rights Seriously,* Cambridge, MA: Harvard University Press, 1977.

Dworkin, Ronald. "Rights as Trumps." In J. Waldron (ed.), *Theories of Rights.* Oxford: Oxford University Press, 1984, 153–167.

Dworkin, Ronald. "Life Is Sacred: That's the Easy Part." *New York Times Magazine,* May 16, 1993.

Elshtain, Jean Bethke. "Reflection on the Problem of 'Dirty Hands'." In S. Levinson, *Torture: A Collection.* Oxford: Oxford University Press, 2004, 77–89.

Engle, Karen. "From Skepticism to Embrace: Human Rights and the American Anthropological Association from 1947–1999." *Human Rights Quarterly,* 23, 3 (2001): 536–559.

Ernst, Gerhard, and Jan-Christoph Heilinger (eds), *The Philosophy of Human Rights: Contemporary Controversies*. Berlin, Germany and Boston, MA: de Gruyter, 2012.

Evans, Brad, and Zygmunt Bauman. "The Refugee Crisis is Humanity's Crisis." *The New York Times*. May 2, 2016, www.nytimes.com/2016/05/02/opinion/the-re fugee-crisis-is-humanitys-crisis.html

Evans, Tony. *The Politics of Human Rights: A Global Perspective*. London: Pluto Press, 2005.

Feinberg, Joel, and Jan Narveson. "The Nature and Value of Rights." *Journal of Value Inquiry*, 4, 4 (1970): 243–260.

Felice, William F. *Taking Suffering Seriously: The Importance of Collective Human Rights*. Albany, NY: State University of New York Press, 1996.

Fine, Sarah, and Lea Ypi. *Migration in Political Theory: The Ethics of Movement and Membership*. Oxford: Oxford University Press, 2016.

Foot, Philippa. "The Problem of Abortion and the Doctrine of the Double Effect." *Oxford Review*, 5 (1967): 5–15.

Foucault, Michel. *The Archaeology of Knowledge*. New York: Pantheon Books, 1972.

Foucault, Michel. *Wrong-Doing, Truth Telling: The Function of Avowal in Justice*. Translated by S. W. Sawyer. Chicago, IL: University of Chicago Press, 2014.

Freeman, Michael. "The Philosophical Foundations of Human Rights." *Human Rights Quarterly*, 16 (1994): 491–514.

Freeman, Michael. *Human Rights: An Interdisciplinary Approach*. Cambridge: Polity, 2002.

Friedman, Maurice. *Martin Buber's Life and Work: The Later Years 1945–1965*. New York: E. P. Dutton, 1983.

Gadamer, Hans-Georg. *Truth and Method*. New York: Continuum, 1997 [1960].

Gearty, Conor. *Can Human Rights Survive?* Cambridge: Cambridge University Press, 2006.

Gewirth, Alan. "The Basis and Content of Human Rights." In A. Gewirth, *Human Rights: Essays on Justification and Applications*. Chicago, IL: University of Chicago Press, 1982, 41–78.

Gilabert, Pablo. *Human Dignity and Human Rights*. Oxford: Oxford University Press, 2018.

Glendon, Mary Ann. *Rights Talk: The Impoverishment of Political Discourse*. New York: The Free Press, 1991.

Glendon, Mary Ann. *A World Made New: Eleanor Roosevelt and the Universal Declaration of Human Rights*. New York: Random House, 2002.

Glendon, Mary Ann. "Reclaim Human Rights." *First Things: A Monthly Journal of Religion and Public Life*, Aug/Sept (2016): 19–21.

Golder, Ben. *Foucault and the Politics of Rights*. Stanford, CA: Stanford University Press, 2015.

Goodhart, Michael. *Human Rights: Politics and Practice*, 3rd edn. Oxford: Oxford University Press, 2016.

Goold, Benjamin J., and Liora Lazarus. *Security and Human Rights*. Portland, OR: Hart, 2007.

Gordimer, Nadine. "Reflections by Nobel Laureates." In Y. Danieli, E. Stamatopoulou, and C. Dias (eds), *The Universal Declaration of Human Rights: Fifty Years and Beyond*. Amityville, NY: Baywood, 1999.

Gordon, Joy. "The Concept of Human Rights: The History and Meaning of its Politicization." *Brooklyn Journal of International Law*, 23, 3 (1998): 689–791.

Gordon, Neve (ed.). *From the Margins of Globalization: Critical Perspectives on Human Rights*. Lanham, MD: Lexington, 2004.

Gregg, Benjamin. *Human Rights as Social Construction*. Cambridge: Cambridge University Press, 2011.

Gregg, Benjamin. *The Human Rights State: Justice Within and Beyond Sovereign Nations*. Philadelphia, PA: University of Pennsylvania Press, 2016.

Griffin, James. *On Human Rights*. Oxford: Oxford University Press, 2008.

Haas, Michael. *International Human Rights: A Comprehensive Introduction*, 2nd edn. New York: Routledge, 2014.

Habermas, Jürgen. "Kant's Idea of Perpetual Peace: At Two Hundred Years' Historical Remove." In C. Cronin, & P. de Greiff (eds), *Inclusion of the Other: Studies in Political Theory*. Cambridge, MA: MIT Press, 1998, 165–202.

Habermas, Jürgen. *Between Naturalism and Religion: Philosophical Essays*. Cambridge: Polity, 2008.

Hart, H. L. A. "Are There Any Natural Rights?" *The Philosophical Review*, 64, 2 (April, 1955): 175–191.

Hart, H. L. A. *The Concept of Law*. Oxford: Oxford University Press, 1961.

Hasson, Kevin J. "Religious Liberty and Human Dignity: A Tale of Two Declarations." *Harvard Journal of Law and Public Policy*, 27, 1 (Fall, 2003): 81–92.

Hayden, Patrick (ed.). *The Philosophy of Human Rights: Readings in Context*. St. Paul, MN: Paragon House, 2001.

Hobbes, Thomas. *Leviathan*. Edited by I. Shapiro. New Haven, CT: Yale University Press, 2010 [1651].

Hohfeld, Wesley. "Some Fundamental Legal Conceptions as Applied in Judicial Reasoning." *Yale Law Journal*, 23 (1913): 16–59.

Hohfeld, Wesley. "Fundamental Legal Conceptions as Applied in Judicial Reasoning." *Yale Law Journal*, 26 (1917): 710–770.

Holder, Cindy, and David Reidy. *Human Rights: The Hard Questions*. Cambridge: Cambridge University Press, 2013.

Holt, Robin. *Wittgenstein, Politics and Human Rights*. London and New York: Routledge, 1997.

Honderich, Ted. "John Stuart Mill's *On Liberty* and a Question about Liberalism." In T. Honderich, *On Political Means and Social Ends*. Edinburgh, UK: Edinburgh University Press, 2003, 4–23.

Hopgood, Stephen. *The Endtimes of Human Rights*. Ithaca, NY: Cornell University Press, 2013.

Horkheimer, Max, and Theodor Adorno. *Dialectic of Enlightenment*. Translated by E. Jephcott. Stanford, CA: Stanford University Press, 2002 [1947].

Human Rights Watch. "BROKEN PEOPLE: Caste Violence Against India's 'Untouchables'." Human Rights Watch Report, March, 1999, https://www.hrw.org/reports/1999/india

Human Rights Watch. "We Have No Orders to Save You": State Participation and Complicity in Communal Violence in Gujarat." Human Rights Watch Report, April, 2002, www.hrw.org/reports/2002/india/gujarat.pdf

Hunt, Lynn. *Inventing Human Rights: A History*. New York and London: W. W. Norton, 2008.

Ignatieff, Michael. *Human Rights as Politics and Idolatry*. Princeton, NJ: Princeton University Press, 2001.

Ignatieff, Michael. "Is the Human Rights Era Ending?" *The New York Times*, February 5, 2002, www.nytimes.com/2002/02/05/opinion/is-the-human-rights-era-ending.html

International Commission on Intervention and State Sovereignty. *The Responsibility to Protect*. Ottawa, ON: International Development Research Centre, 2001.

Ishay, Micheline. *The History of Human Rights: From Ancient Times to the Globalization Era*. Berkeley, CA: University of California Press, 2004.

Ishay, Micheline. *The Human Rights Reader: Major Political Essays, Speeches, and Documents from Ancient Times to the Present*. 2nd edn. New York: Routledge, 2007.

Israel, Jonathan I. *Democratic Enlightenment: Philosophy, Revolution, and Human Rights 1750–1790*. New York: Oxford University Press, 2011.

Joseph, Peter. *The New Human Rights Movement*. Dallas, TX: BenBella Books, 2018.

Kamm, Francis. "Harming Some to Save Others." *Philosophical Studies*, 57, 3 (1989): 227–260.

Kant, Immanuel. *Groundwork for the Metaphysics of Morals*. Edited and translated by A. W. Wood. New Haven, CT: Yale University Press, 2002 [1785].

Kennedy, David. "The International Human Rights Movement: Part of the Problem?" *European Human Rights Law Review*, 6 (2001): 245–267.

Kennedy, David. *The Dark Sides of Virtue: Reassessing International Humanitarianism*. Princeton, NJ: Princeton University Press, 2004.

Kennedy, David. "Reassessing International Humanitarianism: The Dark Sides." In A. Orford (ed.), *International Law and Its Others*. Cambridge: Cambridge University Press, 2006, 131–155.

Kleingeld, Pauline. *Kant and Cosmopolitanism: The Philosophical Ideal of World Citizenship*. Cambridge: Cambridge University Press, 2012.

Kraynak, Robert P., and G. Tinder. *In Defense of Human Dignity: Essays for Our Times*. Notre Dame, IN: University of Notre Dame Press, 2003.

Kretzmer, D., and E. Klein. *The Concept of Human Dignity in Human Rights Discourse*. The Hague, The Netherlands: Kluwer Law International, 2002.

Kristeva, Julia. *Hatred and Forgiveness*. New York: Columbia University Press, 2010 [2005].

Kymlicka, Will (ed.). *The Rights of Minority Cultures*. Oxford: Oxford University Press, 1995.

Kymlicka, Will. "The Good, the Bad, and the Intolerable: Minority Group Rights." *Dissent* (Summer, 1996): 22–30.

Langlois, Anthony J. "The Narrative Metaphysics of Human Rights." *International Journal of Human Rights*, 9, 3 (2005): 469–487.

Lear, Jonathan. *Radical Hope: Ethics in the Face of Cultural Devastation*. Cambridge, MA: Harvard University Press, 2006.

Leibich, Andre. "Minority as Inferiority: Minority Rights in Historical Perspective." *Review of International Studies*, 34, 2 (2008): 243–263.

Lenin, Vladimir Ilyich. "What Is To Be Done?" In *Lenin's Collected Works*. Translated by J. Fineberg and G. Hanna. Moscow: Foreign Languages Publishing House, 1961 [1902], 347–530.

Levinas, Emmanuel. *Entre nous. Essais sur le penser-à-l'autre*. Paris: Grasset, 1991.

Levinson, Sanford (ed.). *Torture: A Collection*. Oxford: Oxford University Press, 2004.

Li, Xiaorong. "'Asian Values' and the Universality of Human Rights." *Philosophy and Public Policy Quarterly*, 16 (1996): 18–23.

Locke, John. *Two Treatises of Civil Government*. Edited by R. Ashcraft. London: Routledge, 1989 [1689].

Lutz-Bachman, Matthias, and Amos Nascimento. *Human Rights, Human Dignity, and Cosmopolitan Ideals: Essays on Critical Theory and Human Rights*. Farnham, Surrey: Ashgate, 2014.

MacKinnon, Catharine. *Are Women Human? And Other International Dialogues*. Cambridge, MA: Harvard University Press, 2006.

MacKinnon, Catharine et al. *Are Women Human?* March 7, 2011, https://nationalhumanitiescenter.org/on-the-human/2011/03/are-women-human/

Macklin, Ruth. "Dignity is a Useless Concept: It Means No More than Respect for Persons or their Autonomy." *The British Medical Journal (BMJ)*, 327, 7429 (December, 2003): 1419–1420.

Malpas, J., and N. Lickiss. *Perspectives on Human Dignity: A Conversation*. Dordrecht, The Netherlands: Springer, 2007.

Margalit, Avishai. *The Decent Society*. Cambridge, MA: Harvard University Press, 1996.

Maritain, Jacques. *The Rights of Man and Natural Law*. New York: C. Scribner's Sons, 1943.

Martinich, A. P. *The Two Gods of Leviathan: Thomas Hobbes on Religion and Politics*. New York: Cambridge University Press, 1992.

Marx, Karl. "On the Jewish Question." In K. Marx and F. Engels, *The Marx-Engels Reader*. New York: Norton & Company, 1978 [1844], 26–46.

Marx, Karl, and Friedrich Engels. *The German Ideology*. Moscow: Marx-Engels Institute, 1932 [1846].

Meckled-Garcia, Saladin, and Basak Cali. *Legalization and Human Rights*. London: Routledge, 2005.

Mégret, Frédéric. "The Disabilities Convention: Human Rights of Persons with Disabilities or Disability Rights?" *Human Rights Quarterly*, 30, 2 (May, 2008): 494–516.

Milanovic, Branko. *Global Inequality: A New Approach for the Age of Globalization*. Cambridge, MA: Harvard University Press, 2016.

Mill, John Stuart. *On Liberty*. In *The Collected Works of John Stuart Mill, Volume XVIII – Essays on Politics and Society Part I*, edited by J. Robson.. Toronto, ON: University of Toronto Press, 1977 (1859), 213–310.

Mill, John Stuart. *The Subjection of Women*. In *The Collected Works of John Stuart Mill, Volume XXI – Essays on Equality, Law, and Education*, edited by J. Robson. Toronto, ON: University of Toronto Press, 1984 [1869].

Mill, John Stuart. *Utilitarianism*. In *The Collected Works of John Stuart Mill, Volume X – Essays on Ethics, Religion, and Society*, edited by J. Robson. Toronto, ON: University of Toronto Press, 1985 [1861].

Monshipouri, Mahmood. *Islamism, Secularism and Human Rights in the Middle East*. Boulder, CO: Lynne Rienner, 1998.

Montero, A. Reis. *Ethics of Human Rights*. New York: Springer, 2014.

Morris, Benny. *The Birth of the Palestinian Refugee Problem, 1947–1949*. Cambridge: Cambridge University Press, 1988.

Morsink, Johannes. *The Universal Declaration of Human Rights: Origins, Drafting, and Intent*. Philadelphia, PA: University of Pennsylvania Press, 1999.

Moyn, Samuel. *The Last Utopia: Human Rights in History*. Cambridge, MA: Harvard University Press, 2010.

Moyn, Samuel. "The Future of Human Rights." *Sur – International Journal on Human Rights*, 11, 20 (2014): 57–64.

Moyn, Samuel. *Not Enough: Human Rights in an Unequal World*. Cambridge, MA: Belknap Press of Harvard University Press, 2018.

Mutua, Makau. "Savages, Victims, and Saviors: The Metaphor of Human Rights." *Harvard International Law Journal*, 42, 1 (2001): 201–245.

Mutua, Makau. *Human Rights: A Political and Cultural Critique*. Philadelphia, PA: University of Pennsylvania Press, 2002.

Nickel, James W. *Making Sense of Human Rights*, 2nd edn. London: Blackwell, 2007.

Nussbaum, Martha. "Capabilities and Human Rights." *Fordham Law Review*, 66, 2 (1997): 273–300.

Nussbaum, Martha. "Women and Cultural Universals." In M. Nussbaum, *Sex and Social Justice*. New York: Oxford University Press, 1999, 29–54.

Oberman, Kieran. "Immigration as a Human Right." In S. Fine and L. Ypi (eds), *Migration in Political Theory: The Ethics of Movement and Membership*. Oxford: Oxford University Press, 2016, 32–56.

Okin, Susan Moller. "Feminism, Women's Human Rights, and Cultural Differences." *Hypatia*, 13, 2 (1998): 32–52.

Ophir, Adi. "Documentation as an Act of Resistance." *Davar (Hebrew)* (May–June, 1991).

Orend, Brian. *Human Rights: Concept and Context*. Peterborough, ON: Broadview, 2002.

Pappé, Ilan. *The Ethnic Cleansing of Palestine*. Oxford and New York: Oneworld, 2006.

Parekh, Serena. *Hannah Arendt and the Challenge of Modernity: A Phenomenology of Human Rights*. New York: Routledge, 2008.

Paskins, Barrie. "What's wrong with torture?" *British Journal of International Studies*, 2, 2 (July, 1976): 138–148.

Perry, Michael. *The Idea of Human Rights: Four Inquiries*. Oxford: Oxford University Press, 1998.

Perugini, Nicola, and Neve Gordon. *The Human Right to Dominate*. Oxford: Oxford University Press, 2015.

Piketty, Thomas. *Capital in the Twenty-First Century*. Cambridge, MA: Belknap Press, 2014.

Pleasants, Nigel, and Gavin Kitching. *Marx and Wittgenstein: Knowledge, Morality and Politics*. New York: Routledge, 2002.

Pogge, Thomas. "An Egalitarian Law of Peoples." *Philosophy and Public Affairs*, 23, 3 (July, 1994): 195–224.

Pogge, Thomas. "How Should Human Rights be Conceived?" In T. Pogge, *World Poverty and Human Rights*. Cambridge: Polity Press, 2002, 52–70.

Pogge, Thomas. *World Poverty and Human Rights*, 2nd edn. Cambridge: Polity Press, 2008.

Pogge, Thomas. "The Hunger Games." *Food Ethics*, 1, 1 (June, 2016): 9–27.

Pogge, Thomas. "Fighting Global Poverty." *International Journal of Law in Context*, 13, 4 (Special Issue, December, 2017): 512–526.

Powers, Maggie. "Responsibility to Protect: Dead, Dying, or Thriving?" *The International Journal of Human Rights*, 18, 8 (2015): 1257–1278.

Press, Eyal. "In Torture We Trust?" *The Nation*, March 31, 2003, www.thenation.com/article/torture-we-trust/

Rajagopal, Balakrishnan. *International Law from Below: Development, Social Movements and Third World Resistance*. Cambridge: Cambridge University Press, 2003.

Rancière, Jacques. "Who Is the Subject of the Rights of Man?" *South Atlantic Quarterly*, 103, 2–3 (2004): 297–310.

Rawls, John. *A Theory of Justice*. Cambridge, MA: Harvard University Press, 1971.

Rawls, John. "Justice as Fairness: Political not Metaphysical." *Philosophy and Public Affairs*, 14, 3 (Summer, 1985): 223–251.

Rawls, John. *Political Liberalism*. New York: Columbia University Press, 1993.

Rawls, John. "The Law of Peoples." *Critical Inquiry*, 20, 1 (Autumn, 1993): 36–68.

Rawls, John. *The Law of Peoples*. Cambridge, MA: Harvard University Press, 1999.

Raz, Joseph. "On the Nature of Rights." *Mind*, 93, 370 (April, 1984): 194–214.

Raz, Joseph. "Human Rights Without Foundations." *University of Oxford Faculty of Law Legal Studies Research Paper Series*, Working Paper, 14 (March, 2007): 1–20.

Reddy, Sanjay, and Thomas Pogge. "How Not to Count the Poor." Initiative for Policy Dialogue Working Paper Series, 2009, https://doi.org/10.7916/D8P274ZS

Reilly, Niamh. *Women's Human Rights*. Cambridge: Polity Press, 2009.

Rioux, Marcia H., Lee Ann Basser, and Melinda Jones. *Critical Perspectives on Human Rights and Disability Law*. The Hague, The Netherlands: Martinus Nijhoff, 2011.

Rorty, Richard. *Philosophy and the Mirror of Nature*. Princeton, NJ: Princeton University Press, 1979.

Rorty, Richard. "Human Rights, Rationality, and Sentimentality." In S. Shute and S. Hurley, *On Human Rights: The Oxford Amnesty Lectures*. New York: Basic Books, 1993, 111–134.

Rosen, Michael. *Dignity: Its History and Meaning*. Cambridge, MA: Harvard University Press, 2012.

Rousseau, Jean-Jacques. *The Social Contract*. Translated by M. Cranston. Harmondsworth, England: Penguin Books, 1968 [1762].

Sangiovanni, Andrea. *Humanity Without Dignity: Moral Equality, Respect, and Human Rights*. Cambridge, MA: Harvard University Press, 2017.

Scott, Joan Wallach. *Only Paradoxes to Offer*. Cambridge, MA: Harvard University Press, 1996.

Sen, Amartya. "Equality of What?" The Tanner Lectures on Human Values. Stanford, CA: Stanford University Press, 1979, 197–220, http://hdrnet.org/43/1/sen80.pdf

Sen, Amartya. "Elements of a Theory of Human Rights." *Philosophy and Public Affairs*, 32, 4 (October, 2004): 315–356.

Sen, Amartya. "Human Rights and Capabilities." *Journal of Human Development*, 6, 2 (2005): 151–166.

Shapiro, Ian. *The Evolution of Rights in Liberal Theory*. New York: Cambridge University Press, 1986.

Shelton, Dinah. *Regional Protection of Human Rights*. Oxford: Oxford University Press, 2008.

Shlaim, Avi. "The Debate about 1948." *International Journal of Middle East Studies*, 27, 3 (August, 1995): 287–304.

Shue, Henry. "Torture." *Philosophy and Public Affairs*, 7, 2 (Winter, 1978): 124–143.

Shue, Henry. *Basic Rights: Subsistence, Affluence, and U.S. Foreign Policy*, 2nd edn. Princeton, NJ: Princeton University Press, 1996.

Sikkink, Kathryn. *Evidence for Hope: Making Human Rights Work in the 21st Century*. Princeton, NJ: Princeton University Press, 2017.

Simmons, William Paul. *Human Rights Law and the Marginalized Other*. New York: Cambridge University Press, 2011.

Singer, Peter. "Escaping the Refugee Crisis." *Project Syndicate*, September, 2015, www.project-syndicate.org/commentary/escaping-europe-refugee-crisis-by-peter-singer-2015-09?barrier=accesspaylog

Slim, Hugo. *Killing Civilians: Method, Madness, and Morality in War*. New York: Columbia University Press, 2008.

Smith, Michael J. "Humanitarian Intervention: An Overview of the Ethical Issues." In J. H. Rosenthal (ed.), *Ethics and International Affairs: A Reader*. Washington DC: Georgetown University Press, 1999, 271–295.

Smith, Rhona K. M. *Textbook on International Human Rights*. Oxford: Oxford University Press, 2003.

Spellman, A. B. "Interview with Malcolm X." Interview held on March 19, 1964. Printed in *Monthly Review* (May, 1964).

Spivak, Gayatri Chakravorty. *Outside in the Teaching Machine*. New York: Routledge, 1993.

Spivak, Gayatri Chakravorty, and Judith Butler. *Who Sings the Nation-State? Language, Politics, Belonging*. Oxford: Seagull Books, 2007.

Stamos, David. *The Myth of Universal Human Rights: Its Origin, History, and Explanation Along with a More Humane Way*. Boulder, CO: Paradigm Publishers, 2013.

State Council of the People's Republic of China, Information Office. "Human Rights in China." *Beijing Review* (November 4, 1991): 8–45.

Steiner, Henry J., and Philip Alston. *International Human Rights in Context: Law, Politics, Morals*, 2nd edn. New York: Oxford University Press, 2000.

Syse, Henrik. *Natural Law, Religion, and Rights: An Exploration of the Relationship Between Natural Law and Natural Rights, with Special Emphasis on the Teachings of Thomas Hobbes and John Locke*. South Bend, IN: St. Augustine's Press, 2007.

Tasioulas, John. "On the Nature of Human Rights." In G. Ernst and J.-C. Heilinger (eds), *The Philosophy of Human Rights: Contemporary Controversies*. Berlin, Germany and Boston, MA: de Gruyter, 2012, 17–60.

Tasioulas, John. "Towards a Philosophy of Human Rights." *Current Legal Problems*, 65, 1 (2012): 1–30.

Tasioulas, John. "On the Foundations of Human Rights." In R. Cruft, S. M. Liao, and M. Renzo (eds), *Philosophical Foundations of Human Rights*. Oxford: Oxford University Press, 2015, 45–70.

Tatum, Dale C. *Genocide at the Dawn of the Twenty-First Century*. New York: Palgrave Macmillan, 2010.

Tawney, R. H. *R. H. Tawney's Commonplace Book*. Edited by J. M. Winter and D. M. Joslin. Cambridge: Cambridge University Press, 1972.

Taylor, Charles. "A World Consensus on Human Rights?" *Dissent* (Summer, 1996): 15–21.

Thomson, Judith Jarvis. "Killing, Letting Die, and the Trolley Problem." *The Monist*, 59, 2 (April, 1976): 204–217.

Tilley, John J. "Cultural Relativism." *Human Rights Quarterly*, 22, 2 (May, 2000): 501–547.

Tindale, Christopher. "The Logic of Torture." *Social Theory and Practice*, 2, 3 (1996): 349–374.

Tomalty, Jesse. "Remedial Responsibility for Severe Poverty: Justice or Humanity?" *Journal of Applied Philosophy*, 34, 1 (February, 2017): 89–98.

Tomuschat, Christian. *Human Rights: Between Idealism and Realism*. Oxford: Oxford University Press, 2003.

Topolski, Anya. "Relationality as a 'Foundation' for Human Rights: Exploring the Paradox with Hannah Arendt and Emmanuel Levinas." *Theoria and Praxis*, 2, 1 (2014): 1–17.

United Nations Committee on Economic, Social and Cultural Rights. "Statement on Poverty and the ICESCR." New York: UN Economic and Social Council, 2001.

United Nations Human Rights Council. "Human Rights, Sexual Orientation and Gender Identity." A/HRC/RES/17/19, New York: UN, 2011, https://undocs.org/A/HRC/RES/17/19

United Nations Human Rights Council. "Protection Against Violence and Discrimination Based on Sexual Orientation and Gender Identity." A/HRC/RES/32/2, New York: UN, 2016, https://undocs.org/A/HRC/RES/32/2

United Nations Office of the High Commissioner for Human Rights. "Human Rights Dimension of Poverty." New York: UN, n.d., www.ohchr.org/en/issues/poverty/dimensionofpoverty/pages/index.aspx

United Nations Office of the High Commissioner for Human Rights. "What are Human Rights?" New York: UN, n.d., www.ohchr.org/en/issues/pages/whatarehumanrights.aspx

US Department of State. "The Voluntary Principles on Security and Human Rights." 2000, https://2001-2009.state.gov/g/drl/rls/2931.htm

de Waal, Alex. *Mass Starvation*. Cambridge: Polity, 2018.

Waldron, Jeremy. *"Nonsense Upon Stilts": Bentham, Burke, and Marx on the Rights of Man*. New York: Methuen, 1987.

Waldron, Jeremy. "How to Argue for a Universal Claim." *Columbia Human Rights Law Review*, 30, 2 (1999): 305–314.

Waldron, Jeremy. "Torture and Positive Law: Jurisprudence for the White House." *Columbia Law Review*, 105, 6 (October, 2005): 1681–1750.

Waldron, Jeremy. *Dignity, Rank, and Rights (The Berkeley Tanner Lectures)*. Oxford: Oxford University Press, 2012.

Wallace, Rebecca (ed.). *International Human Rights: Text and Materials*. London: Sweet & Maxwell, 1997.

Washburn, Wilcomb E. "Cultural Relativism, Human Rights, and the AAA." *American Anthropologist*, 89, 4 (December, 1987): 939–943.

Wheeler, Nick. *Saving Strangers: Humanitarian Intervention in International Society*. Oxford: Oxford University Press, 2000.

Whelan, Daniel J. *Interdependent Human Rights: A History*. Philadelphia, PA: University of Pennsylvania Press, 2010.

Wittgenstein, Ludwig. *Tractatus Logico-Philosophicus*. Translated by C. K. Ogden. London: Routledge & Kegan Paul, 1922.

Wittgenstein, Ludwig. *Philosophical Investigations*. Edited by G. E. M. Anscombe and R. Rhees; translated by G. E. M. Anscombe. Oxford: Blackwell, 1953.

Woods, Kerri. *Human Rights*. New York: Palgrave Macmillan, 2014.

World Medical Association. "Declaration of Tokyo – Guidelines for Physicians concerning Torture ..." World Medical Association, 1975, www.wma.net/policies-post/wma-declaration-of-tokyo-guidelines-for-physicians-concerning-torture-a

nd-other-cruel-inhuman-or-degrading-treatment-or-punishment-in-relation-to-de
tention-and-imprisonment/

Zivi, Karen. *Making Rights Claims: A Practice of Democratic Citizenship.* New
York: Oxford University Press, 2012.

Žižek, Slavoj. "Marxist philosopher Slavoj Žižek explains why we shouldn't pity or
romanticize refugees." Interview by A. Merelli. *Quartz,* September 9, 2016, https://
qz.com/767751/marxist-philosopher-slavoj-zizek-on-europes-refugee-crisis-the-left-
is-wrong-to-pity-and-romanticize-migrants/

Žižek, Slavoj. *Refugees, Terror and Other Troubles with the Neighbors.* Brooklyn,
NY: Melville House, 2016.

Index

AAA *see* American Anthropological
  Association (AAA)
absolutism 25–6, 37–9, 79, 91–2, 216,
  221, 226
Adorno, Theodor 124n6
affiliation 82, 88n10, 128–9
African Commission on Human and
  People's Rights 19
African Court of Human and People's
  Rights 20
Agamben, Giorgio 203–4
agreement theories 214–15
Akram, Susan 150n24, 150n26
American Anthropological Association
  (AAA) 93–4, 97, 101–2, 122, 221
American Bill of Rights 8, 18, 30n3,
  94, 204
American Constitution 18, 30n3
American Declaration of Independence
  8–10, 18, 30n3,170, 204–5
Améry, Jean 182
Amnesty International 117–18
Annan, Kofi 185
Anti-Semitism 113, 124n6, 192
Arab–Israeli conflict, 150n21, 172; *see
  also* Israeli–Palestinian conflict
Arendt, Hannah xx–xxi, 10–12, 13, 131,
  142, 144, 145–6, 150n18, 203, 207–8
Asian values 95–6, 102–3, 105n2
asylum 22, 138, 140–5, 171
autonomy 33, 44n6, 47, 79, 121, 123n2,
  131, 132, 136, 183, 186–7, 200, 214,
  217; individual 64, 128, 128; Kantian
  42–3; of disabled 136–7

Balibar, Etienne xx, 203–9, 209n11,
  209n12, 231n3
Basch, Linda 16n3
Bauman, Zygmunt 16n3, 138, 144–5

Beitz, Charles xiii, 88n14, 213–15
Benhabib, Seyla 16n3, 150n15
Bentham, Jeremy 57n1, 58n5
Berlin, Isaiah 72n1
Bernstein, J. M. 209n12
Blanc, Cristina 16n3
Boersema, David xvi
Brecher, Bob 180–182, 187n6
Bretton Woods Conference 163
Brown, Wendy xxi, 129–30, 149n4, 192,
  194–6
B'Tselem 176–8, 187n5, 234, 235n2
Buber, Martin 8
Buchanan, Allen xvii, 88n14, 212–13
Buddhism 15, 100–1, 112
Burggraeve, Roger 203, 208n9
Burke, Edmund 57n1
Butler, Judith 16n3, 124n10

capability: approach xix, 80–3, 84, 87,
  88n5, 88n10, 128–9, 135, 164, 229;
  and functioning 82–3; and human
  rights 83
capitalism 104, 112, 194, 221, 228, 230,
  231n14; global 143
Categorical Imperative 42–3, 77
Catholic 112, 113
CFS *see* Committee on World Food
  Security (CFS)
Chinese White Paper (1991) 96
Christian/Christianity 15, 41, 91, 101,
  104, 198
civic rights *see* civil rights
civil–political human rights 20, 21,
  22–26, 31n9, 83, 109, 124n3, 131,
  139, 170, 178; and economic–social–
  cultural rights xviii, 7–8, 63–4, 87,
  95–6, 103, 128, 141, 152, 160,
  166–167, 224, 227

civil rights xviii, 8–10, 118; and human rights 8–12, 207–8; definitional characterization of 9; Hannah Arendt and 11–12, 13, 145; Malcolm X and 10–11; movement 10; refugees' 142, 150n13; women's 131

civil society 9–10, 117, 172; global 216; organizations of 117, 219

civilians 29–30, 186

Clinton, Hillary 125

colonialism 102, 103–5, 122, 162, 220, 221–2; anti- 24

Committee on World Food Security (CFS) 165

communitarianism 95

Confucian 15, 100–1

Conley–Zilkic, Bridget 188n16

consequentialist theories 64–5

Constitution of Medina (622) 18

consumer price index (CPI) 163

contract 19, 21, 23, 26, 28, 26, 64, 120, 187, 216; in Hobbes 49; in Locke 50–1; in Rawls 55–7; social 9–10, 16n9, 55, 57, 65

contractualism 35, 65–6, 173

Convention on the Elimination of All Forms of Discrimination against Women (1979) 107, 116, 127, 133

Convention on the Prevention and Punishment of the Crime of Genocide (1948) 28, 186

Convention Relating to the Status of Refugees (Refugee Convention, 1951) 139–41, 146–8, 150n23

Convention on the Rights of Persons with Disabilities (Disabilities Convention, 2006) 107 132, 133–8

Convention against Torture (1984) 179

"corporation view" of groups 110

CPI *see* consumer price index (CPI)

Corradetti, Claudio xvii

Creationism 115

crimes against humanity 20, 113, 185–6, 188n19, 188n20

Cruft, Rowan xvii

cultural diversity 38, 97–8, 99, 121–2, 221

cultural relativity xix, 37, 88n8, 94–6, 98, 101, 128, 221, 227; descriptive 91–2, 95

Cushman, Thomas xvii

Dalit 113

Darwin, Charles 87

Davidson, Scott 208n9

Davies, Norman 16n3

Davis, Michael 181

decent society (Rawls) 154–6, 157, 159

Declaration on the Elimination of Violence against Women 28

Declaration on the Rights of Indigenous Peoples 120–3

democracy 54, 101, 167, 168n11, 207, 222; liberal 11–12, 222; political right to 159, 213

democratic: non- 96, 154, 222; society 23, 25, 86–7, 154, 213; system of government 25, 100, 104, 218

democratization 104

deontological theories 64–5

Derrida, Jacques 208n10

Dershowitz, Alan 180–1

development 108, 121–3, 164–7, 168n2, 168n11; economic 103; ideology 104–5; sustainable 27–8, 167

Dickens, Charles 167–8

dignity xix, xxi, 12, 15, 17n11, 21–3, 40–43, 44n6, 44n7, 44n9, 69, 73–6, 80, 82, 93, 102, 126, 128, 136–7, 161, 167–8, 182, 198, 205, 222, 229

disability rights xix, 27, 107, 125, 131–8, 141, 144, 149n7

discrimination 22, 26, 86, 114, 126, 132, 144, 146, 152, 194–5, 229; anti- 132, 144; against disabled 136–7; in education 28; in employment and occupation 28; against groups 125; against indigenous 122–3; against groups 125; against minorities 112–19; non- 82, 120, 132, 134, 136–7; racial 27, 107, 112–13, 118, 124n5, 131; against refugees 140; religious 28, 113–14, 154; against sexual minorities 115–18; torture based on 179; against women 27, 28, 107, 116, 125, 127, 131, 133

Donnelly, Jack xvi, 105n4, 119

Douzinas, Costas 208n9

Dummett, Michael 144

duties 23, 31n9, 43, 47, 51–2, 84, 110, 217; correlativity of human rights to 25, 60–69, 77; in *The Law of Peoples* 155; institutional xix, 84–88, 88n12, 213; moral/ethical 65, 142, 233; relation to rights of 69–71, 87, 202–3, 214; state's 134, 137, 140–2, 146, 185

Dworkin, Ronald xix, 25, 38, 65, 67–8, 72n3, 74–5

economic rights xvi, xvii, 10, 25, 95, 103, 152, 227–30; global 151–69

economic–social–cultural human rights 83; and civil–political rights xviii, 7–8, 63–4, 87, 95–6, 103, 128, 141, 152, 160, 166–7, 224

education 8, 53, 81, 85, 121–123, 129, 133, 144, 147, 151–2, 156, 166–7, 168n11, 197, 217, 228–9; discrimination in 28; right to 7, 9, 23, 79, 136–7, 141, 160–1, 177; religious 114–115, 141; sentimental 198–99

egalitarianism 65, 155, 157–9, 161–2, 229

Elshtain, Jean 180

emergency, concept of 69; public 26, 170, 178; state of 69, 173

Enlightenment 4, 38, 47, 77, 99, 108, 124n6, 199, 200, 234

equality xx–xxi, 12, 18, 21–3, 35, 40, 43, 72n2, 74, 80, 88n6, 88n7, 96, 98, 111, 121, 155, 158, 193, 195, 207, 223, 225, 228–30; freedom/liberty and 7–8, 16n5, 16n6, 21, 47–8, 56, 168n7, 196, 205–6, 231n15; equal opportunity 56, 153; equal rights 12, 56, 102, 115, 118, 126–7, 132, 136, 144, 213; in Dworkin 67–69; in Hart 65–67; in Hobbes 50; in Locke 51; in Mill 54; in Rawls 55–7, 155–6, 160; of disabled 132, 134–8; of women 127–8, 130, 168n11

Equaliberty (Balibar) 205–6

Ernst, Gerhard xvii

ethics xx, xxii, 18, 34–5, 37, 39–40, 44n4, 47, 54, 63–4, 77, 91–2, 102, 124n11, 140–1, 143–4, 161, 174, 180, 184, 188n8, 188n12, 191, 208n7, 212, 214, 219–20, 227, 233; Dewey's 235; Kant's 41–43; Levinas's 201–3; meta– 197, Rawls's 55–57

ethnic cleansing 150n22, 185–6

Eurocentrism 208n5, 223

European Council Commissioner for Human Rights 19

European Court of Human Rights 20

European Union 144, 217–18

exploitation 162, 194–5; of disabled 134; workplace 127; women's 133

externalism 37

Feinberg, Joel 44n6

feudalism 192–3

Foot, Philippa 188n8

Foucault, Michel xx, 200–3, 208n8, 231n6

foundationalism 191, 210, 213, 215; anti– 196–9

freedom 8, 21–22, 25, 33, 35, 64, 74, 87, 96, 137, 152, 225; in AAA statement 94; from arbitrary arrest 56; in Arendt 145, 207; of assembly 56, 82; of association 171; in Balibar 205–6; in Brown 130, 196; and capabilities 80–3; of choice of occupation, income, and wealth 57, 129; of conscience 26, 56, 68, 114, 155; in Dworkin 68; and equality 7–8, 16n5, 23, 47–8, 56; 68, 72n2, 168n7, 205–6; from exploitation, violence, and abuse 134; of expression 96, 134, 171; in Gewirth 78–80; in Hart 66–7; in Hohfeld 62; individual 47, 64; indigenous 123; to leave and re-enter 7, 138–9; in Locke 51; in Marx 193–4; in Mill 54; of movement 6, 7, 9, 39, 57, 68, 81, 138–40; 133, 171, 177, 182; in Nussbaum 80–3; negative and positive 63, 128; of opinion 133–4, 207; of the person 56; from poverty 166–8; in Rawls 56, 153, 155, 159; of religion 7, 18, 26, 81, 114, 141; from retroactive laws 26; sexual 195; from slavery 134, 155; of speech 18, 56, 68, 81–3, 159; of thought 7, 26, 39, 56, 114, 159; from torture 134, 180, 182; and well-being xix, 78–80, 84

French Declaration of the Rights of Man and Citizen (1789) 8, 18, 31n3, 170, 193; Balibar on 204–7

Gadamer, Hans-Georg 106n8

Galt, John 58n5

Gaza Strip 147

Gearty, Conor 224, 226, 231n12

Geneva Conventions 29–30, 146, 186

Gewirth, Alan xix, 77–80, 84

Glendon, Mary Ann 30n7, 31n13, 217–8

globalism 37

Global Resources Tax (GRT) 161–2

God 9, 10, 11, 15, 30n3, 41–2, 44n7, 50–2, 74–7, 88n1

Golan Heights 147

Golder, Ben 208n8

governance 104, 164, 219, 230–1

Griffin, James xvii, 88n14

group rights xix, xxi, 25, 48, 107–12, 124n3, 125; collective version of 110; denial of 110; external and internal violations of 110–1, 183; in ICCPR

109, 120–1; as human rights 109–10, 132, 213; in ICSECR 109, 120–1; indigenous groups 120–3; individual rights and 111–2, 114, 119, 122–3, 208n2, 233; in UDHR 109; women's rights as 131

GRT *see* Global Resources Tax (GRT)

Habermas, Jürgen 208n10
habilitation and rehabilitation: of disabled 134, 136; of refugees 143, 148
Hague Conventions 29, 186
Hammurabi's Code 18
Hart, H. L. A. xix, 64, 65–7
Heilinger, Jan-Christoph xvii
Hinduism 15, 113; caste system 113
Hirschmann, Nancy 149n2
Hobbes, Thomas xix, xxi, 4, 16n9, 48–50, 51–2, 55–7, 58n3, 58n4, 65, 77, 153, 173, 192; psychological egotism 35
Hohfeld, Wesley 59–60, 63, 65, 70; Hohfeldian scheme 60–3
Holocaust 3, 113
homosexual identity 195
Holder, Cindy xvii
Honderich, Ted 58n6
Hopgood, Stephen 224–5
Horkheimer, Max 124n6
Hugo, Victor 167–8
human: concept of 32–4; emancipation 194, 196; nature 9, 57, 93, 95, 100, 196–8, 201, 206; sacredness of 74–6
human rights: community xx, 4, 13–14, 105, 217–8, 219–20, 223, 227; concept of 3–4, 14, 40, 83–4, 91, 96, 191, 208n10, 220–1; critiques of 191–209, 210–12, 217–20, 220–3, 223–31, 232–5; culture xiii, 197–9 223; definition of 9, 12, 40, 73, 109, 167, 180, 210, 229; dignity and 40–3; *see also* dignity; discourse of 12, 100, 104–5, 109, 191, 210, 214, 217; education 198–9; essence of 91, 138, 212–13, 215, 231; foundations of 9, 14–16, 35, 73–6, 84, 100, 136, 197, 206–7, 208n10, 213, 215; historical story of 3–4, 8, 216; idea of xviii, xix, xxiiin3, 24, 39, 40–1, 52, 74, 94, 103, 109, 144, 166, 191, 199, 200, 203, 214, 227, 232; justifications of xix, 14, 34–7, 73, 79, 92, 212; language of xiv, 13, 162, 206, 220, 227; liberalism and *see* liberal; liberalism; narrative of

xvii, 222; political facets of *see* political emancipation; political equality; political rights; political systems; political theory; politics; practice of xvii–xviii, 212, 218, 225; relativism of *see* relativism; sacredness of 18, 30n3; substance of 87, 98, 213, 218; terminology of xviii, 50, 68, 73, 80, 215, 217, 219; universalism of *see* universalism
human rights, categories of: 6–8; absolute xix, 9, 21, 22, 25–26, 71, 72n4, 105n5, 144, 170–171, 178, 180; civil–political *see* civil–political human rights; economic–social–cultural *see* economic–social–cultural human rights; human/civil 8–12
human rights, theories of: Arendt's 10–2, 207–8, *see also* Arendt; Balibar's 204–7; Beitz's political practice 213–5; Buchanan's international law 212–3; Nussbaum's and Sen's capability approach 80–3; Foucault's 200–1; Gewirth's two basic moral rights 77–80; Pogge's institutional duties 84–88; liberal *see* liberal; liberalism; religious 74–77; Rorty's sentimental 196–9
human rights, types of: disability 131–138, *see also* disability rights; global economic 151–68; group 108–112, *see also* group rights; indigenous 119–123, *see also* indigenous; LGBTQ+ 115–8; migrants 142, *see also* migrants; migration; minority 112–119, *see also* minority rights; refugee 138–149, *see also* refugee(s); religious 113–5; security 170–1; women's 125–131, *see also* women's rights
Human Rights Watch 117–18, 124n7, 124n8, 172
humanism 77, 101, 144, 201; anti– 200, 201; post– 200
humanitarianism (humanitarian) 15, 28, 143, 184–5, 218–9, 220, 231n7; intervention xx–xxi, 95, 172, 182–7, 188n12, 219; law *see* international humanitarian law
humanity/humankind 3, 6, 12, 15, 101, 104, 112, 127, 150n15, 161, 185, 197, 231n15; in crisis 138, 145; Foucault on 200–1; Kant on 43; Levinas on 203

hunger 96, 164, 188n21; poverty and 162, 167, 228, 231n13

ICC *see* International Criminal Court (ICC)
ICCPR *see* International Covenant on Civil and Political Rights (ICCPR)
ICESCR *see* International Covenant on Economic, Social and Cultural Rights (ICESCR)
ICISS *see* International Commission on Intervention and State Sovereignty (ICISS)
ICJ *see* International Court of Justice (ICJ)
Ignatieff, Michael 216–17, 224
IHL *see* international humanitarian law (IHL)
IHRL *see* International Human Rights Law (IHRL)
immigration 144, 173, 219, 225
immunity 99; Hohfeldian 60–2
imperialism: anti– 24; cultural 102; moral 102; universalism as 101–5; Western x, 102–3, 220–223
indigenous: groups/peoples 105, 109, 120–121, 125; individuals 122–3; rights xix, 28, 107, 119–23, 144
individual rights xi, 24, 49, 50, 54, 57, 67, 69, 84, 111, 119, 122–3, 125, 175, 182, 188n12, 194, 226; vs. group rights 109, 111–2, 119–20, 122, 208n2 *see also* human rights
individualism 4–5, 50, 93, 95, 101, 108–10, 131, 153, 196–7, 202–3, 208, 213, 217
inequality 72n2, 231n14, 67; Brown 130, 195; Gewirth 79; Hart 67; Moyn 228–30; Rawls 56, 153, 156–8, 160; mitigation of global 161–2
INGOs *see* international non–governmental organizations (INGOs)
institution/s: intergovernmental 218–9; of human rights xiii, 117, 224–5; institutional theory xi, 84–88, 88n12, 162
instrumentalism 35, 71; theories of 64–5
Inter–American Commission on Human Rights 19
Inter–American Court of Human Rights 20
interest/s 35, 42, 54, 57, 75, 84, 96, 129, 132, 155–9, 161, 170, 184, 193–4, 195,

201, 213, 214, 225–7; Raz 69–71; security as 170–2, 175–7; theories 63, 65
International Bill of Human Rights 20–6, 227; Universal 166
International Commission on Intervention and State Sovereignty (ICISS) 185, 188n15
international community 119–20, 156, 183–5
International Convention on the Elimination of All Forms of Racial Discrimination (1965) 107, 112
International Court of Justice (ICJ) 20, 30
International Covenant on Civil and Political Rights (ICCPR) 20, 25–6, 31n16, 39, 108–9, 112, 116, 120–1, 131, 133–4, 139–40, 142, 146, 166, 170–1, 178–9, 188n11, 226–7
International Covenant on Economic, Social and Cultural Rights (ICESCR) 20, 25, 108–9, 112, 131, 133–4, 140, 142, 166, 169n14, 188n11, 227
International Criminal Court (ICC) 20, 30, 186
International Criminal Tribunal for Rwanda 30
International Human Rights Law (IHRL) xviii, 14, 18, 19–28, 116, 118, 123, 173, 174, 177, 187, 212–13, 216, 224
international humanitarian law (IHL) xix, 28–30, 30n6, 146, 186–7, 212
international non–governmental organizations (INGOs) 222
International Poverty Line (IPL) 163, 165
interventionism *see* humanitarian
IPL *see* International Poverty Line (IPL)
Islam/Muslim 15, 41, 91, 112, 113, 115, 119, 173, 198, 233
Israel 30n5, 146–149, 176–8, 187n5
Israel–Palestine 146–9, 176–8, 187n4, 226, 233–5
Israeli–Palestinian conflict 150n22, 226, 231n12

Judaism (Jewish) 15, 41, 91, 112, 115, 192, 233
justice: access to 134; Brown on 196; domestic 153–4, 156–7, 162; global 34, 154–60, 162, 228; human rights as fight for 219–20, 230, 232; Mill on 53; Rawls on 55–57, 153–160

Kamm, Frances 188n8
Kant, Immanuel 33, 41–3, 44n9, 55, 63, 65, 74, 77, 92, 136, 198
Kennedy, David 218–20, 224, 231n7
Kristeva, Julia 150n15

Langton, Rae 149n2
Laws of Noah 18
Lear, Jonathan 124n11
legal framework of human rights 18–31; humanitarian law 28–30; hyper–legalization 218; International Bill of Human Rights 20–26; international human rights law 19–20; international human rights instruments 26–8; international legal system 160, 212–13; enforcement 19–20, 30, 85, 131, 213, 216
Lenin, Vladimir 231n10
Levinas, Emmanuel xx, 200–3, 208n9
LGBTQ+ 107, 115–8, 124n10, 125
Liao, S. Matthew xvii
liberal: basis of human rights 111, 168n7; tension on intervention 184, 188n12; Hobbes as 48–50, 52, 58n4; rights 48, 59, 154, 160, 194–5; rights tradition xix, xxii, 4, 93, 103–4, 108, 197; societies 129–30, 154–7, 159; underpinnings of human rights 47–58
liberalism xiii, xix–xxi, 7–8, 16n5, 47–8, 64, 128–30, 158–60, 162, 192, 194, 196–7, 202–3, 222; Arendt against 11–12; Balibar and 204–6; Brown on 149n4, 194–6; classical 47, 173, 203–4; domestic 159–60; Dworkin on 67–68; Foucault against 200–1; freedom and equality in 47–48, 56, 67–8, 168n7; ideology of 112, 191, 194; and illiberalism 111, 115, 159; individual rights in 4, 47, 51, 205–6 52, 54, 57, 67, 93, 152–3, 166, 187, 220; international 159–60; Levinas and 201–3; Locke as father of 50–52; Marx on 192–4, 203; Millian 52–55; neo– 228, 230; paradoxes of 192–6, 223; Pogge on 156–8, 160–2; political xv, 4, 50, 55–6, 59; in Rawls 55–57, 80, 153–160; and religion 115
liberty xvii, 6, 8, 9–10, 16n6, 18, 22, 31n10, 123, 134, 152, 170, 173, 178, 187n1, 193–4, 207, 225; in Balibar 205–6; in Dworkin 67–8; and equality 8, 47–8, 67–8, 205–6; in Hobbes 49, 52; in Hohfeld 61–2; in Locke 52, 56; in Mill 52–54; of movement 139; negative and positive 72n1; principle of liberty, in Rawls 153; of conscience 154, 159

Li, Xiaorong 97, 101–2, 105n2
Locke, John xv, xvii, 4, 10, 16n9, 31n10, 48, 50–2, 55, 56, 57, 65, 77, 153, 170, 173, 187n1, 192
Lockwood, Heidi 149n2
Lyotard, Jean–Francois 208n10

MacKinnon, Catharine 126–7, 149n2
Macklin, Ruth 44n6
Magna Carta (1215) 18
market fundamentalism 228
Martinich, A. P. 58n4
Marx, Karl xx, 33, 48, 192–3, 195, 196, 203, 210–11
Marxism 112, 143, 194
maximalism, of duties 87
MDGs *see* UN Millennium Development Goals (MDGs)
Mégret, Frédéric 133–4, 137–8, 149n7, 149n8
migrants 145; rights of 28, 111, 119, 131, 138
migration 138, 141–2, 182, 188n14, 203, 230; Arendt on 145; Bauman on 144–5; Dummett on 144; global 143; workers 27, 107, 125
Milanovic, Branko 231n14
Mill, John Stuart xix, xxi, 8, 48, 52–5, 56, 58n5, 58n6, 65, 153
minimalism, of duties 87
Minimum Age Convention 28
minority rights xix, 107, 109, 110, 112–19, 125; *see also* human rights, theories of
modernism 210, 232; post– 145, 200; critique of 200
moral: dilemma 180, 191; foundations and justification of human rights 14, 35, 37, 63–4, 78, 84–86, 137, 174, 201, 215; imperialism 102; realism 92; relativism 37, 92, 98–9, 105n6, 220–1; rights 36, 65–9, 78, 84, 207, 212; universalism 105n2
moral theory 35, 37, 44n2, 65, 73; consequentialism 65; contractualism 35, 65; deontology 35, 65; egalitarian 65; Gewirth's 77–80; instrumentalism 35; Kant's 42–4; utilitarianism 52–4, 65

morality 23, 34–5, 47, 77–8, 199;
  Gewirth's definition of a 77; and
  religion 75, 88n3
Mormonism 91
Morris, Benny 150n22
Morsink, Johannes 30n7, 31n13
Moyn, Samuel 16n1, 224, 228–30

Nancy, Jean–Luc 208n10
Narveson, Jan 44n6
nation–state 5, 16n3, 141–2, 188n9, 206;
  global system 144, 183, 187, 188n10
natural law 14, 50, 66; and natural
  rights 47–52, 77, 84
natural rights xvii, 9, 10, 18, 47, 47–8,
  57, 64–5, 77, 84, 192, 208n1; in
  Hobbes 49–0: in Hart 65–7; in Locke
  50–1; in Hobbes and Locke 52; in
  Marx 192–3
negative rights (duties) vs. positive 31n9,
  63–5, 87, 128
neoliberal/ism 230, capitalism 228
Nickel, James xvi
Nussbaum, Martha xix, 84, 128, 149n3,
  180; capability approach 80–3, 88n5,
  88n6, 88n9, 88n10, 128, 135, 187n7

objectivism 37, 44n4, 92
Orend, Brian xixn1, 88n3, 88n12, 235n1

Palestine 30n4, 176–7, 187n4, 226,
  231n12, 233–4; Palestinian refugees
  146–50
Palestine Liberation Organization 226
Pappé, Ilan 150n22
Perry, Michael xvii, 75–6
personal security 170, 176, 182, 225–6;
  vs. national/state security 170–1
philosophical analysis 62, 71; of human
  rights 76; of law 65; of security 173–4
philosophical critique of human rights
  xviii, xx, 191–209; alternative dis-
  courses 200–3; anti–foundationalism
  196–9; paradoxes of liberalism 192–6;
  political philosophy 203–8
philosophy of language 126, 218
Piketty, Thomas 231n14
pluralism 37, 133, 137–8, 155–6
Pogge, Thomas xix, 44n3; on global
  resource tax (GRT) 161–2, 183;
  institutional theory of human rights
  84–7; on poverty 163–5, 167, 168n12;
  on Rawls 156–62, 168n5
political emancipation 193–4, 196

political equality 12, 206
political rights 25, 56–7, 67; democratic
  159; economic rights and 25, 95, 152;
  see also civil–political human rights
political systems 85, 154, 205, 208; in
  Rawls 56–7
political theory/thought 5, 13, 16n3, 26,
  32, 35, 55, 63, 67, 174, 188n9, 192,
  194, 208n7, 214; classical 205; liberal
  57; modern 183; realist 184;
  Western 194
politics xxi, 13–14, 35, 204, 207, 231n3;
  and human rights xii, 6, 104, 131,
  201, 209n11, 210, 214, 216, 224, 227;
  international 6, 12, 184; in Rawls 57;
  real–life politics 173, 175 204, 232;
  and religion 16
positive rights (duties) 154; vs. negative
  rights see negative rights
poverty xx, 140, 183, 227–8, 183,
  227–8; alleviation, elimination,
  eradication of 64, 162, 164, 167, 228;
  counting, measuring, and assessing
  162–6, 168n12; definition of 163–4,
  166–7, freedom from 166–8; "halving" 165; as human rights issue 151–
  3, 166, 168n5, 169n16; and hunger
  162, 164, 167, 188n21, 228, 231n13;
  income 163–4; multidimensional 151,
  168n1; trends in 164–5
power 13, 200, 224; in Brown 129–130;
  global/world 6, 224; governmental 53;
  in Hobbes 48–49, 50; Hohfeld on
  60–62; of human rights 218–20, 225;
  in Locke 51; in Mill 53–54; political
  35, 48, 223; state 50, 226
PPP see purchasing power parity (PPP)
Press, Eyal 187n7
Principle of Generic Consistency 77–80
principle of liberty (Rawls) 153
privacy 22, 79, 126, 133, 182, 195, 225
privilege 4, 15, 51, 99, 120, 141;
  Hohfeldian 60–2
prostitution, trafficking and 133
psychological egotism (Hobbes) 35
purchasing power parity (PPP) 163

racial discrimination 27, 112–3, 118,
  124n5, 131–2; convention against
  107, 112–3
racism 15, 96, 118, 142, 144, 195;
  Malcolm X's 10
Rajagopal, Balakrishnan 104–5, 231n9
Ramcharan, Bertrand 176, 187n3

Rancière, Jacques 203
rationality (rational): in children 33;
    essence in humans 33, 47, 132, 197; in
    Foucault 200; in Gewirth 77–9; in
    Hobbes 49–50, 52; in Kantian ethics
    42–3, 77; in Levinas 203; in Rawls 57;
    Rorty on 197–9
Rawls, John xix, xxi, 16n9, 35, 44n3, 48,
    55–7, 153–161, 166, 168n4, 214–15;
    basic rights 56–7, 159–60; domestic
    justice 56–7, 153–4; international
    justice 154–6; and liberalism 55–57,
    58n4, 80, 153–60; Pogge's –critique of
    156–160
Raz, Joseph xix, 69–71, 213–16, 231n4,
    231n5
Reddy, Sanjay 163–4
refugee(s): Agamben on 203–4; Arendt
    on 144–6; definition of 139, 141–2,
    145–6, 149n10; Dummett on 144;
    Jews as 145–6; numbers of 138;
    Palestinian 146–9, 149n9, 150n22,
    150n23, 150n24; policies 219; rights
    xix, xxi, 28, 107, 111, 125, 138–46,
    150n12, 182, 201
Reidy, David xvii
relativism 37–8, 40, 44n5, 88n4, 92,
    96–9, 105n1, 235; absolutism *vs.* 37;
    in AAA 94; cultural 40, 94–6, 103,
    109, 129, 197; Li on 105n2; moral/
    normative 92; in Rorty 197–8; Taylor
    on 99–101, 105n6; universalism *vs.*
    xv, 37, 40, 92, 93–6, 102–4, 198,
    220–1; universalism–relativism
    continuum 97–101; Waldron
    on 97–9
religion (religious) 91, 100, 205, 220, 235;
    Buddhism 15, 100–1, 112; Catholic
    112, 113; Christianity 15, 41, 91, 101,
    104, 198; Confucian 15,
    100–1; and dignity 41; discrimination
    22, 26, 113, 126, 139–40, 154;
    foundation/justification of human
    rights xxii, 74–7; freedom of 7, 18, 22,
    39, 81, 114, 141; Hinduism 15, 113;
    Hobbes and Locke on 52; and human
    rights 14–6, 30n3, 44n7, 113–8, 131;
    Islam/Muslim 15, 41, 91, 112, 113,
    115, 119, 173, 198, 233; Judaism/
    Jewish 15, 41, 91, 112, 115, 192, 233;
    and liberalism 115; Mormonism 91
Renzo, Massimo xvii
Responsibility to Protect (R2P) 172,
    185–7, 187n2

rights: general/special 64; Hart on 65–7;
    interest theory of 63; in law (Hoh-
    feld) 59–62; positive/negative 63; Raz
    on 69–71; sovereign's 49; theories of
    59–72; trumps (Dworkin) 67–9; will
    theory of 63; *see also* human rights
Roberts, Lani 149n2
Rorty, Richard xx, 197–200, 203, 208n4
Roseman, Mindy Jane 149n2
Rousseau, Jean–Jacques 4, 16n9, 33, 55
Rwanda 184, 185; International
    Criminal Tribunal for 30

Schiller, Linda 16n3
Scott, Joan 192, 196
security xx, xxi, 170–82, 227; dilemma/
    pseudo–dilemma 173–8; Gearty on
    226–7, 231n12; –3, 225, 182–3, 187n3,
    187n5; human rights engagement with
    225–7; individual/personal to state/
    national 170–1; torture xxii, 178–82;
    Wall (Israel–Palestine) 176–8,
    226, 235n2
Security Wall (case study) 176–8,
    226, 235n2
self–determination 24–5, 108–9, 120–1,
    123n2, 183
Sen, Amartya 80, 84, 88n5, 88n6,
    88n7, 128
sex (sexual): violence 81, 127, 130;
    discrimination 22, 26, 55, 113, 126,
    140, 229; functions of 82; and gender
    identity 112, 115–7, 119; orientation
    107, 112, 115–7, 118, 131, 195;
    satisfaction 81
Shapiro, Ian 50, 58n3
Shlaim, Avi 150n22
slavery 15, 22, 30n2, 55, 94, 96, 98, 101,
    110, 155, 162, 186; right against 7, 26,
    39, 134, 171, 178; sexual 111, 126–7,
    186
Smith, Michael 184, 188n12
social contract 9–10, 16n9, 55, 57, 65
sodomy 195
solidarity 220, 225; in Bauman 145; in
    Moyn 229; in Rorty 199; in Žižek 143
sovereignty (sovereign) xx, 95, 103, 104,
    120, 141–2, 206; concept of 183; in
    Foucault 200; and humanitarian
    intervention 182–7; human rights *vs.*
    183–4, 186–7, 188n12, 213, 215; in
    Hobbes 49–50, 52, 58n3; in Locke 51;
    in Rawls 57; rights of 49, 58n3
Spellman, A. B. 10

Spivak, Gayatri 16n3, 129, 194
Stanford Encyclopedia of Philosophy 8
stateless(ness) 138, 142, 144–5,
    150n17, 207
structuralism 200, post– 200
subordination, of women 130–1,
    194–5
surveillance 178, 225, 227
sympathy 199, 235
systematic: method xvi, xviii, xx–xxiii,
    22, 27, 200; philosophy xix–xx

Tasioulas, John xvii, 88n14
Tawney, R. H. 75–6
Taylor, Charles xv, 97, 99–101,
    105n6
Ten Commandments 18
terrorism 172–173, 176, 178, 183, 186,
    226; war against 173m 226,
    180–1, 226–7
Thomson, Judith 188n8
ticking bomb scenario 180–1, 187n6
Tokyo Declaration (1975) 179
Tomalty, Jesse 168n3
Topolski, Anya 208n9
torture xx–xxii, 97, 178–82, 225;
    absoluteness of right/prohibition
    against 26, 39, 105n5, 171, 178–9, 180;
    Brecher on 180–2, 187n6; Convention
    against 179; definition of 179, 181;
    and dignity 182; legitimacy of 180,
    187n7; right not to be subjected to/
    prohibition against 7, 22, 96; as war
    crime and crime against humanity 186
totalitarianism, Hannah Arendt on
    11–12, 145
trafficking 28, 126–7, 133
trolley problem 180, 188n8

UDHR *see* Universal Declaration of
    Human Rights (UDHR)
UNCCP *see* United Nations
    Conciliation Commission on
    Palestine (UNCCP)
UN 2030 Agenda for Sustainable
    Development (2015)
    27–8, 167
UN Commission on Human Rights
    93, 120
UN Conciliation Commission on
    Palestine (UNCCP) 147
UN General Assembly 10, 20, 24, 28,
    30n4, 116, 120, 139, 146, 148,
    150n25, 185

UN Human Rights Council 19,
    116–117, 120
UN Millennium Declaration (2000)
    27–8, 164, 167
UN Millennium Development Goals
    (MDGs) 165, 167
UN Millennium Summit (2000) 164
UN Office of the High Commissioner
    for Human Rights (OHCHR) 116,
    118, 166, 168n13, 176
UN Relief and Works Agency for
    Palestine Refugees (UNRWA) 147,
    150n23
UN Sustainable Development Goals
    (SDGs) 167
United Nations 19, 20, 23, 24,
    26–7, 28, 30, 107, 112, 117,
    138, 164, 185, 188n15,
    222, 224
Universal Declaration of Human Rights
    (UDHR, 1948) 3, 20–6, 30n7, 31n10,
    31n12, 38, 40, 73–4, 91, 93–4, 96, 103,
    108–9, 113–16, 120, 122, 123, 125–7,
    131, 133–5, 136, 138, 140, 142, 146,
    151–2, 166–7, 170, 178, 188n9,
    188n11, 204–5, 220–1, 227, 229,
    231n15, 234
universalism (universality) of human
    rights xix, xxi, xxii, 3, 9–10, 14,
    17n12, 18–19, 22, 30n2, 31n8, 37–40,
    79, 88n8, 91–106, 112, 113–4, 122,
    220–3, 233–5; and disability rights
    135–8; Donnelly on 105n4; Li on
    105n2; for refugees 143–4; *vs.*
    relativism xix, 37, 40, 92–7, 102–4,
    198, 220–1; Taylor on 99–101, 105n6;
    universalism–relativism continuum
    97–101; for women 126–9; naïve
    universalism 221; Waldron on 97–9;
    Western/imperialistic xv, 101–5, 198,
    220–3, 235
UNRWA *see* United Nations Relief and
    Works Agency for Palestine Refugees
    (UNRWA)
utilitarianism 57, 58n5, 65, 67, 88n13,
    92, 143; in Mill 52–5; non– 75

veil of ignorance 55, 153, 155–6
violence 79, 81, 224; against disabled
    134; anti– 10; in ethnic cleansing 186;
    in India 124n7, 124n8; governmental
    230; non– 101; against persons based
    on sexual orientation or gender
    identity 117–18; policing 225; political

226; in poverty 152; against women 28, 130

"Voluntary Principles on Security and Human Rights" 171

Waldron, Jeremy xix, 44n9, 97–9, 101–2, 179n4
de Waal, Alex 188n21, 231n13
war crimes 20, 185–6, 188n18, 188n21, 231n13
West Bank 147, 177, 187n5
Wittgenstein, Ludwig 211, 231n1, 231n2
women's rights xix, xxi, 9, 15, 28, 30n2, 107–8, 125–31, 194–6; Brown on 129–31, 194–6; in capabilities approach 127–9; and discrimination

27–8, 107, 116, 149n3; as human rights (MacKinnon) 125–7, 149n2; Mill on 54; religious violations of 114
World Bank 163–6, 168n1, 168n8, 168n12
worldlessness 145
World Summit (2005) 185; Outcome Document 188n14
World War II xvi, 4, 18–9; post– 138–9, 184, 217

X, Malcolm 10–11

Zerilli, Linda 149n2
Žižek, Slavoj 143, 150n16